Managing Global Financial and Foreign Exchange Rate Risk

John Wiley & Sons

Founded in 1807, John Wiley & Sons is the oldest independent publishing company in the United States. With offices in North America, Europe, Australia, and Asia, Wiley is globally committed to developing and marketing print and electronic products and services for our customers' professional and personal knowledge and understanding.

The Wiley Finance series contains books written specifically for finance and investment professionals as well as sophisticated individual investors and their financial advisors. Book topics range from portfolio management to e-commerce, risk management, financial engineering, valuation and financial instrument analysis, as well as much more.

For a list of available titles, please visit our Web site at *www.WileyFinance.com.*

Managing Global Financial and Foreign Exchange Rate Risk

GHASSEM A. HOMAIFAR

WILEY

John Wiley & Sons, Inc.

This book is printed on acid-free paper. ∞

Copyright © 2004 by John Wiley & Sons, Inc., Hoboken, New Jersey. All rights reserved.

Published simultaneously in Canada.

For general information on our other products and services, or technical support, please contact our Customer Care Department within the United States at 800-762-2974, outside the United States at 317-572-3993 or fax 317-572-4002.

Wiley also publishes its books in a variety of electronic formats. Some content that appears in print may not be available in electronic books.

For more information about Wiley products, visit our Web site at *www.wiley.com*.

Library of Congress Cataloging-in-Publication Data

Homaifar, Ghassem.
  Managing global financial and foreign exchange rate risk /
Ghassem A. Homaifar.
    p. cm.—(The Wiley finance series)
  Includes bibliographical references and index.
    ISBN 0-471-28115-8 (CLOTH)
    1. Foreign exchange. 2. Foreign exchange rates. 3. Risk management.
    4. Foreign exchange—United States. 5. Foreign exchange rates—United States.
    6. Risk management—United States. I. Title. II. Series.
  HG3851.H63   2004
  332.4'5—dc22   2003015159

Printed in the United States of America.

10 9 8 7 6 5 4 3 2 1

To my wife and daughters

contents

CHAPTER 4
Application of Options and Futures for Managing Exposure   **75**

CHAPTER 7
Swaps   177

CHAPTER 8
Translation, Transaction, and Operating Exposure   217

CHAPTER 9
Debt, Equity, and Other Synthetic Structures   **253**

preface

R isk taking is the foundation of the capitalist economy as it is positively correlated to the reward for entrepreneurial behavior. Risk management in the twenty-first century integrates mathematical and physical science along with that of behavioral finance and economics. The end result is a mushrooming set of derivative products where price is contingent on the behavior of underlying assets, such as stocks, bonds, commodities, currencies, indices, and other exotic instruments. The market for derivatives plays an ever-increasing important role in transferring risk from risk-averse individuals and institutions to those who are willing to take it for a profit. Risk taking and risk management are balanced in the marketplace by regulatory oversight, as bank and financial services industry regulators continue to search for an optimum balance that protects the integrity of the banking system and provides regulatory capital relief while enhancing the return on capital to financial institutions.

This book is intended to provide readers who already have an understanding of the time value of money the opportunity to venture into the exciting and often mysterious world of global derivatives. In various derivative textbooks, the price-generating function of derivatives is expressed as a highly complex mathematical manipulation that is unintelligible to a broad audience. This endeavor is intended to bridge the gap between theory and practice by focusing on understanding various derivatives for managing exposure to foreign exchange, commodity price, interest rate, and credit and weather risks.

The objective is to present a coherent analysis of the various risks that a multinational firm faces in an integrated global market and to consider active risk management approaches for mitigating exposures to commodity price, foreign exchange, equity price, and interest rate changes within the context of value creation for its stakeholders. Numerous real-world examples are employed to illustrate how derivatives can be used to mitigate risks. To those whose work has been cited throughout this book, I am indebted for their contributions to the knowledge base that has revolutionized the practice of risk management. Wall Street's brightest minds continue to respond to changes in the regulatory landscape, changes in tax laws, and changes in business and financial risks with further innovations in derivatives and financial engineering.

This book is organized into 12 chapters. Chapter 1 provides an overview. Chapter 2 addresses the balance of payments (BP) equilibrium and managing exposures related to the disequilibrium in the various components of BP. Some preliminary results for the U.S. balance of payments are presented and compared to recent evidence from the emerging market economies of Southeast Asia.

Chapter 3 outlines a simple and unified framework for the dynamic process of international rate parity relationships along with managing exposures induced due to changes in foreign exchange rates. Furthermore, the economic consequences of the partial and incomplete exchange rate pass-through provide interesting observations and challenges for U.S. multinational corporations. This chapter concludes with a framework for the macrodetermination of the exchange rate linking the real sector of the economy, where production takes place, with the financial markets and monetary policy formulation by the Federal Reserve Board, where financing is encouraged (discouraged).

Chapter 4 lays out the foundation of option pricing in a fairly simple context and its application for managing risk. Hedging foreign-denominated cash inflows and outflows using call and put options provides the reader with opportunities to challenge the conventional wisdom of hedging and not hedging. The question of whether to hedge or not to hedge explains the cost and benefits of hedging with options vis à vis hedging with forward or futures contract. The chapter concludes with an example of covered call, protective put, and zero collar and its implications for managers.

Chapter 5 outlines the principles of futures pricing and application for dividend-paying instruments such as stock index and currency futures. The pricing formulation prepares, in a relatively nontechnical way, the foundation for the understanding of the relatively complex derivatives instruments discussed throughout the book. Nondividend-paying futures such as gold, silver, and other commodity futures are priced in the context of cost of carry model.

Anticipatory hedging with various futures, such as stock index, currency, and commodities, is provided in the context of illustrative cases that permits readers to follow the peculiarities of the futures and forward contracts as well as highlighting their idiosyncrasies. The final section of the chapter presents some of the most recent evidence on the forward and futures prices.

Chapter 6 presents principles of pricing and application of interest rate futures, such as Treasury bills, notes, bonds, and Eurodollar futures, for managing exposure due to interest rate and price risk. The shape of the term structure of interest rates provides readers with various theories of the interest rates as the foundation of the interest-sensitive derivative instruments that has revolutionized the financial services industry in the last two decades. The price volatility of bonds such as duration and convexity provides readers with a clear and coherent analysis of these important factors in active bond portfolio management. The delivery process in the futures market illustrates the institutional aspects of the cheapest-to-deliver bonds in the Treasury notes and bonds market.

Arbitrage and risk transfer from hedgers to speculators in interest rate futures market in the context of easy-to-follow examples provide readers with an in-depth analysis of this important subject. Hedging with a duration-based approach illustrates the application of the various interest rates futures using long and short hedges for managing exposure to interest rate risk.

Chapter 7 lays out the foundation of the swaps. In the finance nomencla-ture, selling an asset and buying another asset simultaneously, and vice versa, is a swap. The markets for interest rate and currency swaps are some of the most inno-vative in the world. A new breed of swaps are introduced in the over-the-counter market in restructuring assets/liabilities, and mitigating and transferring risk. This chapter provides an extensive analysis of the valuation of the plain-vanilla inter-est rate and currency swaps and their application to interest rate risk management. Pricing and valuation of caps, floors, collars, and corridors along with their appli-cation is presented in a framework that can be easily understood by readers with a minimal background in the time value of money. Valuation and application of swaptions is highlighted with numerous examples and graphical illustrations. The swap risks and exposure associated with swaps can be substantial, as regulatory authorities have imposed capital reserve in protecting the soundness of the bank-ing system in swaps transactions that used to be treated off balance sheet and footnoted in the past. Currency swaps are analyzed along the same lines as their interest rate counterpart in a plain-vanilla type and embedded with various options making them callable, cancelable, exchangeable, and so on.

Chapter 8 analyzes the effect of the unexpected change in exchange rates: on the single-period cash flows (transaction exposure), multiperiod cash flows (operating exposure), and accounting-induced changes in the consolidated bal-ance sheet (accounting exposure). This chapter unifies the fundamentals of hedg-ing transaction, economic (operating), and translation (accounting) exposures with various derivatives in a user-friendly framework. The chapter highlights managing transaction exposure for Lufthansa Airlines' acquisition of aircrafts from Boeing in 1985 by a cost-benefit analysis of various hedging instruments for mitigating airline exposure to foreign currency exchange rate risk. The chapter also reviews the current literature on the practice of U.S. multinational corporations in regard to their hedging activities on such firms as DuPont and Nike. Analysis of value at risk (VAR) for the exposures related to changes in commodity prices, interest rates, and market risk are illustrated with numerous easy-to-follow examples. The mandate of regulatory authorities in bank supervision requiring banks to hold capital reserve for risky assets have increased the importance of VAR analysis for financial and nonfinancial corporations.

Chapter 9 outlines the nonstandard debt derivatives developed in the over-the-counter market to transfer risk, to mitigate reinvestment rate risk, to transfer the prepayment risk from a class of bond to other classes, to mitigate price and exchange rate risks, to increase liquidity, to reduce agency costs, to reduce trans-action costs, and to reduce tax burden circumventing regulatory restrictions. The nonstandard derivative products offer opportunities in the financial market to enhance the yield and reduce the risk if properly combined with other assets in the portfolio. Therefore, they demand an understanding of the underlying factors that determine their value. The reward is higher, as is the risk of the individual derivative product. It is imperative to fully understand the pricing mechanism before committing the capital. Pricing inverse floaters along with floaters and their application in an active bond portfolio management is illustrated at the outset.

Numerous examples explain using inverse floaters to create synthetic fixed rate. Mortgage and asset-backed derivative securities, as well as the price, yield, and prepayment risks, provide the idiosyncrasies of these instruments. The chapter also analyzes prepayment risks such as extension and contraction risks. The interest-only (IO) and principal-only (PO) securities derived synthetically from fixed rate instruments reveal an interesting phenomena regarding their price and yield relationship. This chapter concludes with the equity-linked debts and the implication for global diversification and liability management with such derivatives as caps, floors, collars, and swaptions.

Chapter 10 provides an overview of options on the interest rates, currencies, indices, and commodity futures products, such as options on spreads position on the Eurodollar futures, the Treasury futures, the currency futures and commodity futures. The currency options that began trading at the Philadelphia Exchange in 1982 to respond to the needs of multinational corporations for hedging currency exposure as well as to the needs of arbitrageurs and speculators to garner speculative profits (losses). Options in the interest rate products were introduced by the Chicago Mercantile Exchange in 1985. Various options positions for hedging and speculating are illustrated using real-life exposures. The options on futures are very similar to the options on equities and are priced accordingly using standard Black-Scholes options pricing formula. Spreads positions, such as bear spreads, bull spreads, butterfly spreads, box spreads, short straddle, long straddle, strips, and straps, are illustrated with numerous examples. The final section of the chapter discusses exotic options, variants of the ordinary options where the spot price, strike price, maturity, and/or volatility of the options are embedded with options. For example, the text discusses allowing the spot price to be determined by its behavior over the option period as opposed to one price at the expiration or exercise date (whichever comes first) or by making the spot price path-dependent, where the frequency of trading or number of days that options have for expiration to be used for establishing average spot price.

Chapter 11 discusses credit derivatives and default insurance, the new breed of on– and off–balance sheet financial instruments of the last five years that allow banks and other financial corporations to transfer or assume credit risk on a specific "reference" asset or portfolio of assets. The increased application of the derivatives has raised concerns about the default risk properties of these instruments. These concerns have been mitigated by the Bank for International Settlement, as it imposed a risk-based capital ratio in 1992, requiring banks to hold capital reserves to cover the unexpected losses on the current and future replacement cost of these instruments in the event of default. The number of credit derivatives is growing as new instruments are developed by financial engineers in response to changes in regulatory climate, taxes, increased volatility, and change in supply and demand condition. Credit derivatives enable the parties to reduce credit exposure without physically removing assets from the balance sheet. For example, loan sales and unwinding or assignment of loans require consent and notification of the counterparty. However, transactions on credit derivatives are confidential and do not require notification of the customer, thereby separating the fiduciary relationship from risk management decisions. The credit derivatives discussed in this chapter, such as credit default swap, synthetic collateralized loan obligations, asset swaps, total return swaps, and credit-linked notes, allow efficient allocation of economic capital, resulting in diversification of risk and improved shareholder returns.

Chapter 12 reviews some of the recent exotic innovations in credit and weather derivatives. The regulatory changes in treatment of derivative transactions, whether booked in the bank balance sheet or in the bank trading desk, continue to have significant impact on the return on capital as the Bank for International Settlement searches for an optimum capital reserve requirement that protects the integrity of the banking system as well as providing sufficient regulatory and economic capital relief. The chapter starts with a discussion of highly leveraged transactions, such as credit spread forward, credit spread options, option on credit exposure, asset swap switch, and callable step-ups. These derivative products are designed to transfer risks synthetically in the capital markets. Numerous examples illustrate pricing and application of transfer and convertibility protection. A discussion of emerging market bonds and stripped Brady bonds follows. Finally, the chapter presents pricing and application of weather derivatives.

I am indebted to my 2002–2003 MBA class at Middle Tennessee State University for reading various chapters and providing valuable input for improving the clarity of the material. I am grateful for those who provided case studies. My thanks and appreciation go to Reuben Kyle, Larry Farmer, Jeannie Harrington, Lee Sarver, Frank Mitchelo, James Feller, Mahmoud Haddad, Bichaka Fayissa, John Lee, Mamit Deme, Albert Deprince, Emily Zietz, Kenneth Hollman, Amy Daly, Natasha Bradford, David Brown, Todd Horton, Michael Deweese, Rob Whitley, Kathryn Mackorell, Pichet Panee, Melissa Wilson, Chris Curry, Butch Nunely, and Rich Stone for their insightful comments on various chapters and to my graduate assistants, Yan Liu and Zhijie Qi, for research support. I remain solely responsible for any remaining errors. Special thanks to my editor, Sheck Cho, for his valuable input that improved the clarity of my presentations, and to Karen Ludke, Sujin Hong, and Jennifer Hanley for editorial assistance at John Wiley & Sons. Last but not least, I remain indebted to my wife and daughters for their unconditional support.

CHAPTER 1

Global Markets: Transactions and Risks

This chapter outlines the foundation of this book in managing and mitigating various exposures that a firm faces in a global context. What is truly revealing is that exposure is defined by *Webster's New World Dictionary* as "the fact of being exposed in a helpless condition to the elements."[1] The elements can be (unforeseen) macro- or microfactors unique to the company. Fortunately, for events that might be unforeseen, such as death or natural disasters, the markets have developed various types of insurance for managing and transferring those risks to risk arbitrageurs (various types of insurance companies). What remains to be managed is the macrorisk—market risk that cannot be avoided, but can at times be mitigated—and microrisk—the unique risk that is peculiar to a company—which needs to be managed properly.

Exposure has increased for the major players in the market as the world economy has seen a major restructuring of financing transactions since March 1973 (the beginning of floating rate arrangement). The increased volatility of exchange rates and innovations in derivative products has created opportunities and challenges to corporations. Exhibit 1.1 shows the percentage monthly change in yen/$ exchange rates 1957 through 2002. Notable in the exhibit is the beginning of the floating rate arrangement in 1973 and the subsequent significant

EXHIBIT 1.1   Monthly Percentage Change ¥/$ (1957–2002)

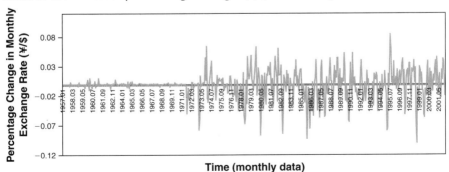

increase in the volatility of the exchange rate, particularly in the periods 1973–74, 1979–80, and 1995–96. The percentage changes in the yen/$ exchange rate appears to be randomly distributed. Chapter 3 provides further discussion of the implications of this randomness for decision making.

The absence of volatility in the foreign exchange market for yen/$ prior to the floating rate arrangement is also notable. This period coincided with the fixed exchange rate arrangement of 1945 to 1971 known as the Bretton Woods Arrangement, while allowing occasional dollar devaluations in 1934 when dollar devalued to $35/ounce of gold from $20.67/ounce to remedy a huge U.S. deficit. The dollar was devalued to $38/ounce of gold on December 17–18, 1971, in an agreement that came to be known as the Smithsonian Agreement. Despite these devaluations, March 1973 marks the end of a fixed exchange rate arrangement where the British pound and Swiss franc were allowed to float respectively on June 1972 and January 1973. By June 1973, the dollar lost an average of 10 percent.

Most firms were able to rise to the occasion, adapt to the new challenges, and prosper. Some have not fared so well; in extreme cases, firms have become dinosaurs unable to adapt to environmental changes and face extinction. Savings and loans (S&Ls) and Laker's Airline are the classic examples of the dinosaurs unable to mange their exposure.

SAVINGS AND LOANS PROBLEMS

S&Ls had high-duration assets on the left-hand side of the balance sheet in the form of mostly fixed rate mortgages, while they were funded on the right-hand side of the balance sheet with mostly low-duration, short-term floating rate demand deposit and fixed rate time deposits of two to five years maturity. Exhibit 1.2 provides the monthly change in basis points for one-year Treasury bills (T-bills) since 1953. The monthly basis point change in one-year T-bills dramatically increased in the late 1970s due to double-digit inflation, which raised the exposure for the financial institutions, particularly the S&Ls.

EXHIBIT 1.2   One-Year Monthly First Difference for T-Bills (1953–2002)

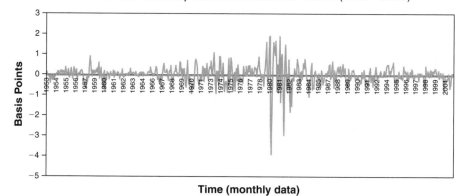

For years, when the yield curve was upward sloping, it paid for S&Ls to borrow short term and lend long term. However, the double-digit inflation of the late 1970s and concurrent rise in short-term interest rate as well as recession of the early 1980s and the slowdown in economic activities reduced the incentive to borrow, squeezing profits and reversing the fortunes of the S&Ls. The high interest rates of the late 1970s and early 1980s produced an inverted yield curve in 1982, where the yield curve was downward sloping (i.e., the short-term rate was higher than the long-term rate), forcing the entire industry into bankruptcy. After the S&L debacle, the market witnessed creation of a new breed of instruments (e.g., floating rates loans, floater and inverse floater, and an array of other derivatives in the bond markets to remedy prepayment risk), where the risk of rising interest rates shifted to borrowers, thereby increasing the probability of borrowers' default. The risk of the mismatch of assets/liabilities in the case of S&Ls did not disappear; banks simply transferred it to individual borrowers.

The mismatch of revenue and cost also create exposure for a firm, where the revenue is denominated in one currency and cost is incurred in another currency. Laker's Airline was the victim of this mismatch. A weak dollar in the early 1970s made travel to the United States a bargain for British travelers, raising revenue of Laker's Airline and inducing it to borrow U.S. dollars to purchase new aircrafts. Exhibit 1.3 shows the rate of monthly percentage of pound devaluation (revaluation) over the period 1957 to 2002.

The dollar strengthened against the British pound by the early 1980s, making travel to the United States very expensive and increasing the pound cost of the dollar to service the dollar-denominated debt. Laker's Airline was hit by a double whammy, which forced the company into bankruptcy.

AGENCY PROBLEMS

Domestic or multinational corporations can be defined as a portfolio of various activities, where each activity is intended to produce payoffs in sustaining and

EXHIBIT 1.3   British Pound Monthly Rate of Devaluation (Revaluation) (1957–2002)

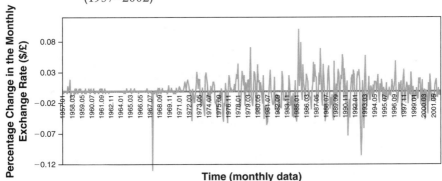

creating value for stakeholders. In organizing various activities, firms issue claims to the assets of the corporations to various claimants based on priority of claims. Here stakeholders develop a comprehensive system of checks and balance to ensure that one class of claimants, such as creditors, is protected against the abuse of power of another class of claimant, such as stockholders. The agency relationship defines the governing principle to settle claims between principal and agent, stockholders and bondholders, management and the stockholders, management and the employee, and management and any other injured party. The cost associated with managing and mitigating agency-related risk can be substantial. However, without an appropriate and well-defined agency relationship that defines the contractual obligations of various claimants, firms run the risk of lengthy legal battles that drain their scarce resources and destroy value.

The conflict of interest between the parties in an agency relationship gives rise to agency-related problems and costs. In the context of two individuals in an agency relation such as marriage, conflict of interest lands the parties in divorce court for the resolution and division of assets (physical and human) and liabilities. To alleviate agency-related problems and associated costs, a party that wishes to establish agency relation with another party might require a "prenuptial agreement." In the case of firms, such an agreement can be an exposure management vehicle to avoid the cost and pain arising in the future in the event of dissolution of the agency relationship.

In the context of domestic or multinational firms, the conflict of interest between stakeholders and management needs to be managed and mitigated. Whether management acts in the best interests of stockholders or creditors or pursues its own self-interest by giving the firm's officers large severance packages or golden parachutes in the event of corporate buyout or merger is an empirical issue. Stakeholders in most firms design a compensation scheme to direct management actions toward maximizing value of the firms and manage stakeholders' exposure to abuses by management.

"Monster Mess"

The conflict of interest between Arthur Andersen consulting as a consultant and auditor to Enron is the classic example of an agency problem leading to eventual bankruptcy of Enron Corporation. According to Bethany McLean:

> [P]olitics are almost beside the point. As a financial scandal, Enron is much bigger than anyone imagined—and, more important, the factors that enabled it haven't gone away. Systematic conflicts of interest are more pervasive and corrosive than either Congress, regulators, investors, or the press appreciate. Watkins's letter makes it clear that the partnerships and off-balance-sheet entities that Enron created weren't used to "reduce risk," as the company claimed repeatedly last fall. They were used to cook the books, plain and simple.[2]

Due to operational and locational diversifications and various regulatory requirements, multinational corporations are far more exposed to agency-related problems and associated costs than their domestic counterparts. Executives of Japanese multinational corporations usually sit on the boards of other companies and are far more effective in managing agency-related costs between management and unions than their North American counterparts. Domestic or multinational firms should strike a balance between the costs and benefits of agency relationship; when entering into additional agency relationships, the marginal cost of additional agency relationship should be equal to marginal benefits realized.

TYPES OF MARKETS

Markets for Real Assets

In this market individuals and corporations organize their economic activities efficiently for producing real goods (tangible) such as food, clothing, and shelter and (intangible) services such as counseling, education, and other services for allocation and distribution in meeting the demands of the society. Producers employ factors of production—labor, raw materials, and capital—in such a way that pays for the cost of the factors and leaves a profit for producers. Here value is created and opportunities expanded, and the welfare of individuals in the society is increased. The price mechanism is the governing principle in addressing the three basic questions of the market economy: what to produce, how to produce it, and for whom to produce it. The price mechanism ensures the production of goods and services that the economy demands and is willing to pay for it.

Markets for Financial Assets

Market for financial assets is where the capital is distributed and channeled from lenders (investors) to ultimate users of capitals (borrowers): individuals, corporations, and other entities. Corporations issue claims to assets of their companies in the form of bonds and stocks for acquiring long-term capital or issue short-term vehicles such as commercial papers, banker's acceptance (known as money market instruments), for securing short-term debts. The capital is expected to be channeled in such a way that maximizes the welfare of the economic system, where the most promising projects are funded based on their merits. Projects that produce more payoffs than their costs create value for the providers of capital. Examples of these markets are stock markets, bond markets, and the foreign exchange spot market, where the underlying asset is the spot exchange rates representing claims on the purchasing power of one currency relative to another currency.

Markets for Derivatives

Where value is neither created nor destroyed, it is simply transferred from one party to another in a given transaction. The derivatives market is also known as the zero-sum game market, where the gain of one party is exactly equal to loss of another party. Derivatives derive their value from the underlying assets, such as stocks, bonds, commodities, or foreign currency spot exchange rates. Derivatives markets perform two valuable functions: (1) transfer risk and (2) price discovery. Without the markets for derivatives, the financial and real markets are not complete and may not function efficiently in managing, mitigating and transferring risks. Derivatives markets are sometimes referred to as speculative markets, where two parties take offsetting positions based on their own expectations. The profit and loss potential is symmetrical and can be devastating to the well-being of individuals or corporations.[3]

Derivatives markets serve to provide valuable information to participants for taking current actions to remedy expected problems in the near future. These markets enable individuals and corporations and other agencies to discover today the expected market consensus of what future interest rate, commodity prices, stock or bond prices, or foreign currency exchange rate will be. This price discovery mechanism provided by the derivatives markets is essential for planning, procuring, and executing production as well as for managing and mitigating exposure to various risks. Exhibits 1.4 and 1.5 highlight the price discovery mechanism of derivatives markets and the link between markets for financial assets and derivatives.

As shown in Exhibit 1.4, the U.S. Treasury 90-day T-bills zero-coupon interest rate was 1.82 percent as of March 20, 2002. The forward interest rate for the 90-day T-bill futures in Exhibit 1.5 for June 2002 priced on March 20, 2002, at current price of 97.765 is to yield 2.235 percent (100 − 97.765). In Exhibit 1.5, the T-bill forward interest rate is derived from International Money Market (IMM) index of 97.765 at current reading translates into 100 minus the IMM index of 97.765 to yield 2.235 percent. The Eurodollar interest rate futures the most actively traded future for June 2002 delivery priced at

EXHIBIT 1.4   U.S. Treasuries (spot)
Wednesday, 20 Mar 2002, 10:31 A.M. EST

Bills		Mat Date	Previous Price/Yield	Current Price/Yield	Yld Chg	Prc Chg
3 month		6/20/02	1.80(1.83)	1.79(1.82)	−0.01	−1
6 month		9/19/02	2.03(2.08)	2.03(2.08)	0.00	0

Notes/ Bonds	Coupon	Mat Date	Previous Price/Yield	Current Price/Yield	Yld Chg	Prc Chg
2 year	3.000	2/29/04	99−00(3.54)	98−28+(3.60)	0.06	−0−04
5 year	3.500	11/15/06	95−04+(4.67)	94−27+(4.74)	0.07	−0−09
10 year	4.875	2/15/12	96−28(5.28)	96−13(5.35)	0.06	−0−15
30 year	5.375	2/15/31	94−31+(5.73)	94−17(5.77)	0.03	−0−15

Source: www.bloomberg.com.

EXHIBIT 1.5   Wednesday, 20 Mar 2002, 10:32 A.M. EST

Interest Rate Futures	Time	Current	CHG	Open	Hi/Lo	Prev
90DAY EUROS FUTR	10:21	97.500	−0.005	97.540	97.550	97.505
Jun 02					97.495	
13-week Treasury bill futures		97.765		97.89	97.89/97.75	
Jun 02						

Source: Chicago Mercantile Exchange.

97.5 on March 20, 2002, in the Chicago Mercantile Exchange (CME) is to yield 2.5 percent.

The T-bills futures are predicting that the short-term interest rate is expected to go up by 41.5 basis points. The interest rate futures has priced as of March 20, 2002, a short-term interest rate hike by the Federal Reserve Board by as much as 50 basis points to take place by June 2002. The price discovery function of derivatives is a reminder to the participants of the markets that those who wish to borrow short term in the near future should take advantage of the lower rate right now, or those who have a line of credit at the floating rate may consider converting to the fixed rate before the rates go up.

TYPES OF TRANSACTIONS

Spot Transactions

Most transactions in every economy are spot for immediate delivery of the goods or services for cash or credit in transactions involved in the markets for real assets or the markets for financial assets. The spot transaction may take place in an organized exchange, such as New York Stock Exchange (NYSE) or at an over-the-counter exchange such as Nasdaq for the financial assets such as stocks, bonds, and bills. The only difference between the spot transaction in real and financial markets is that the transaction is personal in the former and impersonal in the latter. For example, the parties to a transaction involving the purchase and sale of 100 shares of IBM stock remain anonymous to one another. The purchase and sale of vehicles by buyer and seller is personal where the buyer takes the delivery in return for immediate payment.

Other transactions may call for delivery to take place some time in future provided that the terms of the contract—that is, the price, the size, the time of delivery, settlement, and any other agency-related provisions—are negotiated today between the two parties. In still other scenarios the parties may arrange that no physical delivery of the goods takes place and the parties to settle their transactions on cash basis on or before the delivery date. These types of transactions are executed in the forward, futures, or options markets.

Options Transactions

A unilateral transaction where one party has the right but not the obligation to buy (to call) or to sell (to put) real or financial assets at a specific price (strike price) for a given future delivery period is called an option transaction. Insurance companies (e.g., life, property casualty, and other specialized companies) have underwritten put options (i.e., life insurance, health, fire, etc.) in individual life, and assets (i.e., property and vehicles) for centuries for profit. For example, motor vehicle insurance that an individual buys is a put option, which gives the right to the individual to sell the vehicle to an insurance company at strike price (the price at which the car is insured) in the event of an accident in which the vehicle is totaled. The insurance company that sold the put option in this case is obligated to perform and purchase the vehicle at the strike price even though the vehicle is nearly worthless. However, when individuals borrow against their real assets by leveraging their portfolio to purchase financial assets such as stocks, they are effectively buying a call option on the underlying assets. In the event stock price goes down, the brokerage firm will liquidate the position to recover the money that was lent unless the individual can put up more money to avoid being squeezed out of the margin position.

Options on financial assets such as stocks, bonds, bills, indices, currency, commodities, and interest rate futures take place in an organized exchange where the counterparty risk is eliminated. Examples of such markets are the Philadelphia Options Exchange and CME. In these markets, value is transferred from one party to another in a zero-sum game where the gain of one party is exactly equal to but opposite of the other party's loss.

Forward Market Transactions

Forward market transactions are over-the-counter transactions between two or more parties where buyer and seller enter into an agreement for future delivery of something of value priced today. The parties are obligated to perform on the settlement or delivery date. The earliest forward transactions occurred during the early days of civilization where crop producers entered into informal and non-standardized arrangements to buy or sell at current market price for delivery in the future.

Without an organized exchange for the execution of a transaction in the forward market and without any formal and standardized arrangement detailing provisions of the transaction (size, settlement date, and actual physical delivery of the goods or services), agency-related problems, including costs arise, should one party to the transaction fail to perform. Thus forward transactions can be risky. Although forward transactions these days take place between individuals or corporations and usually major banks or financial institutions, the counter-party risk still raises the exposure of the banks or the financial institutions to possible non-performance risk. To alleviate the problems associated with counterparty risk, inconvenience of physical delivery, and storage-related cost, an organized forward exchange was created. The transactions in the organized forward exchange came to be known as futures.

Futures Transactions

While a transaction in the forward market is personal, futures contracts provide impersonal transactions between two parties in an organized, orderly, and cost-efficient exchange market. They enter into an agency contract to buy or sell claims on financial or real assets known as derivatives. Because the exchange of value takes place in an organized physical location, the contracts are standardized to size, settlement date, and other agency-related provisions at the current spot price for delivery in the future.

Clearinghouses created by member participants of the organized exchanges ensure the integrity of the transactions and eliminates the counterparty risk by marking individual transactions to market on a daily basis. This daily settlement requires transfer of value from one individual to another individual in a zero-sum game. As current futures price (spot) changes daily as a result of the change in the underlying value of the assets (real or financial) due to various macro- or microfactors, the profit or loss is recognized and is posted to an individual account by the clearinghouse. Exhibit 1.6 provides a partial list of contracts traded in the four different organized futures exchanges in the United States and the United Kingdom.

EXHIBIT 1.6 Partial Lists of Contracts Traded in Four Different Futures Exchanges

LIFFE[a]	NYMEX[b]	CME[c]	CBOT[d]
STIR[e]	Energy-related	Currency futures	Long-term bonds
Long-term bonds	contracts	and options	Municipal bond index
SWAPS	Gold, silver	Interest rate futures	Commodities
Equity and index	Aluminum	and options	10-year notes
Commodity	Palladium	Index futures	
Options	Platinum	and options	
and futures	Copper	Commodity futures	
		and options	
		Weather futures	
		and options	

[a] London International Financial Futures and Options Exchange.
[b] New York Mercantile Exchange.
[c] Chicago Mercantile Exchange.
[d] Chicago Board of Trade.
[e] STIR refers to short-term interest rate contracts traded at LIFFE.

TYPES OF RISKS

Macrorisk

Macrorisk is the risk of being in the market, which cannot be avoided but can be managed. All domestic and multinational corporations (MNCs) face macroeconomic-induced risk, such as general downturns in economic activity, changing political landscape, war and peace, natural disasters, or international terrorism, that affect individual attitudes and expectations, which in turn causes change in consumption, investment, and financing decisions. As the attitude of individuals or firms toward risk and uncertainty change, so does their attitude about how much to save or consume and invest/or finance over time. In times of prosperity, economic agents consume more and expand production, while in the downturns and times of recession and increased uncertainty, they withhold from such activities.

The degree to which firms are exposed to macrorisk is entirely dependent on the nature of their business and is believed to be proportional to the expected payoff from their endeavor. For example, some firms are more prone to higher macrorisk than others and expect to do better in good times and worse in a down turn in economic activity.

Foreign Exchange Risk

Foreign exchange risk is unique to MNCs as the foreign-denominated cash inflows or outflows must at some time in the future be converted to the domestic currency of the operating unit, creating a windfall gains or losses. Direct foreign investment (DFI) in the form of acquiring foreign real assets (i.e., buying a plant overseas or building manufacturing facilities) to take advantage of imperfections in offshore markets and portfolio investment in stocks, bonds, and bills and other short-term assets entails opportunities for greater return (exchange gains) and higher risk due to foreign exchange losses.

Currency exchange risk—the economic, transaction, and accounting consequences of the fluctuation of exchange rates—strongly impacts many businesses. In the early 1980s, the tight monetary policy of Paul Volker, chairman of the Federal Reserves, resulted in high real interest rates in the United States compared to other countries. This in turn resulted in a high value of the dollar compared to other currencies, making the U.S. dollar relatively very strong and U.S. exports very expensive and unattractive to foreigners. Consequently Caterpillar, historically a world leader in the construction of heavy equipment, found itself at a disadvantage compared to its main competition Komatsu, a Japanese manufacturer of hydraulic excavators. Later in the 1980s, the strong dollar eased inflationary pressure in the U.S. economy, leading to lower inflationary expectations and a decline in the long-term U.S. interest rates. The value of the dollar also fell sharply following the September 1985 Plaza agreement in New York, as the Group of Five (G-5) central banks (the United States, Japan, Germany, France, and the United Kingdom) decided to put downward pressure on the value of U.S. dollar by selling dollars from their inventory to buy other foreign currency. This led to U.S. capital flight, as foreign investors were no longer interested in trading their currencies for dollars to invest in U.S. financial assets.

In 1986 Caterpillar had a $100 million profit on foreign exchange due to favorable weak U.S. dollar exchange rate that turned its $24 million operating loss into a $76 million profit for the year. As a result of this experience, Caterpillar established a special unit for managing currency risk exposure.[4]

Other companies did not fare as well. Lufthansa, the German airline, contracted with Boeing to purchase 20 aircrafts for $500 million in January 1985. Fearing revaluation of the U.S. currency, which could increase the deutsche mark cost of the planes, Lufthansa purchased dollar forwards in the foreign exchange market. In fact, however, the dollar devalued against the German mark. The forward contracts cost Lufthansa $140 to $160 million more for the planes than if it had simply waited and purchased the dollars on the spot market.[5]

To appreciate the severity of losses that firms experience due to unexpected changes in spot and forward rates, Exhibit 1.7 lists foreign exchange losses and events for a number of institutions around the world.

EXHIBIT 1.7   Foreign Exchange Loss

Company (home country)	Transaction-inducing Loss	Date	Approximate Loss	Description
Kashima Oil (Japan)	Futures	1993	$1.5 billion	Speculative losses stemming from loss of internal control
Abbott Lab (U.S.)	Foreign exchange	1993	$41.29 million	Loss due to unfavorable exchange rate
Telephones de Mexico (Mexico)	Foreign exchange	1994	$218 million	Loss due to unfavorable exchange rate movement
Bank Negara (Malaysia)	Futures	1993	$2.1 billion	Speculative loss in foreign currency futures
Allied Lyons (U.K.)	Foreign exchange options	1991	$219 million	Speculative loss from unauthorized option hedging
Viking Star (Bahamas)	Foreign exchange	1991	$31.4 million	Unfavorable exchange rate movement
Showa Shell (Japan)	Foreign exchange	1993	$1.54 billion	Affiliate of Shell conceals FX loss for years

Source: Company reports and various newspapers.

Does foreign exchange risk raise the cost of capital and lower the optimum debt ratio for MNCs?[6] The author's own research provides evidence to the contrary. Due to the ability of MNCs to exploit imperfections in the product, factor, and financial markets across international boundaries, they are able to earn monopoly rents. This is evidenced by higher market to book value ratio for MNCs relative to domestic corporations, as documented elsewhere.[7] This result does not negate the fact that MNCs attach higher hurdle rates for analyzing cash flows of foreign projects as higher risk-adjusted required rate of return of foreign projects embody additional premium for foreign exchange risk.

Political Risk

Political risk refers to a changing political landscape and its effects on the way individuals or firms conduct business in the world market. New political arrangements may impose various restrictions on the flow of goods and services. The risk of takeover or expropriation of foreign-owned assets or nationalization of foreign assets as proxy for political risk has been mitigated by a disciplining mechanism of the international capital market. The capital market has ensured and insulated capital providers from such risk by imposing grave penalties on perpetrators of such acts by simply refusing capital, the lifeblood of progress to the nations engaged in such acts. This risk was significant in the past, and multinational firms used to spend precious resources identifying, quantifying, and micromanaging it in cases involving acquisitions, foreign direct investment, and portfolio investment.

Greater integration of the world financial markets, global securitization, liberalization of trade, innovations of new financial products, and expansion of opportunities in a global environment have reduced and presumably eliminated the need for consideration of political risk for all practical purposes. The increased volatility in the financial markets due to a floating exchange rate arrangement since 1973 and greater interdependency of global economies have created new opportunities as well as additional risks associated with innovative derivatives. These four risks can be classified in an agency relationship context:

1. *Counterparty Risk.* The risk that one of the parties to the agency contract will fail to perform for whatever reasons and does not fulfill its financial obligations.[8]

2. *Liquidity Risk.* Associated with the lack of an efficient secondary market in which a long or short position can be liquidated without substantial discount at current market price.

3. *Rollover Risk.* The risk of being forced to close out the position without being able to renew the contract at the market prevailing price or rate. This risk is also synonymous with the availability of the fund. For example, a financial institution may extend a six-month fixed rate loan to a party and be able to fund the loan for three months; the institution is exposed with the risk of availability (rollover) for the funding of the loan for the next three months.

Some type of hedging in the forward or futures market is necessary to mitigate the risk of higher interest rate in the next three months.

4. ***Risk Risk.*** The risk of not knowing and understanding the ramifications of the type of the agency relation one has entered and the risks entailed in such relationship. The risk of not understanding the risk of security the (long or short) position one has taken.[9]

While most of these risks have been eliminated in the derivative markets in which the trade takes place in organized exchanges, the risks of over-the-counter transactions remain fairly substantial worldwide. Furthermore, the greater interdependencies among various economic units and the increase in the use and abuse of derivatives as well as greater coordination of fiscal and monetary policies in the context of various treaties (i.e., European Union, North American Free Trade Agreement, Asian Free Trade Agreement, and Economic Cooperation of West African Economies) have created an environment in which a shock to a local economy can easily spread to other trading partners.

NOTES

1. See *Webster's New World Dictionary of the American Language,* 2nd edition (New York: Simon and Schuster, 1980).

2. Bethany McLean, "Monster Mess," *Fortune,* February 4, 2002.

3. The speculative loss in the futures market for Bank Negara the central Bank of Malaysia was in excess of $2.1 billion in 1993. The loss for British Merchant Bank of Barings stemming from the speculative transactions by Nick Leeson, the Barings head of the trading division in Singapore, was in excess of $1.2 billion, forcing the bank into bankruptcy. The Baring was acquired in the bankruptcy.

4. Gregory J. Millman, *The Floating Battle Field: Corporate Strategies in the Currency War* (Amacom, l990).

5. Ibid.

6. Eiteman, Stonehill, and Moffett (2001, P-3) maintain that the foreign exchange risk raises cost of capital and lower optimal debt ratio for MNCs without substantiating the above hypotheses.

7. Homaifar, Zietz, and Benkato (1998) find that in contrast to conventional wisdom, MNCs employ less long-term debt in their capital structure than their domestic counterparts (DCs), which corroborates with Lee and Kowk's (1988) evidence that MNCs have lower debt ratio than domestic corporations. MNCs appear to have higher agency cost of debt than DCs. This evidence is consistent with those of Myers (1977) and of Lee and Kowk. MNCs have more nondebt tax shelter than DCs. According to Homaifar et al., the significant difference in tax shelter ratio between MNCs and DCs implies that the MNCs are better equipped to arbitrage institutional restrictions than DCs for the purpose of reducing their tax liabilities.

8. Credit Suisse First Boston counterparty to forward ruble/dollar contract fails to deliver dollars when the Russian government froze access to dollars in August 1997.

9. Orange County, California, retirement plan invested in derivative interest rate futures for enhancing the yield of the portfolio expecting interest rate to fall. This transaction was speculative in nature and was not intended to hedge or transfer risk. The interest rate actually did go up against the expectation of the retirement fund and the result was the loss of nearly $1.7 billion when interest rate futures liquidated for massive loss in December 1994. The retirement planner did not realize a priori what risk is entailed in interest rate futures transaction.

CHAPTER 2

Balance of Payments Exposure Management

Balance of payments (BOPs) provides a summary of all transactions involving real goods, services, financial assets (portfolio investments such as stocks, bonds and bills, etc.) and direct investments (i.e., foreign acquisitions, joint ventures, divestitures), capital (import/export), and transfer payment in cash or in kind between any two individuals, corporations, government entities, and countries over a specific period. Goods and services flow from one country to another to fulfill the individual's desire to consume what is not available or cannot be produced competitively in the importing local economy and the producer's desire to expand production in the exporting country to earn a profit. The trade takes place when one party acquires the know-how and technology to produce goods or services far more efficiently than another party.

The theory of comparative advantage provides reasonable explanations of why countries trade with one another. The pattern of trade between countries can provide a guiding principle for the resurgence of trade rooted in the theory of comparative advantage. Based on this theory, it pays to specialize in the production of certain goods or services and to trade these goods and services with others, where they have comparative advantage in production of those goods and services. The various regional free trade agreements (FTAs), such as the North American Free Trade Agreement (NAFTA), and the Asian Free Trade Agreement (AFTA), have provided a competitive advantage through a reduction or elimination of tariffs and quotas to a member country at the cost of a nonmember. This excerpt from the *Wall Street Journal* as of April 4, 2002, highlights the argument:

> Unlike multilateral trade accords where all members of the World Trade Organization are treated equally, bilateral and regional "free trade" deals create inequities by granting preferential treatment to some countries at the expense of others. This is why economists call FTAs by another name, preferential trade agreements. The effect of such agreements is that production of goods shifts from countries that have a comparative advantage to countries that are less efficient producers but have been given a competitive advantage through lowered tariffs.[1]

Free trade is not a zero-sum game, since the parties realize real gain and enhance their own welfare by producing in the areas for which they have achieved specialization, thereby producing at a minimum average cost. For example, U.S. manufacturing technology sectors have acquired comparative advantage in the production of goods requiring a highly skilled labor force and trading these goods for goods that its trading partners produce more efficiently.

It is important to distinguish between absolute advantage and comparative advantage. While most of U.S. trading partners in Latin America, Southeast Asia, and Eastern Europe have absolute advantage in hourly wages in manufacturing, U.S. manufacturing has absolute advantage in productivity (output per man-hour). The wage or productivity alone (absolute advantage) cannot be used as an argument in favor of protectionism; the ratio of the productivity over wage (comparative advantage) may dictate which goods or services the United States buys from its trading partners and the goods and services it sells. For example, wages in Mexico are much lower than those in the United States, and so is Mexico's productivity. Thus, Mexico buys goods and services from countries where the ratio of productivity over wage is greater than its own and sells goods and services where its productivity over wage is greater than its trading partners. It is no surprise that the United States buys steel and automobiles from Japan and sells food, lumber, aircrafts, and semiconductors. Exhibit 2.1 provides some preliminary evidence on the behavior of U.S. exports and imports from its major trading partners during the 1961 to 2001 period.

It appears that the United States imports more goods from its trading partners than it sells, thereby running a deficit, which is financed by issuing an IOU to trading partners in the form of short- or long-term financial assets. This creates exposure. The deficit appears to be much larger with Japan followed by Canada and Mexico. The United States experiences a small deficit against France and Germany and almost no deficit against the United Kingdom. The larger the deficit, the greater the chances that interest rates need to go up to entice creditors to extend the short- or long-term credit.

EXHIBIT 2.1   Behavior of U.S. Exports and Imports with Major Trading Partners (1996–2001)

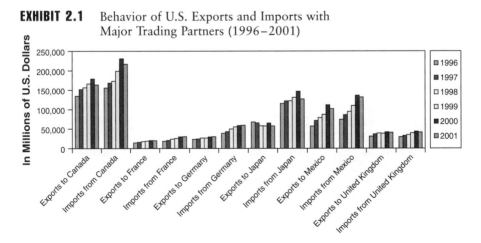

The rising cost of financing the current account deficit, particularly financing at the floating rate coupled with the availability (rollover) risk, is especially acute for emerging economies and economies plagued with high inflation. Fabio de Olivera Barbosa, Brazilian secretariat of the National Treasury, sums up this argument:

> The turbulence involving emerging economies in general, and Brazil in particular, deeply affected country access to international capital markets. The magnitude of change can been seen in the widening spreads for sovereign bonds. In June 1997, the Treasury issued a global, thirty-year bond with a 395 basis point spread; two years later, a global, ten-year bond was bearing an 850 basis point spread. The spread is over and above the equivalent dollar denominated bond of the same maturity.[2]

When a trading partner exhausts all of its options to acquire financing in the private sector, lenders of last resort—the International Monetary Fund (IMF) or the World Bank—may provide funding; however, it may impose various "austerity" restrictions on the borrower that may or may not be in the best interest of the borrowing country.

BALANCE OF PAYMENTS AS A SOURCE AND USE OF FUNDS

Balance of payment is the summary of all international transactions between residents of one country with the rest of the world community, as each transaction is recorded as a credit and debit over a specific period. BOP is virtually a source and use of fund statement as an accounting identity, where the sources of funds are those transactions that increase the purchasing power of a nation that must equal use of fund, those transactions that reduce the purchasing power of a country. The export of goods and services creates source of funds and the import of goods and services produces the use of funds. The export of goods, services, and capital generates demand for the currency of the exporting country and supply of foreign currency as foreign buyers use their own currency to purchase the currency of the exporter to pay for the export. Likewise, the import of goods, services, and capital generates supply of currency of the importer and demand for foreign currency to settle transactions. Therefore, any imbalance in the supply of and demand for the currency of the export and/or import creates temporary disequilibria and exposure to currency and interest rate risks.

COMPONENTS OF BALANCE OF PAYMENTS

Current Account

The current account summarizes all transactions on the net balance of the trading of goods and services, net balance of income on direct investment and portfolio investment, and net transfer payments in cash or in kind over a specific period. When a country runs a deficit in its current account by issuing claims to the assets acquired, it is essentially supplying more of its currency in the market than the market demands. This phenomenon creates an excess demand for the currency of the country where more goods and services are imported from than exported and simultaneously increases the excess supply of currency of the country running the deficit. The excess supply of currency as a result of a trade imbalance induces a chain reaction in the financial markets, leading to the eventual devaluation of the country's currency to eliminate the excess supply in a floating rate environment.

Capital Account

The capital account summarizes transactions on the net direct foreign investment and net portfolio investment in stocks, bonds, T-bills, and other net short- or long-term financial assets of private sector and/or government agencies over a specific period. The net current and capital account make up the overall balance of a nation. However, since the floating rate arrangement of 1973, the short-term capital account has become increasingly volatile, leading to the importance of the basic balance composed of net current account and the long-term capital account (net).

Official Foreign Exchange Reserve

This is the central bank's portfolio holding of foreign currencies, gold, and other certificates and near money, such as special drawing rights (SDRs), issued as a form of reserve credit to members by the IMF; a member can borrow from other members up to 625 percent of the member's allocation. The ability of a country's central bank to maintain its currency at a desired exchange rate is directly related to the amount of reserve it has accumulated as a buffer against temporary disequilibria. Countries experiencing chronic and persistent deficits in their current accounts are forced to tap into their reserves to maintain their currency value, thereby dwindling reserves and running the risk of severe depreciation. Depreciation can be a double-edged sword, beneficial to exports as goods and services become attractive to foreigners and detrimental to the economy as import prices go up (in addition, domestic producers will find this as an opportunity to raise their product price) and inflation occurs in the economy.

However, countries with a surplus in their current account normally build up their reserves and enjoy the benefits of a strong currency that can be anti-inflationary as import prices fall and local producers are forced to maintain the price of their domestic production at current price.

Statistical Discrepancy for Errors and Omissions

This category is created to balance source and use of fund statements due to transactions involving barter (i.e., an exchange of service for service) and underground economic activities (i.e., smuggling, money laundering, and other illegal transactions) where no entry is made on the port of entry as to the value of the goods over a specific period of time. The components of BOP that produce the balance of payments equation can be summarized as:

$$\text{Current account} + \text{Capital account} + \text{Official reserve}$$
$$+ \text{Statistical discrepancy} = 0$$

Exhibit 2.2 (the cumulative four-quarter balances), which shows the U.S. current and key components of capital account as well as statistical error in year 2001, is taken from the Federal Reserve Bank of St Louis.

CURRENT ACCOUNT AND ECONOMIC FUNDAMENTALS

The relationship between current account and economic fundamentals is discussed briefly in the following section. However, in the interest of clarity and to provide a foundation on which later analysis will be more meaningful, here we approach the relationship from a different angle—the current account summarizing all transactions originating in the asset markets between a country's residents and the rest of the world. Demand for a particular good in the asset market is a function of price, income, and price of substitute goods, where the quantity demanded of a good is inversely related to its price and directly related to price of substitute goods and income.

The same principle is applicable to the demand for imports and supply of exports originating in current account with few exceptions, such as the role of government and the action it can take to promote or curb trade by eliminating trade barriers or by imposing tariff and quota. What about the exchange rate? The exchange rate is theoretically the ratio of the prices of baskets of identical goods

EXHIBIT 2.2 U.S. Balance of Payments 2001
(in billions)

Merchandise Trade: −$426.515	+	
Balance on Service: +$78.803	+	
Balance on Investment Income: −$19.114	+	
Balance on Net Transfer: −$50.501	+	
Current Account	=	− $417.427
Foreign Direct Investment in U.S.: $157.934	+	
Portfolio Investment in U.S.: $514.212	+	
U.S. Direct Investment Overseas: −$156.018	−	
U.S. Portfolio Investment Overseas: −$97.661	−	
Capital Account excluding Reserves	=	+ $418.467
Capital Account including Reserves		+ $455.895
Statistical Discrepancy		− $ 39.196

Source: The Federal Reserve Bank of St. Louis.

and services in two different currencies. In reality, such baskets do not exist due to differences in individual tastes across the globe. The factors inducing change in current account can be summarized as:

- Exchange rate ≈ ratio of two prices
- Income
- Government
- Expectations ≈ consumer confidence

Other factors, such as inflation and the unemployment rate, affect the exchange rate and consumer confidence respectively and shape individuals' expectations about their own state in particular and the state of the economy in general. As the state of the economy improves (income rises), consumer confidence rises, propelling consumer propensity to consume and spend, including acquiring more foreign goods and services imported from overseas. These actions cause a deficit in the current account.[3] Factors such as income and expectations are interrelated.

Exchange Rate

As the dollar weakens against foreign currencies, requiring more dollars to acquire foreign currency, the goods and services made in the United States become relatively more attractive to foreign buyers. In this scenario, exports are expected to improve as the domestic goods become cheaper for foreigners to acquire and imports are expected to fall as foreign goods and services tend to be more expensive, thus creating an increase and improvement in the current account balance. This simplistic analysis assumes among other things that the pass-through from the exchange rate to prices of goods and services in the exports and imports sector of the economy is complete and simultaneous. For example, suppose the dollar appreciates by 5 percent against all other currencies. If the export price goes up by 5 percent and the import price goes down 5 percent immediately following dollar appreciation, then the pass-through is complete and simultaneous. The evidence for the U.S. economy and its implications for managing exposure is contrary to this analysis. This important issue is discussed in Chapter 3.

Government

The government can and does play an important role in shaping policies that lead to improving overall economic activities in a democracy. For years, the struggling U.S. steel industry has been lobbying Congress for the imposition of a tariff and/or quota on imported cheap steel from other countries to protect domestic producers. Such actions have a common denominator: They make imported foreign steel from countries where Congress has imposed a tariff more expensive compared to that of those given preferential treatment of no tariff or less tariff and also invites domestic producers to raise their prices. This action, assuming it is not reciprocated by tariff-impacted countries (i.e., other countries imposing no tariff on U.S. goods), is expected to reduce imports and help exports, thereby improving the current account balance for the United States.

CAPITAL ACCOUNT, EXPECTATION, AND INTEREST RATE

The capital account tends to be interest rate and yield sensitive. Expectations also play a major role for making foreign direct investment and portfolio investments by U.S. individuals and institutions overseas as well as their foreign counterparts in the U.S. markets. Investors seeking a better return overseas are usually attracted to emerging economies with a promise of expected high yield. In particular, the short-term capital account is highly sensitive to interest rate and yield in emerging market stocks and bonds markets. The so-called hot capital in pursuit of high returns moves swiftly from one country to another and retreats at the sign of any weakness and financial crises, creating substantial exposure to users and providers of capital. This example shows the net capital inflows (+) to the United States during the year 2001:

2001.1	347.006
2001.2	226.927
2001.3	57.718
2001.4	263.806

This example vividly reflects the impact of the September 11 attack on the World Trade Center on the quarterly net capital inflows to the United States. The net capital flow dramatically fell to $57.718 billion by the end of the third quarter as foreign investors divested their portfolio investment in the United States due to rising concern regarding international terrorism and its adverse impact on the performance of the overall U.S. economy. However, foreign investors returned to the U.S. market as the pace of investment in the United States rose over and above the pre-September 11 to $263.806 billion by the fourth quarter of 2001. It appears that the world capital market has treated the September 11 as an isolated event (i.e., unsystematic risk).

U.S. BALANCE OF PAYMENTS: RECENT EVIDENCE

Exhibit 2.3 provides some interesting patterns of U.S. current and capital account as a percentage of fourth-quarter gross domestic products (GDP) over the 1961 to 2001 period. The current account is the balance of country's income derived from exports and expenditure due to imports. While current account as a percentage of GDP is painting a widening deficit over time, the net capital account provides a picture of an economy that has attracted long- and short-term net capital in the form of foreign direct investment, portfolio investment, and other

EXHIBIT 2.3   U.S. Annual Current and Capital Account as
Percentage of the Fourth Quarter GDP

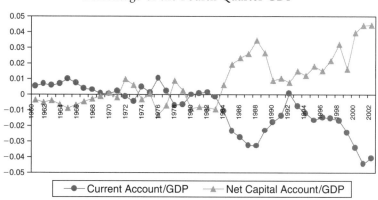

short- or long-term capital to finance the deficit. The excess supply of U.S. currency created as a result of the deficit in current account appears more than offset by the excess demand for the U.S. dollar in the capital account.

In the 1960s, the current account as a percentage of GDP was positive, ranging from .5 percent in 1960 to 0.2 percent by the end of 1970. The capital account, however, was negative, ranging nearly −0.3 percent to −0.2 percent during the same span. International trade, the sum of exports and imports, was nearly 5 percent of GDP in the mid-1960s. In the 1970s to 1980s, the pattern of U.S. trade remained fairly the same as in the 1960s with gradual increase in international trade; the current account as percentage of GDP remained positive in all years except 1971, 1972, and 1977 to 1979; capital account behaved opposite of the current account during the same period, as indicated in Exhibit 2.3.

The 1980s witnessed a gradual deterioration in the current account; in particular, the deficit in the current account reached 3.24 and 3.28 percent of GDP by 1986 and 1987. However, the capital account was positive, reaching 2.6 and 3.4 percent of GDP during the same period.[4] The 1980s coincided with the defense buildup of the Reagan presidency, a rising annual budget deficit, and the tripling of the national debt by the end of 1989. While nominal interest rates had fallen significantly by the mid-1980s due to falling inflation and inflationary expectations, the real interest rate remained fairly attractive. Coupled with a strong U.S. dollar and a rising equity price, enormous foreign capital was invested in the United States to finance a huge twin deficit, in current account and in the annual government budget.

In the 1990s, the current account continued to behave as it had in the 1980s, except for 1991, when the current account turned into a small surplus due to the huge transfer of receipts from the U.S. allies in the Gulf War to pay for the execution of the war. By the late 1990s and the beginning of 2000 and 2001, the deficit in the current account ballooned to 3.4, 4.4, and 4.0 percent of the GDP; the surplus in the capital account more than offset the deficit during the same period. The international trade as a percentage of GDP by 2000 in the United States reached nearly 20 percent of the GDP.

The deficit in the current account can cut both ways. Assuming a nation's productive capacity increases as a result of importing more capital (i.e., goods, services, and credit) and net capital flows are used to build up a country's infrastructure and foreign reserve, it follows that the deficit and the resulting exposure to interest rate and exchange rate changes will not adversely effect the economy. The deficit and resulting exposure in this scenario is a value-creating phenomenon; in financial terms, it is a positive net present value. The increase in imports over exports is invested at the rate exceeding the cost of funding the deficit. However, a deficit can be harmful to the well-being of an economy if an increase in the deficit is used primarily to finance current, not future, consumption. In such a case, the resulting exposure to interest rate and foreign exchange risk can be devastating. In the scenario discussed, the deficit is invested at the rate below the cost of capital in the negative net present value projects.

EXPOSURE RELATED TO CAPITAL ACCOUNT

Exposure in the capital account is related to the foreign direct investment and portfolio investment overseas. The return of the original capital and the capital gain or loss, royalties, and interest income are exposed to foreign exchange risk as well as interest rate and market risk, creating opportunities for a windfall gain as a result of favorable exchange rate movements and falling interest rates or losses stemming from unfavorable exchange rate and rising interest rates.

Example: Suppose a U.S. money manager invests in one-year bonds denominated in British pounds promising an 8 percent interest rate. Assume the pound appreciates by 5 percent during the year. The return to the U.S. investor as defined in Equation 2.1 is 13.40 percent.

The returns realized by U.S. investors investing in foreign assets (i.e., stocks, bonds, bills, and other long-term instruments) are related to:

$$\boxed{\text{Interest, dividend, capital gains (losses)}} +/- \boxed{\text{Foreign exchange gains/losses}}$$

$$(1 + \text{Return in \$}) = (1 + \text{Return in £}) \, (1 + \% \text{ change in exchange rate})$$

(2.1)

Ignoring the covariation of the return in foreign currency and percentage change in dollar value of pound, the rate of return in dollars will be simply equal to 13 percent—the sum of 8 percent interest and windfall gain due to favorable exchange rate movement of 5 percent.

The risk as measured by the variance of Equation 2.1 will be:

$$\text{Volatility in \$} = \text{volatility in £} + \text{volatility of percentage change}$$
$$\text{in \$/£ exchange rate}[5]$$

The volatility (variance) of the return realized by the U.S. investor is directly related to the volatility of the U.K. interest rate as well as the volatility of the percentage change in exchange rate.

Suppose the pound devalues by 50 percent, due to a weakness in its economic fundamentals and a huge protracted deficit in its balance of payments, causing a substantial hike in the interest rate, which results in an increase in nonperforming loans due to an inability of the borrowers to service their debt, thereby inducing a crisis in the U.K. banking sector. This in turn causes a substantial drop in the rate of return to U.S. investors as defined by Equation 2.1 to −46 percent, the sums of 8 percent interest, −50 percent loss due to unfavorable foreign exchange rate movements, and −4 percent due to the interaction term between interest rate in pound and percentage change in exchange rate.

In this scenario, U.S. investors will most likely divest their holdings of British-denominated bonds, causing massive flight of capital and further depreciation of the pound. The spillover contagion effect to U.S. providers of capital to British borrowers can range from massive losses to U.S. institutions as British borrowers default as U.S. institutions realize large losses in their portfolio investments due to rising interest rates and the falling market value of stocks and bonds, inducing a banking crisis in the United States.

Brazilian Experience

The current account deficit in Brazil and the devaluation of its currency in January 1999 is at the center of the Brazilian currency crisis. The current account as a percentage of GDP began to deteriorate starting in 1994, and by 1998 the deficit reached nearly −.037 percent of the GDP, as shown in Exhibit 2.4.

The Brazilian currency (real), which at times was relatively overvalued against the U.S. dollar, started a significant downward spiral particularly in 1998 to 2000, losing more than 50 percent of its value since its inception in 1995. As seen in Exhibit 2.5, the real remained fairly stable since its inception; however, it nearly depreciated by over 25 and 27 percent compound rate between 1988 and 1999.

According to Brazil's central bank, by 1999, 59.6 percent of the domestic debt to finance deficit was in the form of overnight borrowing at the floating rate interest. No wonder the significant increase in current account deficit and subsequent

EXHIBIT 2.4   Current Account as a Percentage of GDP

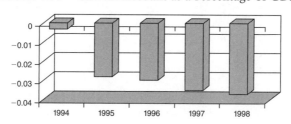

EXHIBIT 2.5   Rate of Depreciation of Brazilian Real (1995–2000)

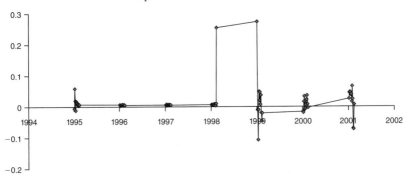

speculative attack on the Brazilian real was not coincidental. This excerpt from the secretariat treasury of Brazil points in the right direction as to the cause of Brazilian financial crisis of 1998–1999:

> The bulk of the federal budget deficit in Brazil is financed by domestic capital markets, mostly through bonded debt. After 1994, which marked the beginning of the Real Plan and the successful process of macroeconomic stabilization, it was clear that the federal government's debt management strategy should be adapted to the new environment. By that time, public debt structure was almost fully indexed—most of it to inflation indexes, the exchange rate, or to floating short-term interest rates; nominal, fixed-rate instruments represented no more than 6 percent of total outstanding debt. At that point, the basic strategy was to modify the domestic debt structure by gradually increasing the share and average maturity of fixed-rate instruments.[6]

The Brazilian central bank was at the center of the Brazilian financial turbulence, where short-term debt financing mitigated the long-term structural deficit problems. This action of the central bank amounted to planting a ticking time bomb in the Brazilian economy, expected to go off at any time without warning. The exposure to interest rates changes could have been mitigated by changing the composition of debt and lengthening the duration of the bond issues, particularly reducing the size of the overnight borrowing and restructuring the debt by reducing the central bank's adverse selection of accepting more poor risk associated with short-term borrowing than long-term fixed rate borrowing. The currency crises and the risk associated with them are directly related (co-vary) with the interest rate risk and associated banking crises that they entail.[7]

The run on currency and speculative attack by short sellers and arbitrageurs following the deterioration of the country's economic fundamentals, such as prolonged deficit in the current account, budget deficit, high inflation, and high interest rates, lead to currency crises.[8] The central bank's reaction to currency crises can lead to a crisis in the banking sector as weak banks with substantial nonperforming loans are forced into bankruptcy due to rising interest rates. The central bank's attempt to shore up the supply of its own currency, however, using finite reserve to save the currency from speculative attack, and its attempt to tighten monetary aggregate by raising interest rates while simultaneously providing liquidity to the banking system in order to bail out the weak banks led to the creation of excessive money, higher inflation, and interest rates that chocks up the economy.[9]

Currency and interest rate risks and the ensuing crises can result from the way the imbalances in the current account are financed in booming economic times. When the imbalance is financed primarily with large capital inflows and short-term credit from large foreign banks at times of economic growth and rising prosperity, the return on investment is usually greater than the cost of capital. However, as the boom ends and foreign short-term capital retreats as a result of actual and expected severe currency devaluation and as the cost of servicing foreign currency–denominated loans skyrocket and bankruptcies mounts, solvency of local banks is put in doubt due to currency and banking crises.[10]

Currency Crisis in Southeast Asia

The currencies of Thailand, South Korea, Indonesia, Malaysia, and the Philippines were severely depreciated during 1997 and 1998, ranging as high as -52.6 percent for the Korean won and as low as -34.4 percent for the Philippine peso. The capital flows to the region in the form of foreign direct investment, portfolio investment, and bank loans that fueled the engine of the economic growth in the 1980s and much of the 1990s were reversed due to the severity of the currency devaluation and the fallout in the equity markets as capital flight from the region led to retrenchment of the exposed capital to both currency and interest rate risk.

According to Kowai, the influx of global private short-term "hot" capital in search of high-yield, inflow of unhedged capital to finance domestic credit boom, insufficiently regulated domestic financial markets with highly leveraged corporations, and increasing political uncertainty made East Asian economies vulnerable to external shocks in the period preceding the crisis.[11] Implicit or explicit government guarantees provided financial institutions with the incentive to borrow excessively, encouraged excessive risk taking, and created "moral hazard" problems for borrowers and lenders. Furthermore, the fixed exchange rate arrangement in the precrisis period provided the illusion that foreign currency–denominated loans at lower interest rates as compared to higher interest rates at home were immune from the exchange rate and interest rate risks.[12]

It appears that the currency crisis in East Asia was due to systematic failures in several key areas, and supervisory institutions of banks and finance companies lacked the moral courage and incentives to take actions that could have prevented the chaos or at least reduced the extent and severity of the crisis.

Corsetti, Pesenti, and Roubini provide a link between the current account (CA) deficit as a percentage of GDP and extent of the depreciation of the currencies in East Asia during 1997, as shown in the Exhibit 2.6.[13]

EXHIBIT 2.6 Current Account/Gross Domestic Product and the Percentage Changes in Exchange Rates

	1996	1996–97
Korea	−4.82%	−52.6%
Indonesia	−3.3	−49.6
Malaysia	−3.73	−35.2
Philippines	−4.67	−34.4
Thailand	−8.51	−44.4
China	0.52	0.0
Hong Kong	−2.43	0.0
Singapore	16.23	−16.1
Taiwan	4.67	−15.9

Source: G. Corsetti, P. Pesenti, and N. Roubini, "What Caused the Asian Currency and Financial Crisis?" *Japan and the World Economy* (October 1999): 305–373.

According to Corsetti and associates, countries with severe devaluations in 1996–1997 experienced a high current account deficit in the 1990s financed primarily with short-term debt. South Korea and Thailand financed only 10 and 16 percent of the current account deficit with long-term direct foreign investment. The short-term foreign liabilities to major foreign banks as a percentage of reserve at the end of 1996 was 213 percent for South Korea, 181 percent for Indonesia, 169 percent for Thailand, 77 percent for the Philippines, and 47 percent for Malaysia, based on an estimate provided by Corsetti and associates. The current account for China, Hong Kong, Singapore, and Taiwan were near zero or positive; therefore, these countries were not affected as much or as severely as the other five countries in the region. Since short-term capital flows are highly sensitive to expectations of higher yield, they also run the risk of quick reversal when expectations fail to materialize.[14]

Exhibit 2.7 presents short-term foreign liabilities as a percentage of international reserve for the five Asian Economies.

EXHIBIT 2.7 Short-Term Foreign Liabilities/International Reserves

	Indonesia	Malaysia	Philippines	South Korea	Thailand
June 1990	2.21	.22	3.18	1.06	.59
June 1994	1.73	.25	.41	1.61	.99
June 1997	1.70	.61	.85	2.06	1.45

Source: Bank for International Settlement, International Monetary Fund.

Short-term foreign liabilities exceeded international reserves for Indonesia, South Korea, and Thailand, an indicator of international bankers' refusal to roll over credit; thus these countries would not have had enough reserves to meet their short-term obligations. When the value of short-term international debt denominated in hard currency exceeds the liquidation value of assets in hard currency, a country's financial system is internationally illiquid. That is the way in which assets are financed in the emerging economies, and the mismatch of the assets' maturity and that of the foreign liabilities is at the center of the Southeast Asian crises.[15]

Current account deficit can be a source of extending economic growth beyond the country's own means. The capital imported from overseas economies in the form of DFI, portfolio investment, and bank loans has provided the necessary ingredients for the creation of jobs and opportunities in the U.S. economy as well as a fair rate of return to the providers of capital. So long as the imported capital is invested in increasing productive capacity of a country where the cost of capital is less than return on capital, the deficit in current account is essentially a value-producing phenomena. This has been the case for the U.S. economy so far.

EXCHANGE RATE ARRANGEMENTS, DOLLARIZATION, AND PEG

Several countries, particularly those hard hit with chronic inflation such as Brazil and Argentina, have attempted to establish a currency regime that protects the purchasing power of their currency. With the exception of Hungary, these countries and their respective currencies are pegged to the U.S. dollar, as shown in Exhibit 2.8.

There are more than eight different currency regimes in the world. Countries move from one regime to another in hopes of finding a system of exchange

EXHIBIT 2.8   Currencies Pegged to U.S. Dollar

Country	Currency	Currency Pegged to
Argentina	peso	U.S. dollar
Bahamas	dollar	U.S. dollar
Barbados	dollar	U.S. dollar
Bermuda	dollar	U.S. dollar
China	yaun	U.S. dollar
Hong Kong–China	HK$	U.S. dollar
Hungary	forint	Composite of European currencies
Saudi Arabia	riyal	U.S. dollar

Source: International Financial Statistics, International Monetary Fund, Washington D.C., July 1999.

rate that can provide financial stability and maintain the purchasing power of their currency.[16] For example, the South Korean won was pegged to the U.S. dollar prior to its collapse in 1997; thereafter, the Korean won was allowed to float against other currencies.

Prior to 1991 Argentina was in a managed exchange rate regime. After 1991 it established a currency board that fixed the exchange rate against the U.S. dollar at a one-on-one ratio, requiring the central bank to maintain a 100 percent reserve in the form of dollars or gold for every peso issued by the government. While the IMF and World Bank hailed this policy early on, the 100 percent reserve requirement imposed an unnecessary burden to an economy with a relatively small foreign sector. Since Argentina was required to either earn a dollar or attract a dollar in the form of DFI or portfolio investment to issue pesos, Argentina's monetary policy was completely dependent on the U.S. monetary policy.

In addition, the central bank allowed Argentineans to hold dollar-denominated savings and checking accounts, thereby creating excessive demand for dollars. The Argentineans, weary and distrustful of their government and their own currency, continued to accumulate U.S. dollars, making maintenance of the peg at a one-to-one ratio impossible. The currency board system, aimed at providing stability for Argentina's economy, was destined to collapse. Exhibit 2.9 shows the distribution of outstanding bank certificates of deposit (CDs) held in the banking system in U.S. dollars as a percentage of total deposits as of 1992 to 1999 reported by Argentina's central bank.

The exhibit clearly indicates the Argentinean preference for the U.S. dollar as opposed to their own currency. The ownership of the dollar-denominated CDs held by individuals and institutions is nearly in the low 60s as a percentage of the total up until 1995, and the percentage grows to the low 70s from 1996 to 1999. For example, by December 1999, of the 47.82 billion total CDs, $34.32 billion were denominated in U.S. currency, and only 28 percent of total CDs were in pesos. CD holders knew more about the real value of the peso than the

EXHIBIT 2.9   Ownership of
Dollar-Denominated Time
Deposits by Argentineans

Year	Dollar-Denominated Time Deposit as a Percentage of Total
1992	.61
1993	.58
1994	.61
1995	.65
1996	.72
1997	.72
1998	.70
1999	.72

currency board, despite the higher interest rates differential in favor of the peso, and they demonstrated this by holding more dollars than pesos. Exhibit 2.10 shows the interest rate differential between Argentina's monthly 30- to 59-day central bank time deposit rate and U.S. 90-day time deposit rate as of 1992 to 2002.

The higher interest rate differential and the greater volatility in Argentina's peso reflect the higher risk premium due to exchange rate risk and sovereign risk. Particularly notable is the rising interest rate differential to nearly 14 percent by early 1995 that is attributed to the spillover effect from the 1994 currency and banking crises in Mexico. The interest rate differential remained under 5 percent for part of 1995 and throughout 1999 with a small spike in the 1997 due to the Asian crises and the 1998 Russian ruble devaluation. Finally, the interest rate differential approached nearly 30 percent with the collapse of the peso and rising inflation in 2001.

It appears that there was no money illusion, at least for those individuals and institutions holding CDs denominated in U.S. dollars, despite a relatively higher interest rate denominated in pesos. The term "money illusion" refers to the inability of individuals to distinguish between lower interest rates in hard currency (dollars) and higher interest rates in soft currency (pesos).

Since the supply of dollars was limited, the demand for dollars by all individuals far exceeded the supply. The result is familiar: The peso has to devalue and the dollar has to appreciate, and that is exactly what happened.

Argentina's Peso Doomed to Collapse

After nearly four years of recession with an unemployment rate of 20 percent, and ballooning foreign debt at $141 billion, Argentina decided to devalue the peso in early December 2001, at the urging of the IMF. The peso lost more than

EXHIBIT 2.10   Interest Rate Differential: Argentina and the United States

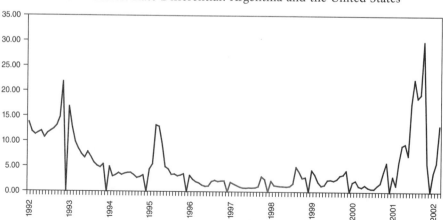

70 percent of its value, to 3.1 pesos per U.S. dollar. According to a *Wall Street Journal* report, massive devaluation resulted in a default of Argentina's $141 billion in loans from major foreign banks and a banking holiday on December 1 to avoid a run in the banking system.[17] Devaluation reignited the inflation and inflationary expectations in Argentina, for years hidden by the currency board. Exhibit 2.11 provides the percentage change in consumer and producer price index in Argentina from 1995 to 2002.

While inflation appeared to be under control, nearly falling to zero by 1996 and under zero (deflation) for much of the 1999–2000 period under the currency board, it was essentially bottled as a genie trying to get out. After the collapse of the peso, the consumer (retail) inflation rate exceeded 24 percent. Had the peso been allowed to adjust at least periodically to macroeconomic forces, the gradual transition to a system of independent float that the current government in Argentina is seeking would have been less painful and costly.

This is not to say that the currency board and/or any other fixed exchange rate regime are inherently untenable. On the contrary, fixed and managed exchange rates may provide financial stability that policy makers in different countries seek, provided that the imbalance in the current account is used to finance projects that pay more than they cost. It is, however, absolutely impossible to require a system with significant differences in socioeconomic, political, and market structure as compared to the U.S. structures to be dollarized overnight.

Exhibit 2.12 provides a clue as to the collapse of the peso and failure of the currency board to maintain and restore stability in the formerly inflation-ravaged economy of Argentina. The current account deficit as a percentage of

EXHIBIT 2.11   Argentina's Producer and Consumer Price Changes (1995–2002)

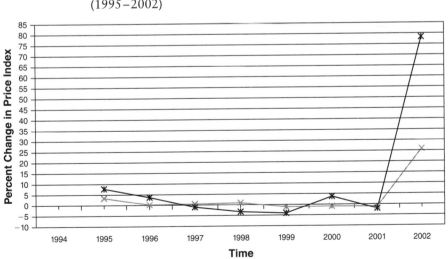

EXHIBIT 2.12   Argentina's Current Account as a Percentage of GDP

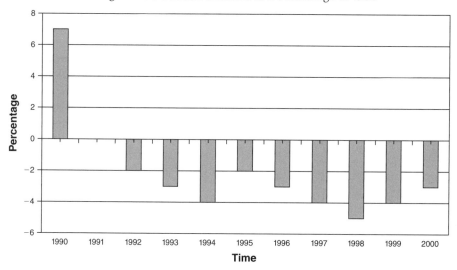

GDP continued to deteriorate and reach over −5 percent by 1995; this was followed by the recession of 1996–1997 and the next three years. The overvalued peso choked the export sector by making goods produced in Argentina extremely uncompetitive, thereby aggravating and prolonging the recession.

The IMF, as a lender of last resort, is requiring Argentina to cut spending as a precondition of extending additional lines of credits.

MANAGING BALANCE OF PAYMENT EXPOSURE
IN THE EMERGING MARKET ECONOMIES

The imbalance in the current account and the way in which it is financed is at the center of various crises, starting with the devaluation of the Mexican peso in 1994, the Russian currency devaluation of August 1998, the Brazilian currency devaluation of January 1999, the Southeast Asian crisis of 1996–1997, and more recently Argentina's financial and currency crisis of 2002. The external debt of emerging and developing economies is financed primarily either through short-term or long-term jumbo loans syndicated by large banks at a floating rate (usually LIBOR—London Interbank Offering Rate—plus spread). There is almost no distinction between short-term and long-term credit as known in the West (short-term credit is usually at a floating rate, while long-term credit is at a fixed rate) as related to the extension of credit to emerging market economies.

The one distinction between short- and long-term credit is related to rollover risk. This risk is mitigated in long-term debt at least until maturity. At times, short-term credit has to be rolled over at the maturity of the short-term debt at the then-current interest rate denominated in a major foreign currency. While individual and corporate borrowers in the West have the option of refinancing their long-term debt when rates fall, such an option usually is not available to borrowers in emerging market economies. Here is the problem. The banks, especially in the United States and Europe during the aftermath of the savings and loan debacle, learned a valuable lesson and started to pass the interest rate risk to the ultimate borrower. The risk did not disappear; indeed it has increased as the exchange rate has become more volatile since the floating rate arrangement of 1971.

For emerging market economies, external borrowing coupled with the excessive use of leverage by corporate borrowers and associated interest rate risk and foreign exchange rate risk has been a recipe for disaster, as seen in the 1990s. Corporate borrowers in emerging market economies need to restructure their balance sheets through an equity for debt swap to reduce their debt/equity ratio. This restructuring increases equity and reduces interest charges for servicing debt. It will be in the best long-term interest of the suppliers of foreign capital, particularly large banks, to afford the same options to users of capital in emerging markets that they offer to their own market; that is, to extend long-term credit at a fixed rate denominated in foreign currency to emerging market economies with the option to refinance the loan when and if it is profitable for the borrowers to do so. In this scenario, creditors are protected from the interest and foreign exchange risk and borrowers are locked at the fixed foreign–denominated interest rate, where the cost of servicing debt is known and borrowers can take steps to manage exposure to both types of risk.

Case Study

KAIROS CAPITAL

by James Feller, Yan Liu, and Zhijie Qi

Merlina Katapodis stared through her office window, scarcely noticing the murky haze that spread over Athens. The Areopagus rose in the distance, but the unusually dank morning rendered the mountain indistinct. Deep in thought, she pondered her first major assignment with Kairos Capital, a private investment partnership comprising a number of extremely wealthy and powerful shipping magnates. At the moment, she felt little of the ambitious drive that had launched her into her current position.

Katapodis had returned to her native Greece only two months before and had been recruited by George Condoratos, Kairos Capital's primary managing partner. Condoratos was especially impressed with the undergraduate business degree she had earned from a major American university and the graduate work she had done at the London School of Economics. Although Katapodis had not completed the master's degree requirements, she felt confident that

(continues)

her academic background in international economics would provide her with the appropriate analytical tools to identify exceptional investment opportunities in developing countries. After only one week on the job, her eagerness had been replaced by apprehensiveness. Her academic background, while impressive on paper, had primarily emphasized abstract modeling and theory. Moreover, she had concentrated on the socioeconomics of Latin American countries, and while she considered herself an expert in this area, she knew little about the emerging nations of Africa and Asia. Thus, she was dismayed when she received Condoratos's e-mail naming China as the focus of her initial investigation. The memorandum was terse, offering no particular guidance, and only one restriction: that she present, on paper and orally, the results of her first-stage analysis on Thursday afternoon of the following week. Two of the nine days had passed, and she had not, except for some halfhearted exploratory forays, accomplished anything of substance. Her attempts to elicit suggestions from the other analysts had been politely rebuffed, as all three were currently involved in their own assignments and facing their own deadlines. Additionally, although it was not outwardly apparent, they were loath to disclose the methods on which their own success depended, and perhaps even jealous of Katapodis's educational background and beginning salary.

Katapodis swiveled her chair from the bleak window view back to her desk and noticed the framed adage, in Greek script, that had provided her with inspiration in past difficulties. Attributed to Heraclitus, it bluntly stated, in English translation: "Many fail to grasp what is right in the palm of their hand." As she considered the years of dedicated study she had spent and the expertise she did possess, her doubts began to dissipate. She mused to herself, "Well, I'll start with what I can do, and learn the rest on my own as I go." Katapodis clicked the mouse, and began.

See Exhibits 1 through 3 for China's balance of payment from 1989 to 1998.

THOUGHT QUESTIONS

1. Did China have a merchandise (goods and services) trade surplus or deficit? What is the trend?
2. Was China's current account in surplus or deficit?
3. Relate the percentage change in current account to the percentage changes in the all-urban Consumer Price Index during the same period. Was there a positive or a negative relation between the two?
4. Did China have a financial account surplus or deficit?
5. What is the current account deficit or surplus as percentage of GDP?
6. How devaluation of China's currency affected the current account balance?
7. Calculate the index of real exchange rates for China (assuming base year of 1994 and the index is set at 100).

EXHIBIT 1 Current Account (Units: US$, Scale:: Millions)

During Period	Goods Exports: F.O.B.	Goods Imports: F.O.B.	Trade Balance	Services: Credit	Services: Debit	Balance on Goods and Services	Income: Credit	Income: Debit	Balance on Goods, Services, and Inc.	Current Transfers, NIE: Credit	Current Transfers: Debit	Current Account, N.I.E.
1989	43220.00	-48840.00	-5620.00	4603.00	-3910.00	-4927.00	1894.00	-1665.00	-4698.00	477.00	-96.00	-4317.00
1990	51519.00	-42354.00	9165.00	5855.00	-4352.00	10668.00	3017.00	-1962.00	11723.00	376.00	-102.00	11997.00
1991	58919.00	-50176.00	8743.00	6979.00	-4121.00	11601.00	3719.00	-2879.00	12441.00	890.00	-59.00	13272.00
1992	69568.00	-64385.00	5183.00	9249.00	-9434.00	4998.00	5595.00	-5347.00	5246.00	1206.00	-51.00	6401.00
1993	75659.00	-86313.00	-10654.00	11193.00	-12036.00	-11497.00	4390.00	-5674.00	-12781.00	1290.00	-118.00	-11609.00
1994	102561.00	-95271.00	7290.00	16620.00	-16299.00	7611.00	5737.00	-6775.00	6573.00	1269.00	-934.00	6908.00
1995	128110.00	-110060.00	18050.10	19130.30	-25222.80	11957.60	5191.26	-16965.10	183.75	1826.73	-392.09	1618.39
1996	151077.00	-131542.00	19535.00	20601.00	-22585.00	17551.00	7318.00	-19755.00	5114.00	2368.00	-239.00	7243.00
1997	182670.00	-136448.00	46222.00	24569.00	-27967.00	42824.00	5710.00	-16715.00	31819.00	5477.00	-333.00	36963.00
1998	183529.00	-136915.00	46614.00	23895.00	-26672.00	43837.00	5584.00	-22228.00	27193.00	4661.00	-382.00	31472.00

EXHIBIT 2 Capital Account (Units: US$, Scale: Millions)

During Period	Capital Account: Debit	Capital Account, N.I.E.	Direct Investment Abroad	Direct Investment in Rep. Econ., N.I.E.	Portfolio Investment Assets	Portfolio Investment Liabilities, N.I.E.	Other Investment Assets	Other Investment Liabilities, N.I.E.	Financial Account, N.I.E.	Net Errors and Omissions
1989	n.a.	n.a.	-780.00	3393.00	-320.00	140.00	-229.00	1519.00	3723.00	114.61
1990	n.a.	n.a.	-830.00	3487.00	-241.00	n.a.	-231.00	1070.00	3255.00	-3205.17
1991	n.a.	n.a.	-913.00	4366.00	-330.00	565.00	-156.00	4500.00	8032.00	-6766.93
1992	n.a.	n.a.	-4000.00	11156.00	-450.00	393.00	-3267.00	-4082.00	-250.00	-8211.15
1993	n.a.	n.a.	-4400.00	27515.00	-597.00	3646.00	-2114.00	-576.00	23474.00	-10096.40
1994	n.a.	n.a.	-2000.00	33787.00	-380.00	3923.00	-1189.00	-1496.00	32645.00	-9100.25
1995	n.a.	n.a.	-2000.00	35849.20	79.00	710.40	-1081.00	5116.19	38673.80	-17823.20
1996	n.a.	n.a.	-2114.00	40180.00	-628.00	2372.00	-1126.00	1282.00	39966.00	-15504.00
1997	-21.00	-21.00	-2563.00	44237.00	-899.00	7842.00	-39608.00	12028.00	21037.00	-22121.80
1998	-47.00	-47.00	-2634.00	43751.00	-3830.00	98.00	-35041.00	-8619.00	-6275.00	-18901.80
1998	-2417.00	n.a.	2841.00	-35465.00	-5441.00	n.a.	-3150.00	-28.00	-18901.80	-18901.80

EXHIBIT 3   Overall (Units: US$, Scale: Millions)

	Overall Balance	Financing	Reserve Assets	Use of Fund Credit and Loans	U.S. CPI	Chinese CPI	Exchange Rate	GDP
1989	−479.39	479.39	558.37	−78.98	4.83	18.33	4.72	358086.4
1990	12046.80	−12046.80	−11555.00	−491.80	5.40	3.06	5.22	355180.9
1991	14537.10	−14537.10	−14083.00	−454.03	4.23	3.54	5.43	397810.2
1992	−2060.15	2060.15	2060.15	n.a.	3.03	6.34	5.75	463126.3
1993	1768.62	−1768.62	−1768.62	n.a.	2.95	14.58	5.80	597144.8
1994	30452.80	−30452.80	−30452.80	n.a.	2.61	24.24	8.45	553614.6
1995	22469.00	−22469.00	−22469.00	n.a.	2.81	16.90	8.32	703081.5
1996	31705.00	−31705.00	−31705.00	n.a.	2.93	8.32	8.30	818064.2
1997	35857.20	−35857.20	−35857.20	n.a.	2.34	2.81	8.28	899328.5
1998	6248.15	−6248.15	−6248.15	n.a.	1.55	−0.84	8.28	946346.7

Source: International Financial Statistics.

NOTES

1. *Wall Street Journal,* April 4, 2002.
2. He spoke at the Atlanta Fed eighth annual conference on financial markets: Financial Crises, October 17–19, 1999, in Sea Island, Georgia.
3. On the other hand, when the state of the economy falters, consumer confidence is shaken, thereby reducing economic activities and producing weak economic fundamentals that could lead to investor panic and financial crises in the extreme. See Radlet and Sachs (1998a, 1998b), Furman and Stiglitz (1998).
4. See Whitt (1998), who reaches a similar conclusion.
5. Here the interest rate risk in dollar and pound is defined as the variance of the underlying interest rates, while assuming zero covariance between the pound interest rate and percentage change in the exchange rate.
6. Federal Reserve Bank of Atlanta conference: Financial Crises, 1999.
7. See Kowai et al. (2001) Development Economic Research Group World Bank.
8. See for example: Krugman (1979) and Obstfeld (1986) who argues that currency crises can occur in a country with a sound economic fundamentals due to self-fulfilling prophecy as modeled by Diamond and Dybvig (1983).
9. The link between banking and currency crisis is documented in a study by Kaminsky and Reinhart (1999).
10. See for example: McKinnon and Pill (1996) and Krugman (1998a).
11. See Kowai (1998).

12. Nominal interest rate averaged 16% in Thailand during 1991–96, while U.S. risk-free rate was 4.5% plus spread of 2.6% for currency and macrorisk factors for the loans denominated in U.S. dollar.

13. Corsetti, Pesenti, and Roubini (1999).

14. The return on invested capital according to Organization of Economic & Community Development (OECD) (1998) report was below cost of capital for two thirds of Korean Chaebol prior to collapse of the Korean won.

15. See Radlet and Sachs (1998) and Chang and Velasco (1998) for supporting evidence.

16. According to International Financial Statistics, International Monetary Fund, more than 38 countries are in the system of exchange rate arrangement similar to Euro zone, 8 countries maintain a currency board with an implicit legislative requirement to maintain a specific currency at fixed exchange rate provided that monetary policy of the country be strictly in line with the policy of the currency to which it is pegged, 7 countries have a pegged exchange rate allowing +/− 1 percent fluctuation around the central rate, 8 countries have a system of crawling peg allowing periodic adjustment to the central rate to which it is pegged, 25 countries maintain managed float, and more than 48 countries have independent float.

17. *Wall Street Journal,* January 11, 2002.

CHAPTER 3

Foreign Exchange Rate Dynamics: Managing Exposure

FOREIGN EXCHANGE MARKETS

The foreign exchange market is the complex network of global over-the-counter institutions and structures that facilitates exchange of one currency for another (transfer of purchasing power), management of exchange rate risk (transfer of foreign exchange risk) from hedgers to risk arbitrageurs, and exchange rate determination. The foreign currency exchange market is the largest and least regulated market in the world. Unlike the stock and commodity markets, it operates with no supervisory or regulatory oversight. The volume of daily transactions in spots, outright forwards, and swaps far exceeds the volume of daily stocks and bonds traded in the organized exchanges worldwide.

The foreign exchange market is geographically dispersed, extending from Sydney, Australia, to Tokyo, Singapore, and East Asia, Moscow, Western Europe, New York, Chicago, and San Francisco. The market is relatively thin when trading begins in the Far East and is far more liquid when the last hours of trading in Europe coincide with trading in the United States due to differences in the time zones. Exhibit 3.1 shows the proportion of individual currency turned over daily in the global foreign exchange market.

The U.S. dollar makes up 45, 41, 41.5, and 43.5 percent of the total daily turnover shares for April 1995 through April 1998, respectively, of the global foreign exchange market activity.[1] The deutsche mark and Japanese yen rank second and third in the period of 1995 to 1998 in terms of their respective position in the global foreign exchange market activity.

FOREIGN EXCHANGE TRANSACTIONS

A foreign exchange market transaction is composed of *spot, outright forward, and swaps.* Exhibit 3.2 presents the global daily foreign exchange market turnover by types of transaction as reported by the Bank for International Settlements (BIS) in 1989 through 2001. Average daily turnover for all currencies was $1.1369 trillion,

EXHIBIT 3.1 Currency Distribution of Global Foreign Exchange Market Activity[a]

	Percentage Shares of Daily Turnover			
	April 1989	April 1992	April 1995	April 1998
U.S. dollar	90	82	83	87
Deutsche mark[b]	27	40	37	30
Japanese yen	27	23	24	21
Pound sterling	15	14	10	11
French franc	2	4	8	5
Swiss franc	10	9	7	7
Canadian dollar	1	3	3	4
Australian dollar	2	2	3	3
ECU and other EMS currencies	4	12	15	17
Other currencies	22	11	10	15
All currencies	**200**	**200**	**200**	**200**

[a] Whenever reported on one side of transactions. The figures relate to reported "net-net" turnover, that is, they are adjusted for both local and cross-border double-counting, except in 1989, for which data are available only on a "gross-gross" basis.
[b] Data for April 1989 exclude domestic trading involving the deutsche mark in Germany.

Source: Bank for International Settlements, Central Bank Survey of Foreign Exchange Market Activity, 1999 Basle.

EXHIBIT 3.2 Global Foreign Exchange Market Turnover[a]

	Daily Averages in April (in billions of U.S. dollars)				
Instrument	1989	1992	1995	1998[b]	2001
Spot transactions	317	394	494	568	387
Outright forwards	27	58	97	128	131
Foreign exchange swaps	190	324	546	734	656
Estimated gaps in reporting	56	44	53	60	36
Total "traditional" turnover	**590**	**820**	**1,190**	**1,490**	**1,210**
Memorandum item:					
Turnover at April 2001 exchange rates[c]	570	750	990	1,400	1,210

[a] Adjusted for local and cross-border double counting.
[b] Revised.
[c] Non-U.S. dollar legs of foreign currency transactions were converted into original currency amounts at average exchange rates for April of each survey year and then reconverted into U.S. dollar amounts at average April 2001 exchange rates.

Source: Bank for International Settlement, Basle, Switzerland.

of which 43 percent involved spot transactions, 9 percent over-the-counter forward transactions, and 48 percent foreign exchange swaps as of April 1995.

The average daily turnover grew by 27 percent over the three-year period, to $1.4415 trillion in April 1998; however, the distribution of over-the-counter forwards has remained stable at 9 percent, and foreign exchange swaps make up more than 51 percent of all transactions in the foreign exchange market.

Spot Transactions

A spot transaction involves the exchange of one currency for another. For example, the U.S. dollar for the euro or the Japanese yen, at an agreed exchange rate to be settled in cash in two business days between two counterparties. Spot transactions account for nearly 40 percent of all transactions in the foreign currency exchange market. For example, Kodak needs to pay £10 million to a British supplier in a spot transaction. The foreign exchange dealer in New York has quoted the pound as:

Bid: $1.5210; Ask: $1.5240

Kodak pays $15.24 million in two business days to settle the spot transaction at the ask rate of $1.5240. The foreign exchange dealer's profit from this spread in dollars terms is $30,000.

Outright Forward

An outright forward is an over-the-counter transaction involving the exchange of one currency—for example, the British pound with another, say, the euro, at the forward exchange rate determined today for the delivery to take place for cash settlement in more than two business days. Nearly 10 percent of all transactions in the FOREX market are forward contracts.

Example: Hedging with Forward Contract. Nissan manufacturing enters into a forward contract with the Bank of America today to sell 350 million yen at a forward price determined today. Nissan will deliver yen in 31 days to the Bank of America. The bank has the following quote for 31 days yen forward:

Bid: 121.32; Ask: 122.40

In 31 days, Nissan delivers the yen and receives $2.8595 million at the ask price of $122.40. The unhedged payoff is risky and depends on the value of the yen when it is converted to U.S. dollars; however, the hedged payoff at the ask price of 122.40 yen is locked in and Nissan will receive $2.8595 million at the maturity of the forward contract, as illustrated in the Exhibit 3.3.

The payoff on an unhedged position could be higher or lower depending on the exchange rate prevailing on the maturity of the yen receivable. It is possible for the unhedged position to provide more dollar receivables at the exchange rate below the forward rate ask price of 122.40 yen/$; however, at the exchange rate above 122.40 the hedged position with an over-the-counter forward contract

EXHIBIT 3.3   Forward Hedge and Unhedged Positions

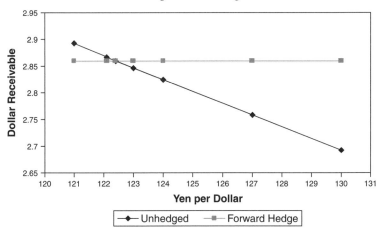

provides more dollars for the receivable denominated in foreign currency. The following excerpt from the *Wall Street Journal* provides an interesting story of the changing corporate expectations and the strategy they follow for hedging their receivables or payables denominated in foreign currency:

> Companies are "not as concerned" now that the yen will slip towards ¥140.00 by mid-year and some instead expect the Japanese currency to hold in a trading range of between ¥120.00 and ¥135.00, Woolfolk added. U.S. companies that obtain a large chunk of their revenues in foreign currency engage in hedging to protect against swings in exchange rates that may erode their earnings, mainly by buying forward or options contracts that insure against currency movements beyond specific levels.[2]

Forward Rate Agreement—An Approximation.   Consider these quotes in the interbank Eurocurrency interest rates for dollar, pound, Swiss franc, and euro:

	U.S. dollar	U.K. sterling	Swiss franc	Euro euro
30 days	$5\frac{3}{4}-5\frac{7}{8}$	$5\frac{5}{8}-5\frac{6}{8}$	$4\frac{7}{8}-5$	$5\frac{1}{2}-5\frac{5}{8}$
60 days	$6-6\frac{1}{8}$	$6\frac{1}{8}-6\frac{1}{4}$	$5\frac{1}{8}-5\frac{1}{4}$	$5\frac{7}{8}-6$
90 days	$6\frac{1}{4}-6\frac{3}{8}$	$6\frac{1}{2}-6\frac{5}{8}$	$5\frac{4}{8}-5\frac{5}{8}$	$6\frac{1}{4}-6\frac{3}{8}$

The 30-day forward rate prevailing in 60 days in dollars and other currencies can be estimated using these approximations.

Ninety-day fixed rate borrowing can be defined as the average of the 60-day rate and the 30-day forward rate 60 days hence. To manufacture a forward rate, the long-term rate has to be set equal to the geometric average of the short-term rates. For example, a 90-day rate has to be equal to the geometric average of a 60-day rate and 30-day forward rate prevailing 30 days hence. However, the simple approximation in Equation 3.1 provides a useful framework for estimating forward rates:

$$Lt\ (\text{rate}) = \frac{(St\ (\text{maturity}) \times St\ (\text{rate})) + (FR\ (\text{maturity}) \times FR)}{\text{maturity of } (St\ (\text{rate}) + FR)} \quad (3.1)$$

where

Lt	= the long term
St	= the short term
FR	= the forward rate
30-day forward rate in \$	= 7.125%
90-day rate	= $((60 \times 60\text{-day rate})$
	$+ (30 \times 30\text{-day forward rate}))/90$
$6\frac{3}{8}$	= $((60 \times 6) + (30 \times 30\text{-day forward}))/90$

The 60×90 forward rate (30-day forward rate in 60 days) is produced schematically as:

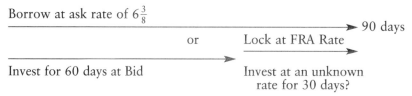

Borrow at ask rate of $6\frac{3}{8}$ → 90 days

or   Lock at FRA Rate

Invest for 60 days at Bid   Invest at an unknown rate for 30 days?

Hedging with the Forward Rate Agreement.

The forward rate agreement (FRA) is an over-the-counter instrument to hedge interest rate risk. The total daily transaction in the over-the-counter interbank market for FRA was \$66 and \$74 billion as of April 1995 and 1998, respectively, and as a percentage of total 7.5 and 5.85 percent during the same time periods.[3]

The bank selling FRA is guaranteeing the 30-day forward at 7.125 percent in the previous example. The buyer of FRA is indirectly guaranteed the rate at 7.125 percent in 60 days. However, if the actual rate exceeds the agreed rate by 1.5 percent in 60 days, the losing party, in this case the buyer of the FRA, gets compensated by the present value of the difference in 60 days, since the buyer of the FRA has to pay at the spot 1.5 percent more to acquire the capital needed. If the rate in 60 days falls by 1.375 percent, the buyer of the FRA in 30 days will be borrowing at spot at 1.375 percent below the agreed rate, and the present value of this amount has to be sent to the seller of the FRA in 60 days. Assuming the buyer of the FRA wished to borrow \$10 million in 60 days for only 30 days and to protect itself from rising interest rates, it buys a 60×90 FRA at 7.125 percent and in 60 days the 30-day rate at the spot is 9.125 percent. The losing party, in this case the buyer of the FRA, will receive the present value of the difference in 60 days:

$$\text{Cash received by the losing party} = \frac{10M\ [(.02)\ (30/360)]}{(1 + 09125 \times 30/360)} = \$16,540.95$$

The buyer of FRA in 60 days will be borrowing \$10 million at 9.125 percent for 30 days. The interest cost will be equal to \$76,041.66; however, in 60 days, it will receive $16,540.95 from the seller of the FRA that can be invested at the borrower's opportunity cost. Assuming the money received can be invested at 9.125 percent, the total out-of-pocket cost of this loan will be equal to $59,375, which is exactly equal to interest cost of the loan at 7.125 percent. The buyer of the FRA is locked in at 7.125 percent no matter which way interest rates move.

Foreign Exchange Swaps

A spot/forward spot is a contract involving two counterparties to exchange currencies in principal amount only in two business days at the predetermined exchange rate for cash settlement at the expiration of the contract (the short leg) and reversal of the exchange of the same two currencies at the rate agreed by the two parties and at a date in the future (e.g., three business days; known as long leg), provided that the rate for the long leg is different from the rate prevailing at the conclusion of the short leg. When the short leg of the swap is more than two business days, then the swap is a forward/forward swap.

A FOREX swap also can be described as the portfolio of long and short positions entered simultaneously at two different dates prevailing in the future, for example, 30 and 60 days, and at the rate determined today, that is, 30 and 60 days forward rate, respectively. In the over-the-counter market for forwards and swaps, any particular date can be arranged with the swap dealer (usually a major bank).

Example: An importer needs £1,000,000 in 60 days for only 30 days to pay for an outstanding obligations entered with a British supplier. The importer can buy a 30-day FRA in 60 days as of today, can wait and borrow in 60 days by paying the prevailing spot rate, or it can enter into a foreign exchange swap agreement. Suppose the importer sells £1,000,000 60 days forward at $1.5210/£ and simultaneously buys £1,000,000 90 days forward at $1.5278/£. This swap transaction is borrowing in disguise for 30 days at fully collateralized basis at the U.S. rate of 5.36 percent per annum. This is the implied 30-day forward repo rate, as the importer is selling pounds 60 days forward with the agreement to buy it back in 90 days as follows:

$$(1 + \text{repo rate}) = \frac{\$1.5278/£}{\$1.5210/£}$$

The actual 30-day rate in 60 days could be higher or lower than 5.36 percent. Furthermore, the unhedged position produces availability risk (the risk that the capital may not be easily available) for the importer that is mitigated in the forward/future markets. The notional principal in this example is £1,000,000. The ratio of the buying rate of $1.5278/£ and the selling rate of $1.5210/£ after being annualized is the interest rate denominated in dollars. By selling forward, one essentially is borrowing (financing), and by buying forward, one is equivalently lending (investing) at a predetermined rate that fixes (locks) the cost of borrowing. Foreign exchange swaps make up nearly 50 percent of all the transactions in the FOREX market.

Example: Forward/Forward Swap.   Haynes Company needs to borrow £100,000 for 30 days, 60 days from today. Haynes can wait and borrow at the current market rate in 60 days, which could be higher or lower than the prevailing 30-day rate, or it can enter into a forward/forward swap that can fix the cost of borrowing today. Haynes enters into a swap agreement by buying 90-day pounds forward at $1.5280/£ and simultaneously selling 60-day pounds forward for $1.52/£. Haynes pays $152,800 and receives $152,000 and has the use of £100,000 for 30 days at a fully collateralized basis at the rate of 6.32 percent annualized. Haynes is paying dollars and receiving pounds and the swap dealer paying pounds and receiving dollars:

FOREIGN EXCHANGE MARKET FUNCTIONS

The previous example analyzed the type of transactions in the foreign exchange market. Each transaction is intended to provide a particular function. For example, a spot transaction is intended to transfer *purchasing power* from one party to another. A forward transaction is intended to *transfer risk* from one party to another. Transferring risk is hedging that is intended to reduce the exposure to foreign exchange risk. A swap transaction is essentially a *financing* at a fully collateralized basis.

FOREIGN EXCHANGE QUOTATIONS

Foreign exchange daily quotations are reported in the major newspapers for all major currencies. In direct quotes, the currencies are quoted in terms of U.S. dollar per foreign currency. Indirect quotes or European term are quoted in terms of foreign currency per U.S. dollar equivalent. The direct quote provides the value of the foreign currencies from the perspective of U.S. investors in terms of dollar per foreign currency, while the indirect quote refers the foreign currency value per U.S. dollar from the perspective of foreign investors. Exhibit 3.4 provides the direct and indirect quotes for Japanese yen and British pound spot, one-, three-, and six-month forward rates as of May 17, 2002.

In the exhibit, the forward exchange rate as a measure of the market consensus of the future exchange rate for the British pound and Japanese yen indicates that the dollar is expected to strengthen against the pound, while weakening against the yen in the next one to six months as of Friday, May 16, 2002, based on current and expected future information. The pound is said to be trading at discount against the U.S. dollar in the forward market for 30 to 180 days forward as reflected in the direct quote. The dollar is trading at a premium against the pound and at a discount against the yen, which is reflected in the indirect quote (European term) in the exhibit. The consensus for the future exchange (forward) rate may change as new information comes to market and as individuals and institutions evaluate that information in pushing the exchange rate into the new direction.

CROSS-EXCHANGE RATE

Based on Exhibit 3.4, the cross-currency exchange rate can be estimated from the perspective of the Japanese investor as yen/dollar and of the British investor as pound/dollar as the yen/pound:

$$\frac{125.92}{.6858} = 183.61 \text{ ¥/£}$$

The spot exchange rate yen per pound should be 183.61; deviation provides an opportunity for riskless arbitrage in the currency exchange market. Likewise, the various cross-currency forward rates can be calculated as the ratio of the one-, three-, or six-month forward yen/$ and one-, three-, or six-month forward pound/dollar:

$$\frac{125.72}{.6870} = 182.99 \text{ ¥/£}, 181.72 \text{ ¥/£}, \text{ and } 179.70 \text{ ¥/£}.$$

These cross-currency exchange rates are direct quotes from the Japanese investor's perspective, and the indirect quote will be the ratio of the one over the direct quote. Cross-currency forward rates as a forecast of future rates show an appreciation of the yen against the British pound as fewer yen are required to pay for one unit of British pound.

EXHIBIT 3.4   Foreign Exchange Quotations

	Fri	Thu	Fri	Thu
	$/¥		¥/$	
Japan (yen)	.007942	.007802	125.92	128.17
1-month forward	.007954	.007814	125.72	127.97
3-months forward	.007979	.007839	125.32	127.57
6-months forward	.008025	.007883	124.61	126.85
	$/£		£/$	
Britain (pound)	1.4582	1.4570	.6858	.6863
1-month forward	1.4556	1.4544	.6870	.6876
3-months forward	1.4501	1.4489	.6896	.6902
6-months forward	1.4421	1.4408	.6934	.6941

Source: Investor's Business Daily, May 17, 2002.

BID AND OFFER QUOTATIONS IN THE INTERBANK MARKET

In the over-the-counter market for foreign exchange, the quotes for the spot and forward transactions are provided by major foreign exchange dealers in terms of the bid (buy) and offer (ask) price on the major currencies in which the dealer is making market. The dealer stands to buy at the bid price, and simultaneously sell at the offer price, earning an arbitrage profit. The currency may be quoted outright with a price that reflects all decimals, or it may be quoted as point's quotations, as shown in Exhibit 3.5.

In the interbank market for foreign exchange, the dealer may quote outright as $1.4582–99 per unit of British pound. In this case the dealer is indicating that it is willing to sell pounds at $1.4599 and simultaneously buy at the bid price of $1.4582, while quoting the one-, three-, and six-month forward in a point quotation as −26 to −21, −81 to −54 and −161 to −128. The points with the negative sign signal deductions from the spot rate to arrive at the respective forward rate of varying maturities. When the point's quotations are given and are positive, the dealer is signaling that points need to be added to the spot rate to arrive at a particular forward rate.

ARBITRAGE IN THE FOREIGN EXCHANGE MARKET

Temporary deviations in the spot and forward rates provide an opportunity for major foreign exchange dealers, other individuals, and corporations to engage in arbitrage. Major banks around the world have trading divisions in which currency traders make markets in the foreign currency exchange around the clock for the clients as well as their own accounts. In private banks, compensation is tied to individual performance in generating arbitrage profit. In central banks, foreign exchange dealers receive fixed remuneration; they make market in millions of dollars in major currencies without being concerned with profits or losses in any given daily transactions. Central bank dealers buy and sell a particular currency in lots of $10 to $20 million or more to achieve certain objectives (i.e., stability, reduced volatility, to push the currency in certain direction against speculative attacks on dollar, pound, or yen).

MAJOR PLAYERS IN THE FOREIGN EXCHANGE MARKET

Exhibit 3.6 shows the currency trading and distribution of market share of the major financial institutions. It shows that J.P. Morgan, Citigroup, and Deutsche Bank have nearly 30 percent of the $1.2 trillion daily trading of the foreign exchange market transactions involving spots, forwards, and swaps. Currency trading by central banks and others accounts for over 40 percent of the total foreign exchange trading. The fall in the daily turnover from a high of 1.5 to 1.2 trillion reflects the growing use of electronic trading in the interbank market (see Exhibit 3.7).

EXHIBIT 3.5 Spot and Forward Quotations for Yen and British Pound in the Interbank Market

	$/f[a]			f/$	
	Offer	Bid		Bid	Offer
Japan (yen) spot	.007942	.0078666		125.92	127.12
1-month forward	.007954	.0078833		125.72	126.85
3-months forward	.007979	.0078989		125.32	126.60
6-months forward	.008025	.0079403		124.61	125.94
Point's quotations					
1-month forward				−20 to −27	
3-months forward				−60 to −52	
6-months forward				−131 to −118	

	$/f			f/$	
	Bid	Offer		Bid	Offer
Britain (pound) spot	1.4582	1.4599		.6849784	.685777
1-month forward	1.4556	1.4578		.6859652	.685777
3-months forward	1.4501	1.4545		.6875215	.6896076
6-months forward	1.4421	1.4471		.6910373	.6934332
Point's quotations					
1-month forward	−26 to −21				
3-months forward	−81 to −54				
6-months forward	−161 to −128				

[a] $/f refers to dollar-per-foreign currency.

EXHIBIT 3.6 Foreign Exchange Market Major Players and Distribution of Their Shares

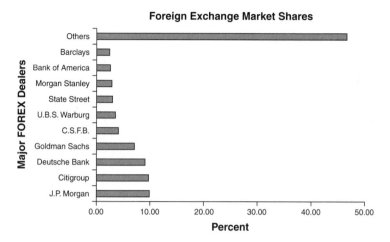

Source: Euromoney: Bank for International Settlement.

EXHIBIT 3.7 Daily Turnovers

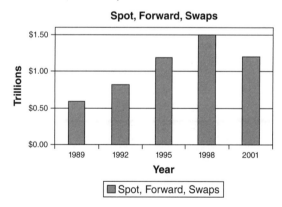

Source: Euromoney: Bank for International Settlement.

Triangular Arbitrage

It is possible for the foreign exchange rate spot or forward delivery in the interbank market to be out of sync temporarily. Arbitrageurs will try to align the currency by buying and selling the undervalued or overvalued currency. Suppose the bid–ask price for the pound/dollar, yen/dollar, and yen/pound is quoted as follows by banks in the United Kingdom, the United States, and Japan.

Currency	Bid	Offer
£/$	.69103	.69343
$/¥	.00794028	.00802503
¥/£	182.85	183.92

The yen appears to be nonaligned as the cross-currency implied exchange rate for the bid and offer price for ¥/£ respectively has to be equal to 179.70–182.24. Using the dollar, an arbitrageur needs to buy pounds and then use pounds to buy the cheap-currency yen as the pound is quoted at a premium against the yen in the cross-currency interbank market as compared to implied cross-exchange rates as illustrated in the following diagram:

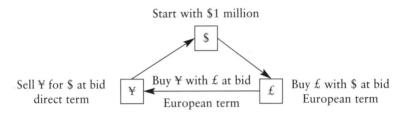

This triangular arbitrage generates $3,293.91 profit provided that the arbitrageur started with $1 million and follows the process illustrated.

SPECULATIVE TRANSACTIONS

Currency market speculative transactions are involved in buying or selling currency (long or short), expecting currency to appreciate or depreciate in the near future. For example, a currency trader expects pounds to devalue in the next 60 to 90 days based on his private forecast of a weaker pound. The trader sells £2 million 90 days forward at $1.562/£; the pound appreciates to $1.57812/£ in the next three months against the expectation of the speculator, at which time the short seller buys pounds at the spot market at $1.57812/£.

The loss in this speculative transaction is −$32,040. Had the speculator taken the opposite position—that is, buying pounds 90 days forward at $1.562/£ and selling the pounds three months later at $1.5781/£—the speculator would have realized a profit of $32,040, before transaction cost as demonstrated in Exhibit 3.8.

FOREIGN EXCHANGE LOSS

The speculative currency trading losses suffered by Allied Irish Bank's U.S. subsidiary in February was $750 million. A FOREX trader at Ireland's largest bank had taken a huge long position on the yen's rise in 2001, but when the dollar continued to climb against the yen, the losses piled up.[4]

EXHIBIT 3.8   Profit (Loss) in Speculative Long and Short Position

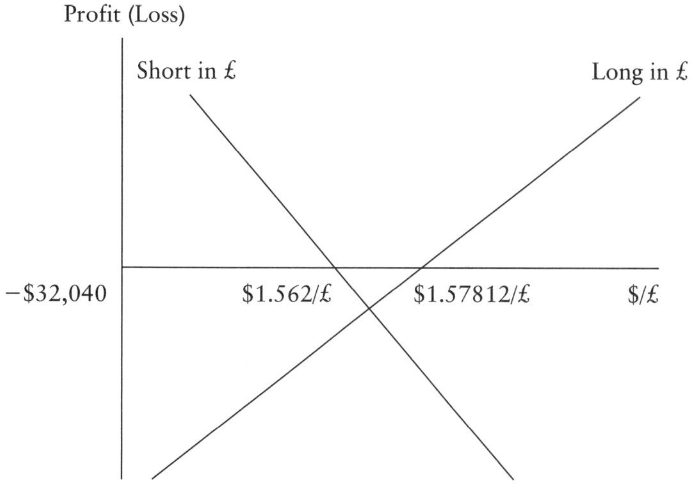

Profit (Loss)

SETTLEMENT RISK

Settlement risk is one of the important issues in the FOREX sector of the over-the-counter market. With the global launch of the Continuous Linked Settlement (CLS) network in July 2002, the FOREX payment and collection process is set to be aligned. To date, the settlement of the FOREX trade in different time zones has resulted in a delay between the pay and receive legs.[5] The CLS mechanism allows the two payment legs of the FOREX trade to be made simultaneously. This eliminates the time lag between the two legs of the FOREX trade, which lies at the center of FOREX settlement risk.[6]

SPOT RATE AND THE LAW OF ONE PRICE

An exchange rate is the ratio of the two prices for the identical basket of goods and services denominated in two different currencies. The dynamics of the two baskets are different, as each basket has to respond to the underlying fundamentals—the macroeconomic factors discussed in Chapter 1—as well as the factors unique to a particular economy (i.e., microfactors and the type of exchange rate arrangements in place in the respective economy).

According to the Law of One Price, assets of the same risk class are expected to provide the same rate of return; otherwise arbitrageurs simultaneously buy inexpensive assets and sell short the overvalued asset and earn riskless profit. Assume a basket of goods and services is currently priced in the United Kingdom at £100 and the identical basket of goods and services in the United States is priced at $150. It then follows from the Law of One Price an implied exchange rate of

$1.50 per British pound as the ratio of the two baskets of goods and services denominated in dollar and pound.

$$\text{Price in } \$ = \text{Price in } £ \times \$/£ \tag{3.2}$$

The spot exchange rate implied $\$/£$ in Equation 3.2 is predicated on the assumption that the price in the respective country is determined in a competitive market and absent of any imperfections (i.e., government intervention and regulatory impediments). This is the absolute version of the purchasing power parity (PPP). The exchange rate implied from Equation 3.2 is the ratio of the two price indices. The identical purchasing power in dollars and pounds for U.S. and U.K. residents in the Equation 3.2 is predicated on the assumption that the exchange rate $\$/£$ is indeed the ratio of the two price indices in dollars and pounds, not distorted by market imperfections. Any deviations from parity will lead to riskless arbitrage in a frictionless market.

BIG MAC INDEX

The Economist has devised an index of McDonald's denominated in currencies in which there are McDonald's franchises owned by McDonald's Corporation worldwide. The price of the burger is usually the simple average of the prices in 120 different locations worldwide. According to the Law of One Price, the price of an identical basket of goods, in this case the Big Mac, has to be equal in dollar terms worldwide. Unlike gold, which is traded worldwide, the Big Mac is nontradeable when there is a deviation from the Law of One Price and arbitrageurs are unable to take advantage of price disparity in different worldwide location. For example, the ratio of the prices in the United States and United Kingdom for the Big Mac is an implied parity exchange rate and as compared to actual exchange rate can provide a rough approximation as to whether a currency is over- or undervalued. According to *The Economist*, "In the history of Big Mac index, the dollar has never been more overvalued."[7] Exhibit 3.9 shows the Big Mac index for the 2002 period.

According to the Big Mac index, the dollar appears to be overvalued against Argentina's peso by 68 percent, as the price of Big Mac is equal to $.78 and $2.49 respectively in Argentina and the United States (($.78/$2.49) − 1 = −.68). The dollar appears to be overvalued against most emerging market economies and the Australian dollar, while it is undervalued against the Swiss franc by 53 percent, the British pound by 16 percent and the euro by 19 percent. The truth is that the price in the market for real assets is not usually determined at least for classes of goods in a competitive environment as the government intervenes in the process of price determination or regulatory requirements impose additional cost on the producer, which ultimately has to be passed to consumers.

However, supply and demand forces competitively determine the price in the financial market for financial assets such as stocks and bonds, with central banks reacting to economic fundamentals by changing the short-term interest rates, which inversely affect the value of financial assets.

EXHIBIT 3.9 Big Mac Index

The Hamburger Standard

	Big Mac prices		Implied PPP^a of the dollar	Actual dollar exchange rate 23/04/02	Under (−)/over (+) valuation against the dollar, %
	in local currency	in dollars			
United States^b	$2.49	2.49	—	—	—
Argentina	Peso 2.50	0.78	1.00	3.13	−68
Australia	A$3.00	1.62	1.20	1.86	−35
Brazil	*Real* 3.60	1.55	1.45	2.34	−38
Britain	£1.99	2.88	1.25^c	1.45†	+16
Canada	C$3.33	2.12	1.34	1.57	−15
Chile	Peso 1,400	2.16	562	655	−14
China	Yuan 10.50	1.27	4.22	8.28	−49
Czech Rep	Koruna 56.28	1.66	22.6	34.0	−33
Denmark	DKr24.75	2.96	9.94	8.38	+19
Euro area	€2.67	2.37	0.93^d	0.89§	−5
Hong Kong	HK$11.20	1.40	4.50	7.80	−42
Hungary	Forint 459	1.69	184	272	−32
Indonesia	Rupiah 16,000	1.71	6,426	9,430	−32
Israel	Shekel 12.00	2.51	4.82	4.79	+1
Japan	¥262	2.01	105	130	−19
Malaysia	M$5.04	1.33	2.02	3.8	−47
Mexico	Peso 21.90	2.37	8.80	9.28	−5
New Zealand	NZ$3.95	1.77	1.59	2.24	−29
Peru	New Sol 8.50	2.48	3.41	3.43	−1
Philippines	Peso 65.00	1.28	26.1	51.0	−49
Poland	Zloty 5.90	1.46	2.37	4.04	−41
Russia	Rouble 39.00	1.25	15.7	31.2	−50
Singapore	S$3.30	1.81	1.33	1.82	−27
South Africa	Rand 9.70	0.87	3.90	10.9	−64
South Korea	Won 3,100	2.36	1.245	1,304	−5
Sweden	SKr 26.00	2.52	10.4	10.3	+1
Switzerland	SFr 6.30	3.81	2.53	1.66	+53
Taiwan	NT$70.00	2.01	28.1	34.8	−19
Thailand	Baht 55.00	1.27	22.1	43.3	−49
Turkey	Lira 4,000,000	3.06	1,606,426	1,324,500	+21
Venezuela	Bolivar 2,500	2.92	1,004	857	+17

^{a} Purchasing power parity; local price divided by price in United States.
^{b} Average of New York, Chicago, San Franciso, and Atlanta.
^{c} Dollars per pound.
^{d} Dollars per euro.

CENTRAL BANK INTERVENTION

The foreign exchange market is the market where the price of a currency is determined by supply and demand forces for the independently floating currencies and needs to be distinguished from the stock market. While government intervention in the stock market has been limited to extreme cases involving events triggering a shot down of the market, central banks intervene in the foreign exchange market to maintain an exchange rate within a desirable range, whether such attempts prove successful or not. On three occasions, the U.S. central bank between 1982 and 1985, attempted to weaken the U.S. dollar, without much success, by selling dollars to buy other currencies. While coordinated policy can prove successful in realigning currency value, intervention by individual central banks may prove futile. The events of the 1990s and various crises provide evidence in support of these arguments that central bank intervention usually distorts the currency values for only a short period and economic fundamentals coupled with expectations ultimately determine the currency values.

Exhibit 3.10 provides the level of the U.S. dollar index against major currencies during the 1973 to 2002 period. The dollar index appears to be fairly stable throughout the period, except for 1980 to 1985, when the dollar revalued against most major currencies and the dollar reversed after the September 1985 Plaza Agreement when the G-5 central bankers collectively decided to sell dollars and buy other currencies to weaken the U.S. currency. The coordinated selloff of dollars achieved the objectives of the G-5 central bankers, as the dollar continued to weaken against major currencies. In February 1987 the Louvre Accord provided a consensus that the dollar had been realigned and needed to be supported to achieve stability.

Although the U.S. dollar plunged in late 1985, the rise in the price of imports was unusually slow or weak, as foreign exporters tried to cut their profit margins to maintain their shares of the market.[8] The pass-through from the U.S. exchange rate to import price and volume was delayed for nearly 12 months following the dollar devaluation.[9] This phenomenon is known as a J-curve; the trade balance deteriorates following an initial devaluation of currency and later improves the

EXHIBIT 3.10   Trade Weighted Index of U.S. Dollar Against
Major Currencies (1973–2002)

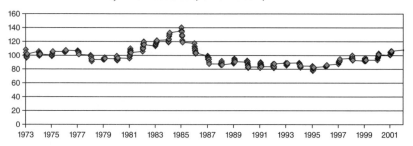

trade balance as exports become attractive and import prices rise after a long delay and fall in import volume, as shown in Exhibit 3.11.

Suppose at time t_0 the central bank devalues the currency. The merchandise trade balance actually deteriorates following devaluation to lower level at time t_1; however, improvement in the balance is delayed until time t_2. This long delay for U.S. data takes nearly 14 to 18 months from the initial devaluation to the improvement in the trade balance.[10]

Exhibit 3.12 provides the monthly percentage of change in the trade-weighted index of U.S. dollars against major trading partners as of 1973 to 2002. Rising volatility and a lack of any particular patterns and randomness of the percentage change in the exchange rate is the result of the independently floating exchange rate arrangement of the early 1970s to which the U.S. currency belongs.

The set of all prices for all goods and services in the real and financial markets that makes up the price index is determined uniquely in each subsegment of the market subject to constraints imposed by the environment in which the segment operates. Some prices are very competitive in one market, while the same product produced elsewhere is not competitive; some products are uniquely produced in one market and not produced at all in other markets due to technological constraints. The exchange rate in practice is the ratio of the prices of the unidentical products produced in two different countries.

Example: Assume there are only five products produced in United States and United Kingdom: oil, steel, soybeans, milk, and chicken. Suppose the United States

EXHIBIT 3.11 J-Curve

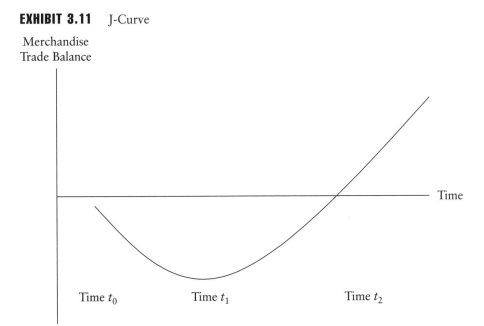

EXHIBIT 3.12   Percentage Change in the Value of Trade Weighted Index
of U.S. Dollar (1973–2002)

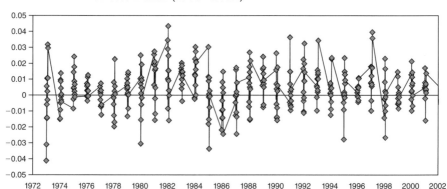

provides a direct subsidy to dairy and soybean producers and an indirect subsidy to steel producers in the form of giving them protection from cheaper steel
produced overseas by imposing tariffs and quotas on steel imported from other
countries. However, the United Kingdom does not provide any subsidy, direct or
indirect, to its own producers with the exception of oil, which is indirectly sub-
sidized. The lower price for dairy products in the United States is distorted and
does not take into account the true cost of production. The higher price for steel
in the United States is also distorted by giving local producers an opportunity
to raise their prices to match the higher price of steel produced elsewhere, induced
by imposition of tariff. Therefore, the price index in the United States and the
United Kingdom is distorted, leading to a distorted exchange rate between dollars and pounds. Having recognized the imperfections induced by government
actions in distorting the prices, let us analyze the impact of inflation, interest
rates, and other factors such as competition and institutional arrangements on
the exchange rate.

RELATIVE VERSION OF PURCHASING POWER PARITY

In this context assume prices are rising at a faster rate in the United Kingdom than
in the United States, requiring £110 to acquire the same basket of goods and services that used to cost £100 one year ago. The identical basket in the United States
that used to cost $150 one year earlier now costs $157.50. The implied exchange
rate based on the Law of One Price has to be equal the ratio of $157.50/£110
or $1.4318/£.

In this scenario, the loss of purchasing power is due to higher inflation in
the United Kingdom relative to the United States, requiring 10 percent more
pounds to purchase the same basket of goods. U.S. consumers also experience
loss of purchasing power in dollars by 5 percent, as they need $157.50 to acquire

the basket of goods and services that used to cost $150 domestically. However, there will be a transfer of purchasing power from the United Kingdom to the United States (provided that the exchange rate adjusts to a new equilibrium as predicated by the PPP). British goods become relatively more attractive as import prices fall and export prices rise (pass-through is complete) due to relative loss of purchasing power by U.K. residents and relative gain of purchasing power by U.S. residents buying cheaper imports, as illustrated in Exhibit 3.13.

The foreign exchange market therefore transfers purchasing power between the two countries as spot, and the expected future exchange rate changes due to changing economic fundamentals and change in expectations. The relative PPP holds when the implied exchange rate derived is the ratio of the prices at time 1 (future price) in Exhibit 3.13 denominated in dollars and pounds, that is, $1.4318/£. Therefore, it follows from the exhibit that the expected or future exchange rate S_1 is related to current spot rate S_0 times the ratio of the one plus the respective inflation rates $\Pi_\$$, Π_f, in the United States and the United Kingdom, that is the expected exchange rate S_1 is as defined in Equation 3.3.

$$S_1 = \frac{S_0\,(1 + \Pi_\$)}{(1 + \Pi_f)}$$

$$S_1 = \frac{\$1.50/£\,(1 + .05)}{(1 + .10)} = \$1.4318/£$$

(3.3)

The approximate version of the relative PPP implies that the percentage change in the exchange rate is equal to inflation differentials as shown in Equation 3.4.

$$\frac{(S_1 - S_0)}{S_0} = (\Pi_\$ - \Pi_f)$$

(3.4)

where

S_1 and S_0 = spot rates direct quote at time 1 and zero
$\Pi_\$$ and Π_f = inflation rates in dollars and foreign currency

EXHIBIT 3.13 Relative Version of Purchasing Power Parity

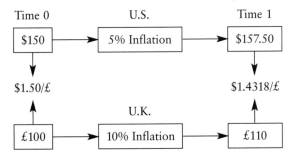

Exhibit 3.14 graphically represents the approximation in Equation 3.4.

The PPP line is the locus of all points where the percentage of change in exchange rates in direct quote is identical to the inflation differentials denominated in dollars and foreign currency. Deviations from the parity line provide an opportunity to buy goods and services from the country whose currency has not appreciated or depreciated according to the inflation differentials and in violation of the Law of One Price. For example, points that are to the left of PPP line, such as A, where the inflation differentials are positive, that is, about 3 percent (the U.S. rate is higher than the foreign rate by 3 percent), while foreign currency has appreciated by 4 percent against the dollar: $(S_1 - S_0)/S_0 = 4$ percent.

This scenario makes foreign goods and services more expensive for the United States to purchase; likewise, U.S. goods and services become attractive for foreigners to purchase until the parity is restored. The U.S. dollar must appreciate by 1 percent against foreign currency to maintain parity. The loss of purchasing power by U.S. residents in buying foreign goods and services in this scenario persuades them not to buy expensive imports. The gain in purchasing power of foreign individuals due to the fact that their currency buys more of the U.S. dollar induces them to purchase more goods and services imported from the United States. The higher demand for U.S. goods and services leads to a greater demand for the dollar and its appreciation. To the left of the PPP line, purchasing power transfers from the U.S. to foreign countries continues until the exchange rate parity is maintained.

EXHIBIT 3.14   Parity Relationship

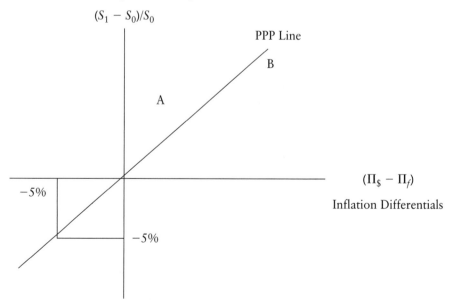

To the right of the PPP line, such as B, there is a transfer of purchasing power from foreign countries to the United States as foreign currency fails to appreciate by the amount of inflation differential, making foreign goods and services relatively more attractive for the United States to buy. This scenario continues until the parity is achieved and there is no transfer of purchasing power from one country to the other. Most evidence tends to reject the relative version of the PPP in the short run, while providing some support for the long term.[11]

EXCHANGE RATE PASS-THROUGH

The relative version of the PPP requires that the changes in price level be simultaneously reflected in the exchange rate. In fact, the price changes are not reflected in exchange rate and the pass-through is incomplete. For example, the U.S. price level changes by +3 percent while the dollar may or may not devalue by 3 percent. The competition and agency relationship that defines the contractual relationship between exporter and importer and currency of the denomination of the import affect the degree of the pass-through. For example, during times of rising yen value, Japan's multinational corporations cut their base price in yen to maintain their market share in the United States and Europe.

Example: Suppose a Lexus is priced at 3.5 million yen, the current spot is 100¥/$. Assuming the yen appreciates to 90¥/$, the dollar price of the Lexus will rise from $35,000 to $38,889 in a complete pass-through. However, at this price Lexus might lose business to competing cars, and, therefore, the price in the United States may go up to $37,100. The price in the United States is increased by only 6 percent while the yen appreciated by 11.11 percent. The pass-through is incomplete, and the degree of pass-through as the ratio of the change in U.S. price and the change in the exchange rate or .06/.1111, is 54 percent.

The exporter has three options regarding how much of the increase in import price due to its own currency appreciation it is willing to absorb:

1. Absorb all of the increase in import price by cutting its profit margin and/or cost; zero pass-through.

2. Absorb none of the increase in import price and pass all of the increase to the exporter; 100 percent pass-through.

3. Absorb some of the increase and pass the remaining to the importer; partial pass-through, under 100 percent.

Exhibit 3.15 provides the yen-per-dollar index over the 1971 to 2002 period. The yen continued to revalue against the U.S. dollar until mid-1995, reaching nearly 80 yen per dollar. The pass-through from the exchange rate to import price was partial, as major Japanese multinational companies, such as Sony, Mitsubishi,

EXHIBIT 3.15   Yen/Dollar Exchange Rates over Time

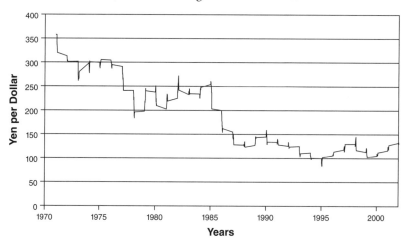

Kumatsu, and Toyota, absorbed some of the increase in import prices, since in a complete pass-through the price of the Japanese import price would have been extremely uncompetitive. The yen revalued in nominal term from 358¥/$ in 1971 to 80¥/$ by the mid-1990s, nearly 77 percent appreciation.

The invoicing practice also helps to explain the partial pass-through. The International Monetary Fund reports that nearly 70 percent of U.S. imports are denominated in dollars. For example, 48 percent of Japanese exports were not denominated in yen in 1986.[12] Furthermore, U.S. imports are acquired in contracts that fix prices in dollar terms for extended periods that delay the pass-through from exchange rate to import prices.[13]

Exhibit 3.16 shows new evidence in favor of the partial exchange rate pass-through in U.S. manufacturing industries during the sample period 1980 to 1991. The coefficients for the complete pass-through are expected to be equal to unity and zero for no pass-through. The pass-through coefficient is as high as 88 percent for stone, glass, and concrete products and as low as 8 percent for lumber and wood products. The average coefficient for all industries is equal to 42 percent, implying that for every 1 percent change in the U.S. dollar, 0.042 percent of the change is passed to the importer and the manufacturer absorbs 0.058 percent of the change in the price. The industries with products that are highly capital intensive, that is, specialized products, are able to pass-through the greater proportion of the change in price due to change in exchange rate to the importer, while industries in which there is stiff competition from other producers overseas find it difficult to pass-through the change in exchange rate to the price they charge to the importer. For example, U.S. apparels face tough competition from their southern neighbors, as the small coefficient of pass-through of 10.68 percent reveals. It looks like U.S. apparels absorb nearly 89.32 of the increase in price by cutting cost or profit margins.

EXHIBIT 3.16   Exchange Rate Pass-Through Coefficients for Selected U.S. Manufacturing

Industry Code (SIC)	Industry	Pass-Through Coefficient
20	Food and kindred products	0.2485
22	Textile mill products	0.3124
23	Apparels	0.1068
24	Lumber and wood products	0.0812
25	Furniture and fixtures	0.3576
28	Chemicals and allied products	0.5312
30	Rubber and plastic products	0.5318
31	Leather products	0.3144
32	Stone, glass, concrete products	0.8843
33	Primary metal industries	0.2123
34	Fabricated metal products	0.3138
35	Machinery, except electrical	0.7559
36	Electrical and electronic machinery	0.3914
37	Transportation equipment	0.3583
38	Measurement instruments	0.7256
39	Miscellaneous manufacturing	0.2765
Average		0.4205

Source: Jiawan Yang, "Exchange Rate Pass-Through in U.S. Manufacturing Industries," *Review of Economics and Statistics* 79 (1997), MIT Press: 95–104.

SPOT EXCHANGE RATE AND NOMINAL INTEREST RATE

The capital account, the financing vehicle for the current account, is interest sensitive. Therefore, capital moves from one location to another not only at the expectation of the higher yield but also at the promise of higher returns. Assuming a frictionless competitive capital market, the real return on capital after adjusting for the change in exchange rate and inflation has to be the same worldwide. The evidence is to the contrary. Real rate differentials are significant, and the market is far from the "textbook" definition of perfectly competitive.[14]

Example: Assume nominal interest rates in U.S. and euro zones are expected to be 4 and 5 percent respectively next year and current spot rate is $1/euro. Invoking the Law of One Price requires that the terminal (future) value of the investment in dollars and euros has to be identical in one period in the future; that is, there should be parity in dollars and euros return. Exhibit 3.17 shows $100 equal to 100 euro.

The exchange rate S_1 is the ratio of the future value of two investment denominated in dollars and euros at the respective expected interest rate of 4 and 5 percent at time 1. The International Fisher Parity (IFP) is maintained provided that the expected future exchange rate is equal to the ratio of the two investments, as illustrated in Exhibit 3.17. In that scenario, regardless of the currency of the choice, the return realized in dollars and euros will be the same at 4 percent for a U.S. investor trying to take advantage of higher nominal interest rate in foreign currency.

In this example, if the U.S. investor converts $100 to 100 euros at the current spot and invest the euros at 5 percent, the proceed of 105 euros will convert to U.S. dollars at $.9905/euro; the expected future income will be equal to $104, which is identical to the investment at home at the home rate of 4 percent. It then follows that the expected spot rate in the future S_1 is the ratio of two present values (the current spot rate of S_0 times the ratio of the one plus nominal interest rate denominated in dollar and foreign currency) as expressed in the Equation 3.5.

$$S_1 = \frac{S_0 \ (1 + R_\$)}{(1 + R_f)} \tag{3.5}$$

where

$R_\$$ and R_f = interest rates in dollar and foreign currency

The crucial assumption in the maintenance of the IFP is predicated on the equality of the real interest rates worldwide and that nominal interest rates are unbiased predictors of future inflation.[15] The real rate of interest is related to productivity of labor and capital. There are vast sectoral differences in a given economy's labor productivity as well as differences worldwide.

FORWARD EXCHANGE RATE AND COVERED INTEREST PARITY

A great deal of empirical evidence supports or is against the efficiency of the foreign exchange for forward rates. Parity exists when the forward rate is the rational expectation of all individuals and embodies no risk premium over time. Suppose

EXHIBIT 3.17   International Fisher Parity

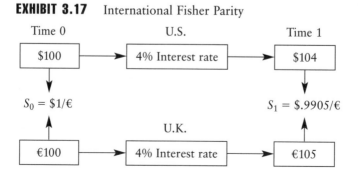

the expected interest rate in dollars and pounds will be 4.5 and 6 percent respectively in one period in the future. The current spot rate is $1.4582/£, which is the ratio of two identical baskets of goods and services denominated in dollar and foreign currency and priced today (ratio of two present values). Invoking rational expectation and zero risk premium, the forward rate has to be equal to the ratio of two futures values denominated in dollars and pounds. In this example, assume £100 is invested and its dollar equivalent is $145.82 in the respective currency as shown in Exhibit 3.18. The forward interest rate parity (IRP) relationship as is defined as the ratio of two future values denominated in dollar and foreign currency in Equation 3.6.

$$F = \frac{S_0\,(1 + R_\$)}{(1 + R_f)} \tag{3.6}$$

where

F is the parameters as defined previously.

The forward premium or discount $(F - S_0)/S_0$ is in direct quote and in equilibrium has to be approximately equal to interest rates differential in Equation 3.7.

$$\frac{(F - S_0)}{S_0} \cong (R_\$ - R_f) \tag{3.7}$$

The forward premium or discount $(S_0 - F)/F$ is in the European term and may need to be annualized.

The implied forward pound ($1.4376/£) in Exhibit 3.18 is in a discount of approximately −1.5 percent, since fewer dollars are required to buy the pound. Interest rate differential is also −1.5 percent, as illustrated in the IRP relationship in Exhibit 3.19.

The IRP line is the locus of all points that in equilibrium the forward premium or discount has to be equal to the interest rate differential and any temporary deviation results in a riskless arbitrage. For example, any point to the left of the IRP line, such as X, indicates that the forward premium or discount in foreign currency exceeds the interest rate differential in dollar and foreign currency and investors realize riskless arbitrage profit by borrowing dollars and investing in foreign currency and selling foreign currency forward. In Exhibit 3.19 suppose the actual quoted forward exchange rate is equal to $1.50/£. The forward pound is

EXHIBIT 3.18   Forward Interest Rate Parity

EXHIBIT 3.19   IRP Relationship

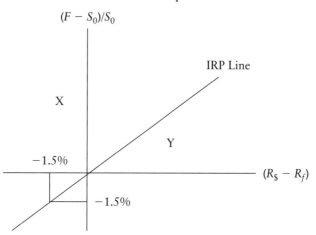

in premium. Other things remaining equal, borrowing $145.82 to buy £100 and investing pounds for one year at 6 percent while selling pounds forward at $1.50/£, there will be a $6.62 riskless arbitrage profit for the strategy just described.

However, the points to the right of the IRP line, such as Y, refer to a situation where the forward premium or discount in foreign currency is below the interest differential in dollars and foreign currency, and it pays to borrow foreign currency and invest in U.S. dollars and sell the dollar forward for a riskless arbitrage profit.

Example: Suppose interest differentials in dollars and Swiss francs are 4 percent per annum (U.S. and Swiss interest rates are 7 and 3 percent, respectively), and Swiss francs (SF) are in 1.4 percent premium against dollar, with a spot rate at $.633/SF and one-year forward in SF is $.6419/SF. There is deviation from parity and the strategy just described will result in a riskless arbitrage profit of SF 25,164.35, provided that the arbitrageur borrowed SF 1,000,000 at 3 percent and invested the proceeds in dollars at 7 percent while selling dollars forward for SF at $.6419/SF.

Interest rate parity as an equilibrium relationship between forward premium or discount and interest rates differential requires two crucial assumptions:

1. Rational expectations
2. Absence of risk premium

"Rational expectations" assume that investors in the United States would not be fooled by higher nominal interest rates in the United Kingdom as they see the higher rate that is contaminated with higher inflation and the covered interest parity (CIP) arbitrage will be zero net present value investment for them. As seen in Exhibit 3.19, if we assume U.S. investors convert dollars for pounds at the spot rate, invest the proceeds in pound-denominated bonds at 6 percent interest, and sell pound one-year forwards today to hedge against foreign exchange rate risk at the forward rate of $1.4376/£, they realize exactly $152.38, which is identical to the future value of the investment had the investors invested in the bond denominated in U.S. dollars. The riskless arbitrage profit in a competitive capital market has to be equal to zero.

"Absence of risk premium" requires that the forward rate does not embody a risk premium constant or time varying that the forward rate does not deviate from the ratio of the two futures value, as is seen in Exhibit 3.19. Uncertainty about the future course of the exchange rate can account for observed deviations from the covered interest parity hypothesis. It is likely that the uncertainty will be greatest when exchange rates change dramatically compared to recent historical trends. In such an environment, the actions of currency speculators can be expected to lead to deviation from the CIP simply because speculators are still in the process of adapting to the change. Not only will they have temporary problems forecasting the exchange rate without systematic error, but they are also likely to demand risk premia because of it.[16]

FORWARD PREMIUM OR DISCOUNT FOR SELECTED CURRENCIES

Exhibit 3.20 provides the observed behavior of the forward premium or discount and interest rates differential between the U.S. dollar and the yen, pound, and Spanish peseta as of September 10, 1998. The Japanese yen appears to be overvalued against the U.S. dollar, as the three forward rates are in a premium exceeding the interest rate differential. All three observations for the yen are to the left of the IRP line. As demonstrated earlier, it pays to borrow dollars and buy yen while investing yen at a Japanese yen rate and selling it forward for riskless arbitrage profit. Since deviations from parity are relatively small, large institutional investors will be able to take advantage of small deviations to make arbitrage profit, whereas the larger bid and ask spread in the interbank market makes it almost impossible for small investors to benefit from such events.

The forward market for foreign exchange for a one-month peseta and pound and three-month Spanish peseta appears to be in line with the interest parity relationship.

EXHIBIT 3.20   Forward Premium (Discount) and Interest Rates Differential

	Yen	Pound	S/peseta
1 month forward	5.4 (5.7)	−1.9 (−1.9)	1.2 (1.2)
3 months forward	4.8 (5.3)	−1.9 (−1.8)	1.2 (1.2)
1 year forward	4.5 (5)	−1.8 (−1.6)	1.6 (1.5)

Source: Figures are interest rate differential and forward premium (discount) in parentheses vs. U.S. dollar, September 10, 1998, *Financial Times.*

INTERNATIONAL PARITY RELATIONSHIP

Assuming the following parameters, the international parity relationships can be illustrated in Exhibit 3.21.

$$S_0 = \$1/€$$
$$S_1 = \$.9903/€$$
$$F = \$.9903/€$$
$$R_\$ = 4\%$$
$$R_f = 5\%$$
$$\Pi_\$ = 2.5\%$$
$$\Pi_f = 3.5\%$$

The euro is in a 1 percent discount against the dollar due to a 1 percent higher nominal interest rate, which is reflected in the inflation differential of 1 percent. The real interest rate is 1.5 percent in both dollars and euros. Percentage changes in the exchange rate and forward premium or discount are identical. Therefore, international parity ex ante is in line with its theoretical counterpart.

REAL EXCHANGE RATE

The nominal exchange rate adjusted for the inflation rates in two different economies provides a measure of the economy's real cost of producing goods for consumption and goods for export over the given period. The real exchange rate E_r is defined as the nominal exchange rate E_n adjusted for the inflation differentials in two economies, as illustrated in the Equation 3.8.

$$E_r = E_n \, (P_f/P_\$) \tag{3.8}$$

where

P_f and $P_\$$ are price indexed in a foreign currency and dollars, respectively.

EXHIBIT 3.21   International Parity Relationship

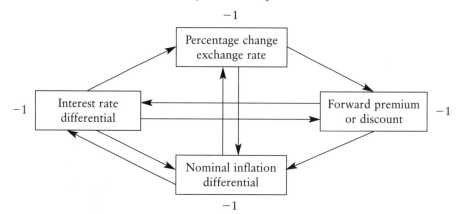

Since a nominal exchange rate is the ratio of the price index denominated in dollars and foreign currency, $P_\$/P_f$, it then follows that the real exchange rate has to be constant and equal to unity, as shown in Equation 3.9.

$$E_r = (P_\$/P_f)\,(P_f/P_\$) = 1 \qquad (3.9)$$

A real exchange rate can be viewed as a measure of an economy's true competitiveness as compared to other economies. When the U.S. real exchange rate appreciates against all other currencies, the cost of producing exports rises, thereby making U.S. exports uncompetitive in the world market. Exhibit 3.22 provides preliminary evidence of the behavior of the real exchange rate for several major currencies over the period 1989 to 1998, with 1995 as the base year with the real exchange rate at 1 or 100 percent. The real exchange rate is by no means constant and deviates from unity substantially for all of the currencies in the sample periods.

The U.S. dollar and British pound appear to have appreciated in real terms by 34.5 and 10.6 percent respectively between the base year of 1995 through 2001. U.S. exports were relatively more competitive prior to the base year as compared to the years following 1995, making exports extremely uncompetitive as reflected in widening the current account deficits. Japanese exports before and after the base period of 1995 appear to have been extremely uncompetitive as the real exchange rate appreciated by 33.8 percent relative to the base year in 2001. The Japanese real exchange rate in 1989 appears to have appreciated by 50 percent as compared to the base year, making exports very uncompetitive, as reflected in the decade of recession in Japan and falling equity prices. The widening U.S. trade deficit in the 1990s and the years 2000 and 2001 (see Exhibit 2.3) may be attributed to the appreciation of the real exchange rate, making U.S. goods relatively expensive for the trading partners.

EXHIBIT 3.22 Real Exchange Rates for Major Currencies

	Canada	France	Germany	Japan	Singapore	U.K.	U.S.
1989	86.0	129.5	134.1	150.3	140.7	94.2	109.3
1990	85.9	111.4	116.3	157.4	129.9	85.6	104.7
1991	82.8	114.1	119.0	144.6	122.8	89.1	103.5
1992	89.6	106.7	107.0	136.4	115.7	89.9	101.2
1993	95.2	114.4	113.7	120.2	114.8	107.8	104.7
1994	102.4	112.3	113.1	110.7	107.2	103.3	103.4
1995	100.0	100.0	100.0	100.0	100.0	100.0	100.0
1996	100.6	103.5	106.5	118.9	100.8	102.1	104.3
1997	101.4	118.4	121.5	129.4	104.6	96.1	112.0
1998	108.6	119.3	123.8	140.4	119.8	93.5	120.0
1999	109.3			124.2	121.6	99.0	119.3
2000	109.4			119.2	123.5	105.2	125.2
2001	113.5			133.8	128.3	110.6	134.5

Source: Author's own estimates, real exchange rate index set at 100 for 1995.

Canada appears to have gained relative competitiveness, as shown by the relatively smaller increase in its real exchange rate (13.5 percent) as opposed to 34 percent compared to its main trading partner, the United States. France's and Germany's exports appear to be relatively more competitive than those of the United States, as their respective real exchange rate have appreciated by nearly 19 and 23 percent between 1995 and 1998. The real exchange rate remains over 100 for all years preceding the base year of 1995 for both countries, implying that their exports, particularly Germany's, remained relatively uncompetitive. Exhibit 3.23 provides a graphical representation of the real exchange rate for the selected countries.

REAL EXCHANGE RATE AND EAST ASIAN CURRENCY CRISIS

Corsetti et al. have provided the estimate of the real exchange rate relative to U.S. dollar for the Southeast Asian economies with 1990 as the base year and real rates for all countries set at 100.[17] Real exchange rates for eight Southeast Asian economies are presented in Exhibit 3.24. Taiwan is excluded as IFS does not provide any data for this economy. With the exception of Hong Kong and Singapore, all other countries experienced significant appreciation in real exchange rates. For example, the real exchange rate of South Korea, Indonesia, Malaysia, Philippines, and Thailand, appreciated by 131.8, 134.5, 43.6, 37.9, and 81 percent respectively between 1990 and 1997 (see Exhibit 3.24). These countries saw erosion of their competitiveness in exports and bore the brunt of the crises in the currency market in the collapse of their currency and ensuing fallout in the financial and banking sector.

Relative to South Korea, Indonesia, and Thailand, China enjoyed a comparative advantage in this period over its regional trading partners in the form of cheap labor and relatively inexpensive currency, thereby capturing the export markets

EXHIBIT 3.23   Real Exchange Rates of Industrial Countries (1989–2001)

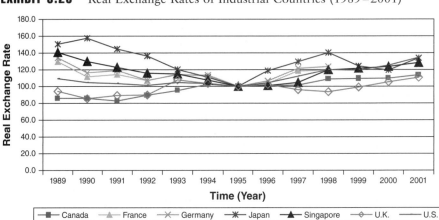

EXHIBIT 3.24   Real Exchange Rates for East Asian Economies (1991–1996)

	South Korea	Indonesia	Malaysia	Philippines	Thailand	China	Hong Kong	Singapore
1990	100	100	100	100	100	100	100	100
1991	101.27	99.83	100.62	83.72	98.54	104.72	93.16	94.40
1992	106.73	103.93	95.06	85.05	99.90	106.72	93.51	94.96
1993	110.84	104.18	99.43	95.29	100.58	99.83	94.95	93.13
1994	106.35	109.43	93.80	82.59	96.91	133.69	93.65	83.51
1995	106.39	114.07	93.49	89.08	96.79	140.18	93.40	81.90
1996	115.60	119.50	93.20	88.66	98.51	151.09	96.07	81.69
1997	231.84	234.55	143.62	137.93	181.05	157.90	96.13	96.87

Source: Author's own estimates using end of the period exchange rates from IFS, real exchange rate index set at 100 for 1990.

lost by others, particularly in the steel market at the expense of South Korea and the apparel market to the detriment of Indonesia and Malaysia. Singapore and Hong Kong were not as hard hit as the other countries in the 1997 crisis, perhaps because of a surplus in the current account and buildup of their foreign reserve compared to the other countries, which faced significant deficits and dwindling foreign exchange reserve.

Case Study

REAL-WOOD FURNITURE, INC.

by Lee Sarver[*]

"Well, there goes my weekend," Mary S. Lytle-Lamm thought glumly as she started back toward her office. With a mint-shiny MBA from Pacific Northwest University, she had joined Real-Wood Furniture, Inc., only three weeks earlier and had hoped to feel her way gradually into the job of financial analyst. (After all, doing finance in class and doing it with real money—other people's, at that—are two very different things!) Evidently, it was not to be. Still awed by the prospect of "doing it for real," she had been trying to determine the most efficient and businesslike arrangement for the objects on her desk, when her new boss, the director of accounting and finance, stuck his head through her door at about 10:30. "Whatever you're doing can wait. Grab a notepad and come along." With that he headed down the hall. Lytle-Lamm reached the conference room only a few steps behind him and stopped dead. "More new faces," she thought, "a lot of them. What's going on?" Waved to a seat without introduction, she soon realized that whatever it was, it seemed urgent.

[*]Middle Tennessee State University   *(continues)*

Real-Wood Furniture began as a hobby. Its founder—a civil engineer with the U.S. Bureau of Reclamation—had built furniture and cabinets in his suburban Spokane garage beginning in the 1970s. Appreciative friends and family persuaded him to go into business during the 1980s, and by 1996 the firm—which sold to decorators and independent shops as far away as northern California—had grown to 120 employees. Because the firm's founders and senior managers still did not think of themselves as business professionals, they had recently begun hiring people with formal training like Lytle-Lamm and her boss.

For years Real-Wood had bought most of its raw materials—wood solids—locally, with more attention to convenience and quality than to cost. (The founder and chairman still never missed an opportunity to sneer about "sawdust-and-glue boards with a photo of wood stuck on." He scorned even hardwood-solids-and-veneers construction.) However, as the firm's market grew, competition sharpened and cost control became an issue. Accordingly, while maintaining relationships with longtime suppliers, Real-Wood had relied increasingly on newer, more capital-intensive, lower-cost Canadian mills to meet its needs. Because imported wood had until recently constituted only a small part of the firm's costs—skilled labor was by far the largest—and because it negotiated long-term contracts, the management of Real-Wood had not felt much concern about foreign exchange risk. The firm's managers were not naive; they simply had other priorities. As it turned out, that had just changed.

The new U.S. administration had just announced a 27 percent tariff on imported Canadian lumber, ostensibly to protect domestic mills from "unfair" competition. At the same time—presumably to head off protests from both Canadians and their erstwhile customers—the U.S. Trade Representative gave assurances that exceptions could be made in cases of hardship. How they could be obtained and how they would work was not yet clear, although the local congressman blandly assured his constituents that business could proceed as usual. These were the events that had precipitated today's unplanned meeting of the management of Real-Wood with the firm's bankers and other outside advisors.

However important everyone realized it had become for the firm to analyze its international position from a strategic perspective, that was, in fact, merely the background to this meeting. In the foreground was a particular deal. Several of the Canadian mills supplying Real-Wood had joined together to offer the firm delivery of a large shipment of assorted hardwoods before the effective date of the tariff. Essentially, they offered to consolidate several orders—some not due for almost a year—for delivery in 90 days at most, with payment of $2.5 million Canadian due then. Such a large delivery would help the firm to postpone facing the costs of the tariff, perhaps even until an exception was obtained or policy changed again.

However, there was no way the proposed shipment could be worked in to the production schedule anytime soon; if the wood could not be sold or bartered to other firms, it would have to be stored. Even the latter course was feasible, since Real-Wood had just finished a new curing facility. (Insurance for this surge in inventory would be covered for a year under the blanket policy the firm purchased when construction began.) Lytle-Lamm's boss confirmed that Real-Wood's cash balance would be stretched to cover the approximately $1.4 to 1.6 million U.S. dollars necessary. At this point, the firm's lead banker, Morgan J. Pierpont, who was present at the meeting, announced that the lenders he represented were more than willing to provide the financing. Eventually the deal was approved, and the real issue became exactly how the firm should structure the transaction. Several alternatives were discussed.

"The simplest thing for us to do is nothing," said the production manager. "I mean, let's take delivery of the wood, buy the Canadian dollars when we need them, and get on with building furniture. After all, how much can happen in the space of 90 days?"

The purchasing manager jumped in. "Maybe we can negotiate a price in U.S. dollars!" When Lytle-Lamm's boss observed that the Canadians would surely raise their asking price, if they had to bear the exchange risk—assuming that they would even discuss it—he countered, "But *they* approached *us!* After all, they have the most to lose from the tariff. Besides, if they've made a number of similar proposals to other customers, they might generate enough volume to get a good rate."

"Well, maybe we can, at that. That's your department; you know those people," answered Lytle-Lamm's boss, "but it still seems like a long shot. Good luck. But what I do know we can do today—and for exactly how much—is hedge." In response to several pairs of raised eyebrows: "For example, we can buy Canadian dollars forward. Morgan can get us a quote or we can shop around." Pierpont smiled without humor. "Or we can buy Canadian dollar futures." "Heck, we can even borrow Canadian dollars and park them in a CD for 90 days. Right, Morgan?" Pierpont nodded. "And Mary can figure out the best course." He looked in her direction and everyone else's glance followed his. All eyes were on her. "Right, Mary?"

Lytle-Lamm's self-confidence returned during lunch, since she had spent the time thumbing through her old class notes (now yogurt-stained). When she returned to her office, she found a single handwritten sheet on her desk (see Exhibit 1), with some numbers and the notation, "Sorry to put you on the spot. Got these from Morgan. Work out our alternatives. Let's take care of this before quitting time today." Lytle-Lamm opened a new spreadsheet and grinned. "Maybe I will have a weekend, after all."

Foreign Exchange Rates

Canadian dollar, spot	1.5728
Canadian dollar, 3-month forward	1.5783
Canadian dollar, 4-month futures	1.5828

Money Market Rates

3-month rate, Canada	2.83% per annum
3-month rate, United States	1.70% per annum

THOUGHT QUESTIONS

1. a. What, in general, is exchange risk?
   b. What risk does Real-Wood face specifically?
2. a. What is political risk?
   b. Is political risk confined exclusively to international transactions?
   c. Do only less-sophisticated Third World governments pose political risk?
3. a. Distinguish between hedging and speculation.
   b. In what sense does failure to hedge constitute speculation?
   c. Could Real-Wood profit by not hedging?
4. How does hedging resemble diversification? How does it differ?
5. a. Are the exchange rates in Exhibit 1 direct or indirect quotations?
   b. Calculate the corresponding direct/indirect quotations.
6. a. What is purchasing power parity?
   b. If a Big Mac costs $1.99 (on average) in the United States, what should it cost (on average) in Canada?
7. a. Distinguish spot and forward rates.
   b. What is meant by a forward premium or discount?
   c. What does the forward rate imply about the expected future spot rate?
8. a. What is the relationship between inflation and interest rates in one country?
   b. What is the relationship between inflation and interest rates between two countries?
   c. What is the relationship between inflation and exchange rates between two countries?
9. a. What is covered interest rate parity (CIRP)?
   b. According to the Exhibit 1, does CIRP hold between Canada and the United States?
   c. If CIRP does not hold, where can you earn the best return?
10. Evaluate Real-Wood's alternatives.

NOTES

1. Central Bank Survey of Foreign Exchange and Derivatives Activity 1998, Bank for International Settlement, Basle, May 1999.
2. John Perry, "Corporate Hedgers Shift to Anticipate a Weakening Dollar," *Wall Street Journal*, May 14, 2002.
3. Bank for International Settlements, Central Bank Survey of Foreign Exchange and Derivatives Activity 1998, Basle, May 1999.

4. *Euromoney,* March 2002.

5. With the launch of new CLS network, "members can settle trades and net positions in each 24-hour period through its payment-versus-payment process in the books of a central entity," notes Daniel Koh, head of trading at Standard Chartered Singapore, one of the member banks of CLS Bank International.

6. *Euromoney,* March 2002.

7. *The Economist,* May 15, 2002.

8. See, for example, Mann (1986), Krugman and Baldwin (1987), and Rosensweig and Koch (1988), pp. 2–15.

9. The evidence of delayed reaction of the change in exchange rate and the import price and volume is documented in a study by Rosensweig and Koch, pp. 2–15.

10. This has been documented by Rosensweig and Koch.

11. See, for example, the classic studies by Gailliot (1971) and Lothiar and Taylor (1996).

12. International Monetary Fund, Washington, DC, 1987.

13. See Bilson (1983).

14. See Cumby and Obstfeld (1981), Frankel (1982), Mishkin (1984), Cumby (1988), and Marston (1997) for classic studies of real interest rate differentials and deviation on uncovered interest parity.

15. Schwebach and Zorn (1997) provide a simple algorithm challenging the Fisher nominal interest rate as sums of the real rate and inflation premium (constant). Assuming uncertain inflation, the authors provide alternative algorithm consistent with observed behavior and explain why nominal interest rate is not an unbiased predictor of future inflation.

16. See Zietz and Homaifar (1994, 1995), who find evidence that the respective forward rates particularly for the German mark and Swiss francs in the period from 1976 to 1984 were close to the theoretical values.

17. Corsetti et al. (1999).

CHAPTER 4

Application of Options and Futures for Managing Exposure

In the financial and currency exchange markets, options continue to play a significant role in transferring risk from those who happen to dislike risk (risk averse) to those who will take it for a profit. Most of the over-the-counter (OTC) options underwritten by various insurance companies (i.e., property casualty, life, health, fire, etc.) are put potions, which provide protection against unforeseen losses. For example, buyers of an option seeking protection on their residence are essentially paying a premium for the right, not the obligation, to sell the property back to the seller of protection (i.e., put writer, the insurance company) in the event of an occurrence, such as a fire, that reduces the value of the property below the price at which the property was insured (i.e., the strike price). The writer of the put option is obligated to perform (i.e., pay the injured party) up to the amount of the protection purchased. Exhibit 4.1 shows the payoff of the buyer and writer of the put option.

The options market or the markets for derivatives are zero-sum game markets. The buyer of the put option as shown in Exhibit 4.1 pays a small premium and gets protection when the value falls below the strike price. The seller of the put option sells protection to a large number of people for a small premium, diversifies its risk, and has the benefit of the law of large numbers, making everybody better off without making some people worse off through the transfer of risk. The put option is out of the money (OTM) above the strike price, where the option will not be exercised; it is at the money (ATM) in the region between the strike price and the price at break-even, where the option will be exercised. The put option is in the money (ITM) at any point below the break-even point.

DETERMINANTS OF THE OPTION PRICE (PREMIUM)

In the foregoing analysis, the premium for the put options is directly related to the:

- Strike price
- Volatility
- Time to expiration

EXHIBIT 4.1   Payoff of the Buyer and Writer of the Put Option

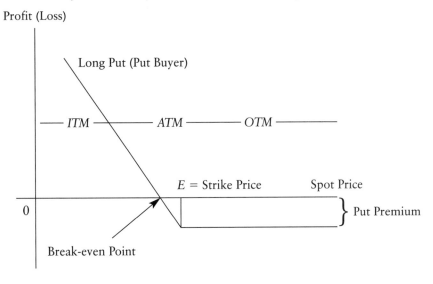

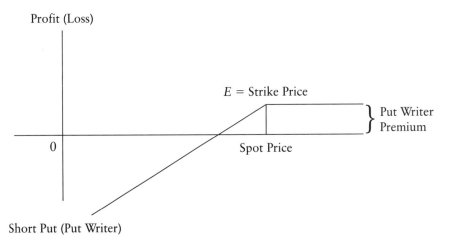

It is inversely related to the:

- Time value of money (interest rates)
- Spot price

The higher the strike price, the more protection one wishes to acquire and, therefore, the higher the premium is expected to be, other things remaining constant. The higher the risk (volatility), the higher the premium will be. It is no accident that the premium on life insurance for males and females in the same age group is not identical, as the average female life expectancy is higher by nearly four years; thus, females pay a relatively smaller premium to get the same amount of coverage. Other things remaining the same, smokers pay a higher premium compared to nonsmokers of the same gender, because the probability of dying earlier than the policy expiration date is greater with the former. The longer the time period for the protection, the greater the premium will be, other things remaining the same.

Like stocks and bonds, the put price (premium) is inversely related to interest rates. The higher the opportunity cost of capital, the smaller the premium is expected to be. Finally, with other things remaining the same, the higher the spot price relative to the strike price is, the smaller the put price (premium) is expected to be.

OPTIONS TRADED IN ORGANIZED EXCHANGES

Options traded, like their close cousin in the over-the-counter market, are essentially priced the same way and respond to the same underlying factors that determine the put/call price (premium). However, the risk or the volatility measure in over-the-counter options is easier to classify and quantify than the volatility of options in organized exchanges on the underlying assets such as stocks, bonds, commodities, indices, interest rates, currencies (spot or futures), and other options. In organized exchanges, the historical standard deviations or implied volatility is used as a proxy for the measure of risk. Exhibit 4.2 presents estimates of the implied volatility for the euro, Japanese yen, Swiss francs, British pound, Canadian dollar, and Australian dollar.

Estimates of the implied volatility are used with other parameters discussed earlier to determine the price of a put/call from the Black-Scholes option pricing formula. For example, the Philadelphia Exchange (PHLX) allows end users to customize all parameters of a currency option trade, including choice of exercise price, customized expiration dates of up to two years, and premium quotation as either units of currency (i.e., cents per pound) or percent of underlying value.

EXHIBIT 4.2   Implied Volatility Rates for Foreign Currency Options[a]

	05/31/02 Implied Vols					
	1 Week	1 Month	2 Months	3 Months	6 Months	12 Months
EUR	9.4	9.3	9.7	9.8	10.1	10.3
JPY	10.5	9.3	9.1	9.0	9.0	9.1
CHF	10.1	10.0	10.2	10.3	10.4	10.6
GBP	5.1	5.5	5.9	6.1	6.8	7.2
CAD	5.7	6.0	6.1	6.2	6.2	6.2
AUD	9.5	9.6	9.7	9.8	9.9	10.1
GBPEUR	5.6	5.8	6.0	6.0	6.1	6.2
EURJPY	8.6	8.1	8.3	8.4	8.8	9.1

[a] This release provides survey ranges of implied volatility mid rates for at the money options as of 11:00 A.M. The quotes are for contracts of at least $10 million with a prime counterparty. Federal Reserve Bank of New York.

PHLX offers standardized options on six major currencies, with American- or European-style exercise; maturities range from monthly to two years, with a choice of midmonth or month-end expiration.

As can be seen from the pricing of the Black-Scholes formula in Exhibit 4.3, 90-day options are priced at $.045 and $.025 respectively for a call/put on the British pound, assuming historical volatility of 12 percent based on the estimates of the annualized standard deviations of currency return for 1979 to 1994.[1] Exhibit 4.4 presents the author's own estimates of historical volatility for six major currencies for the periods 1971 to 1986 and 1987 to 2001. As shown, the Canadian dollar is the least volatile currency with the smallest standard deviation in both periods. Volatility measured by the standard deviation of the changes in currency spot rates has remained fairly stable in both subperiods, in the range of 8 to 10 percent, with the exception of the Canadian dollar.

The call and put price, assuming an implied volatility of 6.2 percent based on the estimate provided by the Federal Reserve Bank of New York for the 90-day British pound, other factors remaining the same, will be $.029 and $.01 per unit of British pound, respectively. The price of both the put and the call decline by 60 percent and 35.56 percent, respectively, when the historical volatility of 12 percent was replaced by the implied volatility of 6.2 percent. The call and put price, P, is the sum of the intrinsic value and time value:

$$P = \text{Intrinsic value} + \text{Time value}$$

In Exhibit 4.3 the put has zero intrinsic value; the spot price is above the strike price and has .025 time value. Likewise, the call has .02 intrinsic value, since spot price is greater than the strike price by 2 cents, and the remaining .025 is due to the time value.

EXHIBIT 4.3   Black-Scholes Option Pricing

	Call	Put
Price	.045	.025
Delta	.598	−.397
Gamma	4.41	4.41
Theta (per/day)	0	0
Vega	.003	.003
Rho	.002	−.002
Option type	Regular	
Exercise	European	
Asset	Currency	
Interest rate $%	1.85	
Foreign rate %	2	
Volatility (%)	12	
Time to expiration (yrs)	.25	
Strike Price	1.43	
Spot Price	1.45	

EXHIBIT 4.4   Estimates of Historical Volatility for Major Currencies

	Annualized Standard Deviations of Currency Return	
	1971–86	Period 1987–2001
Aus dollar	0.0810	0.075
Can dollar	0.032	0.037
Swiss franc	0.105	0.101
Jap yen	0.092	0.10
Brit pound	0.082	0.086
Euro		0.087

Source: Author's own estimate.

SENSITIVITY OF PUT AND CALL PRICE TO UNDERLYING FACTORS

Exhibit 4.3 shows the price sensitivity of call and put to changes in the spot price as delta of the option. Delta is always in the range of zero to 1. It is nearly zero for both OTM options (call and put). The put option delta is in the range of zero to −1. The delta is in the median range for the ATM options and closer to unity when the options are ITM.

Gamma   Exhibits the price sensitivity of the delta to changes in the spot price. That is, the rate at which delta is changing.

Theta   Measures the sensitivity of the option price (premium) to the unit change in time (rate of time deteriorations). As time approaches the expiration of the contract, the value of the option (the time value, not the intrinsic value) is nearly equal to zero.

Vega   Measures the sensitivity of options to changes in volatility. Volatility is the most important parameter in the pricing of both put and call options. This is the only parameter where the input is a guesstimate.

Rho   Measures the price sensitivity of call and put options to changes in interest rate differentials. The call option is directly related to domestic interest rates and inversely related to foreign interest rates (dividend yield in the case of dividend-paying stocks); the put option, however, is inversely related to domestic interest rates and directly to foreign interest rates (dividend yield). In Exhibit 4.3, as interest rate differentials increase, the call and put premium is expected to change by .002 and −.002, respectively. The payoff on the long and short call is illustrated in Exhibit 4.5.

Call options are rights but not obligations to purchase something at a certain price (called an exercise or strike price) and for a specific period. Buying season tickets for college ball games can be considered a call option, where people

EXHIBIT 4.5   Payoff on the Long and Short Call

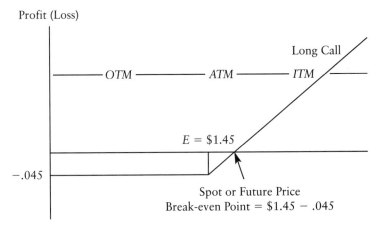

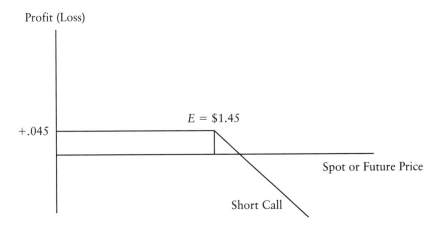

have the right to go to the ball game but no obligation to do so; people also have the right to sell their tickets on eBay to the highest bidder (scalping) and the right to swap tickets for concert tickets. The earnest money a person puts up in making an offer to purchase a house is a call option; the buyer has the right, but not an obligation, to purchase the property at a specific price to be concluded at a specific time. If the buyer decides to walk away, he or she loses only the earnest money. Call and put options are linearly related to one another in the put/call parity, as shown in Equation 4.1.

$$P + S = C + PV(E) \qquad (4.1)$$

where

P = put price
C = call price
S = spot price
$PV(E)$ = present value of the strike price

The currency call or put option is similar to dividend-paying stocks, where both the foreign interest rate and the domestic interest rate affect the value of call and put. Therefore, the present value of the strike price is:

$$PV(E) = \frac{E\,(1 + R_{ff})}{(1 + R_f)}$$

where

R_{ff} = foreign risk-free interest rates
R_f = domestic risk-free interest rates

Assuming that the foreign and domestic risk-free interest rates are identical and the call and the put have the same strike price, the call and the put premium will be the same in the put/call parity paradigm.

Illustration 4.1

OPTION HEDGE

It is June 8 and Excom Corporation has submitted a bid on a contract in Amsterdam for 12.5 million euros receivable in two months, provided that the bid is accepted. The company believes that its chances for winning the contract are better than 75 percent. The company wishes to protect its contingent receivable by buying put options from the Chicago Mercantile Exchange (CME). The put option premium on the August put at strike price of $.9450 is equal to 1.84 cents in the CME, as seen in Exhibit 4.6.

HEDGING STRATEGY

June 8: Buy 100 put options in euro futures at CME (each contract is for delivery of 125,000 units of euro) at strike price of $.9450/euro for a total premium of $230,000.

$$.0184 \times 12,500,000$$

Result

Excom will be ensured that its receivables will be $11,582,500.00 at its minimum (floor) when the put option is exercised on the August expiration date, assuming the expiration spot rate is $.90/euro.

Excom makes a profit of $3,325 per put option, the difference between the $.9266/€ (strike price minus the put premium) and $.90/€ × 125,000 (size of one contract to buy euros in the futures market).

XYZ receivable will be identical to its unhedged position less the premium of $230,000 when the spot rate on the euro is over and above the strike price of $.9450/€ and Excom lets the option expire on the August expiration date for a European-type option, assuming a spot rate of $1/€. In this scenario, the receivable will convert to $12,270,000, that is, equal to spot exchange of euro for $12.5 million less the cost of insurance ($230,000 premium paid for the put option).

EXHIBIT 4.6   Option on Foreign Currency Futures

EURO FX (CME)
125,000 euros; cents per euro

Strike Price	Calls			Puts		
	Jun	Jly	Aug	Jun	Jly	Aug
9350	0.88	1.29	—	0.00	0.78	1.30
9400	0.38	1.02	1.57	0.00	1.01	1.56
9450	0.01	0.79	1.35	0.13	1.28	1.84
9500	0.00	0.61	—	0.62	—	—
9550	0.00	0.47	0.98	—	—	—
9600	0.00	0.36	0.84	1.62	—	—

Estimated Volume Total: **6,191**
Volume for Thursday   **Calls   2,598   Puts   2,419**
Open Interest for Thur   **Calls   44,177   Puts   40,034**

Source: Wall Street Journal, June 8, 2002.

FUNCTIONS OF OPTIONS AND FUTURES

Markets for options and futures provide a number of valuable functions in an economy:

- Risk management: hedging
- Speculation
- Leverage
- Reduced transaction cost and increased efficiency
- Price discovery
- Regulatory arbitrage

Transactions (short and long) in the options and futures market allow individuals and corporations to perform various functions. For example, short selling can be viewed from several different perspectives as a means of:

- Speculating
- Financing
- Hedging

Speculating

Speculating is where the short seller borrows the underlying asset to be shorted and sells with an explicit agreement to buy the asset back later at a lower or higher price in a speculative transaction. In this case the short seller expects the price to drop so it can buy the asset back at a lower price than it sold the asset for. If its expectation materializes, the short seller makes a profit; otherwise it incurs a loss.

Technically short sellers are required to provide some money (margin)—as high as 50 percent of the value of the underlying asset in the spot markets for stocks and bonds to as low as less than 1 percent in the futures market. In essence, the derivatives market provides an opportunity to leverage one's position in the market. Leveraging can cut both ways, leading to higher profits and higher losses.

For example, John Doe believes that the IBM stock priced at $95 per share will drop in the next three months. He wants to short 100 shares of IBM. Therefore he deposits $4,750 in his brokerage account and wishes to sell 100 shares of IBM short. Having secured the margin money, his broker borrows 100 shares of IBM from another brokerage firm and sells 100 share of IBM at $95.

The short seller has to buy back 100 shares in the future. If the stock drops to $80 per share or goes up to $110, the short seller may decide that it is time to unwind the short position by buying the shares back, so the broker can return the borrowed shares. The outcome is a fair game. The short seller either makes $1,500 or loses $1,500 in this scenario.

Financing

Short selling can be viewed as a means of financing. For example, government security dealers buy Treasury securities in the regularly scheduled treasury auction. To finance the purchase, the security dealer sells the underlying asset—for example, T-bills—to a municipality for one week and agrees to repurchase the security after one week at a slightly higher price. This short selling can be viewed as a means of financing at a fully collateralized basis. Remember, the dealer is selling at a lower price with an agreement to buy it (repurchase) back later at a somewhat higher price. The spread between what price the dealer sells and buys back as a percentage of initial price, adjusted for the duration of the sell and purchase, is the interest rate that the dealer paid for financing the purchase of the T-bills and is known as a *repo rate*.

The counterparty financing the purchase is effectively entering into a reverse repurchase agreement, or *reverse repo*. For example, suppose a government security dealer wishes to finance the purchase of on-the-run T-bills over one week. The security dealer enters into a repurchase agreement by posting T-bills as collateral and selling securities to a municipality at $998,275 with the agreement to buy them back for $998,750 after seven days. The repo rate is equal to [($998,750/$998,275) – 1] × 52, or 2.47 percent annualized reflecting the credit quality of the collateral. Exhibit 4.7 illustrates the structure of a repurchase agreement.

The lender may require a *haircut,* which is the difference between the value of the collateral and the amount of loan taken by the security dealer against the collateral. The haircut reduces the lender's counterparty risk and reflects the borrower's credit risk. Assuming the collateral in this example has a market value of $1 million, the haircut is $1,725 as a means of providing protection to the lender in the event the borrower is unable to fulfill its financial obligation. In the mortgage market, the haircut used to be as high as 20 percent, with borrowers putting up collateral valued at $100 and borrowing $80 against the posted collateral.

EXHIBIT 4.7   Structure of a Repurchase Agreement

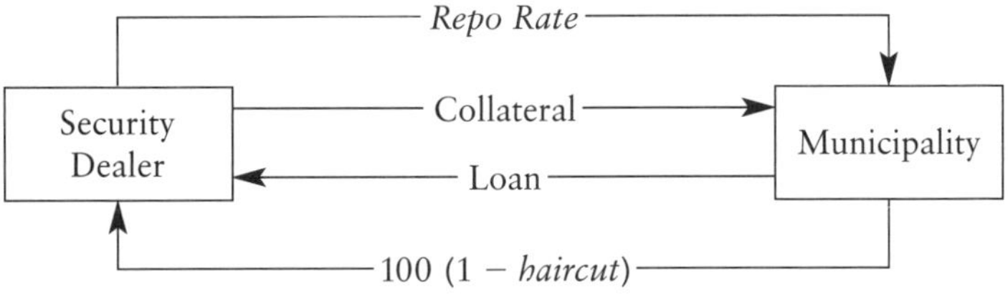

The repurchase agreement in capital markets is used to finance inventory of debt instruments that benefit both buyers and sellers. Buyers usually receive a better interest rate on repos as compared to money market yield, and sellers are able to fund the purchase of the debt instrument at a relatively lower rate than is otherwise available. Hedge funds use the repo market to take advantage of, for example, misspricing of bonds for the 30-year on-the-run and the 29.9-year off-the-run issues, respectively, yielding 6.125 and 6.06 percent in the U.S. Treasury market. A hedge fund buys off-the-run and simultaneously enters into a repurchase agreement over a one-week period. A hedge fund benefits from the low repo rate in its long position, as well as an increase in the price of the underlying off-the-run issue.

A hedge fund simultaneously sells (borrows) the on-the-run issue by entering into a reverse repo over a one-week horizon. In this scenario, the hedge fund receives the collateral in the reverse repo, sells the bond, and uses the proceeds to pay the counterparty. At the end of the contract, reversing the transaction, the hedge fund is obligated to buy back the bond and return it, while receiving the repo rate. The hedge fund benefits if the repo rate is high (it receives interest for lending the bond) in its reverse repo, as well as if there is a falling price of the on-the-run issue.

Hedging

Options and futures provide end users the opportunity to reduce or transfer exposure to various types of risks (i.e., interest rate risk, foreign exchange risk, and market risk). Hedging requires taking an offsetting position, so that an exposed position is protected from rising/falling interest rates or changing exchange rates in one direction or the other. While hedging is essentially buying protection for unforeseen events (similar to insurance), it is costly. Therefore, firms that hedge have good reasons to engage in such activity. Some of the reasons for hedging are obvious, while others are not.[2]

For example, financing a particular transaction requires buying protection from a nonpayment (default). The borrower also can buy a cap in a floating rate note. Furthermore, buying a new car at a dealership requires that the buyer purchase full-coverage insurance if the car needs to be financed. The cap, the credit swap, and buying full coverage are all derivatives designed to mitigate risk. The credit swap enables the buyer of the protection to shift the risk of default to a counterparty. The cap provides protection for a rising interest rate. Buying full coverage ensures that the buyer put the underlying instrument to the seller of the protection in the event the price of the insured instrument falls below the strike price for the insurable events.

To Mitigate the Bankruptcy and Cost of Financial Distress

Firms hedge and transfer their risk to other parties to reduce the variability of their cash flows and probability of large losses that threaten company survival. Since the cost of reorganization and eminent bankruptcy is high, lenders are unwilling to extend credit or require hefty premiums, inducing firms to hedge their business and financial risk, as a dollar of loss in a shaky financial state can cost more than a dollar.

Tax Code

Due to the asymmetric treatment of tax rates as they apply to ordinary income and capital gains, derivatives can be employed to convert one form of income to another to defer capital gains income taxes and arbitrage taxes by shifting income from one subsidiary to another to take advantage of differentials in taxation worldwide. In the fall 1997 Long Term Capital Management (LTCM) entered into a contract with Union Bank of Swiss (UBS), where LTCM agreed to buy a seven-year call option on 1 million shares of its own stock from UBS for $300 million. The boards of both companies approved the deal. The LTCM objective was to convert foreign interest income from its offshore hedge fund into capital gains, defer taxes for seven years, and secure a capital gains tax rate of 20 percent as opposed to the short-term ordinary income tax rate of 39.6 percent. To hedge against the exposure of a rising stock price, UBS purchased 1 million shares of the LTCM stock by borrowing $500 million at LIBOR (London Interbank Offering Rate) plus 50 basis points. In summer 1998 LTCM collapsed and UBS lost nearly $680 million.[3]

Risk Aversion

Risk-averse managers always prefer to avoid a dollar of loss to a dollar of profit. For a risk-averse individual, a dollar of loss is more painful than a dollar of gain. The degree to which managers of large publicly owned corporations are risk averse depends on the agency relationship between managers (the agent) and owners (the stockholders). The embedded options in the managers' compensation packages induce them to increase the market value of the firm and of their own perks without raising the uncertainty of the future cash flows.

Reasons Not to Hedge

Hedging is costly; it entails transaction costs, costs of monitoring the transactions on derivatives, and managerial controls to prevent unauthorized trading as well as costly bid/ask spread in favor of the dealer.

Beginning in 2000, the Financial Accounting Standards (FASB) required, in Statement No. 133, firms to report and recognize derivatives as assets and liabilities on the balance sheet and to measure and report the changes in their market value.[4] Financial and nonfinancial corporations seem to be increasingly using derivatives for risk management.[5]

Short Hedge

Short hedge involves selling derivatives, such as forwards, futures, and options, short to protect the long position that individuals or corporations have or expected to have in the near future, such as receivables denominated in foreign currency. For example, farmers, producers (e.g., oil and natural gas, food processors, portfolio managers), and financial institutions own assets whose value is exposed to various types of risks. These institutions sell derivatives (take short position) to protect the value of the long position.

Consider John Deere, which is exporting goods to the United Kingdom, and an importer that is going to pay in British pounds in the next 90 days. Concerned about the likelihood of the devaluation of the pound, John Deere's treasurer can take a short hedge by selling 90-day pound forward, thereby locking in a specific price for its receivable. If the pound devalues in 90 days, the short hedge produces profit that may remedy the loss incurred in the spot market when receivables are converted at the exchange rate prevailing at that time.

HEDGING RECEIVABLES DENOMINATED IN FOREIGN CURRENCY

Sam Nissan, a major car dealership, has sold 1,000 units of the Altima produced in the Smyrna, Tennessee, plant to a British importer in Birmingham, England. The cars were shipped on October 30, 2001, and the importer has agreed to pay £10 million in January 2002. The treasurer is not trying to remain unhedged, as an unfavorable exchange rate movement may reduce or eliminate the profit margin for all practical purposes, and is contemplating hedging the foreign exchange rate risk. The treasurer's objective in this scenario is to maximize the amount of receivables expected in a three-month period.

Forward Hedging

The 90-day forward rate on a British pound bid rate is quoted at $1.4875/pound, assuming the treasurer expects the spot rate to be between as low as $1.44 to as high as $1.60/pound within the next three months. The forward hedge requires selling pounds forward at the bid price of $1.4785; this locks the dealership in at the total receivable of $14.785 million, as shown in Exhibit 4.8. The exchange rate risk is passed to the seller of the forward contract, usually a major bank.

EXHIBIT 4.8 Short Hedge

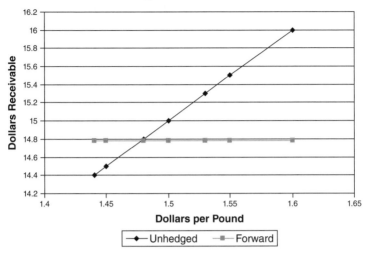

Dollars per Pound

—◆—Unhedged —■—Forward

Illustration 4.2

SHORT HEDGE

Sam Nissan, a major car dealership has sold 1,000 units of the Altima produced in the Smyrna, Tennessee, plant to a British importer in Birmingham, England. The cars were shipped on October 30, 2001 and the importer has agreed to pay £10 million in January 2002.

HEDGING STRATEGY

Oct 30: Sell £10 million forward at bid rate of $1.4785/pound.
January 30: Close out the position.

Result

Sam Nissan will be ensured that its total receivable is $14,785,000. It makes a profit of $285,000 on the forward contract provided that the spot rate is $1.45/pound on January 30. However, had the exchange rate been $1.60/£ on January 30 the forward contract would prove to be costly as compared to the remaining unhedged position. In this scenario, the forward contract backfires resulting in a loss of $1.215 million and receivable in dollars will be no more or no less than $14.785 million.

Protective Put

Nissan is also contemplating another option to hedge exchange rate risk, that is, buying a 90-day put option at a strike price of $1.50/£. This option is quoted at the offer price for 2 cents per unit of British pound. The protective put is intended to produce a payoff similar to an unhedged position for exchange rates above the strike price; however, it provides a floor for the exchange rates below the strike price minus the premium at exactly $1.48/£. In this case, the worst outcome for Nissan is to earn $14.8 million for the receivable denominated in pounds, as illustrated in Exhibit 4.9.

However, at exchange rates above the strike price of $1.50/£, the payoff on the protective put will be identical to the unhedged position less the premium for the insurance.

Covered Call

The treasurer is long in pounds (has receivables denominated in pounds) and therefore can sell call options in British pounds and receive premiums by forgoing the potential for the possible appreciation of the British pound in the next three months. Exhibit 4.10 presents the behavior of the covered call.

Zero Collar

The collar is created by combing a long put and a short call on the underlying instrument, such as stocks, bonds, interest rates, and commodities. The treasurer can finance the long put and the premium of $200,000 associated with a protective put by selling calls and receiving a premium for it to pay for the put, as shown in Exhibit 4.11. Two weeks after buying put options, the pound has moved up to $1.5075/£, and the $1.52 (strike price) call is priced at $.02/£ at the offer. The treasurer finds this price tempting, so he sells the calls on £10 million short and receives $200,000. The zero collar in particular has to be structured so that selling the underlying call short pays for the premium for the put. In this scenario, the upside potential is being sold for a fee to finance the

EXHIBIT 4.9   Protective Put

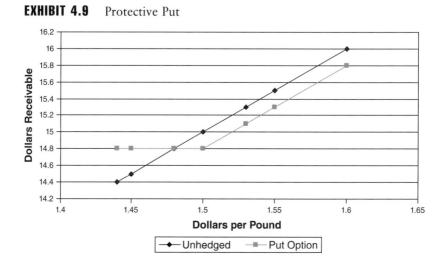

EXHIBIT 4.10 Covered Call

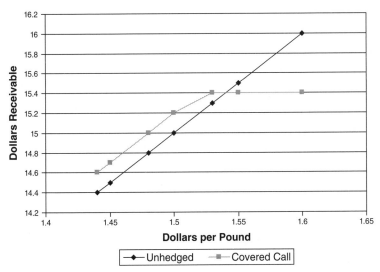

protection sought in buying the long put. Exhibit 4.11 illustrates various payoffs from various hedging instruments.

The collar is producing two expected payoffs that are equal to $15 and $15.2 million regardless of which way the exchange rate is heading. For example, assuming the exchange rate in 90 days turns out to be $1.58/£, Nissan's put expires worthless with the cost of $200,000. However, the call will be exercised, and Nissan is obligated to sell pounds at $1.54/£ ($1.52 strike price plus the 2 cent premium) and realize $15.2 million, assuming that in 90 days the exchange rate is equal to $1.45/£. In this scenario, the call option expires and Nissan can keep the premium; however, the put provides protection at a strike price of $1.50 less a 2 cent premium, leaving exactly $15 million for the receivable.

EXHIBIT 4.11 Payoffs from Various Hedging Instruments

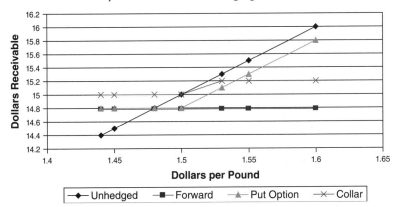

Long Hedges

Long hedges involve buying derivatives (taking long position) in forwards, futures, and options to minimize future outlays, such as payables in the near future denominated in foreign currency, or to lock in a price now for the goods a firm is expected to purchase some time in the near future.

For example, American Airlines (AA) wishes to purchase 2.5 million metric tons of fuel oil in the next two years. It can enter into a forward contract that fixes the price of fuel oil for the next two years by buying fuel oil forward (futures) for the duration of the forward contract. AA buys the fuel oil in the spot market paying the spot price; however, it either receives a rebate (if the spot price is greater than the fixed forward price) or pays (if the spot price is less than the fixed forward price) to the seller of the forward contract the difference between the contract price and the prevailing spot price.

If the fuel oil price goes up, the losing party, here AA, pays the higher spot price and receives a rebate that is equal to the price differential (spot price and contract price) from the seller of the protection, who in this case may be an oil company. However, if the price of the fuel oil drops below the contract price, AA is buying fuel oil at spot at a lower price but paying the difference between what it paid and what it had contracted for to the losing party, the seller of the forward contract. This is called a commodity swap and will be covered fully in Chapter 7.

Example: It is June 18 and AMD manufacturing company needs 10,000 metric tons of aluminum to meet a contract by September 18. The spot price at the London Metal Exchange (LMEX) is quoted in U.S. dollars per metric ton at the close of trading on Tuesday, June 18:

Aluminum High Spot	$1,344 − 1,344.50
3 Months	$1,365 − 1,365.50

The spot price of aluminum turns out to be $.6096/lb., as the metric ton is equal to 2,204.62 pounds. The manufacturer has two options in this scenario: (1) leave it to the market, do nothing, and buy aluminum at spot by September 18; or (2) hedge the exposure by buying aluminum forward at the ask price of $1,365.50 per metric ton. Suppose the price of aluminum turns out to be $1,392 per metric ton on September 18; AMD closes out the futures position for gains of approximately

$$10,000 \times (1,392 - 1,365.5) = \$265,000$$

on the 100 futures contracts. AMD pays on the spot market on September 18, a sum total of $13,920,000 to purchase 10,000 metric tons of aluminum; however, its long hedge has saved the company $265,000. The total cost to AMD is $13,655,000, ($13,920,000 less the profit of $265,000 on the long futures). Alternatively, suppose the aluminum price on September 18 is $1,350 per metric ton. AMD loses on the long futures hedge by

$$10,000 \times (1,350 - 1,365.5) = -\$155,000$$

The total cost to AMD is equal to $13,650,000 ($13,500,000 to buy 10,000 metric tons of aluminum at the spot price of $1,350 per metric ton on September 18 and closing out the futures contract for loss of $155,000). See Illustration 4.3.

Illustration 4.3

AMD manufacturing needs to buy 10,000 metric tons of aluminum to satisfy its contractual obligations to its suppliers by September 18. The spot price of aluminum is $1,344 per metric ton and the 90 days future is at offer $1,365.50.

HEDGING STRATEGY

June 18: buy 100 futures contract (each contract is for delivery of 100 metric tons) on aluminum at ask price of $1,365.50

Sept 18: Close out the position.

Result

AMD will be ensured that its cost will be $1,365.50 per metric ton. AMD makes a profit of $265,000 on the futures contract, provided that the spot is $1,392 per metric ton on September 18. AMD loses $155,000 on the futures contract, assuming the spot is $1,350 per metric ton on September 18.

AMD is better off hedging its exposure to market risk by concentrating on manufacturing efficiency and not speculating on whether the spot aluminum price will be lower or higher in 90 days. Like all other companies, AMD cannot predict future prices in foreign currency, interest rates, or commodity prices. Companies should concentrate their activities where they have comparative advantage and leave risk taking to those that are equipped to do so.

The analysis just provided assumes that the forward and the futures contracts are identical. In reality, there are some differences regarding OTC forwards and their cousins in the organized exchanges for futures contracts. Among other things, profits and losses in organized exchanges are marked to market on a daily basis by the clearinghouse to both parties taking long and short positions. The OTC forward profit or loss is recognized at the settlement date.

SPECULATION ON THE FUTURES PREMIUM OR DISCOUNT

This type of speculation involves simultaneously buying and selling two forward or futures contracts maturing, for example, in three and six months. The speculator is only interested in the spread between the three- and six-month contract and the direction at which it is believed the spread is going to go, based on the economic fundamentals. For example, the speculator believes that the spread (premium or discount) between the three- and six-month forward or futures contract will widen and therefore wants to buy longer-term forward or futures and simultaneously sell shorter-term ones. The forward or futures premium may widen due to increases in interest rate differentials between dollar interest rates and foreign interest rates.

The increase in the interest rate differentials could be due to rising U.S. rates or falling foreign interest rates. In this case the foreign currency is expected to be traded at a premium in the forward or futures market, assuming interest parity relationship holds. However, if a company expects that the spread (premium or discount) will be narrowing (interest rates differentials are decreasing), it will take a long position in the shorter maturity (three months here) while selling the six-month futures short. This type of spread transaction is designed to reduce and limit the risk (reward) of loss (gains) to the speculator.

Example: It is June 7, 2002, and the Swiss franc is $.6423 at spot. A speculator, examining the currency futures, believes that the spread between September 2002 and December 2002 will widen. The speculator buys 20 December contracts at $.6446 and simultaneously sells 20 September contracts at $.6436.

The speculator is long and short in 2.5 million Swiss francs for delivery on the third Wednesday of the delivery month. The speculator holds both long and short positions for three months; then the September contract expires on the third Wednesday and closes out at spot price of $.6535, while the December contract has three months to expiration and has to be liquidated at the prevailing three-month futures contract price. Exhibit 4.13 illustrates three possible prices for the three-month futures assuming the rates are expected to decline from $.6575 to $.65 in the third scenario.

When the spread between the two futures prices widens, as in scenario 1, the swap transactions buying the longer-term maturity and shorting the shorter-term maturity produce a profit of $7,500. However, if the spread narrows, as in scenarios 2 and 3, the swap transactions are respectively producing negative payoffs of $2,500 and $11,250.

The speculator would have structured the swap differently provided that he or she believed that the spread between the two futures or forward contracts would be narrowing. In this scenario the speculator buys the near maturity while

EXHIBIT 4.12   Currency Futures

Contract	Month	Last	Change	Open	High	Low	Vol	Open/Int
Swiss franc	Jun '02	0.6426s	0.0008	0.6429	0.6454	0.6410	2640e	50592 IMM
Swiss franc	Sep '02	0.6436s	0.0008	0.6430	0.6463	0.6425	401e	7718 IMM
Swiss franc	Dec '02	0.6446s	0.0008	0.6446	0.6446		2	87

Source: FutureSource, June 7, 2002.

EXHIBIT 4.13   Speculative Gains or Losses on Foreign Exchange Swap

	1	2	3
Prices at the End of Three Months	**Futures = $.6575** **Spot = $.6535**	**Futures = $.6535** **Spot = $.6535**	**Futures = $.65** **Spot = $.6535**
Six-Month Long	+$32,250	+$22,250	+$13,500
Three-Month Short	−$24,750	−$24,750	−$24,750
Swap	+$7,500	−$2,500	−$11,250
Contract Months	March, June, September, December, and two additional near-term months		
Last Trading Day	Friday before the third Wednesday of month		
Settlement Date	Third Wednesday of month		
Daily Price Limits	None		

shorting the long maturity; if his or her expectation materializes, then profit will be earned. Exhibit 4.14 presents various currency futures contract specifications.

HEDGE RATIO

So far it has been assumed at least implicitly that the entire exposure to various types of risks is hedged by taking an offsetting position with an identical amount of forward, futures, or options. The hedge ratio was assumed to be equal to unity. However, in reality, there may not be an instrument that moves in tandem with the underlying assets in the forward, futures, or options market. The hedge ratio defines the sensitivity of the underlying assets (exposed to various risks) with that of the underlying forward, futures, or options. That is, the hedge ratio measures degrees of the linear relationship between the exposed assets and derivative instruments used to provide protection for the underlying asset.

EXHIBIT 4.14   Philadelphia Board of Trade Currency Futures Contract Specifications

	Australian Dollar	British Pound	Canadian Dollar	Japanese Yen	Swiss Franc
Symbol	ZA	ZB	ZC	ZJ	ZS
Contract Size	100,000	62,500	100,000	12,500,000	125,000
Quotations	Cents per unit	Cents per unit	Cents per unit	Hundredths of a cent per unit	Cents per unit
Mimimum Price Change	$10	$6.25	$10	$12.50	$12.50

For example, the exposed position is payable/receivable denominated in Swiss francs. The Swiss franc forward, futures, and options on futures are available in the OTC as well as the organized exchanges, and the hedge ratio can be estimated as shown in Exhibit 4.15.

The slope of the relationship in Exhibit 4.15 is the hedge ratio denoted as h.[6]

The simple linear relation between the spot (S) and futures (F) is defined algebraically in Equation 4.2.

$$S = c + hF \qquad\qquad (4.2)$$

where

c and h are respectively the intercept and slope coefficient in a simple regression.

The gold spot and gold futures for an August 2002 contract are used in a simple regression as in Equation 4.2. The regression produced R^2 of 98.5 percent, implying that 98.5 percent of the variations in the dependent variable is explained by the independent variable with slope coefficient of 1.06 as the hedge ratio. This hedge ratio is termed minimum variance; no other hedge ratio produces a hedge with a smaller variance, as shown in Exhibit 4.16.

As expected, the relationship between spot and futures has a strong correlation of 99.24 percent. The slope coefficient of 1.06 indicates that for every dollar of gold exposed in the spot market, 1.06 dollar of gold futures has to be shorted in the futures market.

Reduced Transaction Cost

The derivatives market provides opportunities to alter, increase, or decrease and to adjust to the desired position the degree of sensitivity of the market value of

EXHIBIT 4.15   Relationship between Spot and Forward Rates

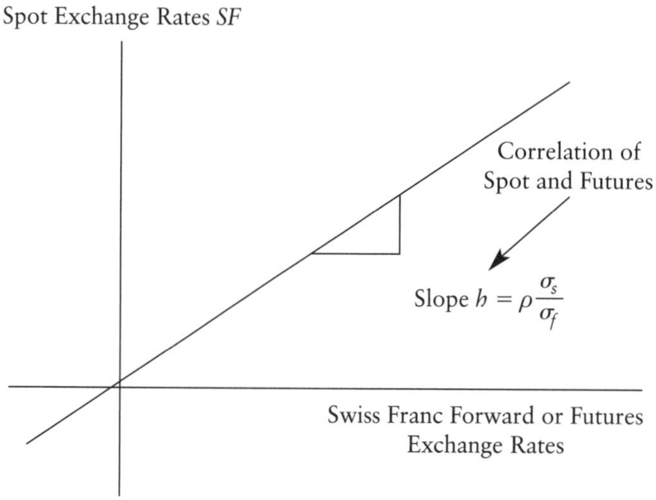

Spot Exchange Rates *SF*

Correlation of Spot and Futures

Slope $h = \rho\dfrac{\sigma_s}{\sigma_f}$

Swiss Franc Forward or Futures Exchange Rates

EXHIBIT 4.16   Regression of Spot Gold on August 2002 Gold Futures

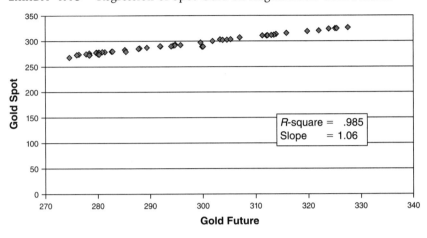

assets (current or expected) or liabilities (payables, current, or expected to be incurred in the future) to changes in market interest rates or changes in market returns at substantially reduced cost. For example, consider a bond portfolio with a duration of a 10.5 years. *Duration* is the price elasticity of the bond with respect to changes in yield. This portfolio is expected to change 10.5 percent in opposite direction for +/−100 basis points change in the yield. The bond portfolio manager believes that the rally in the bond market is nearly over and therefore wishes to shorten the duration of the portfolio to 7.5 years.

Portfolio managers can achieve their objective of reducing duration by selling futures contract without actually selling long-term bonds in the spot market at the bid price and paying transaction costs at both ends and buying intermediate bonds at the ask price in order to shorten duration. The reduced transaction cost increases the potential profits and improves the efficiency of managing and mitigating interest rate risk (see Chapter 6).

PRICE DISCOVERY OF OPTIONS AND FUTURES

Options, forwards, and futures convey information as to the price of the underlying instruments in the future. Trust the option market in pricing financial assets such as stocks, bonds, and commodities. For example, if the 90-day call at the strike price of $30 is priced at $2.5, the stock price conveyed by this premium is to be trusted as opposed to the price in the spot market.

This may seem to be ironic, but in the zero-sum game market, such as options or futures, the parties in this transaction—the long and short call with exactly opposite expectations as to the direction of the stock price in 90 days—are providing a valuable function of discovery of the stock price unintentionally. The short call seller (the writer) believes that the strike price at which she shorted the stock may not be sustained in the near future; likewise the long call buyer (the buyer) believes that the stock price will be greater than the strike price and, therefore, buys the right to purchase the stock at the strike price. The current spot price cannot be greater than $30 (we need to trust this since the short call will receive no more than $32.50 for a share of the stock in the event the long call decides to exercise its right in 90 days for a European call).

REGULATORY ARBITRAGE

The derivatives market allows individuals and corporations to bypass regulatory requirements such as capital adequacy, margin, and reserve requirements imposed by the regulatory agencies and to bypass regulatory restrictions on accounting standards and taxes. For example, hedge funds sell calls on the underlying stocks they own. This provides cash flow from the buyer of the call, while maintaining the possession of the stock with the privilege of receiving dividends as well as the ability to exercise the voting right by forgoing the potential for the higher expected price in the near future. This is an economical way of selling stock that defers taxes and provide some payoff in the form of a premium received as opposed to simply selling the stock at the spot market.

Alternatively, portfolio managers who receive a steady pension flow from various agencies sell put options and receive premiums that obligate them to purchase the underlying assets from the buyer of puts at the strike price. Again, this is an economical way of purchasing the underlying assets, stocks, and bonds as opposed to simply buying the assets for the portfolio.

BINOMIAL OPTION PRICING

[NOTE: The "Hedged Portfolio" section (later in this chapter) is an essential supplement to "Binomial Option Pricing."]

The price (premium) of put and call options can be estimated under risk-neutral conditions. Risk neutrality requires that the portfolio of spot (i.e., stocks, bonds, currencies, etc.) and put options have identical payoff in the risky bivariate states in the future (states 1 and 2). For example, assume the euro spot exchange rate is \$.93/€, and the exchange rate is expected to be either \$1.01/€ or \$.89/€ one period in the future, as shown in Exhibit 4.17.

The put option is OTM in state 1 and therefore has zero time value. It is ITM in state 2 and is worth at least \$.045/€. Combining the delta (Δ) amount of spot with one put option produces a portfolio that is risk neutral in a good (prosperity) or bad state (recession). A portfolio is therefore created in Equation 4.3 with this payoff:

$$\Delta \times (1.01) + 0 = \Delta \times (.89) - .045$$
$$\Delta = -.375$$

(4.3)

EXHIBIT 4.17   Binomial Option Pricing for Put

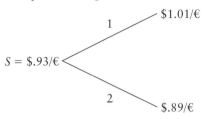

Put option with strike price of $.935/€ is expected to have the following payoffs in the above two states:

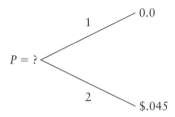

where

P = price of put option

The left side of the equation is a portfolio composed of the Δ amount of spot and one long put with a premium of zero (the put has zero time value in state 1). The right side of the equation is the Δ amount of spot and one long put with the $.045 value (the long put pays $.045 to buy one put as an outflow). The Δ of the put option is between zero and −1. A riskless portfolio is composed of:

Long spot: Δ amount of spot

Long option: 1 put option

Assuming the euro exchange rate moves up to $1.01/€, the value of the portfolio is − $.3788 in state 1. Likewise the value of the portfolio in state 2, where the exchange rate moves down to $.89/€, is also exactly equal to − $.3788, that is, −.375 (.89) − .045 = −.3788. The portfolio is therefore risk neutral, and the payoff from this portfolio in the absence of riskless arbitrage has to be no more than the risk-free interest rate. Suppose risk-free interest rates are equal to 8 and 4 percent, respectively, for the United States and United Kingdom (interest rate differential of 4 percent). We wish to create another risk-neutral portfolio in the current state at time zero by combining the Δ amount of spot and one put option with the price of P to be determined and 90 days to expiration. The payoff from this portfolio (after adjusting for the time value of the money) is identical to the payoff of the other two risk-neutral portfolios in states 1 and 2:

$$\frac{[\Delta\,(.935) + P]\,(1 + .02)}{1.01} = -\$.3788$$

Solving for the price of put option P

$$P = \$.0245/€$$

This price is a rough approximation for the analyst to consider as the intrinsic value of the option is where the time value of the option is assumed to be zero. A portfolio composed of the long in spot and long in put option is expected to produce a payoff similar to the payoff of the protective put discussed earlier. The return from such a portfolio has to be equal to the risk-free rate for nondividend-paying instruments and equal to interest rate differentials for dividend-paying instruments, such as foreign currency, or simply equal to risk-free interest and dividend yield on any dividend-paying stocks.

The call option with the same strike price of $\$.935/€$ and spot prices identical to states 1 and 2 in Exhibit 4.17 is expected to have the payoffs shown in Exhibit 4.18.

The call has $\$.075$ value in state 1 as the spot price exceeds the strike price by $\$.075$; the call has zero value in state 2, and it is OTM. Combining the Δ amount of spot and one short call is expected to produce a risk-neutral portfolio with riskless payoff:

Long spot: Δ amount of spot

Short option: 1 call option

$$\Delta \times (1.01) - .075 = \Delta \times (.89)$$

Solving for $\Delta = .625$

The payoffs in both risk-neutral portfolios in states 1 and 2 are identical to .5563, which is equal to .625 (1.01) − .075 in state 1 or .625 (.89) in state 2. To price the call option denoted C, we need to create another risk-neutral portfolio in the current state (current spot of $\$.93/€$) at time zero whose future value will be identical to the payoff of the other two risk-neutral portfolios in states

EXHIBIT 4.18   Binomial Option Pricing of Call

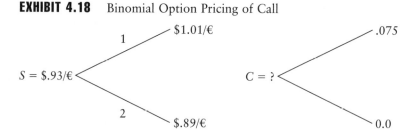

1 and 2, assuming the same 4 percent risk-free interest rate differential and the call has 90 days to expiration:

$$\frac{[.625 \ (.93) - C] \ (1 + .02)}{1.01} = +.5563$$

Solving for $C = .03$

The price of the call option at time zero turned out to be \$.03/€. This price is a rough approximation of the call option as the intrinsic value of the option in the risk-neutral state was ignored. To ensure validity of the results with respect to pricing both call and put options, look at the put-call parity relationship in the Equation 4.4.

$$P + S = C + PV(E) \qquad (4.4)$$

$$PV(E) = E \div \left[\frac{(1 + R_f)}{(1 + R_{ff})} \right]$$

where

P = put price
S = spot price
C = call price
E = strike price
R_f = U.S. risk-free interest rate
R_{ff} = U.K. risk-free interest rate

$$.0265 + .93 = .03 + .935 \left(\frac{1.01}{1.02} \right), \text{ parity approximately holds}$$

HEDGED PORTFOLIO

Combining, for example, 625,000 units of euro with 1 million short calls on the euro will create a hedged portfolio with the following payoffs. The number of units of euro of 625,000 is determined by the hedge ratio of .625, the Δ of the call option in Exhibit 4.18. The current value of this portfolio is therefore:

$$625,000 \ (.93) - 1,000,000 \ (.03) = 551,250$$

The value of the portfolio consists of paying \$581,250 for the 625,000 units of euro and receiving \$30,000 for 1 million short calls. The net cash outlay is equal to \$551,250. If the spot price of the euro goes up to \$1.01/€, the call will be exercised and the value of the hedged portfolio will be equal to 625,000 $(1.01) - 1000,000 \ (.075) = \$556,250$. However, if the spot price of the euro in 90 days falls to \$.89/€, the call will be equal to zero and expires worthless, and the value of the portfolio is equal to exactly \$556,250, that is, 625,000 units of euro at \$.89/€ and zero call value. The return on the portfolio is therefore equal to:

$$\left(\frac{\$556,250}{\$551,250} \right) - 1 \cong .01$$

The return on the portfolio is equal to approximately 1 percent per 90 days, which is equal to a 4 percent interest rate differential between domestic and foreign interest rates. This portfolio is therefore expected to produce a return not greater than the interest rates differentials.

DERIVATIVES APPLICATION IN PRACTICE

The use of derivatives has increased significantly since the start of a new floating rates arrangement in 1973 and rising inflation in the late 1970s in the United States as well as rising oil and gas commodity prices, which prompted a new breed of financial and nonfinancial products that transfer risk from one party to another. Firms use forward contracts for firm commitments, while they use options involving contingent transactions to be executed when and if the actual contingencies arise.

Canada's Barrick Gold was the first mining company to use hedging as a result of various central banks' willingness to lease gold to achieve higher returns. The first generation of the derivatives used by gold mining firms was the synthetic forward contract, which was created by leasing gold from a central bank, selling the gold immediately at the spot market, and using the proceeds to buy a bond with the maturity coinciding with the maturity of the leased gold and with a higher interest rate than the lease rate paid to the central bank (see Exhibit 4.19). The interest rate differential can be considered as a riskless arbitrage profit.

Suppose Barrick leased 10,000 ounces of gold from the Canadian central bank with a promise to return the borrowed gold in 90 days at a lease rate of 4 percent

EXHIBIT 4.19   Constructing Synthetic Forward Contract

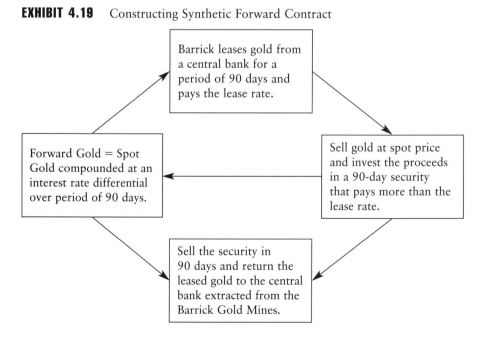

per annum. Barrick simultaneously sells 10,000 ounces of gold at the spot market at $295/ounce and invests the proceeds in 90-day commercial paper at 6.5 percent. The forward gold price in 90 days will be equal to $296.84/ounce, that is, the product of spot price times interest rate differentials of 2.5 percent annually adjusted for the 90 days.

SYNTHETIC FORWARD CONTRACT

The synthetic forward contract allows both parties in this transaction to be better off without making someone worse off. The central bank realizes a positive return on its holding of gold reserves; the gold mining firm mitigates price risk (the risk of falling gold price in the future) and also makes a profit by leasing the gold and subsequent transactions, while borrowed gold is returned by having gold extracted from its mines and returning the borrowed gold to the lender (the central bank).

By 1995 gold mining firms started to use put options to protect the downside risk of lower gold prices in the future.[7] The hedging was intended to reduce the adverse effect of the uncertainty of the gold prices, thereby benefiting lenders of the gold as well as benefiting the producers indirectly as producers were able to get better terms in financing their debt from these lenders.

As of late 1999, Ashanti Goldfield had 10 million ounces of gold hedged, while mining 1 million ounces of gold that year.[8] The company hedged half of its gold reserves based on production estimates for the next 15 years.[9] Ashanti used put options to protect itself against the possibility of falling gold prices. To finance the insurance premium (put option), the company sold call options, effectively creating a zero collar that limits the upside potential and obligates the firm to sell gold at strike price. A rally in the gold price in fall 1999 triggered a margin call by 17 central banks; the company was forced to give banks 15 percent of the ownership of the firm to prevent bankruptcy.[10]

The median (North American Gold Mining Firms) in one sample sells forwards approximately 25 percent of the three-year production for hedging exposure to price risk.[11] Firms that are most likely to hedge have managers holding substantial shares of the stocks; 15 percent of the firms do not employ derivatives.

Delta, Southwest, and American Airlines have all successfully employed various hedging vehicles to reduce and mitigate the financial impact of increased volatility in jet fuel oil prices. For instance, Delta uses the call option to buy fuel oil at a preset strike price contingent on rising jet fuel oil costs. If fuel oil prices rise, the option will be exercised, thereby insulating the company from buying fuel at higher prices. Call options make a profit that pays for the increased cost at the spot market. American Airlines, however, buys options to cap prices above the strike price as illustrated in Exhibit 4.20 as well as swaps that fix the price of fuel oil over the swap period under which it pays or receives, providing protection from the rising fuel cost.

Southwest Airlines has used hedging to a great extent in the last few years. The low-fare carrier has 80 percent of its fuel needs already paid for at oil prices equaling $22 a barrel; unhedged carriers such as Northwest have to pay spot prices around $28 to $29 a barrel as fuel costs continue to be the second highest cost, below the cost of labor.[12]

Manufacturing firms employ derivatives in risk management for smoothing volatilities of earnings and for gaining competitive pricing advantages and efficiency through internal decision making and evaluation.[13] By hedging, multinational firms are expected to increase the certainty of the operating margins. This translates into minimizing the adverse impact of a sudden change in exchange rates on earnings and cash flow.

The following chapters explore the dynamics of futures, options, and other derivatives as they relate to managing various types of exposure to foreign exchange risk. Hedging with derivatives, which is effective for managing short-run exposure to various types of risk, is known as financial hedges. Long-run exposure to unexpected change in exchange rates or unexpected change in interest rates needs to be managed with operational hedges that address the competitive position of multinational corporations across products and markets and are related to a variety of decisions, such as marketing, production, sourcing, geographical location, financing, and investment.[14]

Case Study

APPLICATION OF FUTURES CONTRACTS IN PORTFOLIO HEDGING

Frank Michello*

Mainza Capital Management, a mutual fund company, uses stock index futures contracts to eliminate the risk of losses from declining security prices in its portfolio of assets. The company manages a mutual fund portfolio worth $4.2 billion and has a beta of 0.93. It is now October 1, 2000, and the company is concerned about the performance of the market over the next three months. The company plans to use three-month futures contracts on the Standard and Poor's (S&P) 500 to hedge the risk. Let the current level of the index be 1,388.76 and the December 00 S&P futures, contract settlement value be 1,400.24; one contract is on 250 times the index; the risk-free rate is 5.4 percent per annum, and the dividend yield on the index is 3 percent per annum.

THOUGHT QUESTIONS

1. What is the theoretical futures price for the three-month futures contract for Mainza Capital Management?

2. What three pieces of information are needed to compute the hedge ratio? Based on this information, compute the hedge ratio Mainza Capital Fund must use to eliminate all exposure to market risk over the next three months.

*Assistant professor of finance, Middle Tennessee State University

3. Now consider the consequences of several market scenarios at the final delivery day for the contract. Compute the gain or loss on Mainza Capital Management portfolio if the market at the final delivery day of the contract is:

   a. Index is 5 percent up.

   b. Index is 5 percent down.

   c. S&P index remains unchanged at 1,388.76.

SOLUTIONS TO QUESTIONS

1. The theoretical futures price $F = S_0 \times e^{\wedge}((r - q) \times t)$,

   where

   F = theoretical futures price
   S_0 = spot index price
   e = 2.7183, the natural exponential function
   r = short-term interest rate
   q = dividend yield
   t = number of months to futures expiration/12

   For Mainza Capital Management, the S&P 500 index price is 1,388.76, the short-term interest rate is 5.4 percent, the dividend yield is 3 percent, and the number of months to expiration is 3/12 = .25. Therefore, F = 1,388.76 × exp$^{\wedge}$((.054 −.03) × 0.25) = 1,397.12. The theoretical futures price is the equilibrium price for futures contracts. It is also called the fair price. The theoretical futures price is used to calculate the fair value premium, which is equal to theoretical futures price minus cash (spot) price. For Mainza Capital Management, the fair value price = 1,397.12 − 1,388.76 = 8.36 points. The fair value premium shows how far the futures contract should be trading above or below the cash index, given the expected dividend income for the stocks of the S&P 500, the number of months to expiration for the futures contract, and the short-term interest rate. If the futures' price moves too far above or below the fair value premium band, index arbitrageurs will begin executing trades, which will bring the cash and futures prices back into equilibrium.

2. The three pieces of information needed to compute the hedge ratio are the value of the chosen futures contract, the dollar value of the portfolio to be hedged, and the beta of the portfolio. The hedge ratio, which gives the number of futures contracts the fund manager must sell, is equal to

$$HR = \left(\frac{\text{Dollar value of the portfolio}}{\text{Dollar value of the S\&P futures contract}} \right) \times \text{market beta}$$

$$= \left(\frac{\$4.2 \text{ billion}}{250 \times 1,388.76} \right) \times .93$$

$$= 11,250$$

(continues)

The fund manager must short (sell) 11,250 contracts to eliminate all exposure to market risk.

3. **a.** When rates go up by 5 percent, the index rises to $1.05 \times 1,388.76 = 1,458.198$. Given that the portfolio beta is .93, the portfolio should rise by $.05 \times .93 \times \$4.2$ billion $= \$195,300,000.00$. The dividend on the portfolio is equal to $.03 \times .25 \times \$4.2$ billion $= \$31,500,000.00$. The combined position results in a gain of $\$226,800,000.00$. However, when rates go up, the fund loses on the futures position because of selling the futures contracts short, and they rise in price to 1,458.198 at expiration. The loss from this position is $(1,400.24 - 1,458.198) \times \$250 \times 11,250 = \$163,006,875.00$. The combined position results in a gain of $\$63,793,125.00$.

   b. When rates go down by 5 percent, the index falls to $.95 \times 1,388.76 = 1,319.322$. Given that portfolio beta is .93, the portfolio should fall by $.05 \times .93 \times \$4.2$ billion $= \$195,300,000.00$. This is a portfolio loss. In the futures market, there is a gain. The fund sold 11,250 contracts short at 1388.76. At expiration, the fund will close them at 1,319.322, resulting in an account benefit of $(1,400.24 - 1,319.322) \times \$250 \times 11,250 = 227,581,875.00$. The dividend on the portfolio is equal to $.03 \times .25 \times \$4.2$ billion $= \$31,500,000.00$. The position in the futures market plus the dividends received results in a gain of $\$259,081,875.00$. The combined position results in a gain of $\$63,781,875.00$.

   c. If the market remains unchanged, there is no gain on the stock market (0 percent $\times$ .93 $\times$ \$4.2 billion), but there is a gain in the futures position. The basis will deteriorate to zero at expiration, so that the short hedger has a gain of $(1,400.24 - 1,388.76) \times \$250 \times 11,250 = \$32,287,500.00$. When dividends are included, the net gain is $\$63,787,500.00$.

This scenario shows that hedging protects the fund against unfavorable market movements. By hedging using index futures, Mainza Funds has been able to remove risk arising from market movements and is exposed only to the risk of the securities in its portfolio.

NOTES

1. See Eaker et al. (1996, p. 142).
2. See Froot et al. (1994).
3. See Franklin Edwards (1999).
4. See Gastaneau, Smith, and Todd (2001); Bodnar, Hayt, and Marston (1998); Chowdhry (1995); Schrand and Unal (1998); and Chowdhry and Howe (1999).
5. See Brown (2001), who examined the currency hedging behavior of the U.S. multinational corporations, Bodnar et al. (1998), who find evidence that large

firms are more likely to hedge than their small-firm counterparts; Geczy, Milton, and Schrand (1997), who find evidence that firms with greater investment opportunities are more likely to hedge than those who do not; Allayannis and Weston (2001), who find evidence that firms that use derivatives have higher market value; and Graham and Rogers (2000) and Haushalter (2000), who find that firms that use derivatives employ more leverage.

6. The hedge ratio is the covariance of the spot and futures weighted by the variance of the futures. Assuming the spot and futures move in tandem, then the slope (h) is expected to be equal to 1.

7. See Shepherd (1999).

8. See De Giorgio (1999).

9. See Shepherd.

10. See De Giorgio.

11. See Tufano (1996).

12. See Torbenson (2001).

13. See Brown (2001) for documentation.

14. See Laux, Pantzalis, and Simpkins (2001).

CHAPTER 5

Principles of Futures: Pricing and Applications

The forward or futures price for dividend-paying instruments such as stock index futures or currency futures is priced as a function of the underlying spot as well as any dividend or interest income that accrues to the owners of the physical commodities. The ownership of the physical assets entails costs as well as benefits. Costs can be in the form of opportunity cost, maintenance, tax, insurance, and storage. Among other things, benefits may include the utility of the consumption, realizing rent, royalties, and the ability to secure credit by putting up the instrument as collateral and profiting from temporary shortages. These benefits accrue to the physical owner of the assets and are known as convenience yield. For some commodities, convenience yield is greater than the storage and opportunity cost, and their futures price will be at a discount from the spot price.[1] However, if the opportunity cost and storage is greater than the convenience yield, then the futures or forward price will be at a premium from spot.[2]

COST OF CARRY

Cost of carry includes the opportunity cost, that is, the cost of financing the asset as well as any storage-related costs less any income and royalties derived from the ownership of the physical asset. For nondividend-paying instruments, such as nondividend-paying stock, cost of carry is simply equal to the cost of financing the stock by the brokerage or bank loan interest rates, has zero storage costs, and pays no income. Any nondividend-paying instrument can be converted into a dividend-paying asset in the derivatives market. In the case of nondividend-paying stock, selling call options on the stocks that the owner has can be a means of generating dividends on nondividend-paying stocks. The boundaries between what are dividend-paying and what are nondividend-paying instruments have disappeared in the derivatives market. Cost of carry for dividend-paying instruments, such as foreign currency, is the interest rate differentials in domestic and foreign interest rates. Cost of carry in the stock index is the difference between the financing cost and yield, namely the interest rate and dividend yield.

Derivatives markets provide an increasing range of possibilities for enhancing the return and reduction of risk. For example, nondividend-paying instruments, such as gold and other precious metals, can be converted into dividend-paying instruments through the creation of synthetic forward contracts; nondividend-paying stocks can be converted to dividend-paying types by selling the underlying calls on the stocks. The phenomenal growth of derivatives in risk management is a testimony to the market acceptance of and appreciation for the range of possibilities derivatives have provided risk managers, arbitrageurs, and speculators. Exhibit 5.1 presents the growth of futures traded in the U.S. market alone for mitigating various types of risk in the period from 1990 to 2001.

STOCK INDEX FUTURES

The underlying instruments in stock index futures are stocks in the composite indices such as Standard & Poor's 500 (S&P 500), Nasdaq 100, and other stock indices. The underlying stocks in some of the stock indices pay dividends, and the cost of carry is equal to the opportunity cost of financing the stock (r) less the dividend income (convenience yield) that are assumed to be proportional to the spot price (i). Furthermore, assuming the interest rate and dividend yields are compounded annually, the relationship between F, the future price (forward price), and S, the spot price, can be expressed in discrete time as shown in Equation 5.1.

Now	$1 + r$ (the cost of financing)	Then
S	$1 + i$ (the convenience yield)	F

$$F = S \frac{(1 + r)}{(1 + i)}$$

(5.1)

EXHIBIT 5.1   Growth of Futures in Various Exchanges in the United States (1990–2001)

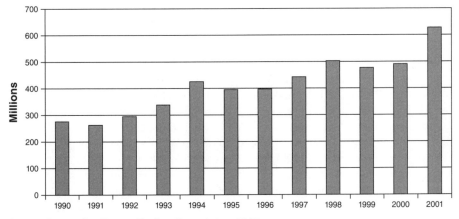

Source: Commodity Futures Trading Commission, 2001.

The simple relationship between future price (F) and spot price (S) in the context of the cost of carry is identical to the forward price of foreign currency derived earlier in Equation 3.6. The future price (F) is directly related to the spot price (S) as well as the cost of financing (the spot) the opportunity cost or the interest rate of r and is inversely related to the dividend yield (i) as a proxy for the convenience yield.[3]

Example: Suppose the S&P 500 index is currently priced at 1,100, the dividend yield is expected to be 2.5 percent, and interest rate as proxies by one-year Treasury is equal to 3.75 percent. What is the price of the three-month index future? The physical owner of the index incurred the interest cost of financing the stock index as a negative return; however, it is entitled to the benefits (the convenience yield) associated with the physical ownership of the instrument, in this case the dividend yield of 2.5 percent. The time to expiration of the future is three months, translated into .25 years. The three-month future price of the index will be equal to:

$$F = 1,100 \frac{(1 + .0375/4)}{(1 + .025/4)}$$
$$= 1,103.41$$

The relationship between F, the futures price, and S, the spot price, can be expressed in continuous time as shown in Equation 5.2.

$$
\begin{aligned}
F &= Se^{(r-i)t} \\
&= 1,100 \times 2.7183^{(.0375 - .025).25} \\
&= 1,103.41
\end{aligned}
\tag{5.2}
$$

where

$e = 2.7183$
$t =$ the time to expiration in year

Wall Street refers to this figure as the fair value of the index. Deviation from the fair value provides opportunities for what has come to be known as index arbitrage. The minimum price change in the 90-day S&P 500 stock index futures is currently $12.5 per one-half "tick" (i.e., 500 times the minimum change in the price of the index that is set at +/−.025). The index futures price is expected to be above the spot price over time in equilibrium, as evidenced by the behavior of the S&P 500 index and the underlying futures on the Friday preceding 1987's Black Monday (see Exhibit 5.2).

INDEX ARBITRAGE

When fair value of the index (also known as theoretical value) is greater than the quoted price—$F > Se^{(r-i)t}$—then the arbitrageur sells the index futures short and simultaneously buys the stocks underlying the index in the same proportion as they are in the spot index. At the expiration of the index future, the

EXHIBIT 5.2 Behavior of S&P 500 Spot and Futures

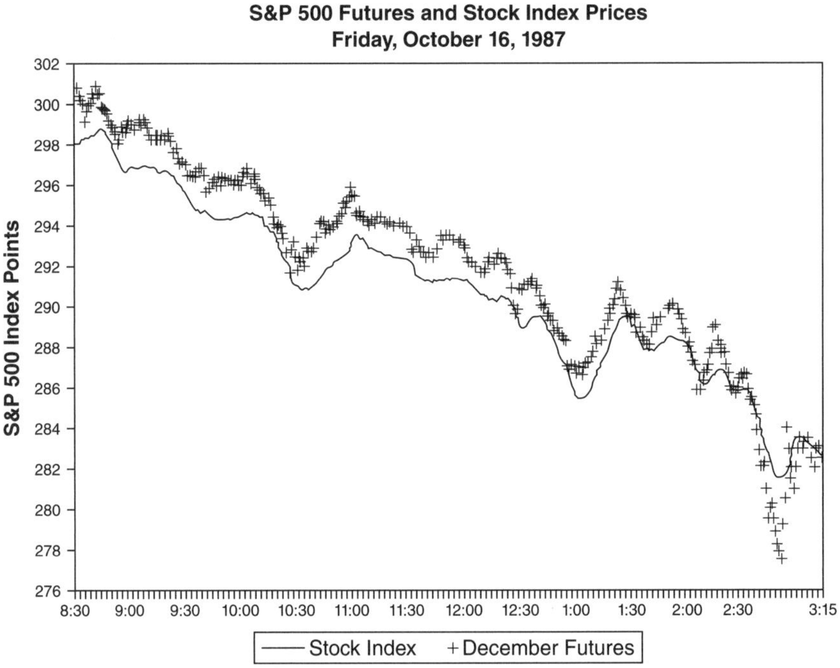

S&P 500 Futures and Stock Index Prices
Friday, October 16, 1987

Source: CME and Standard and Poors.

future price approaches the price of the spot, and the arbitrageur uses the stocks purchased to return the future index shorted. However, if $F < Se^{(r-i)t}$, then it pays to buy the future and simultaneously sell the stocks underlying the index short. At the expiration of the index future, use the index to return shares of stocks that were shorted previously. Buying and selling in both stocks and underlying futures is referred to as program trading. Program trading is at the heart of the spot market's increased volatility and increased efficiency.

The simultaneous transactions of buying and selling in two different markets (spot and future) generated through computerized trading when program trading is initiated takes advantage of deviation from the fair value. This trading aligns the price of the misaligned spot or future and eliminates temporary disequilibrium situations arising in the spot or futures market. Program trading, or the inability of arbitrageurs to trade simultaneously on the spot and futures market, is believed to be one of the reasons for the Black Monday crash on October 19, 1987.[4]

Due to the tremendous increase in the volume of trades on Monday after the October 19 crash (in excess of 604 million shares, far more than the daily average in the New York Stock Exchange (NYSE)), most arbitrageurs were sidelined despite the significant disparity in the price of the S&P 500 spot index and the underlying index futures (see Exhibit 5.3), as time to process trade significantly

EXHIBIT 5.3   Behavior of S&P 500 Spot and Futures on Black Monday

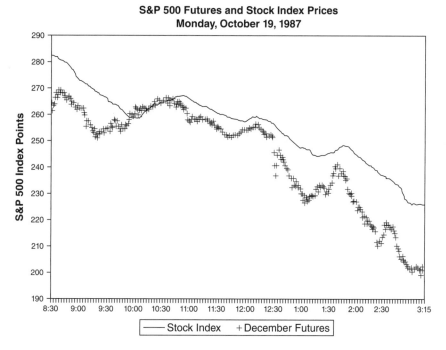

Source: CME and Standard and Poors.

increased, resulting in reduced or no arbitrage in both markets. During most of that Monday, the S&P index futures price was below the S&P 500 stock index. At around 2:30 P.M., the S&P index futures price was at a 35-point discount to the spot index. At the close of business that day, the S&P spot and the S&P index futures respectively closed at 225.06 and 201.50 (see Exhibit 5.3). In the following days, the price of futures aligned with the spot price, consistent with the theoretical price or the fair value.

Index futures and options contracts of the Chicago Mercantile Exchange (CME) closely follow the price of the underlying indices, thereby providing opportunities for managing risk and for speculative profit (loss) for arbitrageurs and individuals. These equity index futures and options contracts are traded in the CME:

E-mini Nasdaq 100

E-mini Russell 2000

E-mini S&P 500

E-mini S&P Midcap 400

FORTUNE e-50

Nasdaq 100

Nikkei 225

Russell 2000

S&P 500

S&P 500/Barra Growth

S&P 500/Barra Value

S&P Midcap 400

S&P/TOPIX 150

CME also trades futures and options on the Goldman Sachs Commodity Index (GSCI).

Example: It is August 2, 2002. The S&P 500 index is at 864.24, and September futures is priced at the close of business at 864.90. The three-month T-bill is priced to yield 1.61 percent. The implied dividend yield on the S&P 500 index can be estimated by taking a natural log of both sides of the future-spot relationship in Equation 5.2.

$$\log \frac{F}{S} = \log e^{(r - i)t}$$
$$\log F - \log S = (r - i)t$$

Plugging the value of the parameters in this relationship, the implied yield in the S&P 500 index is

$$\log 864.90 - \log 864.24 = (.0161 - i)(.25)$$
$$i = 1.29 \text{ percent}$$

The implied dividend yield on the S&P 500 index was derived assuming the appropriate risk-free interest rate is the three-month T-bill rate. The excess interest over dividend yield is only 32 basis points in the example. Most of the dividends in the NYSE are actually paid on the first week of February, May, August, and November of each year.

Had the September futures price of the index been 870, then an arbitrage profit would have been possible as computerized program trading would have initiated these trades:

Futures market: Short September future at 870.

Spot market: Buy stocks underlying the index in the same proportion as they are represented in the index for 864.24.

Result

At the expiration of the future return the purchased stock to cover the short position.

$$\text{Profit} = 500 (870 - 864.24)$$
$$= \$2,880$$

The profit is generated in one contract and represents a riskless arbitrage in the spot and futures market. Arbitrageurs' activity in both markets tend to eliminate these profits and increase the efficiency of the pricing of the spot market. Had the future price been in a significant discount from the fair value, reverse transactions to this scenario—that is, buying future and simultaneously selling the stocks underlying the index—would have secured at no risk some profit, which at the margin has to be equal to zero in an efficient market.

PORTFOLIO INSURANCE

Hedging the portfolio of stocks and bonds can be accomplished with index futures and options. Portfolio managers can effectively insulate the stock or bond portfolio from the unexpected change in the market by selling the appropriate number of index futures to mitigate downside risk over the hedged period. The choice of which index futures to use in hedging the portfolio is dictated by the nature of the underlying stocks in the portfolio. For example, the riskiness of the portfolio in comparison to index futures has to be considered at the outset. The hedge ratio (h) is defined as the change in the spot price with respect to the change in the futures price; it helps to determine the number of futures contracts needed to manage the market risk as well as the efficiency of the hedge, as shown in the Equation 5.3.

$$h = \frac{\Delta S}{\Delta F} \tag{5.3}$$

$$= \beta \left(\frac{S}{F}\right) \tag{5.4}$$

where

β = beta of the underlying exposed asset or portfolio[5] (the index of relative riskiness of the stock or stock portfolio against a broad index, such as S&P 500 index) to be hedged

S = market value of the portfolio of stocks

F = market value of one index futures contract

In Chapter 4 the hedge ratio was defined as the correlation of spot and futures weighted by standard deviation of spot and futures. The transformation from 5.3 to 5.4 is straightforward and can be easily verified.[6] In Chapter 6 the duration-based approach is used to define the hedge ratio.

Example: It is July 17. A portfolio manager at NPR is concerned over the increased volatility of the market and plans to hedge his $430 million growth portfolio over the next three months. The beta of the portfolio is 1.65. The December futures contract for the S&P 500 index is currently quoted at 874.5. The value of each futures contract is 250 times the value of the index. Therefore,

the portfolio manager plans to sell the following number of December futures
contracts using Equation 5.4:

Value of 1 futures contract: $250 \times 874.50 = \$218,625$

$$h = 1.65 \left(\frac{\$430,000,000}{\$218,625} \right)$$

$$= 3,245.28 \text{ rounded to } 3,245$$

The payoff on the long and short positions is demonstrated graphically in
Exhibit 5.4.

The value of the hedged portfolio will be $430 million no matter which
direction stock prices go. For example, if the market drops by 5 percent over
the next three months, the NPR portfolio is expected to drop by 8.25 percent,
because the portfolio is 1.65 times riskier than the average market with a beta
of one. The loss in the cash market of 8.25 percent will be offset by the gain in
the futures shorted, since spots and futures move in tandem over time. The S&P
500 index futures are expected to go down by approximately as much as the
market. The market value of the portfolio drops to $394.525 million (loss of
8.25 percent), and S&P 500 index December futures drops to 830.775. The
results of the hedge are summarized as:

Spot market: July 17
Market value of the portfolio: $430,000,000
Futures market:
Price of S&P 500 index futures: 874.50
Proceeds per one contract at CME: $250 \times 874.50 = \$218,437.25$
Sell 3,245 S&P 500 December futures

EXHIBIT 5.4   Hedging with Futures

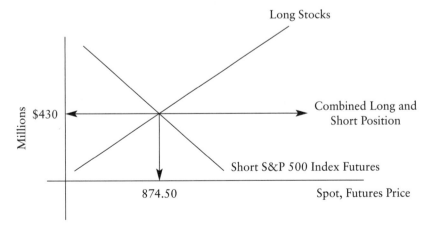

October 21

Spot market: $394,525,000

Futures price: 830.7750

Proceed per one contract: $207,693.75

Buy 3,245 December futures

Results

Spot market: Loss of $35,475,000

Futures market: profit per one contract is $10,931.25

Futures profit: $10,931.25 × 3,245 = $35,471,906.25

Value of hedged portfolio: Spot market: $394,525,000 + profit in the futures
market that is: Long + short = $429,996,906.25

The value of the hedged portfolio is slightly less than $430 million, since the number of futures contracts was rounded down to a whole number. The loss in the spot market was offset by gains in the futures, thereby making the portfolio immune from market risk. However, had the market experienced an increased return of 5 percent over the next three months, the gains in the spot market would have been offset by the losses in the futures markets:

Spot market: October 21

Market value of the stocks portfolio: $465.475 million

Price of the futures: $918.225

Proceeds per one contract: 250 × $918.225 = $229,563.75

Results

Profit in the spot portfolio: $35.475 million

Loss in the S&P 500 index futures: $10,938.75 per one contract

Total loss in the futures = $35,496,243.75

Hedged portfolio: Long + short = $465,475,000 − $35,496,243.75
$$= \$429,978,756.25$$

The hedged portfolio is nearly equal to $430 million due to rounding in the number of futures shorted.

HEDGING WITH STOCK INDEX FUTURES OPTIONS

Individual or a portfolio of stocks and bonds can be hedged with index futures option. The combination of the spot and option (put option) is expected to produce the payoff as:

Long in stock + Long in put = Protective put

Example: Consider J.P. Morgan and Chase stock at $26.38 as of August 8 and January 22.50 put is traded at $2.60. The hedged and unhedged positions have the distributions described below. The payoff or the rate of return on the unhedged portfolio (or security) is spanned over the entire distribution. The hedged portfolio (or security) is truncated at the strike price minus the premium. The put is providing protection below the strike price minus the premium as a floor. In this region any loss in the spot portfolio is offset by the gains in the put option, as a put will be exercised. However, the payoff on the hedged portfolio is identical to the payoff on the unhedged portfolio minus the cost of the protection (the put premium) at any points above the strike price where the put option expires out of the money. The payoff on the hedged and unhedged position for this stock is illustrated in Exhibit 5.5.

The January put provides protection below the strike price of $22.50 for a premium of $2.60 as of August 8. (The investor gets protection below $22.50.) Suppose the J.P. Morgan and Chase stock price drops to $17 per share by the end of December. Investors who hedged their holding of the stock are expected to profit in the option that offsets the losses in the spot position as

$$\$17 + 5.50 - 2.60 = \$19.90$$

Had the stock fallen to $15 per share, the investors have the right to sell the stock at 22.50 minus the premium of $2.60 they paid. In this scenario the investors will end up with $19.90, which is exactly equal to the strike price minus the premium. However, if the stock goes up to $34 per share by January, the put will expire out-of-the-money and the investors' payoffs will be equal to spot price minus the premium.

Example: The portfolio manager of a growth fund with a portfolio worth $200 million in stocks with a beta of 1.65 is concerned about falling stock prices in October and is planning to buy S&P 500 index futures options at a strike price

EXHIBIT 5.5   Hedged and Unhedged Payoff on
                   J.P. Morgan and Chase Stock

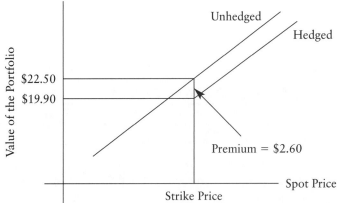

of 900. The October put is quoted at $47.70 (see Exhibit 5.6). Each S&P 500 index futures option contract at the CME is for delivery of 250 times the value of the index. The portfolio manager needs to buy 1,467 put options to protect the value of the portfolio below the strike price of 900 for the S&P 500. The hedge ratio is estimated from Equation 5.4 as:

$$h = \beta_p \left(\frac{S}{F}\right)$$

where

β_p = portfolio beta and is equal to 1.65
S = $200 million
F = $250 × $900
h = 1.65 (200,000,000/225,000)
   = 1,466.67, rounded to 1,467

The cost of buying protection at the CME is 250 × 47.70, or $11,925, for one October put option at the strike price of 900. The cost of 1,467 puts is $17,493,975. This is nearly over 8.75 percent of the value of the portfolio. If the S&P 500 drops by 5 percent from now until mid-October, the portfolio is

EXHIBIT 5.6   Index Futures Options

Index

DJ Industrial Avg (CBOT)

$100 times premium

Price	Aug	Sep	Oct	Aug	Sep	Oct
85	26.00	48.00	...	9.00	31.00	...
86	19.00	42.00	...	13.00	35.00	48.00
87	14.00	35.75	46.00	17.00	38.25	...
88	9.00	30.50	...	23.00	43.50	55.00
89	6.50	26.00	...	30.00	48.80	...
90	4.00	22.00	...	37.50	54.75	...

Est vol 854 Fr 443 calls 309 puts
Op int Fri 8,171 calls 11,056 puts

S&P 500 Stock Index (CME)

$250 times premium

Price	Aug	Sep	Oct	Aug	Sep	Oct
895	...	...	...	...	...	...
900	18.00	39.60	50.10	15.50	37.10	47.70
905	15.50	36.80	...	18.00	39.30	...
910	13.10	34.20	...	20.60	41.70	...
915	...	...	42.30	...	...	...
920	9.10	29.30	...	26.60	46.70	...

Est vol 13,647 Fr 9,599 calls 15,299 puts
Op int Fri 129,926 calls 176,700 puts

Other Options

Nasdaq 100 (CME)

$100 times NASDAQ 100 Index

Price	Aug	Sep	Oct	Aug	Sep	Oct
940	28.00	61.60	...	19.00	58.10	...

Est vol 33 Fr 46 calls 25 puts
Op int Fri 2,272 calls 1,548 puts

NYSE Composite (NYFE)

$500 times premium

Price	Aug	Sep	Oct	Aug	Sep	Oct
488	5.35	18.70	25.25	6.10	19.45	26.00

Est vol 300 Fr 20 calls 419 puts
Op int Fri 1,639 calls 2,941 puts

Source: Wall Street Journal, August 12, 2002.

likely to drop as much as 1.65×5, or 8.25 percent. This portfolio manager is likely to look at the competition, the other portfolio managers, in making such a decision. If hedging is a norm in the industry—that is, if every high-growth fund is expected to hedge some of the time and not hedge at other times—buying some protection during October may be essential. However, if hedging is not a norm in that particular industry, perhaps it does not make economic sense to hedge, especially when others are not hedged for the same type of exposure.

Why is the cost of the hedge so high in this example? Perhaps the increased volatility in a market that is characterized by shaken confidence in Wall Street due to various accounting scandals may be due to a bear market. The increased volatility has substantially increased the put options premium; unless volatility subsides, the protection sellers are going to demand higher premiums.

The portfolio manager in this example can finance the purchase of the put options by simultaneously selling the calls; the premium received for selling the calls pays for acquiring the downside protection. However, by selling calls, the portfolio manager surrenders the upside potential of the stocks in the portfolio. The collared portfolio in the example, assuming the long puts and the short calls are executed at the strike price of 900, is expected to produce payoffs of nearly zero collars as:

$$\text{Long stock} + \text{long put} + \text{short call} = \text{collared portfolio}$$
$$\$200,000,000 - \$17,493,975 + \$18,374,175 = \$200,880,200$$

The cost of buying downside protection (long put) of $47.70 as can be verified from Exhibit 5.6 is more than offset by selling October calls (short calls) at the strike price of 900 for $50.10. Exhibit 5.7 shows the payoff of various hedging instruments.

EXHIBIT 5.7   Behavior of Hedged and Unhedged Portfolio

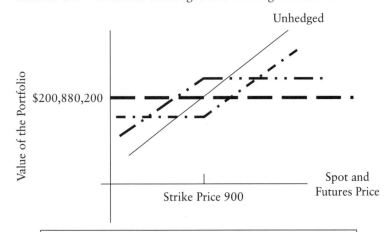

The premiums received for selling 1,467 calls will more than offset the cost of the put options by $880,200:

$$1,467 \times \$50.10 \times 250 = \$18,374,175$$
$$\$18,374,175 - \$17,493,975 = \$880,200$$

Assuming the market drops by 4 percent in the next three months, the growth fund portfolio in this example is expected to drop by 1.65×4 percent, or 6.6 percent. The loss in the portfolio will be equal to $13.2 million. The put options in this scenario will be activated to provide downside protection, while the calls will expire out-of-the-money. The S&P 500 index futures is likely to drop to 864, a 4 percent drop, resulting in a gain of $9,000 per contract, or $13,203,000 for 1,467 put options. The cost of the protection is more than offset by selling calls that will expire for a net gain of $880,200. The value of the collared portfolio will be expected to be:

$200,000,000 − $13,200,000 (loss in the portfolio) + $13,203,000 (gains in put options) + $880,200 (premium received − premium paid) = $200,883,200

The value of the collared portfolio is $3,000 more than Exhibit 5.7 due to rounding of the contracts to a whole number.

BASIS RISK

The actual outcome of the hedged portfolio depends on the behavior of the futures in tracking the value of the spot portfolio. Basis risk needs to be recognized. Basis risk refers to the difference between the spot price (S) and futures price (F) at the inception of the futures contract as well the behavior of the basis over the life of the futures. That behavior is likely to change over time as spot and futures prices continue to change as the underlying factors (i.e., supply and demand), volatility of interest rates (the spot and forward), cost of storage, and convenience yield change over time, as seen in Equation 5.5.

$$\text{Basis} = S - F \tag{5.5}$$

The basis also can be redefined as the difference between futures and spot prices as:

$$\text{Basis} = F - S$$

At the expiration of the futures contract, the futures price approaches the spot price and basis will be equal to zero (see Exhibit 5.8). This can be verified by a simple arbitrage example. For instance, if at the delivery time the spot and futures are not the same, then the asset whose price is higher can be sold short and the asset whose price is lower can be bought, to make delivery for a riskless profit.

The basis risk for financial assets such as interest rate futures, currencies, and stock indices is smaller than the consumption assets. For financial assets, the basis risk is due to the unexpected change in the level of a risk-free interest

EXHIBIT 5.8   Spot and Futures Price

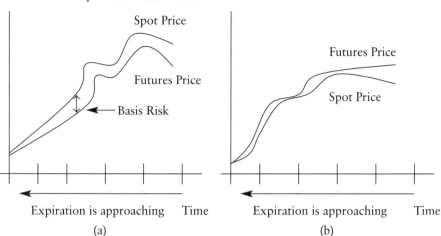

Expiration is approaching   Time   Expiration is approaching   Time

(a)   (b)

rate over time. For consumption assets, the basis risk is greater due to changes in supply and demand conditions as well as storage costs, which can significantly change the convenience yield, resulting in an increase in the basis risk. For exposed assets, the exposure to the hedger is greater if the underlying futures are different from the assets being hedged. In this case the basis risk is likely to be larger.

The underlying factors that contribute to the level of the basis risk essentially determine the spot and futures prices. For instruments whose futures price is related to forward or future rates and yields, such as interest rate, currency, and index futures, the basis risk is related to the volatility of the spot and forward interest rates and is likely to be smaller than consumption assets.

The basis risk is likely to be larger in the hedging instruments that are designed to protect the underlying spot market price movements and require actual delivery. For example, in Treasury futures, more than one type of bond meets the requirements of the exchange and it is the cheapest-to-deliver instrument. Multiple spot prices and futures prices at expiration would likely converge to the spot price of the instrument that is most likely to be delivered.

Exhibit 5.9 presents the actual behavior of the gold spot price and gold futures for the August 2002 delivery at the Commodity Exchange (COMEX).

The gold futures price converges to the spot price approximately four weeks prior to the expiration of the contract. On the expiration date, the futures price is equal to the spot price.

CHANGING THE BETA OF THE PORTFOLIO WITH FUTURES

Futures contracts can be used to achieve a desired or target beta for the portfolio in more economical ways than simply altering beta by buying and selling stocks in the spot market. The buy and sell in the spot market entails transaction

EXHIBIT 5.9   Spot and August 2002 Futures COMEX Gold

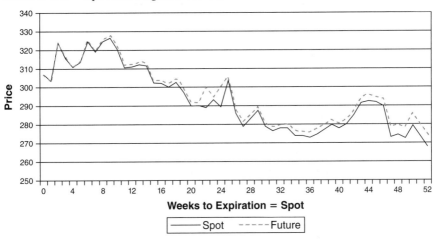

Weeks to Expiration = Spot

Spot -----Future

costs as well as costly bid–ask spreads. Equation 5.6 shows the number of futures contracts needed to achieve the target beta:

$$h = (\beta_t - \beta_p)\left(\frac{S}{F}\right) \qquad (5.6)$$

Suppose the beta of the portfolio (β_p) is equal to 1.65, and portfolio manager intends to achieve a target beta β_t that is equal to 1.40 in three months on July 25. Assume the market value of the spot portfolio (S) is $20 million and the portfolio manager can achieve the target beta by selling S&P 500 index September futures (F) currently priced at 872 short:

$$\text{Number of futures contracts } h = (1.40 - 1.65)\,\frac{20{,}000{,}000}{250 \times 872}$$

$$= -22.92,\ \text{rounded to } -23$$

Selling 23 September futures contracts on the S&P 500 index, the portfolio manager achieves target beta for the portfolio of 1.4. Likewise to achieve the target beta $\beta_t > \beta_p$ of the portfolio beta, the portfolio manager is expected to buy futures contracts in this way: Suppose the target beta is 2.0 in the previous example and portfolio beta is 1.65, all other things remaining the same, the portfolio manager is expected to buy 32 September futures contracts on the S&P 500 index currently priced at 872:

$$h = (\beta_t - \beta_p)\left(\frac{S}{F}\right)$$

$$= (2 - 1.65)\left(\frac{20{,}000{,}000}{250 \times 872}\right)$$

$$= 32.10,\ \text{rounded to } 32$$

ANTICIPATORY HEDGE WITH STOCK INDEX FUTURES

It is August 8 and a conglomerate is contemplating divesting its gas and oil exploration subsidiary within the next three months. The unit will be spun off to reduce the conglomerate's overall riskiness. The gas and oil subsidiary is currently 20 percent of the value of the conglomerate and makes up 25 percent of its overall market risk. Currently the conglomerate has a beta of 2 and total market capitalization of $1.6 billion with 100 million shares outstanding.

Management believes that the actual spin-off may take place in three or more months as a potential acquiring suitor is sought who will pay the highest price. In the meantime, concern over the increased volatility of the market has prompted the manager to look at an alternative, such as the futures market, to provide an avenue for reducing overall risk to 1.50. Currently the S&P 500 index December futures is priced at 905.50 (see Exhibit 5.10). Oil and gas contributes 25 percent of the overall risk, while making up 20 percent of the conglomerate value, or $320,000,000. The number of futures contracts needed to achieve the target beta in three months will be:

$$h = (\beta_t - \beta_p)\left(\frac{S}{F}\right)$$

$$= (1.50 - 2.0)\left(\frac{320,000,000}{250 \times 905.50}\right)$$

$$= -706.79 \text{ rounded to } -707$$

EXHIBIT 5.10   Index Futures

Index Futures

DJ Industrial Average (CBOT)-$10 times average

Sept	8456	8710	8415	8695	255	10705	7450	32,427
Dec	8450	8685	8390	8680	258	10740	7425	573

Est vol 20,314; vol Wed 30,968; open int 33,030, -1,190.
Idx prl: Hi 8717.42; Lo 8430.33; Close 8712.02, +255.87.

S&P 500 Index (CME)-$250 times index

Sept	87670	90700	87400	90570	2970	165670	77130	582,171
Dec	87900	90600	87400	90550	2980	150070	77400	24,036

Est vol 77,434; vol Wed 81,269; open int 626,305, -2,561.
Idx prl: Hi 905.84; Lo 875.17; Close 905.46, +28.69.

Mini S&P 500 (CME)-$50 times index

Sept	87650	90675	87375	90575	2975	117825	77100	347,487

Vol Wed 637,138; open int 347,591, -17,895.

S&P Midcap 400 (CME)-$500 times index

Sept	425.50	436.00	423.50	436.00	10.75	554.00	383.00	16,224

Est vol 760; vol Wed 1,241; open int 16,224, +67.
Idx prl: Hi 435.30; Lo 422.60; Close 435.13, +9.90.

Nikkei 225 Stock Average (CME)-$5 times index

Sept	9820.	9985.	9755.	9965.	40	12100.	9245.	24,904

Est vol 1,386; vol Wed 1,537; open int 24,964, -13.
Idx prl: Hi 9941.01; Lo 9740.43; Close 9799.57, -34.83.

Nasdaq 100 (CME)-$100 times index

Sept	92000	95100	90100	94900	3000	169350	85700	67,324

Est vol 16,634; vol Wed 18,001; open int 67,387, +51.
Idx prl: Hi 948.72; Lo 898.57; Close 947.24, +28.16.

Mini Nasdaq 100 (CME)-$20 times index

Sept	919.5	951.5	900.0	949.0	30.0	1533.0	857.0	173,596

Vol Wed 265,929; open int 173,616, -261.

Source: Wall Street Journal, August 8, 2002.

To achieve the target beta of 1.5, the conglomerate needs to sell 707 December S&P 500 index futures contracts.

COMPETITION FOR SAFEWAY, PLC

Reuben Kyle*

In mid-January 2003, Wal-Mart, the U.S. leading retailer, announced a bid for Safeway PLC, the fourth-largest supermarket chain in the United Kingdom. For Wal-Mart, this move is just the latest in an expansion of its international operations. The huge discount retail company began to look for international opportunities in Mexico, then Canada in the early 1990s. In 1997 Wal-Mart entered European markets in Germany and in 1999 it bought Asda, a U.K. grocer with 229 stores. More recently it purchased a controlling interest in Seiyu, a Japanese supermarket operator.

The bid by Wal-Mart raises a number of interesting issues. First, Wal-Mart would be one of at least four bidders for Safeway. The other three include Tesco, the largest grocery chain in the United Kingdom, William Morrison Supermarkets, and J Sainsbury PLC, the current number-two supermarket firm in Britain. In addition, Kohlberg Kravis Roberts, the Wall Street takeover masters, indicated an interest in Safeway. The result could be a full-scale auction for Safeway.

In March 2003, the British government referred the matter to its Competition Commission to assess the impact of the combination of Safeway with any of the three major supermarket chains in the country. An earlier analysis by the U.K. Office of Fair Trading expressed concern over the impact on competition in local grocery markets but also over the possibility that the resulting big three chains would have 85 percent of the grocery market in the country.

Finally, the merger competition comes at a time when economic conditions are pretty discouraging on all sides of the Atlantic. Safeway's performance in 2002 and in early 2003 were disappointing. In addition, weakness in the U.S. dollar may play a role in the attractiveness of any deal. Between the time of the announcement by Wal-Mart on its interest in Safeway and late spring 2003 the dollar-pound exchange rate fluctuated dramatically.

THOUGHT QUESTIONS

1. Offers by J Sainsbury and William Morrison both are stock deals while Wal-Mart contemplates an all-cash offer. What are the implications for Safeway shareholders?

*Professor, Department of Economics and Finance,
Middle Tennessee State University

(continues)

2. What is the likely impact of multiple bidders for Safeway for that company's shareholders?

3. What is "the winner's curse," and is there a threat of that problem for Wal-Mart?

4. What would a 2 percent swing in the exchange rate mean in an approximately £3 billion deal?

5. What is the likely impact of the competitive issues raised by the British government on a deal for Safeway and on its shareholders?

MANAGING EXPOSURE OF AN INDIVIDUAL STOCK

The exposure to the market risk of an individual stock owned can be mitigated by selling stock index futures or by buying put options. For example, it is August 8 and Jefferson Hedge Fund has 20,000 shares of Microsoft and continues to sell calls on the underlying stocks. The hedge fund in essence continues to produce dividends from nondividend-paying stock such as Microsoft. For the next three months there is no outstanding call on Microsoft, and the hedge fund is concerned over the likelihood of a drop in the stock market of 10 percent or more. Microsoft stock is currently priced at $54 with a beta of 1.3. The S&P 500 index December futures price is 905.50 (see Exhibit 5.10). The hedge fund is going to short six December futures contracts. The number of futures contracts the hedge fund needs to sell in hedging its exposure to the market risk (β) is estimated as:

$$h = \beta \left(\frac{S}{F}\right)$$

where

β = beta of the stock
S = market value of the stock
F = market value of one futures contract
h = 1.3 (20,000 × 54/250 × 905.50)
   = 6.202, rounded to 6 contracts

Exhibit 5.11 summarizes the results of the hedge.

The efficiency of this hedge is equal to 83.81 percent as measured by the ratio of the profits and losses in the spot and futures transactions (i.e., $67,050/$80,000).

CURRENCY FUTURES

Pricing currency futures are similar to the pricing of currency forward discussed in detail in Chapter 3. Here let us consider currency futures in the context of

EXHIBIT 5.11 Hedging Individual Stock with Futures

August 8

Spot price: $1,080,000 (20,000 shares @ $54)

S&P 500 index December futures price: 905.50

Price of one contract: 250 times 905.50 = $226,375

Sell 6 S&P 500 September futures

November 8

Spot price: $1,000,000 (20,000 shares @ $50)

S&P 500 index December futures price: 860.80

Results

Loss of $80,000 in the spot market

Gains in the futures: 6 (250) (905.5 − 860.80) = $67,050

Net loss: −$12,950

---

cost of carry as a dividend-paying instrument where the foreign interest rate can be treated as income and physical ownership or financing the foreign currency as the opportunity cost as defined by domestic interest rate. Since foreign currency is the ratio of two prices denominated in two different currencies, foreign currency futures can be derived from the underlying spot exchange rate, and the respective interest rates can be denominated in domestic and foreign currency. The relation between futures price (F), spot price (S), and domestic and foreign interest rates as denoted by R_d and R_f is:

$$0 \quad \underline{ S \times } \quad \frac{(1 + R_d)}{(1 + R_f)} \quad \underline{ 1 }_{= F}$$

The futures price of the foreign currency (F) in discrete time is directly related to spot prices (S) and its own interest rate (R_d; the opportunity cost), while it is inversely related to the interest income (R_f) as convenience yield over time, as expressed in Equation 5.7.

$$F = S \frac{(1 + R_d)}{(1 + R_f)} \tag{5.7}$$

Assuming domestic and foreign interest rates are compounded continuously, the foreign currency futures can be expressed in Equation 5.8 as:

$$F = Se^{(R_d - R_f)t} \tag{5.8}$$

The relationship expressed in Equation 3.8 is known as the interest rate parity and was discussed in detail in Chapter 3. The violation of the parity provides opportunities for riskless arbitrage profit.

Example: Spot price of the euro is $.95/€. The 91-day futures price of the euro (F) assuming U.S. and euro interest rates of 3 and 4 percent, respectively, compounded continuously, will be equal to:

$$F = .95\, e^{(.03 - .04).25}$$
$$= \$.9476/€$$

The underlying contract on the foreign currency futures is the standardized number of foreign currency that is traded in the organized exchange such as CME, as shown in Exhibit 5.12.[7]

HEDGING WITH CURRENCY FUTURES

To manage foreign currency–induced risk arising from direct investment, portfolio investment or import/export currency futures can provide protection against the foreign exchange rate risk. The exposure to foreign exchange risk in the spot market is managed with currency futures by taking an offsetting position. For example, the exposure to payables denominated in foreign currency can be very costly, as strengthening foreign currency increases cash outflows. Buying foreign currency futures can be one of the means to reduce exposure to this type of risk. The exposure to receivables denominated in foreign currency will be equally harmful to a firm's well-being if the underlying currency weakens, reducing cash inflows. Selling currency futures provides protection against this type of risk. Exhibit 5.13 provides the foreign currency futures quote.

EXHIBIT 5.12   Chicago Mercantile Exchange Currency Futures Contract Specifications (Partial List)

	New Zealand Dollar	Brazilian Real	Mexican Peso	Swedish Krona	South African Rand
Contract Size	100,000	100,000	500,000	2,000,000	500,000
Quotations	Cents per unit	Cents per unit	Cents per unit	Hundredths of cents per unit	Cents per unit
Minimum Price Change	$10	$5	$5	$20	$5
Contract Months	March, June, September, December as well as 9 to 12 consecutive months for some contracts.				
Last Trading Day	Friday before the third Wednesday of month				
Settlement Date	Third Wednesday of month				
Daily Price Limits	None				

EXHIBIT 5.13   Currency Futures

Currency Futures

Japanese Yen (CME)-12.5 million yen; $ per yen (.00)

Sept	.8332	.8349	.8266	.8277	-.0062	.8685	.7495	68,312
Dec	.8337	.8337	.8304	.8311	-.0062	.8885	.7569	1,734

Est vol 3,917; vol Wed 10,862; open int 70,499, -755.

Canadian Dollar (CME)-100,000 dlrs.; $ per Can $

Sept	.6329	.6359	.6304	.6320	-.0016	.6640	.6175	53,520
Dec	.6311	.6337	.6287	.6303	-.0016	.6620	.6190	7,440
Mr03	.6308	.6315	.6275	.6287	-.0016	.6590	.6198	1,765
June	.6264	.6297	.6260	.6272	-.0016	.6565	.6197	638

Est vol 7,360; vol Wed 10,390; open int 63,717, -2,239.

British Pound (CME)-62,500 pds.; $ per pound

Sept	1.5356	1.5384	1.5218	1.5264	-.0078	1.5900	1.3990	32,377
Dec	1.5288	1.5288	1.5142	1.5174	-.0078	1.5720	1.4070	587

Est vol 2,560; vol Wed 6,593; open int 33,004, -261.

Swiss Franc (CME)-125,000 francs; $ per franc

Sept	.6693	.6710	.6600	.6609	-.0080	.6975	.5860	36,644
Dec	.6648	.6660	.6617	.6623	-.0081	.6986	.5875	897

Est vol 3,312; vol Wed 8,900; open int 37,617, -2,519.

Australian Dollar (CME)-100,000 dlrs.; $ per A$

Sept	.5342	.5353	.5295	.5323	-.0029	.5752	.4790	23,352
Dec	.5280	.5295	.5270	.5280	-.0029	.5702	.4980	724

Est vol 750; vol Wed 2,848; open int 24,871, -327.

Mexican Peso (CME)-500,000 new Mex. peso, $ per MP

Sept	.10275	.10285	.10170	.10193	-00007	.10830	.09710	13,723
Dec	.10110	.10110	.10020	.10023	-00007	.10673	.09540	1,547

Est vol 4,265; vol Wed 3,760; open int 15,713, +348.

Euro FX (CME)-Euro 125,000; $ per Euro

Sept	.9730	.9758	.9625	.9641	-.0084	1.0185	.8375	96,350
Dec	.9687	.9713	.9586	.9602	-.0084	1.0129	.8390	4,565

Est vol 9,268; vol Wed 26,643; open int 101,325, -3,625.

Source: Wall Street Journal, August 8, 2002.

Example: It is January 14 and SPC Communication has 43 million New Zealand dollars payable in six months. The treasurer is concerned about strengthening the New Zealand dollar in the next six months. The treasurer buys the New Zealand dollar September futures at $.4325/NZ$. Illustration 5.1 summarizes the results of the hedge.

Illustration 5.1

ANTICIPATORY HEDGING OF STRENGTHENING CURRENCY

It is January 14 and SPC Communication has 43 million New Zealand dollars (NZ$) payable in six months. The treasurer is concerned about strengthening the NZ$ in the next six months.

January 14 spot market
Spot rate: $.4310/NZ$
September futures: $.4325/NZ$
Price per 100,000 NZ$: $43,250
Buy 430 September futures contract

(continues)

Illustration 5.1   *(Continued)*

July 14 spot rate: $.4370/NZ$
Buy 43 million New Zealand dollars at $.4370/NZ$ = $18,791,000
Sell 430 September futures at $.4380/NZ$ = 430 × $43,800

Results
Loss in the spot market: ($18,791,000 − $18,533,000) = (258,000)
Profit in the futures market: 430 × $43,800 − 430 × $43,250 = $236,500
Net loss: −$21,500

The hedge in the case study proved to be prudent in eliminating 91.67 percent of the exposure (236,500/258,000). Had the foreign currency weakened against the treasurer's expectation, the spot market gains would have been nearly offset by losses in the futures market as futures would have been covered for a loss.

ANTICIPATORY HEDGING OF WEAKENING CURRENCY

Currency futures can be used to hedge against a weakening currency position in the market, where income in the form of dividend, interest, royalties, and otherwise is expected to be received in the future in a soft currency. The party with a long position in the soft currency may take an offsetting position in the futures market by selling currency futures. The hedged position eliminates the variability of the exposed position and produces a constant payoff with zero variance.

Example: It is August 8 and a U.S. multinational company is expecting 295 million Mexican pesos for the repatriation of income from a joint venture with a Mexican company in three months. The treasurer is concerned over the likelihood of the peso's devaluation over the next three months. Currently the peso is quoted at $.1027/peso. Exhibit 5.13 quotes the various pesos futures. The treasurer decides to sell December futures short at $.10023. Illustration 5.2 summarizes the results of the hedge.

Illustration 5.2

ANTICIPATORY HEDGING OF WEAKENING CURRENCY

August 8 spot market
Spot rate: $.1027/peso
Receivable at spot rate: $30,296,500
December futures: $.10023/peso

> *Price per 500,000 Mexican peso:* $50,115
>
> Sell 590 December futures contracts
>
> *November 8 spot rate:* $.10985/peso
>
> Sell 295 million Mexican peso at $.10985/peso for $32,405,750
> *December futures:* $.11/peso
> *Price per 500,000 Mexican peso:* $55,000
> Buy 590 December futures at $.11/peso = 590 × $55,000
>
> **Results**
> *Profit in the spot market:* $32,405,750 − $30,296,500 = $2,109,250
> *Loss in the futures market:* 590 × $50,115 − 590 × $55,000 = −$2,882,150
> *Net loss:* −$772,900

The hedge turned out to be very costly, as the exchange rate moved contrary to the treasurer's expectation. Had the treasurer remained unhedged, the receivables would have converted to $32,405,750. However, the loss on the futures in the amount of −$2,882,150 resulted in net receivables of $29,523,600.

ROLLING OVER THE FUTURES HEDGE

Companies that enter into long-term contractual obligations hedge their exposure to market risk by selling short-term futures contracts and at the expiration close out the futures by rolling over into the next futures contracts to buy protection for the unexpected change in the spot price that could adversely affect the hedger. The futures may be rolled over as many times as the hedger finds it necessary to seek protection from unwanted risk. The savings and loans (S&Ls) financed long-term lending by rolling over short-term borrowing profitably as long as the yield curve was upward sloping.

The mismatch of assets and liabilities did not create problems as long as the yield was higher in long-term lending than in short-term borrowing. In essence, the S&Ls rolled over their short-term borrowing to finance long-term investment. This practice came back to haunt the S&Ls in the late 1970s and early 1980s, as the yield curve turned downward sloping and resulted in the collapse of a number of S&Ls.

The rolling over of the futures hedge forward is illustrated by Metallgesellschaft (MG), a major German company in the early 1990s.[8] MG sold a huge number of long-term oil contracts with maturities of 5 to 10 years into futures at a price 6 to 8 cents over the spot price fixed over the life of long-dated forward contracts. MG management, short in the long-dated oil contracts, decided to hedge its exposure by buying short-dated oil futures, and at the expiration of the futures, close out the position and buy the next oil futures by rolling over futures contracts.

This strategy worked as long as oil prices were rising. However, the price of oil dropped under $15 a barrel in 1993, and the futures contract closed out with a massive margin call resulting in a loss of $1.33 billion. MG senior management and its bankers decided that the company needed to abandon the practice of selling oil and fixing the prices up to 10 years into the future, while hedging the exposure by rolling over short-term futures contracts.

While the losses in the futures were short term in nature, the gains in the long-term contracts due to falling oil prices would have been realized on the long-term fixed price contracts. Why did management not use these long-term contracts as a collateral in securing short-term capital to pay for massive margin calls? Perhaps management panicked and did not consider the positive future cash flow to be realized on the long-term fixed contracts as a means of financing short-term cash drains on futures contracts and subsequently closed out all of its hedge position.

Example: It is June 2002 and a privately endowed academic institution in New York believes that it needs to buy 2.1 million gallons of heating oil for winter 2003. The price of heating oil is currently at $.70/gal. Each contract at the NYMEX is for delivery of 42,000 gallons of heating oil. The company buys 50 heating oil December futures at a price of $.71/gal. It bought the nearest futures because distant futures up to one year are not as liquid as the nearest futures, as reflected in a relatively small open interest (refers to the number of contracts outstanding on a particular futures).

Consider the following scenarios for rolling over the futures contracts forward for the academic institution wishing to hedge against rising heating oil price in the future. Assuming the hedge ratio is equal to one (2.1 million gallons of oil is hedged with 50 futures contract where each contract is for delivery of 42,000 gallons of heating oil in the NYMEX) and the price of heating oil by March 2003 is expected to be $.80/gal. The institution closes out December 2002 futures in November at $.73/gal and buys May 2003 futures for $.74. These futures are closed out on April 18 at $.7625/gallon, and the institution buys October 2003 priced at $.77/gal. These contracts are closed out on September 3 at $.7875/gal. Finally the institution buys March 2003 futures on September 18 at $.79/gal and closes them out on February at $.81/gal. Illustration 5.3 summarizes these strategies and the outcome.

Illustration 5.3

ROLLING OVER THE FUTURES FORWARD

It is June 20, 2002 and an academic institution wants to buy 2.1 million gallons of heating oil in winter 2003 to hedge against rising prices in the following winter.

June 20, 2002: The institution buys 50 heating oil December futures.

November 21: The institution closes out December futures and buys 50 May 2003 futures.

April 18: The institution closes out May 2003 futures and buys 50 October 2003 futures.

September 18: The institution closes out October 2003 futures and buys 50 March 2004 futures.

Results

December futures purchased at $.71/gal in June 2002 closed out at $.73 on November 2 for a profit of 2 cents per gallon.

May 2003 futures purchased at $.74/gal in November closed out at $.7625/gal on April 2003 for a profit of 2.25 cents per gallon.

October 2003 futures purchased at $.77/gal in April closed out at $.7875/gal in September 2003 for a profit of 1.75 cents per gallon.

March 2004 futures purchased at $.79/gal in September closed out at $.81/gal in February 2004 for a profit of 2 cents per gallon.

The price of heating oil increased by 10 cents per gallon from June 2002 to winter 2003, while the profit from rolling over futures, ignoring the time value of money, is equal to 8 cents per gallon on the four contracts rolled over forward. The hedge proved to be prudent by insulating 80 percent of the increase in the price of the heating oil to the risk-averse academic institution.

This illustration and previous examples assume that the long or short positions in the futures market are marked to market by the clearinghouse, and any gains are kept in the account, ignoring the time value of money. Losses were covered in the day following the margin calls.

MARKING TO MARKET AND MARGIN

All of the futures contracts traded in the various organized exchanges in the United States and elsewhere are settled through a clearinghouse, thereby eliminating settlement risk or counterparty risk that is present in the over-the-counter forward contracts. To demonstrate how marking to market and margin works, consider a speculator who sells on Wednesday, July 31, five silver August contracts at the Chicago Board of Trade (CBOT) at the close of business at $4.35/oz. Each contract on silver is for delivery of 1,000 ounces of silver. The minimum "tick" is $10 per one contract.

The initial margin is $2,000 per contract with margin maintenance of $1,500 per contract. (The margin on any given day at the close of business has to be $1,500 or more to prevent margin posting.) The speculator deposits $10,000 in its brokerage account and sells five August contracts short. The margin maintenance for five contracts is $7,500. Exhibit 5.14 summarizes the result of the marking to the market and margin operation.

The speculator closes out its position by buying five silver futures at $4.50 on August 20, for a cumulative loss of $500. The speculator deposits $1,250 additional margins for margin calls on August 9, 13, and 15 and had an initial margin of $10,000, and at the closing has a margin balance of $10,750. At the close of business on August 9, the margin has fallen below $7,500 and a margin call of $500 is made to the party with the short position. The following day the margin is posted to the individual account (assuming the speculator wires $500 to its brokerage account).

COMMODITY FUTURES

Pricing commodities futures follows the same principles as pricing other instruments discussed so far. In the context of the cost of carry, the price of commodities futures is related to the price of the underlying spot price (S) plus the costs associated with the physical ownership, such as opportunity cost (r) and cost of storage (z) (assuming these costs are proportional to the spot price) minus the benefits of physical ownership embodied in the convenience yields i.

EXHIBIT 5.14 Marking to Market for a Short Position in Five Silver Futures

Date	Futures Price	Change $	Daily Gains (loss)	Margin Balance $	Margin Call $
July 31	$4.35			$10,000	
Aug 1	$4.40	.05	(250)	$ 9,750	
Aug 2	$4.36	−.04	200	$ 9,950	
Aug 5	$4.50	.14	(700)	$ 9,250	
Aug 6	$4.65	.15	(750)	$ 8,500	
Aug 7	$4.60	−.05	250	$ 8,750	
Aug 8	$4.80	.20	(1000)	$ 7,750	
Aug 9[a]	**$4.95**	.15	(750)	$ 7,000	500[a]
Aug 12	$4.85	−.10	500	$ 8,000	
Aug 13	**$5**	.15	(750)	$ 7,250	250
Aug 14	$4.90	−.10	500	$ 8,000	
Aug 15	**$5.15**	.20	(1000)	$ 7,000	500
Aug 16	$4.95	−.20	1000	$ 8,500	
Aug 19	$4.75	−.20	1000	$ 9,500	
Aug 20	$4.50	−.25	1250	$10,750	

[a] The boldface indicates margin calls and subsequent posting of sufficient margins.

The futures price as denoted by F over t periods will be as follows (see Equation 5.9) assuming the rates are continuously compounded:

$$F = Se^{(r + z - i)t} \qquad (5.9)$$

Example: Suppose the platinum spot is quoted at $510/ounce and risk-free interest rate and storage costs are 4 and 1.5 percent, respectively. Rent can be realized by leasing the platinum to the producer by a major financial institution at the rate of 3 percent per annum. The 91-day futures price of platinum will be:

$$F = 510e^{(.04 + .015 - .03).25}$$
$$= \$513.22$$

Gold and silver futures are priced according to this principle. Gold and silver provide no dividends and entail storage cost as negative income. If this is the case, the convenience yield is expected to be zero. However, the physical ownership provides opportunities as an investment instrument, and at times the owner may be able to take advantage of temporary shortages by selling the commodity at higher prices. These benefits accrue to the physical owner of the asset.

Gold is held as store of value, and central banks are able to lease gold to mining companies and realize positive return as convenience yield. Other precious metals may be leased by the party with the long position with the agreement that the party leasing the precious metals return the leased asset at the end of the leased period. These actions are intended to convert nondividend-paying instrument such as gold to a dividend-paying instrument for manufacturing synthetic forward contracts on gold and other precious metals, described in Chapter 6.

SPREAD POSITION

It is August 7 and a speculator is trying to take spread positions in the platinum futures. Spread involves simultaneously buying and selling two futures contracts with different maturities. The speculator sells short one October 2002 future at $530/troy ounce and simultaneously buys January 2003 at $521.5/troy ounce (see Exhibit 5.17).[9] The contract for platinum is for delivery of 50 troy ounces (5,000 ounces) as shown in Exhibit 5.15. The basis is equal to:

$$\text{Basis} = \$530 - \$521.5$$
$$= \$8.50$$

The basis is likely to change over time. The riskless arbitrage profit is likely to be closer to zero; otherwise arbitrageurs will be selling the October 2002 futures and buying the January 2003 futures. The excess supply of October 2002 futures is likely to push the price lower as more contracts are sold short. The demand for January 2003 is expected to push the price higher and closer to the fair value in Equation 5.9. At the expiration of the October 2002 contract, the short and long positions have to be closed out by covering the short (buying October 2002) and selling the long (January 2003). The market for platinum appears to be inverted (backwardation), as can be verified from Exhibit 5.17. Initial profit of $8.5 \times 5,000 = \$42,500$ per one contract in a spread transaction is most likely to disappear at the expiration of the near futures contract (October futures). Suppose at the expiration the spot price is $531.50, the January futures price is $522.50/troy ounce 1, and the basis is:

$$\text{Basis} = \$531.50 - \$522.50$$
$$= -\$9$$
$$\text{Net profit (loss): } [\$8.50 - \$9] \times 5,000 = (\$2,500)$$

The October short is covered at $531.50/troy ounce for a loss of $1.50/oz, while the December 2003 long will be sold at the expiration of the October contract at $522.50 for a profit of $1/oz. The speculator realized a loss of $2,500 per one contract.

HEDGING WITH COMMODITIES FUTURES

Commodity futures provide risk-averse individuals such as farmers, food processors, grain elevators, manufacturing, financial, and nonfinancial corporations the opportunities for managing risk and provide arbitrageurs with a chance to make speculative profit.

Example: On August 8 a food processor determines that it needs to buy 5 million bushels of corn in each of the following months—September and December 2002; and March, May, and July 2003—at the closing prices shown in Exhibit 5.15. It buys futures contracts in the Chicago Board of Trade to hedge against the rising price of corn. Each contract is for delivery of 5,000 bushels. The initial margin is $2,000 per contract with the margin maintenance of $1,500 per contract. Assuming that the corn price moves one way or the other by more than 10 cents, margin calls will be made to the party with the long or the short position whose initial margin maintenance has fallen below 75 percent of the initial margin of, say, $2,000. The food processor plans to hedge 75 percent of its exposure during the next 12-month period.

The food processor buys 750 contracts for each of the value dates indicated in the example. The margin of $1.5 million ($2,000 \times 750$) is required for each value date. In total, the processor puts up $7.5 million for margins to buy 750 contracts on September and December 2002 and for March, May, and July 2003. These contracts essentially lock the food processor in at the prevailing current futures prices (forward price), eliminating the uncertainty about price changes as well as any potential gains forgone by not having an unhedged position. All contracts were closed out on the 15th calendar day of the contract month at the following prices: September contract = 248.75 cents/bu.; December contract = 255.25 cents/bu.; March contract = 265.50 cents/bu.; May contract = 270.25 cents/bu., July contract = 269.25 cents/bu. Illustration 5.4 summarizes the results of the hedge.

EXHIBIT 5.15 Commodity Futures

Thursday, August 8, 2002

Grain and Oilseed Futures

Corn (CBT)-5,000 bu.; cents per bu.

	OPEN	HIGH	LOW	SETTLE	CHG	LIFETIME HIGH	LIFETIME LOW	OPEN INT
Sept	248.50	250.25	245.25	246.25	-2.75	262.00	205.25	128,888
Dec	259.50	261.50	256.25	257.25	-2.75	272.00	215.00	278,545
Mr03	264.00	265.00	261.00	262.00	-2.50	270.00	224.00	46,191
May	266.50	266.75	264.50	264.50	-2.75	272.50	229.25	11,548
July	268.00	268.75	265.75	266.75	-2.50	273.75	233.75	18,062
Sept	256.00	256.50	253.50	253.50	-1.75	259.00	233.00	3,499
Dec	246.50	247.75	245.00	245.00	-.75	269.00	235.00	15,888
Mr04	252.00	252.00	251.50	251.50	-.50	255.00	242.75	1,227
July	255.50	256.00	255.50	255.50	-.50	259.50	247.75	386
Dec	239.50	239.50	239.00	239.50	.50	260.00	234.00	1,294

Est vol 55,008; vol Wed 71,013; open int 505,528, +190.

Oats (CBT)-5,000 bu.; cents per bu.

	OPEN	HIGH	LOW	SETTLE	CHG	LIFETIME HIGH	LIFETIME LOW	OPEN INT
Sept	180.00	181.00	175.75	177.00	-3.50	186.50	117.50	2,725
Dec	172.50	174.00	171.75	172.00	-.75	183.25	123.00	6,990
Mr03	167.50	167.50	167.00	167.50	-.50	183.00	130.00	1,272

Est vol 677; vol Wed 638; open int 11,157, -94.

Soybeans (CBT)-5,000 bu.; cents per bu.

	OPEN	HIGH	LOW	SETTLE	CHG	LIFETIME HIGH	LIFETIME LOW	OPEN INT
Aug	560.00	562.00	554.50	557.75	-2.25	605.00	425.00	2,663
Sept	551.00	553.00	543.50	545.50	-5.25	580.00	425.00	27,252
Nov	530.00	534.50	521.00	522.75	-7.75	565.00	428.50	100,455
Ja03	531.50	532.50	522.50	523.50	-8.00	562.75	445.00	18,277
Mar	530.00	531.00	523.00	524.50	-6.75	553.50	449.00	15,146
May	530.00	530.00	522.00	524.25	-7.50	554.00	461.00	27,335
July	529.00	530.00	522.00	524.00	-6.25	554.00	450.00	6,772
Nov	504.00	504.00	498.00	498.50	-2.25	525.00	484.00	3,132

Est vol 48,781; vol Wed 59,475; open int 201,018, -1,208

Soybean Meal (CBT)-100 tons; $ per ton.

	OPEN	HIGH	LOW	SETTLE	CHG	LIFETIME HIGH	LIFETIME LOW	OPEN INT
Aug	181.20	182.70	179.50	180.50	-.90	193.00	141.10	5,001
Sept	176.90	177.50	174.50	174.90	-2.00	185.50	139.70	19,363
Oct	168.00	169.00	165.30	166.10	-2.40	180.90	141.50	20,782
Dec	166.00	167.60	163.00	163.90	-2.50	178.00	142.70	50,393
Ja03	165.50	165.80	162.70	163.30	-2.40	175.00	143.50	6,911
Mar	164.30	164.70	161.70	163.00	-1.60	174.60	145.50	6,709
May	162.20	162.80	160.00	161.10	-1.70	172.00	146.00	7,539
July	162.00	162.60	160.00	161.00	-1.30	172.10	147.00	5,774
Aug	160.00	160.00	159.50	159.50	-1.50	170.00	148.00	1,448
Sept	159.50	160.00	158.10	158.10	.40	168.80	148.00	1,002
Oct	156.00	156.00	156.00	156.00	.80	166.00	148.10	457
Dec	156.00	158.00	156.00	158.00	1.00	166.00	148.00	1,300

Est vol 21,100; vol Wed 25,542; open int 126,674, -633.

Soybean Oil (CBT)-60,000 lbs.; cents per lb.

	OPEN	HIGH	LOW	SETTLE	CHG	LIFETIME HIGH	LIFETIME LOW	OPEN INT
Aug	20.10	20.12	19.96	20.00	-.08	20.64	15.62	1,980
Sept	20.12	20.13	19.98	19.99	.11	20.70	15.73	27,712
Oct	20.12	20.18	20.03	20.05	-.10	20.75	15.15	13,810
Dec	20.30	20.39	20.17	20.20	-.10	20.94	16.10	66,984
Ja03	20.30	20.30	20.21	20.21	-.08	20.90	16.35	5,934
Mar	20.30	20.32	20.22	20.22	-.10	20.85	16.70	4,149
May	20.23	20.32	20.26	20.25	-.09	20.90	16.80	8,822
July	20.30	20.33	20.25	20.26	-.07	20.90	16.95	4,550
Dec	19.85	19.85	19.80	19.80	-.10	20.95	19.80	1,987

Est vol 17,090; vol Wed 23,881; open int 136,671, -1,351.

Wheat (CBT)-5,000 bu.; cents per bu.

	OPEN	HIGH	LOW	SETTLE	CHG	LIFETIME HIGH	LIFETIME LOW	OPEN INT
Sept	345.75	350.00	337.00	338.50	-7.75	350.00	271.00	35,641
Dec	357.25	361.75	349.50	350.00	-8.00	365.00	283.50	75,446
Mr03	364.00	366.00	355.00	356.00	-8.75	366.00	288.50	11,768
May	355.00	355.50	348.00	348.00	-5.00	365.00	287.00	573
July	337.00	339.00	332.00	333.00	-4.50	348.50	280.50	6,238

Est vol 34,676; vol Wed 23,697; open int 130,635, +1,766.

Wheat (KC)-5,000 bu.; cents per bu.

	OPEN	HIGH	LOW	SETTLE	CHG	LIFETIME HIGH	LIFETIME LOW	OPEN INT
Sept	383.50	383.50	375.50	377.00	-4.75	383.50	285.50	29,227
Dec	388.50	388.50	380.00	383.25	-3.75	388.50	293.00	38,158
Mr03	387.25	388.00	380.25	383.00	-3.00	388.00	297.50	8,563
May	373.00	374.75	369.00	374.00	1.50	374.75	299.50	920

Est vol 16,151; vol Wed 13,756; open int 80,171, +2,379.

Wheat (MPLS)-5,000 bu.; cents per bu.

	OPEN	HIGH	LOW	SETTLE	CHG	LIFETIME HIGH	LIFETIME LOW	OPEN INT
Sept	388.50	394.00	384.75	385.75	-1.25	394.00	295.00	11,461
Dec	392.00	396.00	388.00	390.25	.25	396.00	305.00	9,370
Mr03	392.00	394.50	386.25	389.25	-1.25	394.50	311.00	7,427
May	385.50	388.00	383.00	383.50	-1.00	388.00	313.00	999

Est vol na; vol Wed 4,821; open int 25,479, +143.

Copper-High (CMX)-25,000 lbs.; cents per lb.

	OPEN	HIGH	LOW	SETTLE	CHG	LIFETIME HIGH	LIFETIME LOW	OPEN INT
Aug	67.30	67.50	67.15	67.25	0.40	82.90	62.90	1,125
Sept	67.30	68.15	67.10	67.50	0.35	88.00	62.95	46,165
Oct	67.80	68.00	67.80	67.75	0.35	85.50	63.60	10,325
Dec	67.90	68.90	67.90	68.30	0.35	83.00	63.50	15,541
Ja03	68.80	68.80	68.80	68.65	0.35	80.10	64.90	1,006
Feb	69.40	69.50	69.40	68.85	0.35	79.95	65.10	935
Mar	69.25	69.50	69.25	69.10	0.35	80.70	65.30	4,256
May	69.85	70.00	69.85	69.65	0.35	81.05	65.80	2,882
June	70.05	70.05	70.05	69.90	0.35	78.40	69.40	711
July	70.40	70.60	70.40	70.10	0.35	80.80	66.80	2,325
Aug	70.80	70.80	70.80	70.30	0.35	77.85	67.40	600
Sept	71.00	71.00	70.65	70.50	0.35	81.00	66.00	2,766
Dec	71.50	71.50	71.50	71.05	0.35	81.60	70.70	3,867

Est vol 13,000; vol Wed 6,981; open int 96,442, +722.

Gold (CMX)-100 troy oz.; $ per troy oz.

	OPEN	HIGH	LOW	SETTLE	CHG	LIFETIME HIGH	LIFETIME LOW	OPEN INT
Aug	314.60	314.60	310.30	310.40	-3.90	331.50	272.60	655
Sept	...	...	...	310.90	-3.90	326.00	302.00	30
Oct	313.70	314.20	310.70	311.20	-3.90	331.50	274.00	13,333
Dec	315.90	316.50	311.90	312.20	-3.90	358.00	268.10	82,967
Fb03	315.10	315.30	313.00	312.90	-3.90	333.70	286.50	8,864
Apr	315.40	315.50	314.30	313.40	-3.90	332.50	281.50	4,279
Dec	318.50	318.50	316.00	315.90	-3.90	359.30	280.00	8,842

Est vol 27,000; vol Wed 47,125; open int 141,866, +1,382.

Platinum (NYM)-50 troy oz.; $ per troy oz.

	OPEN	HIGH	LOW	SETTLE	CHG	LIFETIME HIGH	LIFETIME LOW	OPEN INT
Oct	531.50	540.80	531.50	539.50	6.30	566.00	400.00	5,597

Est vol 1,920; vol Wed 1,363; open int 5,672, +537.

Silver (CMX)-5,000 troy oz.; cnts per troy oz.

	OPEN	HIGH	LOW	SETTLE	CHG	LIFETIME HIGH	LIFETIME LOW	OPEN INT
Aug	...	...	...	463.5	-3.7	541.0	463.5	0
Sept	468.5	469.5	462.5	463.8	-3.7	517.0	412.5	42,319
Dec	472.0	472.5	465.0	466.7	-3.7	613.0	412.0	27,904
Mr03	473.0	474.5	468.0	468.6	-3.7	522.0	417.0	2,511
July	474.0	474.0	474.0	470.6	-3.7	551.0	421.0	4,331
Dec	476.5	478.0	476.5	472.9	-3.8	565.0	419.0	2,278

Est vol 11,000; vol Wed 10,640; open int 83,953, +323.

Petroleum Futures

Crude Oil, Light Sweet (NYM)-1,000 bbls.; $ per bbl.

	OPEN	HIGH	LOW	SETTLE	CHG	LIFETIME HIGH	LIFETIME LOW	OPEN INT
Sept	26.45	26.83	26.28	26.67	0.17	28.18	19.10	101,951
Oct	25.95	26.36	25.85	26.22	0.16	27.61	19.50	84,140
Nov	25.88	26.03	25.68	25.96	0.14	27.25	19.55	25,178
Dec	25.74	25.95	25.50	25.82	0.15	27.05	15.50	50,686
Ja03	25.45	25.63	25.40	25.62	0.15	26.60	19.90	21,671
Mar	25.03	25.26	25.02	25.26	0.15	26.00	20.05	9,206
Apr	24.85	25.10	24.85	25.09	0.15	25.75	20.55	6,871
June	24.60	24.80	24.60	24.76	0.16	25.39	19.82	15,653
Aug	24.33	24.33	24.33	24.49	0.16	24.95	21.16	5,563
Dec	23.90	24.01	23.80	24.05	0.18	24.57	15.92	21,720

Est vol 137,901; vol Wed 192,341; open int 422,063, +1,406.

Heating Oil No. 2 (NYM)-42,000 gal.; $ per gal.

	OPEN	HIGH	LOW	SETTLE	CHG	LIFETIME HIGH	LIFETIME LOW	OPEN INT
Sept	.6565	.6750	.6565	.6724	.0063	.7300	.5390	41,038
Oct	.6769	.6840	.6700	.6825	.0054	.7345	.5460	20,201
Nov	.6820	.6925	.6810	.6915	.0049	.7500	.5570	10,736
Dec	.6900	.6995	.6890	.6985	.0044	.7570	.5660	19,033
Ja03	.6955	.7040	.6950	.7035	.0039	.7510	.5680	11,739
Feb	.6950	.7020	.6950	.7015	.0039	.7441	.5710	9,707
Mar	.6850	.6900	.6850	.6895	.0039	.7261	.5640	6,438
Apr	.6705	.6740	.6705	.6745	.0039	.7041	.5500	3,011
May	.6550	.6550	.6550	.6595	.0039	.6800	.5450	1,959
Aug	.6585	.6615	.6585	.6625	.0039	.6760	.5705	325
Oct	.6705	.6705	.6705	.6745	.0039	.6770	.6290	241

Est vol 38,387; vol Wed 39,277; open int 130,219, +2,474.

Gasoline-NY Unleaded (NYM)-42,000 gal.; $ per gal.

	OPEN	HIGH	LOW	SETTLE	CHG	LIFETIME HIGH	LIFETIME LOW	OPEN INT
Sept	.7546	.7650	.7440	.7554	.0008	.8200	.5788	43,306
Oct	.7235	.7350	.7170	.7288	.0042	.7720	.5815	19,245
Nov	.7070	.7200	.7050	.7148	.0039	.7500	.5523	7,335
Dec	.7050	.7070	.7025	.7068	.0039	.7350	.5700	5,851
Ja03	.6960	.7010	.6960	.7053	.0039	.7300	.5775	2,703

Est vol 46,973; vol Wed 42,530; open int 84,792, -243.

Natural Gas (NYM)-10,000 MMBtu.; $ per MMBtu

	OPEN	HIGH	LOW	SETTLE	CHG	LIFETIME HIGH	LIFETIME LOW	OPEN INT
Sept	2.661	2.800	2.655	2.745	.085	4.770	2.380	62,974
Oct	2.706	2.830	2.705	2.784	.080	4.785	2.410	38,524
Nov	3.070	3.170	3.070	3.134	.068	4.900	2.630	30,173
Dec	3.385	3.480	3.383	3.442	.063	5.010	2.720	32,001
Ja03	3.560	3.640	3.560	3.609	.055	5.049	2.730	28,955
Feb	3.551	3.630	3.540	3.592	.051	4.874	2.700	21,575
Mar	3.525	3.610	3.510	3.566	.047	4.710	2.710	20,487
Apr	3.510	3.560	3.470	[illegible]	[illegible]	[illegible]	[illegible]	[illegible]

Source: Wall Street Journal, August 8, 2002.

Illustration 5.4

TO HEDGE OR NOT TO HEDGE

On August 8 a food processor has determined that it needs to buy 5 million bushels of corn in each of the following months: September and December 2002; March, May, and July 2003. The food processor is concerned about rising prices in the future; therefore it buys corn futures at CBOT.

August 8 futures market

Purchased 750 contracts on corn futures for September at 246.25
Purchased 750 contracts on corn futures for December at 257.25
Purchased 750 contracts on corn futures for March at 262.00
Purchased 750 contracts on corn futures for May at 264.50
Purchased 750 contracts on corn futures for July at 266.75

September 2002 spot market: Sold 5 million bushels of corn for 248.75 cents/bu.
Closed out September 2002 for profit: $5000 \times (248.75 - 246.25) \times 750 =$ $93,750

December 2002 spot market: Sold 5 million bushels of corn for 255.25 cents/bu.
Closed out December 2002 for loss: $5000 \times (255.25 - 257.25) \times 750 =$ $-$75,000

March 2003 spot market: Sold 5 million bushels of corn for 265.50 cents/bu.
Closed out March 2003 for profit: $5000 \times (265.50 - 262) \times 750 = $131,250$

May 2003 spot market: Sold 5 million bushels of corn for 270.25 cents/bu.
Closed out May 2003 for profit: $5000 \times (265.50 - 262) \times 750 = $131,250$

July 2003 spot market: Sold 5 million bushels of corn for 269.25 cents/bu.
Closed out July 2003 for profit: $5000 \times (269.25 - 266.75) \times 750 = $93,750$

Results

The food processor paid the following amounts in the spot market for purchasing 5 million bushels of corn in September and December 2002 and March, May, and July 2003: $12,437,500, $12,762,500, $13,275,000, $13,512,500, and $13,462,500.

Total outlays in the spot market: $65,449,500
Total gains in the futures market: $375,000
Net outlay: $65,074,500

Hedging eliminated nearly 99.4 percent of the exposure to price increases in this scenario, as the hedger was locked in at the predetermined futures prices over the hedge period. The unhedged position would have been $375,000 more costly to the food processor as the cash outlay to buy 5 million bushels of corn at the spot price would have totaled $65,449,500. The cash outlay is equal to $65,074,500 on the locked position with futures contracts, saving the food processor $375,000. The effective cost of the corn purchased in September is the spot price less the gain on the futures:

$$248.75 - 2.50 = 246.25 \text{ cents/bu.}$$

This is identical to the futures price of the September contract purchased on August 8. Similarly, the effective cost of the corn purchased in July is the spot price less the gain on the futures:

$$269.25 - 2.50 = 266.75 \text{ cents/bu.}$$

The 266.75 cents/bu. is exactly identical to the July futures price on August 8, when the hedge position was taken to lock the firm at the futures (forward) price, as can be verified in Exhibit 5.15.

Example: An oil refinery knows that in six months it needs to sell 1.5 million barrels of crude oil. On August 8 the price of oil is $26.65/bbl at the spot market. The refinery is concerned about falling oil prices in the future that is reflected in the inverted crude oil prices in Exhibit 5.15. The crude oil futures is traded at the New York Mercantile Exchange (NYMEX) with 18 consecutive monthly trading, contract size of 1,000 barrels of oil per contract, and an initial margin of $2,700 per contract. The refinery sells 1,500 March futures at a price of $25.20/bbl. The initial margin for these contracts is equal to $4,050,000, and the margin maintenance is set at 75 percent. Illustration 5.5 outlines the result of the hedge.

Illustration 5.5

TO HEDGE OR NOT TO HEDGE

It is August 8 and an oil refinery knows that in six months it needs to sell 1.5 million barrels of crude oil. The refinery is concerned about falling oil prices in the future.

August 8 spot market

Crude oil price: $26.65/bbl
Futures: Sell 1,500 March futures for $25.20/bbl
Proceeds per one contract: $1,000 \times \$25.20/\text{bbl} = \$25,200$
Total proceeds on futures: $1,500 \times \$25,200 = \$37,800,000$

March 15 spot market: Sell 1.5 million barrels of oil for $27
Total proceeds on spot: $1,500,000 \times \$27/\text{bbl} = \$40,500,000$
Buy 1,500 March futures for 27.15
Proceeds per one contract: $1,000 \times \$27.15/\text{bbl} = \$27,150$
Total proceeds on futures: $1,500 \times \$27,150 = \$40,7250,000$

(continues)

Illustration 5.5 *(Continued)*

Results

Loss on the futures: 1,500 ($25,200 − $27,150) = −$2,938,500
Proceeds on the spot: $40,500,000
Net proceeds: $37,561,500

The hedge in Illustration 5.5 proved to be costly, as it turned out the price of oil actually increased, resulting in a loss of −$2,938,500 on the futures contracts shorted as futures were closed out for a loss. The unhedged position would have been far more desirable; however, the refinery was not able to predict accurately crude oil price for the next six months. Would an alternative hedging instrument have provided protection from falling prices as well as an upside potential in the event of rising oil prices? The answer is definitely yes. A put option would have been the better alternative for hedging downside risk in the event oil prices went down. However, buying put options requires paying an up-front fee for securing protection (buying insurance) that treasurers find annoying. In the event that oil prices go up in the future, put options expire out-of-the-money, and a hedged position will be identical to the unhedged position less the premium of the put option.

EMPIRICAL EVIDENCE: FORWARD AND FUTURES PRICES

The relationships between forward and futures prices has been the subject of extensive empirical and theoretical research in the finance literature.[10] The differences between forward and futures prices appear to be small and insignificant for financial futures; for commodities, the forward and futures prices deviate, providing opportunities for arbitrage.[11] Forward and futures contracts are different in many ways due to institutional arrangements in the over-the-counter market for forward contracts and in the organized exchanges in which futures are traded. For example, other things remaining the same, forward and futures contracts do not have the same liquidity. Futures enjoy greater liquidity as compared to their OTC counterpart, the forward contract. The futures prices are marked to market on a daily basis by the clearinghouse, while forward contracts settle at expiration. This presents the counterparty to a forward contract with settlement risk, which is absent in the futures market.[12]

Assuming contango (futures prices are increasing over time) and futures price and interest rates are positively correlated, as the futures are marked to market and proceeds are invested at progressively higher interest rates, the interest earned will make futures contracts more attractive than forward contracts of the same maturity. In this scenario futures price will be greater than forward prices. Likewise, assuming backwardation (futures prices are decreasing over time), the loss on futures will be covered at progressively lower interest rates, the futures contract will be more advantageous to hold than comparable forward contract of the same maturity.

However, if the futures price and interest rates are negatively correlated, then if the proceeds from the rising futures prices are reinvested at progressively lower interest rates, the futures price will be below the forward price of the same maturity. If futures prices are decreasing over time, the losses on the futures are covered at progressively higher interest rates, thereby making futures contracts less attractive to hold than comparable forward contracts of the same maturity. In this scenario the future price will be below the comparable forward price. Assuming interest rates do not change over time and their behavior is completely deterministic, then the forward and futures prices will be identical.

Consider two futures contracts on Platinum Comp and Silver traded respectively at the Chicago Board of Trade (CBOT) and NYMEX, as shown in Exhibits 5.16 and 5.17.

The platinum futures prices are a decreasing function of the time and are known as *backwardation,* while the silver futures prices increase over time for the most distant futures contract and are known as *contango.* These behaviors as well as price series exhibiting both contango and backwardation have been observed for some commodities in the futures market (see Exhibit 5.18).

Why a particular instrument behaves like gold futures in Exhibit 5.18 is related to supply and demand conditions. Why are gold futures for June 2003 traded at $316.3 per ounce and the August 2003 future trades at a lower price of $309.60? No one knows the answer. Why is the convenience yield lower than the cost of storage and opportunity cost in silver futures producing contango? Why is the convenience yield higher than the cost of storage and opportunity cost producing backwardation in platinum futures? The standard answer may be found in the current supply and demand conditions for the commodity. If the current consumption is unusually high and supply is relatively tight, then the current spot is expected to be high and the market expects that, over time, the temporary

EXHIBIT 5.16   Contango Market:
Silver Futures Prices CBOT

Silver	1,000 oz.	Aug 02	$4.05
Silver	1,000 oz.	Oct 02	$4.61
Silver	1,000 oz.	Dec 02	$4.62

Source: FutureSource, August 7, 2002.

EXHIBIT 5.17   Backwardation Market:
Platinum Futures Prices NYMEX

Platinum	Sept 02	—
Platinum	Oct 02	$530
Platinum	Jan 03	$521.5

Source: FutureSource, August 7, 2002.

EXHIBIT 5.18   Contango and Backwardation
in the Gold Futures COMEX

Gold (Day)	Aug 02	$313.00
Gold (Day)	Sept 02	$312.80
Gold (Day)	Oct 02	$313.40
Gold (Day)	Dec 02	$314.70
Gold (Day)	Feb 03	$315.70
Gold (Day)	Apr 03	$315.50
Gold (Day)	Jun 03	$316.30
Gold (Day)	Aug 03	$309.60
Gold (Day)	Oct 03	$310.30

Source: FutureSource, August 7, 2002.

shortages may disappear. In this scenario, the spot price will be above the futures prices, producing an inverted market for the commodity in question.

For example, an unusually cold winter may put upward pressure on the price of heating oil and electricity, thereby pushing the spot prices above the futures prices. Furthermore, why is the convenience yield lower than the cost of storage and opportunity costs on the contracts for September 2002 through February 2003 and significantly higher than storage and opportunity costs for the contracts on June 2003 and August 2003 for gold futures? The economic theory presumably goes back to the underlying supply and demand conditions to provide satisfactory answers for all of these questions.

Case Study

CHOCKLETTO INTERNATIONAL HEDGING

Mahmoud M. Haddad*

You have just been hired by Chockletto International as a risk manager. Chockletto International is a Swiss manufacturer of fine perfume. It imports some of its raw material from the Hawaiian Island Flower Co. of the United States of America. On May 1, 2003, Chockletto International purchased from Hawaiian Island Flower Co. 200 pounds of a specific Hawaiian rose oil to be delivered on November 1, 2003, at total cost of $2,000,000. The USD/CHF exchange rate on May 1 is 0.7233. Current economic forecasts indicate the dollar is expected to continue to strengthen against all major currencies. Chockletto International must maintain its market share of the perfume market and must fulfill its contractual agreement with Hawaiian Island Flower Co.

*Professor of finance, University of Tennessee-Martin

THOUGHT QUESTIONS

1. As a risk manager, you decided to hedge your position in the cash market. How will you use options contracts and/or futures contracts to hedge your position?

2. Using the following information, how would you show the board of directors the advantages and disadvantages of each hedging tool?

Foreign Exchange Rates:

Spot	USD/CHF		0.7233–236
Forward	USD/CHF	1m	40–245
		3m	50–258
		6m	65–275
		12m	80–285

Interest Rates	6 Mos
US$	1.15%–1.16%
CHF	0.90%–0.92%

Option Prices

Put option CHF 6 month	
Exercise price (strike price)	$0.720
Option price	$0.0293

NOTES

1. This type of behavior produces backwardation on the price of the underlying instrument, where the futures or forward price will be at a discount from the spot price.

2. This type of behavior is referred to as normal or contango.

3. Dividend yield is defined as dividend over the current market price.

4. See Barro (1989).

5. The portfolio beta is estimated as the covariance of the portfolio and the market weighted by the variance of the market portfolio as proxied by the Standard & Poor's 500 stock index.

6. In the context of the regression of the spot and futures, the slope coefficient is equal to the beta of the spot and futures. The beta of spot and futures is equal to the covariance of the spot and futures, and covariance is simply equal to correlation times the standard deviation of the spot and futures.

7. Currently 14 currency futures and options are traded at the Chicago Mercantile Exchange. They are: Australian dollar, Brazilian real, British pound, Canadian dollars, Cross Rates euro FX, Japanese yen, Mexican peso, New Zealand

dollar, Norwegian krone, Russian ruble, South African rand, Swedish krona, Swiss franc, and Cross Rates euro pound.

8. See "MG's Trial by Essay," *Risk* (October 1994): 228–234; and Miller and Culp (1995).

9. The *Wall Street Journal,* August 7, 2002.

10. See Houthakker (1957); Telser (1958); French (1983); Chang (1985); Park and Chen (1985); Flesaker (1993); Masiela, Turnbull, and Wakeman (1993).

11. For interest rate futures, Rendleman and Carabini (1979) found that the difference between forward and futures prices are statistically insignificant. Cornell and Reinganam (1981) and Chang and Chang (1990 analyzed foreign currency forwards and futures on five currencies: British pounds, Japanese yen, German marks, Swiss francs, and Canadian dollars. They find statistically insignificant differences between forward and futures prices. However, for commodities futures such as gold, silver, copper, and platinum, Park and Chen found statistically significant differences between forward and futures prices.

12. See Homaifar and Helms (1990).

CHAPTER 6

Interest Rate Futures: Pricing and Applications

Most futures contracts, particularly those traded in various futures exchanges, such as the Chicago Board of Trade (CBOT) and the Chicago Mercantile Exchange (CME), derive their value from the value of the underlying spot market pricing. Weather derivatives are the exception. For example, interest rate futures contracts derive their value from the underlying Treasury bills, notes, and bonds in the spot market; commodity futures, such as gold, silver, oil, and gas, derive their values from the underlying commodity prices; and stock indices futures and municipal bonds futures are directly related to the stock and bond prices actively traded in the spot market.

The underlying macro- or microfactors that determine the price of a given security in the spot market convey the same information to the participants in the futures market for pricing futures in an organized exchange as buyers and sellers determine the futures price in a frenzy that is expected to change as new information arrives or big movers get in an out of their short or long positions. For example, an unexpected increase in interest rates adversely affects the price of bonds in the spot market as well as bills, notes, and bond futures as interest rate futures are likely to increase from their previous level.

Unlike the spot market, where institutional arrangements limit the hours of transaction to seven or eight hours, transactions in the futures market for some futures, such as stocks, is almost continuous, lasting 23.5 hours per 24 hours. While there might be a hint of an upward movement in stock prices at the opening bell of the futures market, there is no directive to uncover which market is following and which is leading when both markets are open for business. When the spot price continues to rise, selling in the futures market (short selling) puts downward pressure on the underlying instrument in the spot market, and prices start to fall. Likewise, when spot prices fall sharply, buying in the futures market helps shore up the supply in the spot market as the trend is likely to be reversed. This analysis hints that the futures market is likely to be leading and the spot market following. However, the dynamics of both markets are so complex that most of the time they defy logic.

TREASURY BILLS FUTURES

Like its counterpart in the spot market, Treasury bill futures are zero coupon bonds whose price behavior reflects the underlying forward interest rates and the factors that are likely to change participants' expectations with respect to the direction of the forward interest rates. T-bill futures contracts with a face value of $1 million and 13 weeks maturity are traded actively at CBOT. Equations 6.1 and 6.2 show the dynamics of their price.

$$\text{Price} = \text{Face value} - \text{Discount} \qquad (6.1)$$

$$\text{Discount} = f \times t \times F \qquad (6.2)$$

where

f = forward interest rate
t = time to expiration in year
F = face value of the futures

Forward interest rates are the unobservable rates derived from the underlying yield to maturity or spot rates (zero arbitrage rates) in the Treasury markets. Assuming the Treasury spot rates for various maturities are upward sloping (i.e., long-term rates are higher than their short-term counterparts), the forward rates will be greater than their spot counterparts. However, if the spot rate curve or the term structure of the spot rates is inverted, then the forward rate derived from the spot rates will be below its spot counterpart. Exhibit 6.1 shows the behavior of the yield to maturity, spot rates, and forward rates.

When the yield is upward sloping, the spot rate is over and above the yield to maturity and the forward rates are greater than the spot rate. However, in the inverted yield market, the reverse is true. That is, the forward rates will be below the spot rates and spot rates below the yield to maturity.

SPOT RATE

The spot rate or theoretical spot is the rate that equates the present value of cash flows from a portfolio of zero coupon bonds to the market value of the coupon-paying debt instrument. For example, any coupon-paying debt instrument can be defined as a portfolio of zero coupon bonds with a maturity corresponding to the maturity of the coupon that is discounted at a portfolio of spot rates. The yield to maturity and spot rate are the same for any zero coupon bond of any maturity. In the Treasury spot market, the zero coupon bonds are the securities with a maturity of one year or less (i.e., 90 and 180 days).

Example: Consider one-, two-, and three-year bonds rated to yield 5, 5.5, and 6 percent, respectively. The first bond is a pure discount issue, and the last two bonds are priced at par (the coupon and yield are identical). All three bonds have $1,000 face values, as shown in Exhibit 6.2.

EXHIBIT 6.1   Behavior of Various Yields over Time

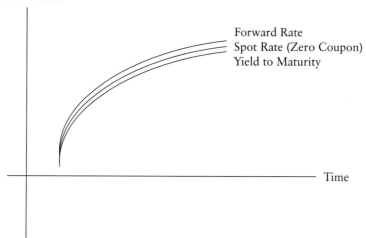

Yield to Maturity,
    Spot, and
Forward Rates

Forward Rate
Spot Rate (Zero Coupon)
Yield to Maturity

Time

Yield to Maturity,
    Spot, and
Forward Rates

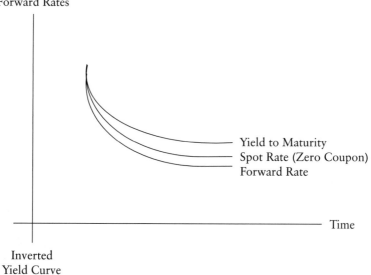

Yield to Maturity
Spot Rate (Zero Coupon)
Forward Rate

Time

Inverted
Yield Curve

EXHIBIT 6.2   Price and Various Interest Rates

Maturity	Coupon	Yield to Maturity	Price	Spot Rates	Forward Rates
1	0	5%	$ 952.38	5	—
2	5.5%	5.5	$1000	? = 5.51%	? = 6%
3	6	6	$1000	? = 6.04%	? = 7.01%

The two-year bond is considered a portfolio of two one-year bonds:

$$\$1,000 = \left[\frac{55}{(1 + .05)} \right] + \left[\frac{1,055}{(1 + ?)^2} \right]$$

The unknown rate is the two-year spot rate, which equates the present value of the cash flow from the coupon-paying instrument to the portfolio of zeros. Solving for the unknown, the two-year spot rate is equal to 5.51 percent. The first coupon (one-year zero coupon bond) was discounted at a one-year spot rate of 5 percent as opposed to 5.5 percent yield to maturity. The second coupon and the principal in two years are discounted at the two-year spot rate of 5.51 percent, preventing riskless arbitrage from stripping coupons. This procedure is known as *bootstrapping* for estimation of the spot rates.

Three-year bonds can be defined as a portfolio of three zero coupon bonds of one, two, and three years to maturity whose present values discounted at respective spot rates must be equal to the present value of the three-year coupon-paying bond:

$$P = \$1,000 = \frac{60}{(1 + .05)} + \frac{60}{(1 + .0551)^2} + \frac{1,060}{(1 + ?)^3}$$

The three-year spot rate can be found by solving for the unknown. The three-year spot rate turns out to be equal to 6.04 percent. The relationship between an n-year spot rate ($R(0,n)$) prevailing at time zero and forward rates ($f(1,n)$), the rate prevailing between time (1 and n), is demonstrated schematically in Exhibit 6.3.

FORWARD RATE

The forward rate is the rate that is expected to prevail in the future between any two adjacent periods. For example, from Exhibit 6.3, the forward rate between periods 1 and 2 and that between periods 2 and 3 can be inferred from the market data. The number of forward rates in n periods will be equal to n $(n - 1)/2$. There are three forward interest rates in Exhibit 6.3: $f(1,2)$, $f(2,3)$, and $f(1,3)$, which are defined as forward rates between years 1 and 2, years 2 and 3, and years 1 and 3.

Example: Consider an individual with a two-year investment horizon who is endowed with $5,000. This individual can invest in a two-year bond, as in

EXHIBIT 6.3   Term Structure of Spot and Forward Rates

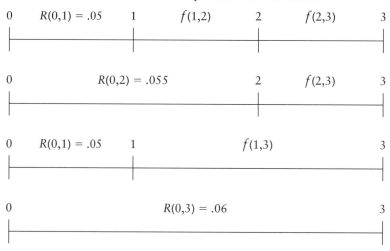

Exhibit 6.2, or in a one-year bond and roll over the proceeds in another one-year bond at a rate that is expected to prevail between years 1 and 2. The payoff from either alternative has to be the same, assuming the absence of riskless arbitrage:

Option 1: Invest $5,000 in a two-year bond, $5,000 $(1.055)^2$ = $5,565.125

Option 2: Invest $5,000 in a one-year bond and at maturity roll over to another one-year bond at the forward rate of $f(1,2)$ that is expected to prevail between years 1 and 2.

The payoff of this option is identical to the payoff of option 1:

$$\$5,000 \ (1.05) \ (1 + f(1,2)) = \$5,565.125$$
$$(1 + f(1,2)) = 1.06, f(1,2) = .06$$

This scenario exposes investors to reinvestment rate risk, which is assumed to be equal to zero under the expectation hypothesis.

Option 3: Buy the three-year bond and sell the bond at the end of two years. There is interest rate risk associated with this option, and the longer the maturity, the greater is the interest rate risk. The expectation theory is plagued with two fundamental flaws, namely *interest rate risk* and *reinvestment rate risk* are both assumed to be zero. Therefore, bonds of varying maturities are perfect substitutes for one another.[1]

Assuming the forward interest rate is greater than 6 percent, it pays to invest in a one-year bond and roll over the proceeds in another one-year security. A riskless arbitrage profit can be realized following this strategy. However, as demand for a one-year forward bonds increases, the price goes up and the yield drops.

Likewise, if the forward interest rate is less than 6 percent, it pays to invest in a two-year bond. As demand for two-year bonds increases, the demand will push its price higher and its yield down until the payoff from either option is identical and arbitrage profit disappears.

The forward rate $(f(2,3))$ can also be estimated from the observed rates in two- and three-year bonds. Let us define any long-term interest rate as the geometric average of the short-term rates. For instance, the two-year rate is defined as the geometric average of two one-year rates: one that is observed and the other that is an unobservable one-year forward rate. Similarly, let us define the n-year rate as the geometric average of n one-year rates as shown in Equation 6.3.

$$(1 + R(0,n))^n = (1 + R(0,1))\ (1 + f(1,2))\ (1 + f(2,3))$$
$$+ \ldots + (1 + f(n - 1, n)) \qquad (6.3)$$

For n equal to 3:

$$(1 + R(0,3))^3 = (1 + R(0,1))\ (1 + f(1,2))\ (1 + f(2,3))$$

Plugging the numbers from Exhibit 6.2 for three- and one-year spots and one-year forward rate $(f(1,2))$, and solving for the $(1 + f(2,3))$ produces:

$$(1 + .06)^3 = (1 + .05)\ (1 + .06)\ (1 + f(2,3))$$
$$(1 + f(2,3)) = 1.0701, f(2,3) = .0701$$

The one-year forward rate prevailing between years two and three is equal to 7.01 percent. This result can be obtained using the observed yield for two- and three-year bonds, as seen in Equation 6.4.

$$(1 + f(2,3)) = \frac{[(1 + R(0,3))^3]}{[(1 + R(0,2))^2]} \qquad (6.4)$$

$$(1 + f(2,3)) = \frac{(1.06)^3}{(1.055)^2} = 1.0701, f(2,3) = .0701$$

The forward rates are the market consensus and are assumed to be unbiased predictors of the future spot rates.

DETERMINANTS OF THE SHAPE OF THE TERM STRUCTURE OF INTEREST RATES

Plotting the yield to maturity, spot rate, and forward rates against various maturities over time, the likely scenario may be a normal upward-sloping term structure. However, sometimes other shapes, such as downward-sloping (see Exhibit 6.4) or relatively flat or hump-shaped yield curves, are observed. The yield curve at any point in time is a snapshot of various debt instruments of varying maturities against time assuming other things such as coupon, default risk, liquidity risk, and maturity risk remain the same.

Various theories have been advanced to explain the shape of the yield curve.[2]

EXHIBIT 6.4 U.S. Treasury Securities (August 1981)

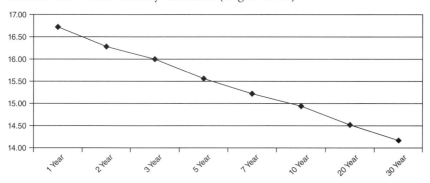

Expectation Theories

Expectations theories can take several forms: pure expectation theory, liquidity premium theory, and preferred habitat theory. Various forms of expectation theories assume the forward rates are the market consensus of the future interest rates and embody no risk premium over time.[3] For example, based on the pure expectation theory, the long-term rate is the geometric average of the portfolio of short-term rates that is expected to prevail in the future. A falling term structure, such as Exhibit 6.4, indicates that the market expects forward interest rates to continue to fall in the near future, as witnessed in the past due to falling inflationary expectations producing an inverted yield curve that was observed on the last business day in August 1981. Likewise, a flat term structure reflects future short-term interest rates that are expected to remain constant, and a rising term structure hints that the short-term interest rates (the forward rates) are expected to go up, producing an upward-sloping scenario for U.S. treasury securities as of October 1982 (see Exhibit 6.5).

The pure expectation theory has been criticized because it assumes that bonds of varying maturities are perfect substitutes for one another. Clearly this is not the case. Longer-term bonds are more prone to higher price and reinvestment rate risk than short-term bonds.

Liquidity Preference Theory

Given the uncertainty about future interest rates and the greater price and reinvestment rate risk associated with long-term bonds, investors are likely to demand higher risk premiums that are expected to increase uniformly as the maturity of the bond increases.[4] Based on this theory, long-term interest rates are greater than the geometric average of short-term rates expected to prevail in the future. An investor's aversion to risk and uncertainty of long-term bonds and preference of greater liquidity of the short-term rates increases demand for short-term debt, pushing their yields down and price up.[5] Similarly, the supply of long-term debt tends to exceed the demand, depressing the price and pushing the yield

EXHIBIT 6.5 U.S. Treasury Securities (October 1982)

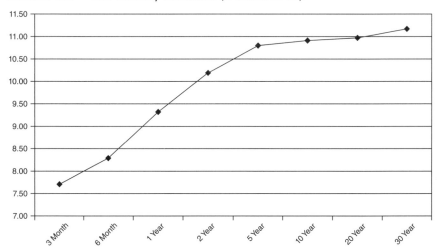

higher, and producing an upward-sloping yield curve. Investors will be enticed to invest in the long end of the bond market if they are compensated by higher rates. The forward interest rate will be a biased predictor of the future short-term interest rates as advocated by the liquidity preference theory.

Preferred Habitat Theory

This theory, advanced by Modigliani and Sutch,[6] assumes that the term structure embodies an expectation of future interest rates as well as risk premium. However, risk premium is not expected to rise or fall uniformly as maturity increases or decreases as advocated by the proponents of the liquidity preference theory. Preferred investment or financing horizon is dictated by the nature of the assets and liabilities of the financial institutions in making asset allocation decisions. Institutions will be enticed to shift from their preferred horizon only if sufficient compensation in the form of higher yield is offered.

For example, life insurance companies have a long-term investment horizon since their liabilities are long term. Property casualty insurers, however, invest in the intermediate segment of the market and will be induced to move into the long end of the market only if a higher risk premium mitigates their aversion to interest rate and price risk associated with long-term bonds.

Market Segmentation Theory

According to this theory, regulatory or self-imposed restrictions dictate asset allocation decisions of the financial institutions to invest in a particular segment of the market. Supply and demand in each segment of the market determines the price, yield, and shape of the yield curve.[7] Borrowers or lenders may not be enticed to shift from one maturity segment to another one, even if opportunities arise from differences in the yield differentials between any two segments.

Bond Price Volatility

Price volatility is measured by the *duration* of a bond, which is equal to the slope of the price yield relationship in Exhibit 6.6 weighted by the market value of the bond. Duration is the price sensitivity of the bond with respect to change in yield and therefore can be considered price elasticity. For that matter, some bonds are more price elastic than others and offer the potential for enhancing yields in active portfolio management.

Duration also can be defined in terms of number of years (as is practiced on Wall Street) as the sum of cash flows (multiplied by the present value of the time) in which each cash flow is recognized, weighted by the market value of the bond. In this context duration measures the size and timing of the cash flows, as seen in Equation 6.5.

$$D = \frac{\left[\dfrac{\displaystyle\sum_{t=1}^{n} (t\,C)}{(1+R)^t} + \dfrac{(n \times F)}{(1+R)^n} \right]}{P} \tag{6.5}$$

where

C = coupon interest (coupon rate times the face value of the bond F)
R = yield to maturity of the bond
P = market value of an n-year bond

The term in brackets is the slope of the price/yield relationship $\Delta P/\Delta Y$.

EXHIBIT 6.6   Price/Yield Relationship

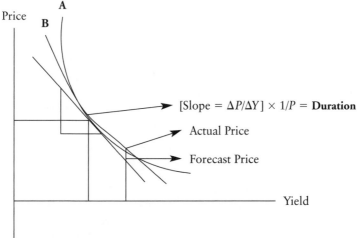

Duration of the three-year bond in Exhibit 6.2 is calculated using Equation 6.3 and is equal to 2.83 years:

$$D = \frac{\left\{\dfrac{(1 \times 60)}{(1.06)} + \dfrac{(2 \times 60)}{(1.06)^2} + \dfrac{(3 \times 60)}{(1.06)^3} + \dfrac{(3 \times 1{,}000)}{(1.06)^3}\right\}}{1000} = -2.83$$

Duration is produced in this equation and is weighted by $(1 + R)$, known as modified duration $(D/(1 + R))$. The modified duration of the bond is equal to 2.67 years. Duration indicates that for every $+/-100$ basis point (1 percent) change in the yield, the bond price is expected to change symmetrically in the opposite direction by $-/+2.67$ percent.

The price/yield relationship in Exhibit 6.6 is a nonlinear convex set because the percentage changes in bond or stock prices or the price of any asset, financial or real, is nonsymmetric, while duration as a measure of volatility is linear, additive, and symmetric.

For example, the price of a stock is currently at $50. The price goes up to $75 for a gain of 50 percent, and the price drops to $50 from $75 for a loss of 33.33 percent. The percentage changes are nonsymmetric. The additive property of duration implies that the duration of the portfolio is the simple weighted average of the duration of individual assets in the portfolio, as each asset is weighted by the market value, not the book value, against the total market value of the portfolio. The symmetric property of duration implies that the extent of the exposure to the bond portfolio as a result of changes in the yield for plus or minus, say, 100 basis points will be the same. The exposure is defined in Equation 6.6 as the changes in the market value of the portfolio of assets or liabilities as $\Delta P = P_t - P_{t-1}$, which is related linearly to duration of the portfolio (D_p) as well as to the market value of the portfolio (P) and to the changes in the yield (ΔY):

$$\Delta P = -D_p \times P \times \Delta Y \qquad (6.6)$$

$\Delta P = -$(modified duration) (market value of the portfolio) (change in yield)

Example: Horizon bond portfolio currently has a market value of $350 million with a modified duration of 9.375 years. The portfolio manager is expecting rates to go up as the outlook of higher growth for the economy is improving. Therefore, the portfolio manager is contemplating shortening the duration of its portfolio to seven years, assuming she is expecting a 50 basis point increase in the yield in the next three to six months. The amount of the exposure for this portfolio is symmetrical and expressed as follows:

$$\Delta P = -9.375\ (\$350{,}000{,}000)\ (+/- .0050)$$
$$\Delta P = +/- \$16{,}406{,}250$$

This portfolio is expected to *decrease* or *increase* in value in excess of $16.4 million for a 50 basis point increase or decrease in the yield because the yield and price are inversely related. When the yield changes are small, duration provides an estimate of the exposure that is close to actual changes in the market value of the portfolio; however, when the yield changes are large, duration under-estimates the actual changes in the price of a bond when the bond price changes in either direction.

Dollar value of one (DVO1) basis point can be estimated using Equation 6.6 for a bond or portfolio of credits. For example, DVO1 for this portfolio is:

$$\Delta P = -9.375 \ (\$350,000,000) \ (+/-.0001)$$
$$= +/- \$328,125$$

The portfolio value is expected to change by $+/-\$328,125$ for every one basis point change in the yield. DVO1 conveys useful information to a portfolio manager, as some proprietary Web sites, such as Bloomberg and Reuters, report these statistics for their member clients.

Consider the three bonds in Exhibit 6.7 the forecasted percentage price changes based on duration and actual percentage price changes for plus or minus 100 basis points change in the yield.

The 20-year pure zero coupon bond has the highest price volatility as reflected in the modified duration of 18.87 years. The actual percentage price change for this bond is -17.60 and $+21.49$ percent respectively for $+/-100$ basis points change in the yield as seen in Exhibit 6.7. The forecast based on duration predicts that the price is expected to change by $+/-18.57$ percent for every 1 percent change in the yield. The duration alone is not sufficient to capture the percentage change in price of bond due to convexity of this bond.[8]

Similarly, the 20-year bond in Exhibit 6.7 has more convexity than the other two bonds, as reflected in the actual price changes for $+/-100$ basis points change in the yield when compared to the other two bonds. The convexity captures the curvature of the price yield relationship, as bond A in Exhibit 6.6 enjoys higher convexity (positive) compared to bond B. The price of the positively convex bond is expected to increase more for a decrease in yield, while the price is expected to drop less in the event of an increase in the yield than a bond with smaller or no convexity.

EXHIBIT 6.7 Actual and Forecasted Percentage Price Changes Based on Duration

Maturity	Coupon	Yield	Price	Modified Duration	Actual % price change for bps +100	Actual % price change for bps -100[a]
3	6	6	1,000	2.67	-2.66	+2.75
20	0	6	306.55	18.87	-17.60	+21.49
25	6	9	703.57	10.62	-9.76	+11.60

[a] Actual percentage price changes are estimated as $(P_n - P_i)/P_i$
where
P_n = new price of the bond
P_i = initial price of the bond

For example, for 3- and 25-year coupon-paying bonds, the actual percentage price changes and the forecast of the percentage price changes based on their respective duration are approximately close, as shown in Exhibit 6.7. For example, the price of a 25-year coupon-paying bond is expected to change by +/– 10.62 percent as reflected in its duration. However, the actual percentage price changes of this bond are respectively −9.76 and +11.6 percent for +/– 100 basis point change in the yield, as seen in Exhibit 6.7.

APPROXIMATE DURATION

When the yield changes are small, the forecast price based on duration is nearly the same as the actual price, as shown in Exhibit 6.6. However, the forecast error increases as changes in yield become substantial. The changes in the yield in reality are relatively small in the market, and approximate duration (D_a) in Equation 6.7 provides a reasonable estimate of the exposure to bond or bond portfolio:

$$D_a = \frac{(P^+ - P^-)}{(2\, P_i\, \Delta Y)} \tag{6.7}$$

where

P^+ = new price of bond when yield increases
P^- = new price of the bond when yield decreases
P_i = initial price of the bond

The approximate duration estimated using Equation 6.7 for the bonds in Exhibit 6.7 is shown in Exhibit 6.8.

With the exception of the long-term 20-year pure zero coupon bond, the approximate duration provides a reasonable estimate of bond volatility. This procedure will be employed throughout the remainder of the book. When the yield changes are relatively high, duration and convexity combined can be used to measure the exposure to the bond or the bond portfolio. Equation 6.8 defines the percentage change in price due to duration and convexity.

$$\Delta P/P = -(\text{modified duration})\,(\text{change in yield}) + \tfrac{1}{2}\,(\text{convexity})$$
$$(\text{change in yield})^2$$

$$\Delta P/P = -D_p \times \Delta Y + \tfrac{1}{2}C \times (\Delta Y)^2 \tag{6.8}$$

EXHIBIT 6.8 Estimates of Approximate Duration

Maturity	Coupon	Yield	Price	Modified Duration	Approximate Duration
3	6	6	1000	2.67	2.709
20	0	6	306.55	18.87	19.54
25	6	9	703.57	10.62	10.68

where
   C = convexity of the bond
   (Other parameters were defined previously.)

The approximate convexity (C_a) is defined in Equation 6.9.

$$C_a = \frac{[(P^+ + P^-) - 2\,P_i]}{P_i\,(\Delta Y)^2} \tag{6.9}$$

The approximate convexity for the 20-year zero coupon bond for $+/-100$ basis points change in the yield is:

$$C_a = \frac{[(252.56 + 372.42) - 2 \times 306.55]}{(306.55)\,(.01)^2}$$

$$= 387.53$$

The percentage change in price due to duration and convexity in Equation 6.8 for the 20-year zero coupon bond will be equal to

$$\Delta P/P = -18.51(+/-.01) + \tfrac{1}{2}\,(387.53)\,(.01)^2$$

$$= +/-.1851 + .0194$$

$$= +.2045, -.1657$$

The actual convexity of this bond is equal to 386.47.[9] The percentage price changes due to duration and convexity combined are respectively $+.2045$ and $-.1657$, which is a substantial improvement over the estimates provided by duration alone in Exhibit 6.7.

PRICING TREASURY BILL FUTURES

Thirteen-week T-bill futures are priced as zero coupon instruments as a pure discount bond sold at discount from its face value of $1 million. The discount was defined in Equation 6.2; it is a function of forward interest rate, time to expiration in year, and face value. T-bill futures contracts provide delivery of 13-week T-bills at settlement and a face value of $1 million. The T-bill delivered by the party with a short position can be a new or seasoned issue. For example, a T-bill futures contract to be settled in six months requires that the party with a short position deliver six months from now a T-bill with a face value of $1 million and 13 weeks remaining to expiration.

For example, consider a T-bill futures contract at the CBOT with an IMM index of 98.125 (forward interest rate of $100 - 98.125$, 1.875 percent). The invoice price of T-bill futures is provided in Equation 6.10.

$$\text{Invoice Price} = \$1,000,000 - .01875 \left(\frac{91}{360}\right) (\$1,000,000)$$

$$= \$995,260.41 \tag{6.10}$$

Currently the minimum price "tick" is equal to 1/2 basis point, and the duration of the 13-week zero coupon bond is equal to its maturity of .25 year. Using Equation 6.6, the change in price of the T-bill future is estimated as:

$$\Delta P = -.25\ (\$1{,}000{,}000)\ (+/-.00005)$$
$$= +/-\$12.5$$

The T-bill futures have a DVO1 of $25, as can be verified using Equation 6.6:

$$\Delta P = -.25\ (\$1{,}000{,}000)\ (+/-.0001)$$
$$= +/-\$25$$

EURODOLLAR FUTURES

Eurodollars are time deposits denominated in U.S. dollars that are deposited in banks outside the United States. The rate on these deposits serves as a benchmark interest rate for corporate funding. The Eurodollar futures contract, developed by CME in 1981, represents a forward interest rate on a three-month deposit of $1 million. The Eurodollar futures contract is now the most actively traded futures contract in the world. Open interest has recently surpassed 4 million contracts.

The measurement of exposure in the futures market for changes in the forward rates as they affect the price of various futures is similar to the convention employed in the spot market. For example, the price of 90-day Eurodollar futures for one "tick"—1/4 basis point change in the yield—is expected to change by $6.25 in either direction as can be verified from Equation 6.6[10]:

$$\Delta P = -.25\ (\$1{,}000{,}000)\ (+/-.000025)$$
$$= +/-\$6.25$$

The exchange allows for the minimum price change of $12.5 in either direction for longer-term Eurodollars. It should be noted that duration of the zeros is always equal to its maturity. Ninety-day Eurodollar or T-bill futures have a face value of $1 million by institutional arrangement and a duration of .25 years by definition.

The IMM index, as defined in Chapter 1, is used to provide the market estimate of the forward interest rate as the difference of 100 minus IMM index:

$$\text{Forward Rate} = 100 - \text{IMM index}$$

August to December futures on the Eurodollar quotation in Exhibit 6.9 from the CME at the last settlement price has the IMM index of 98.175, 98.18, 98.14, 98.12, and 98.065. These index numbers translate to the forward interest rates of 1.825, 1.82, 1.86, 1.88, and 1.935 percent for the various futures contracts. For example, the 90-day October futures price for Eurodollar futures per $100 face value and the IMM index of 98.14 is equal to:

$$100 - .0186\ (.25)\ (100) = 99.535$$

EXHIBIT 6.9   Eurodollar Futures

globex® quotes as of 07/23/02 04:10 P.M. (CST)

| MTH/ | SESSION | | | | PT | EST | PRIOR DAY | | |
STRIKE	OPEN	HIGH	LOW	LAST	SETT	CHGE	VOL	SETT	VOL	VOL
AUG02	98.1625	98.1625	98.155	98.16B	—	−1.5	394	98.175	3289	54509
SEP02	98.185	98.235	98.15	98.235	—	+5.5	9006	98.18	92103	672000
OCT02	—	—	—	—	—	UNCH		98.14	810	7812
NOV02	—	—	—	—	—	UNCH		98.12	25	2594
DEC02	98.07	98.15	97.995	98.13	—	+6.5	7813	98.065	149271	661728

The price of 90-day Eurodollar futures is equal to $995,350 per $1 million face value. There are some differences between Eurodollar and T-bill futures contracts:

- T-bill futures contract price traded at IMM in Chicago at maturity approaches a $1 million face value of the underlying futures contract as if the party with long position (the party that purchased the T-bill futures) will take delivery of the T-bill at maturity. However, the Eurodollar futures is settled at maturity in cash based on the Eurodollar rate (R) prevailing on the second London business day before the third Wednesday of the month. For example, if the 90-day Eurodollar deposit rate at settlement date is equal to 2.125 percent, then the final marking to market will set the contract price by Equation 6.11:

$$10,000 (100 - .25\ R)$$
$$10,000 (100 - .25\ (2.125)) = \$994,687.50$$

(6.11)

- The Eurodollar futures contract is a contract based on interest rates (Eurodollar futures deposit rate), while the T-bill futures contract is based on the price of the T-bill or discount rate. Eurodollar futures are used to estimate the zero coupon LIBOR rates with maturities up to 10 years.

Delivery Process

This is a three-day process involving three parties in the T-notes and T-bond futures. They are the party with long position (the buyer), the party with short position (the seller), and the clearinghouse. The party with the short position can initiate delivery by serving notice to the clearinghouse at any time that begins two business days prior to the first business day of the delivery month and ends two business days before the last business day of the month. The three-day process is:

Day 1. The short serves notice of intention for delivery to the clearinghouse, known as positions day.

Day 2. The clearinghouse notifies both long and short and matches the oldest long to the short that is expected to deliver and invoice the long, known as notice of intention day.

Day 3. The short delivers the cheapest-to-deliver issue to long; in return, the long makes payment to the short and assumes title to the instrument.

Delivery Options

Identification of the deliverable instrument that satisfies the exchange requirements as well as the requirement of the party with the short position which should be the cheapest instrument to be delivered, known as quality option.

Timing Option

This option is afforded to the party with short position the timing in delivery month to deliver.

Wild Card Option

This is the option to deliver after the closing bell at 2 P.M. CST, until 8 P.M. if prices in the T-bond spot drops and the party with short position proceeds to purchase the cheapest issue for delivery.

All three options granted to the party with short position are not provided for free; therefore, the futures price will be lower by the value of these options.

TREASURY NOTES FUTURES

There are three types of futures: 2, 5, and 10 year. The underlying instrument for the two-year futures is a $200,000 par value T-note with no more than two years or no less than 21 months remaining to maturity.

The underlying instruments for the five-year T-notes is a bond with $100,000 par value with an original and remaining maturity of no more than five years and three months and maturity of no less than four years and three months.

The underlying instruments for 10-year T-notes is a bond with a 6 percent hypothetical $100,000 par value T-note with a maturity that is not less than 6.5 years and not greater than 10 years from the delivery date. The delivery options allow the party with the short position to deliver from the set of acceptable T-notes the notes that are the cheapest-to-deliver issue. Exhibit 6.10 presents the CBOT's mechanism for conversion factors for various types of issues in standardizing contracts.

The party with a short position receives:

(Quoted futures price × conversion factor) + accrued interest

The cheapest-to-deliver T-bond is estimated by the party with the short position as the issue from among the acceptable issues having the highest implied

EXHIBIT 6.10 Conversion Factors for
6 Percent Treasury Bonds
Acceptable for Delivery to Meet
the June 2002 Futures Contract

Maturity	Coupon	Conversion Factor
11/15/28	$5\frac{1}{4}$	0.9014
02/15/29	$5\frac{1}{4}$	0.9011
02/15/31	$5\frac{3}{8}$	0.9152
08/15/28	$5\frac{1}{2}$	0.9346
02/15/26	6	1.0000
11/15/27	$6\frac{1}{8}$	1.0160
08/15/29	$6\frac{1}{8}$	1.0166
08/15/23	$6\frac{1}{4}$	1.0296
05/15/30	$6\frac{1}{4}$	1.0335
08/15/27	$6\frac{3}{8}$	1.0482
11/15/26	$6\frac{1}{2}$	1.0633
02/15/27	$6\frac{5}{8}$	1.0797
08/15/26	$6\frac{3}{4}$	1.0948
08/15/25	$6\frac{7}{8}$	1.1084
02/15/23	$7\frac{1}{8}$	1.1317
08/15/22	$7\frac{1}{4}$	1.1445
11/15/24	$7\frac{1}{2}$	1.1828
11/15/22	$7\frac{5}{8}$	1.1889
02/15/25	$7\frac{5}{8}$	1.1992
02/15/21	$7\frac{7}{8}$	1.2078
11/15/21	8	1.2264
08/15/19	$8\frac{1}{8}$	1.2245
05/15/21	$8\frac{1}{8}$	1.2371
08/15/21	$8\frac{1}{8}$	1.2390
02/15/20	$8\frac{1}{2}$	1.2686
05/15/20	$8\frac{3}{4}$	1.2977
08/15/20	$8\frac{3}{4}$	1.3002
08/15/17	$8\frac{7}{8}$	1.2818
02/15/19	$8\frac{7}{8}$	1.2985
11/15/18	9	1.3085
05/15/18	$9\frac{1}{8}$	1.3154

Source: Chicago Board of Trade, June 26, 2002.

repo rate and makes delivery at settlement date. The party with the short position pays to purchase the T-bond:

$$\text{Quoted price} + \text{Accrued interest}$$

The ratio of what the party with a short position receives and pays is equal to one plus the implied repo rate the short earns, similar to the repo rate (the dealer pays) that is implied in a contract where a government security dealer borrows (sell short) to finance the purchase of Treasury securities with an agreement to repurchase the issue from the buyer some time in the future at a higher price. That is, the ratio of quoted futures price × conversion factor/quoted spot price can be interpreted as one plus the implied repo rate.

Example: The quoted futures price is $105-23$. Three bonds with their price and respective conversion factors are provided. Which bond is the cheapest to deliver?

Bond	Price	Conversion Factor
A	127.625	1.308
B	120.25	1.2264
C	110	1.1317

The cheapest to deliver is bond C, producing an implied repo rate of 8.77 percent. The repo rates for bonds A and B, respectively, are equal to 7.82 and 8.35 percent.

TREASURY BOND FUTURES

The underlying instrument is a 20-year hypothetical bond with $100,000 par value and 6 percent coupon that is quoted at 32nds of 1 percent similar to the Treasury spot. That is, the quote of $103-14$ per $100 face value is equal to $103 14/32, or $103.4375. The minimum price changes are equal to 1/32, or $31.25 per $100,000 (see Exhibit 6.11). Any bond with a maturity of over 15 years and not callable within 15 years is acceptable for delivery purposes.

Example: Consider a quoted futures price is equal to $95-08$. The conversion factor for this bond is 1.425 and the bond has $2.5 accrued interest per $100 face value at delivery. The cash paid by the party with the long position and the cash received by the party with short position is equal to:

$$\text{Cash received by the short seller} = 95.25 \times 1.425 + 2.5$$
$$= \$138.231$$

The party with short position in one contract delivers a bond with $100,000 face value and receives $138,231.

At the settlement date of T-bond futures, the seller of the futures contract is required to deliver a 6 percent 20-year hypothetical bond with face value of $100,000. In reality, such a bond may not exist at delivery, and the CBOT

EXHIBIT 6.11 Interest Rate Futures

Interest Rate Futures

Treasury Bonds (CBT)-$100,000; pts 32nds of 100%

Sept	107-12	107-15	106-23	107-01	-16	109-00	96-07	393,067
Dec	105-22	106-06	105-18	105-26	-16	107-00	96-06	48,582

Est vol 164,352; vol Wed 212,429; open int 441,731, -1,904.

Treasury Notes (CBT)-$100,000; pts 32nds of 100%

Sept	111-31	11-315	11-125	11-145	-20.0	112-24	100-25	855,825
Dec	10-045	110-16	10-005	10-025	-20.0	11-055	99-31	146,744

Est vol 355,885; vol Wed 575,534; open int 1,002,572, +30,015.

10 Yr Agency Notes (CBT)-$100,000; pts 32nds of 100%

Sept	107-00	107-09	06-255	106-29	-15.0	107-27	97-19	24,057

Est vol 531; vol Wed 2,138; open int 24,057, -168.

5 Yr Treasury Notes (CBT)-$100,000; pts 32nds of 100%

Sept	111-20	111-20	111-05	11-065	-15.0	112-02	102-17	616,444

Est vol 152,775; vol Wed 219,430; open int 631,841, -9,983.

2 Yr Treasury Notes (CBT)-$200,000; pts 32nds of 100%

Sept	07-012	07-012	06-247	106-26	-7.7	107-07	103-11	106,180

Est vol 7,282; vol Wed 4,857; open int 106,180, +1,520.

30 Day Federal Funds (CBT)-$5,000,000; pts of 100%

Aug	98.310	98.310	98.285	98.295	-.015	98.400	97.465	47,958
Sept	98.39	98.39	98.28	98.35	-.04	98.43	97.27	41,904
Oct	98.47	98.47	98.42	98.43	-.04	98.48	97.75	34,735
Nov	98.51	98.51	98.46	98.47	-.04	98.52	97.56	12,249
Dec	98.52	98.53	98.48	98.49	-.05	98.55	96.60	22,084
Ja03	98.50	98.52	98.47	98.48	-.08	98.58	96.29	3,634

Est vol 23,920; vol Wed 31,981; open int 169,619, +5,542.

10 Yr Interest Rate Swaps (CBT)-$100,000; pts 32nds of 100%

Sept	107-19	108-03	107-19	107-25	-13	108-16	100-08	29,930

Est vol 625; vol Wed 1,094; open int 29,930, +481.

Muni Bond Index (CBT)-$1,000; times Bond Buyer MBI

Sept	105-12	105-25	105-11	105-18	-12	107-03	102-01	4,036

Est vol 205; vol Wed 456; open int 4,036, -56.
Index: Close 106-18; Yield 5.23.

	OPEN	HIGH	LOW	SETTLE	CHG	YIELD	CHG	OPEN INT

Treasury Bills (CME)-$1,000,000; pts of 100%

	OPEN	HIGH	LOW	SETTLE	CHG	YIELD	CHG	OPEN INT
Sept	...	...	...	98.51	-.02	1.49	.02	674

Est vol 0; vol Wed 5; open int 674, -3.

Libor-1 Mo. (CME)-$3,000,000; pts of 100%

	OPEN	HIGH	LOW	SETTLE	CHG	YIELD	CHG	OPEN INT
Aug	98.24	98.25	98.22	98.22	-.02	1.78	.03	21,109
Sept	98.30	98.32	98.28	98.28	-.03	1.72	.03	10,986
Oct	98.34	98.35	98.34	98.35	-.04	1.65	.04	4,453
Nov	98.40	98.40	98.36	98.36	-.03	1.64	.03	3,861
Dec	98.35	98.35	98.30	98.32	-.05	1.68	.05	1,587

Est vol 3,506; vol Wed 6,764; open int 46,254, -500.

Eurodollar (CME)-$1,000,000; pts of 100%

	OPEN	HIGH	LOW	SETTLE	CHG	YIELD	CHG	OPEN INT
Aug	98.28	98.30	98.27	98.27	-.02	1.73	.02	53,825
Sept	98.34	98.35	98.30	98.31	-.03	1.69	.03	730,710
Oct	98.35	98.37	98.32	98.32	-.05	1.68	.05	19,514
Nov	98.36	98.37	98.32	98.32	-.05	1.68	.05	3,352
Dec	98.38	98.37	98.30	98.32	-.05	1.68	.05	705,192
Ja03	98.34	98.34	98.29	98.30	-.05	1.70	.05	1,297
Mar	98.25	98.25	98.14	98.18	-.08	1.82	.08	632,572
June	97.93	97.94	97.81	97.82	-.12	2.18	.12	439,814
Sept	97.47	97.48	97.35	97.37	-.14	2.63	.14	377,225
Dec	96.99	97.00	96.86	96.88	-.16	3.12	.16	284,318
Mr04	96.50	96.56	96.43	96.46	-.14	3.54	.14	183,598
June	96.18	96.23	96.10	96.12	-.12	3.88	.12	163,630
Sept	95.88	95.96	95.86	95.88	-.09	4.12	.09	127,202

Source: Wall Street Journal, July 20, 2002.

conversion convention shown in Exhibit 6.10 can be used to determine which bond is to be delivered. Economics dictates that the party with the short position buy back the security it sold short. Therefore, it has to identify the bond that meets the requirements set by the exchange and is the least expensive bond, that is, the cheapest-to-deliver issue, using a procedure similar to the one described for Treasury notes.

The party with a short position is granted the time in which the actual delivery will take place in the delivery month, which is known as timing option or wild card play. The party with a short position has until 8 P.M. to issue notice of intention for delivery of the cheapest bond to the clearinghouse. Once the notice is served, the settlement price at the closing at 2 P.M., when the trading in the CBOT T-bond futures ceases, will be used as the invoice price. The T-bond spot continues to trade until 4 P.M.

The wild card option gives the right to the party with a short position to proceed with the delivery. If the price of bond declines after 2 P.M. CST and the individual proceeds to buy the cheapest to deliver the bond for settlement. However, if the price of bond does not go down, the party with the wild card option continues to keep the position open until the following day and proceeds with the strategy just described. The delivery options embedded in the futures contract make it difficult for the party with the long position to determine which Treasury bond will be delivered or when it will be delivered.

CONVERSION FACTOR

The CBOT calculates the conversion factor for bonds of varying maturities and coupons as shown in Exhibit 6.10. Let us verify the conversion factor for the issue that will expire on May 15, 2018, with a coupon of 9 1/8: This issue has 16 years and 43 days to maturity as of June 26, 2002. The present value of the cash flow for this bond, assuming that the bond pays semiannual coupon, has exactly 16 years to maturity, and a yield of 6 percent, is shown in Equation 6.12:

$$P = \frac{\sum\limits_{t=1}^{32} (4.5625)}{(1+.03)^t} + \frac{(100)}{(1+.03)^{32}} \qquad (6.12)$$
$$= 131.85$$

Normalizing the present value of the cash flow by the face value (here assumed to be $100) gives us the conversion factor of 1.3185. The conversion factor that is estimated by CBOT for this issue is 1.3154 in Exhibit 6.10. The difference between the two figures reflects the 41 days of accrued interest and the actual date in which the first coupon is expected. Alternatively, the conversion factor of 1.3185 needs to be adjusted downward by the 41 days of interest:

$$\frac{1.3185}{1.0067} = 1.3097$$

Example: Pricing Treasury Bond Futures. The price of T-bond futures is related to the underlying spot price minus the present value of any income and/or royalties (i.e., dividend or interest income) that accrues to the owner of the spot until delivery date and minus the value of any options embedded in the futures contract (i.e., delivery options). To underscore the dynamics of both futures and spot markets and the pricing that emerges, let us look at the actual price for various Treasury spot and futures:

	02 Sep	02 Dec
2-year	106–155	106–177
5-year	110–15	109–190
10-year	110–250	109–130
30-year	105–23	104–17

Source: CBOT Price of Treasury Futures, July 26, 2002, 9 A.M. CST.

	Coupon	Price
2-year	2.25	100–01
5-year	4.375	104–08+
10-year	4.875	103–25
30-year	5.375	100–26+

Source: www.Bloomberg.com, Spot Price for Treasury Securities, July 26, 2002, 10:01 A.M. EDT.

The price for the two-year September futures is equal to $106.4844, while the spot two year is priced at 100 1/32. The differences in the cash and futures price reflect the coupon interest among other things. According to CBOT, the two-year 2.25 percent bond, assuming 6 percent interest, has a conversion factor equal to .9358 as of September 2002. Therefore, the party with short position invoices the party with the long position the product of the current quoted futures on September 2002 futures as of June 26 that is $106.4844 with a conversion factor of .9358 is equal to $99.648. Likewise five-year December futures are priced at $109.5938, while the five-year spot is priced at 104–08+, translating to $104 plus 8/32 and adding 1/64 for the + sign by the Wall Street convention. So 104–08+ = $104 17/64 = $104.2656.

The yield to maturity that is reflected in the cash market for the five-year bond is 3.4391 percent. The futures yield corresponding for this issue on a 6 percent bond is equal to 3.8711 percent.

Five steps can be used to determine the futures price of T-bonds:

1. Adjust the current price of the cheapest-to-deliver bond that has already been identified by the short for the accrued coupon interest income:

$$\text{Invoice price} = \text{Spot price} + \text{Accrued interest}$$

2. Estimate the present value of coupon interest that accrues to the party with the long position up until the delivery time.

3. Subtract step 2 from step 1 and compound the result over the delivery period at the interest rate for the bond in step 1 and over the number of days that delivery will take place from the current time as seen in Equation 6.13.

$$F = (S - PV \text{ of coupon}) (1 + R^*) \tag{6.13}$$

where

S = cash price of Treasury adjusted upward for the accrued interest in step 1

PV of coupon = present value of coupon interest, if any, received between current time and time before delivery discounted at the yield to maturity

F = current futures price

4. Adjust the price of the futures (F) downward from the last coupon to the next coupon after delivery.

5. Divide the step 4 futures price by the conversion factor for the cheapest-to-deliver bond to provide the estimate of the current futures quote.

Example: It is July 26, 2002. Suppose the cheapest-to-deliver bond in a September 2002 T-bond futures contract is a 9.125 percent coupon bond priced at $130.92 with a conversion factor of 1.3154, and delivery is expected to take place by September 28, 2002. Coupon payments are made April 15 and October 15 of each year. Assuming the yield to maturity is 6 percent, semiannual compounding and flat term structure, what is the estimate of the quoted futures price?

Coupon payment	Current time		Maturity of futures	Coupon payment
	103 days	63 days	17 days	
April 15	July 26		Sept. 28	Oct. 15

The last coupon was in 103 days, and the next coupon will be in 80 days. The invoice price is therefore:

$$130.92 + 4.5625 \left(\frac{103}{183}\right) = \$133.49$$

Since the coupon interest is not due to be received from the current time until delivery date, the current or cash futures price (F) is equal to Equation 6.13 with a zero present value of coupon compounded for duration of the futures contract that is 63 days in this example.

$$133.49 \left[1 + .\left(06 \times \left(\frac{63}{365}\right)\right)\right] = \$134.87$$

There is no accrued interest at delivery, since no coupon was received after July 26. Dividing this price by the conversion factor of 1.3154 produces the current quoted futures price (*F*) as of July 26:

$$\frac{134.87}{1.3154} = 102.53$$

ARBITRAGE IN THE INTEREST RATES FUTURES MARKET

The tremendous growth of the futures market may be attributed to the success of the various contracts that continue to come to market in transferring risk from one party to another. Price of the futures, although very volatile at times, more or less represents the collective market consensus in evaluating various macro- or microinformation as it pertains to particular contracts. The opportunities for short-term arbitrage profit push the price of various instruments toward the fair value. The market appears to be more efficient than critics argue.

Innovations are the key in this market, as the derivatives market seeks to debut alternative products that appeal to certain segments of the market and allows risk takers and risk-averse individuals and institutions to mitigate and transfer risk. The market for derivatives is rational, despite behavior that at times appears completely irrational to would-be investors, arbitrageurs, and/or speculators.

PRICING SYNTHETIC FUTURES OR FORWARD

Suppose an underlying instrument currently priced at *S* has zero storage cost (as negative yield), pays a known dividend (has positive convenience yield, i.e., coupon-paying bond, dividend-paying stock, foreign currency that can be invested to earn foreign interest rates, and any other instrument that can be used for consumption or investment purposes by liquidating to take advantage of the favorable price changes), and the interest rate that one can borrow is equal to 4 percent. The three–month futures or forward price of this instrument will be:

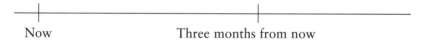

Now   Three months from now

The party who buys three months forward (*F*) is not entitled to any of the costs (storage or insurance) or benefits (convenience yields) associated with the underlying instrument directly. However, indirectly the price of the spot (*S*) has to be adjusted upward for any cost (storage, insurance, and other costs) as denoted by *Z* over the three months and adjusted downward over the three months for the income, royalties, and dividend as denoted by *I* as defined in Equation 6.14.

$$F = (S + Z - I)\,(1 + R)^{t/365} \qquad (6.14)$$

If the storage cost and dividend or interest income is a percentage of the spot price as denoted by Z and I, then this relationship can be restated in Equation 6.15 in continuous time as:

$$F = Se^{(R + Z - I)t} \qquad (6.15)$$

where

$e = 2.7183$
(other parameters are as defined)

Example: Spot price is currently $100 for a dividend-paying instrument with a dividend (I) of $.30 and storage cost ($Z$) of $.25. The interest rate is 4 percent per annum and discrete annual compounding. The price of 90-day futures is estimated using Equation 6.14.

$$F = (100 + .25 - .30)(1 + .04)^{90//364}$$
$$= \$100.92$$

Any deviation from this price indicates that the law of one price is violated and leads to a riskless arbitrage profit.

Suppose our synthetic three-month forward is priced at $103.

> Sell short forward at $103.
> Borrow $100 at 4 percent.
> Purchase spot bond at $100.

In three months, as t approaches zero, forward contract price in Equation 6.14 approaches the price of the spot as $S = F - Z + I$. However, the forward was sold short at 103. At the settlement of the forward contract we have this cash flow:

> $F = \$103$
> $-Z + I = .05$
> Total cash flow $= F - Z + I = \$103.05$
>
> Total outlay for the loan including the interest:
> $100 borrowed to purchase the bond
> $1 interest over 90 days
> Total outlay $= \$101$
> Profit $=$ Cash flow $-$ Outlay
> $\quad\quad\; = \$2.05$

This strategy pays off no matter what the forward or futures price will be in 90 days and involves no initial cash outlay.

However, suppose the forward price is equal to $97.50. In this case it pays to buy the forward and sell short the spot at $100 and invest the proceeds at 4 percent over three months:

> Buy the futures at 97.50.

Sell short the bond at 100.

Invest 100 for three months at 4 percent.

The arbitrageur has $101 cash flow from the settlement of short spot and invests it at 4 percent:

$100

$1

Cash flow = $101

The outlay for the purchase of the forward is $97.50, and .05 dividend net of storage, that can be used to buy back the shorted spot. In 90 days the price of the forward again approaches the spot, which is equal to $S = F - Z + I$. However, the price was negotiated at 97.50, and the total outlay will then be equal to:

$F = \$97.50$. Arbitrageur pays in 90 days to purchase the bond at the settlement date.

$-Z + I = .05$. Arbitrageur pays for storage and receives the income.

Total outlay = $F - Z + I = \$97.55$

Profit = Cash flow − Outlay

= $\$101 - \$97.55 = \$3.45$

The riskless arbitrage profit has to be equal to zero in a competitive market if prices are determined competitively and the law of one price is not violated. The price of $100.92 is considered as a zero arbitrage profit on the forward contract no matter if the arbitrageur takes a long or short position in the forward contract priced competitively. Suppose the arbitrageur shorts the forward and at the settlement the forward contract approaches the spot price of $F - Z + I$, the cash flow can be computed:

$F = 100.92$

$-Z + I = \$.05$

Total cash flow = $100.97

The total outlay to borrow 100 at 4 percent over 90 days to buy the spot will be:

$100, spot price

$.97 interest over 90 days

Total outlay = $100.97

Arbitrage profit = 0

Similarly, assume the arbitrageur follows the opposite strategy of buying the forward at $100.92 and shorting the spot and investing the proceeds at 4 percent. The cash flow and outlay will be:

$100, selling the spot

$.97 interests earned over 90 day at 4 percent

Total cash flow = $100.97

At the settlement of the forward contract in 90 days, the arbitrageur pays the forward contract that is agreed earlier as well as any accrued interest will be:

100.92, price of the forward in 90 days

.05 Accrued interest net of storage

Total outlay = $100.97

Arbitrage profit = 0

Example: The spot gold price is currently at $300/ounce. The Canadian Central Bank is contemplating leasing 300,000 ounces of gold to Barrick at the lease rate of 3.75 percent. Barrick intends to sell the leased gold at the current price and invest the proceeds for six months at the Canadian T-bill rate of 5 percent. At the end of six months Barrick expects to have extracted enough gold to return the lease to the Canadian Central Bank. What is the six-month gold futures (forward) price, assuming storage and other costs are zero?

Using Equation 6.15, the six-month forward price of the dividend-paying gold can be determined as:

$$F = 300 \, e^{\,(.05 + 0 - .0375)\,.5}$$

where

t = .5 year

e = 2.7183

F = $301.89

HEDGING WITH FUTURES: DURATION-BASED APPROACH

Assuming the change in yield is parallel and zero convexity, the change in the price of the interest-bearing futures and spot from Equation 6.6 is:

$$\Delta F = -D_f \times F \times \Delta Y$$
$$\Delta S = -D_s \times S \times \Delta Y$$

where

F = contract price of the futures

D_f = duration of the futures

D_s = duration of the spot

S = market value of the spot

R_f = yield on the futures (the forward rate)

R_s = yield on the spot portfolio

The number of futures contract (h) (the hedge ratio $\Delta S/\Delta F$ shown in Equation 6.16) that is required to hedge spot portfolio is equal to:

$$h = \frac{[D_s \times S \times (1 + R_f)]}{[D_f \times F \times (1 + R_s)]} \tag{6.16}$$

The relationship derived in Equation 6.16 as the hedge ratio ($\Delta S/\Delta F$) is predicated on the assumption that the durations (spot and futures) need to be capitalized by the respective yields in the spot and futures markets. In essence, the modified durations are to be used in arriving at the hedge ratio in Equation 6.16.

Example: Short Hedge. It is July 20 and the portfolio manager is expecting to borrow $27 million in three months over a 180-day period. The portfolio manager is expecting that the interest rate in three months will go up and the cost of financing the 180-day funding will increase. Therefore, he wishes to sell December futures short to hedge against the possible increase in the yield. The choice of which futures contract to use for hedging is important in insulating the changes in the spot market interest rate as well as the amount of the spot to be hedged (the hedge ratio).

The choices are numerous, ranging from T-bill futures to T-notes, T-bond futures, and Eurodollar futures. The choices involving various Treasury issues reflect the forward or futures interest rates on government funding, while the Eurodollar interest rates reflect the time deposit rate on offshore private banks. The futures contract to be used is the Eurodollar December futures in Exhibit 6.11 that is quoted at 98.32, translating to 1.68 percent Eurodollar futures interest rate, as this futures contract is the most liquid of all the futures traded.

The short hedge in the futures market is expected to produce profit if the rates go up as expected. In the spot market, the portfolio manager is expected to pay higher interest rates to acquire the needed funds. However, the short hedge will produce a loss if the rates drop, because the short position has to be covered at a higher price. In the spot market, the portfolio manager is expected to borrow the needed funds at a lower interest rate. The proceeds of the 90-day Eurodollar futures per $1 million contract size is equal to:

$$\$1,000,000 - .25(1.68\%)\,(1,000,000) = \$995,800$$
$$D_s = .5 \text{ year}$$
$$D_f = .25$$
$$R_f = 1.68 \text{ percent}$$

Assuming the current spot interest rate is equal to:

$$R_s = 1.85 \text{ percent}$$

The number of futures contracts to be shorted is derived using Equation 6.16 as the hedge ratio:

$$h = \frac{\left[.5 \times \$27,000,000 \times \left(1 + \dfrac{.0168}{4}\right)\right]}{.25 \times 995,800 \left(1 + \dfrac{.0185}{4}\right)}$$

$$= 54.20 \text{ contracts; rounded to the nearest number} = 54$$

On October 20, the treasurer issues $27 million commercial paper at a discount of 2.35 percent. The proceeds per 100 will be equal to $100 - .50$

(.0235) (100) = $98.825. The proceeds per $1 million will be $988,250. In total the treasurer raises $26.68275 million by issuing a $27 million nonfinancial commercial paper over a six-month period. The IMM index for Eurodollar futures is 97.6, indicating an interest rate of 2.4 percent. The DVO1 of the Eurodollar futures of $25 is identical to that of T-bill futures, as can be verified from Equation 6.6. The Eurodollar interest rate futures has changed by +72 basis points, resulting in a change in price equal to $72 \times -\$25$ or

$$\Delta F = -D_f \times F \times \Delta Y$$
$$= -.25 \ (1,000,000) \ (+.0072)$$
$$= -\$1,800$$

DVO1 × the number of basis point change in yield = $\Delta F, \Delta S$

$$-\$25 \times 72 = -\$1,800$$

Illustration 6.1 summarizes the results of hedging.

Illustration 6.1

SHORT ANTICIPATORY HEDGE

HEDGING STRATEGY

July 20, 2002, spot market
The six-month commercial paper is rated to yield 1.78 percent
Proceeds per $100: 100 − .5(1.78%) (100) = 99.110
Effective yield $(100/99.11)^{365/180} - 1 = .0183$

Futures Market: December Eurodollar futures IMM index is 98.32
Price per $1 million is 1,000,000 − .25(1.68%) (1,000,000) = $995,800
Implied yield $(100/99.58)^{365/90} - 1 = .0172$
Sell 54 Eurodollar futures contracts

October 20, 2002, spot market
Issue $27 million commercial paper at 2.35 percent
Proceeds per $1 million: is $1,000,000 − .5 (2.35%) (1,000,000) = $988,250
Effective yield $(100/98.825)^{365/180} - 1 = .0243$

Futures Market: December Eurodollar futures IMM index is 97.60
Close out the December futures at interest rate of 2.4 percent
Eurodollar delivery is in cash as opposed to T-bill
The final marking to market on the second London business day before the third Wednesday of the month will set the price per $1,000,000: 10,000 (100 − .25 (2.4)) = $994,000
Buy 54 Eurodollar futures contract

Results

Unhedged position: The effective cost of financing six-month commercial paper will be 2.43 percent on October 20.

Hedged position: Profit on the futures per one contract is $995,800 − $994,000 = $1,800

Total profit 54 × $1,800 = $97,200

The proceeds from the issue of the commercial paper on October 20, $26.682750M

The effective proceeds, the cash proceeds plus the profit in the futures: $26,779,950

Implied yield: $(100/99.185)^{365/180} - 1 = .0167$

The hedge in Illustration 6.1 proved to be successful in keeping the effective cost of financing the commercial paper on October 20 at 1.67 percent as the higher cost of financing on July 20 was offset by the profit realized in the Eurodollar futures market.

Example: Long Hedge. It is January 12 and the treasurer of Realvalue is expecting to receive $4.6 million interest and dividend income from various fixed and variable annuities in the next three months. The treasurer is expecting to invest this fund on the intermediate Treasury securities with maturity of 9.5 years, current yield of 4.4 percent, and priced at 103.65.

The treasurer is expecting the interest rate to fall in the next three months; therefore, she wishes to hedge against falling interest rates in three months by buying T-note futures. Currently June T-notes futures are priced at 109−22 or 109 22/32 (109.6875). Since each contract is for delivery of $100,000 face value, the futures price is $109,687.5 per one contract.

The average duration of the portfolio of spot Treasury notes in three months is expected to be 6.75 years. The cheapest-to-deliver bonds in the T-notes contract is expected to be a 10-year 4.875 percent bond with a conversion factor of .912. Currently the yield on this bond is 4.56 percent per annum, and the duration is expected to be 7.34 years at the maturity of the futures contract.

The hedge ratio from Equation 6.16 is estimated as:

$$h = \frac{\left[6.75 \times 4,600,000 \left(1 + \frac{.0456}{4}\right)\right]}{\left[7.34 \times 109,687.5 \left(1 + \frac{.044}{4}\right)\right]}$$

$$= 38.61, \text{ rounded to 39 contracts}$$

On January 12 the treasurer buys 39 June T-note futures contracts, expecting interest rates to drop in three months. If the rates decline, the $4.6 million proceeds have to be invested at a lower interest rate. However, if the Treasury futures price goes up (rates fall), the treasurer makes a profit in the futures that offsets the potential loss due to falling interest rates. If the rates go up in three months, the proceeds can be invested at higher rates; however, the hedging will become a costly insurance as the futures have to be liquidated for a loss that reduces the yield on the spot portfolio.

On April 12 the treasurer invest $4.6 million on the T-notes. The yield is 4 percent and current price is 107–04, 107.125, or $107,125. The Treasury futures price is 111–08, 111.25, or $111,250 per one contract. The treasurer sells 39 June futures and invoices the party with the long position. Illustration 6.2 describes the results of the hedging.

Illustration 6.2

LONG ANTICIPATORY HEDGE

It is January 12 and the treasurer of Realvalue is expecting to receive $4.6 million interest and dividend income from its fixed and variable annuities in April 19. The treasurer is expecting to invest this fund on the 4.4 percent T-notes priced at 103.65 over 9.5 years.

January 12
Spot market: Spot price is 103.65
Price per note: $1036.5
Buy 4,438 notes to be almost fully invested

Futures market: June futures priced at 109–22
Price per contract: $109,687.5
Buy 39 T-note futures

April 19
Spot price: 107.125
June T-notes futures priced at 113–08
Price per contract: $113,250
Sell 39 contracts

Increase in the cost of T-notes: $4,754,207.5 − $4,599,987 = $154,220.50
Profit in the futures: $3,562.5 × 39 = $139,937.5
90 percent of the increase in the cost of the T-notes was covered by profit in the futures.

The long hedge in Illustration 6.2 was effective in managing exposure to interest rate risk and insulated a 90 percent increase in the cost of buying T-notes. The treasurer would have been able to hedge her exposure to a decrease in interest rates using T-bill or T-bond futures. The choice of which instrument to use for hedging has to be analyzed by the correlation of the spot and underlying futures. When spot and futures move in tandem, the correlation between spot and futures is expected to be close to unity and the futures will be able to insulate the adverse movements in interest rates on the value of the spot. Hedging is intended to reduce or eliminate the potential loss due to an increase or decrease in interest rates, which may increase the cost of the issuing debt or decrease the return from the investment in the near future. Hedging is costly and is not intended to maximize the profit or the value of the firm. Insurance is always costly, but not having it may prove to be very costly and at times disastrous. Regulation and/or institutional arrangements sometimes mandate insurance.

Institutional investors such as insurance companies invest in the market, and their investment is dictated by the nature of their liabilities. For example, life insurance companies invest in the long end of the market, since their liabilities are long term.

Example: It is May 9 and a life insurance company has a portfolio of T-bonds currently valued at $35 million with a current yield of 5.6 percent priced at par, 16 years to maturity, and duration that is expected to be 10.41 years in three months. This portfolio has to be liquidated in the next three months to meet the life insurance obligations. The portfolio manager is exposed to interest rate risk in the next three months and therefore wishes to hedge its portfolio with T-bond futures. The current futures price is 105–23, or 105.7188. Since each contract is for delivery of $100,000 face value, the T-bond futures contract price is $105,718.8.

The cheapest-to-deliver bond in the T-bond futures contract is a 7.25 percent bond with 6 percent conversion factor of 1.1445 with a maturity of 19 years and 9 months. The yield on this bond is 6 percent, and duration will be 11.135 years (the approximate duration derived from Equation 6.7) at the expiration of the futures contract in three months.

The treasurer is concerned about rising interest rates in the next three months and wishes to sell T-bond futures to hedge against such eventuality. If interest rates rise in the next three months, the market value of the spot portfolio is expected to fall by an amount approximately equal to the duration of the spot bond (in this case by 8.75 percent per 100 basis points increase in the yield). However, profit will be realized in the short futures because short will be covered at a lower price. If rates had dropped, the market value of the spot portfolio would be expected to go up by 8.75 percent per 100 basis point decrease in the yield. However, futures have to be covered at higher price for a loss. The number of futures contracts that should be shorted depends on the hedge ratio, which is derived from Equation 6.16.

$$h = \frac{-\left[10.41\,(35{,}000{,}000)\left(1 + \frac{.06}{4}\right)\right]}{\left[11.135\,(105{,}718.8)\left(1 + \frac{.056}{4}\right)\right]}$$

$$= -309.81, \text{ rounded to } -310$$

The treasurer needs to short 310 December T-bond futures contracts.

At the expiration of the futures, the treasurer invoices the party with the long position by the product of the futures sold short (quoted futures price) and the conversion factor; in this scenario the short receives $105,718.8 × 1.1445, $120,995.2 and pays $114,351.60 for the cheapest-to-deliver bond per contract. The profit per contract is equal to the difference in what the treasurer receives and pays per contract. In this case, the profit will be equal to $6,643.55 per contract.

On August 9 the yield on the T-bond has increased to 6.125 percent and the proceeds from the bond portfolio are $33,159,978.8, a loss of $1,840,021.2. The profit in the futures is equal to $2,059,503.17. The T-bonds futures have insulated the increase in the yield of the spot portfolio and eliminated the exposure to interest rate increase. Illustration 6.3 summarizes these results.

Illustration 6.3

HEDGING WITH T-BOND FUTURES

It is May 9, and a life insurance company has a portfolio of Treasury bonds currently valued at $35 million with yield of 5.6 percent priced at par and 16 years to maturity. The bonds have to be liquidated in three months to meet obligations.

May 9
Bond market value: $35,000,000
Price of T-bond futures: 105–23
Price per contract: $105,718.80
Sell 310 contracts

August 9
Proceeds of bonds at the spot market: $33,159,978.80
The cheapest-to-deliver bond in the T-bond futures contract is a 7.25 percent priced at $114.35 per $100 face value with 6 percent conversion factor of 1.1445 and 19 years and 9 months at the maturity. The short invoices the long and receives (quoted futures) × conversion factor, $105,718.80 × 1.1445, and pays $114,351.60 per one cheapest-to-deliver contract.
Buy 310 cheapest-to-deliver bonds

Results
Loss of $1,840,021.20 in the spot market
Profit in the T-bond futures: $6,643.56 × 310 = $2,059,503.17
Net profit: $219,481.97

In Illustration 6.3, the hedge insulated the portfolio manager from a higher interest rate as the decline in the value of the portfolio was more than offset by a profit in the T-bond futures.

For a duration-based active bond portfolio management, see the following excerpt taken from *Bondweek:*

> Indiana Farm Bureau Insurance will look to swap out of financials into triple-B utilities on the view that utilities are oversold as a result of Enron-related worries. The Indianapolis-based insurer has an effective duration of approximately 5.58 years. It does not follow a benchmark, but does not like to let duration fall below 5.5 years. It allocates 56.7 percent to corporates, 13.6 percent to utilities, 9.5 percent to CMOs, 8.6 percent to collateralized debt obligations, 3.1 percent to Treasuries, 3 percent to taxable municipal bonds, 2.8 percent to Fannie Mae Delegated Underwriting and Servicing pools, 1.5 percent to asset-backed securities, 7 percent to agency pools, and .3 percent to agencies.[11]

NOTES

1. See Lutz (1940–41).
2. See Homer and Leibowitz (1971).
3. Fama (1976).
4. See Hicks (1946)
5. See Cox, Ingersoll, and Ross (1981).
6. Modigliani and Sutch (1966).
7. See Culbertson (1957).
8. See Chicago Board of Trade (1989).
9. Convexity is defined as the second derivative of the bond with respect to change in yield weighted by the market value of the bond as (dP^2/dR^2) $(1/P)$. The convexity can be calculated as:

$$\left[\frac{dP^2}{dR^2}\right]\frac{1}{P} = \left[\sum_{t=1}^{n}(t)(t+1)C/(1+R)^{t+2} + (n)(n+1)F/(1+R)^{n+2}\right]/P$$

where
  $C =$ coupon interest
  $F =$ face value of the bond
  $R =$ yield to maturity
  $n =$ maturity of the bond
10. See Figlewski (1986), Burghardt et al. (1991), and Fabozzi (1993, 1998).
11. *www.Bondweek.com,* January 7, 2002.

CHAPTER 7

Swaps

The market for swaps is by far one of the most innovative in the world. Swaps are introduced in the over-the-counter market to restructure assets, obligations, and mitigate and transfer risk for those who wish to avoid it to those who are equipped to take it for profit. Since the introduction in 1981 and 1982, respectively, of currency and interest rate swaps, the notional principal outstanding has grown to $4.22 and $57.229 trillion, as of the end of June 2001. Interest rate and currency swaps must be distinguished from foreign exchange swaps, where the parties simultaneously borrow and lend (short and long) in the euro credit market short-term bank deposits denominated in two different currencies with net payment (receipt) of interest at the maturity. The volume of the foreign exchange swaps grew to $13 trillion by the end of June 2001.

Exhibit 7.1 provides the market value of interest rates, options, and currency swaps between 1994 and 2002 as surveyed by the International Swaps and Derivatives Association (ISDA). The notional principal increased more than sevenfold to over $82 trillion by 2002. This tremendous growth reflects the increasing

EXHIBIT 7.1 Market Value of the Interest Rate, Options, and Currency Swaps

Year	Amounts (in trillions of $)
1994	11.303
1995	17.713
1996	25.453
1997	29.035
1998	50.997
1999	58.265
2000	63.0
2001	69.2
2002	82.7

Source: Market Survey Report by International Swaps and Derivatives Association, Inc.

appetite of capital markets for interest rate and currency swaps to manage interest rate and foreign exchange risk.

INTEREST RATE SWAPS

Forward market agreements coupled with borrowing and lending in domestic or foreign currency produces a synthetic derivative known as swaps, involving two parties that finance each other's debt in a single currency at floating for a fixed rate (interest rate swaps) or in two currencies denominated in dollars and foreign currency at fixed for floating rate or fixed for fixed rates (currency swaps).

Swaps can be considered as a low-cost means of refinancing by two parties in which the parties agree to exchange periodic interest (cash flows) on a single currency, fixed for floating or floating for floating, based on different indices as interest rate swaps in the future. The interest rate swaps tend to change and alter the financial obligations of the firm denominated in floating rates to the interest rates denominated in fixed rates and vice versa.

Interest rate swaps experienced growth of 73.69 percent between 1998 and June 2001, reflecting a tremendous increase by banks and nonbank institutions in hedging interest rate risk as well as risk taking by speculators (see Exhibit 7.2).

Currency swaps increased from $2.31 trillion in June 1998 to $4.22 trillion by the end of June 2001, reflecting a 82.68 percent growth in the same periods, despite a decline of $2 trillion in the overall over-the-counter (OTC) foreign exchange derivatives from 1998 to 2001.

A forward contract to buy 100,000 barrels of oil at 27.50/bbl for delivery in nine months can be considered as a swap transaction. The parties to the transaction are obligated to perform, requiring the buyer to pay $2.75 million in exchange for receiving 100,000 barrels of oil no matter what the spot price of oil is in nine months. This agreement is the simplest form of swap involving the exchange of one cash flow (i.e., $2.75 million for 100,000/bbl at spot price in nine months). The buyer's exposure to price changes in the oil market is transferred to the seller of the forward contract as the buyer is locked in to the forward price of 27.50/bbl oil. An extension of a forward contract to a multiperiod, where the parties agree to exchange periodic cash flows on designated dates and designated price at some future dates, produces swaps.

FORWARD RATE AGREEMENT

A forward rate agreement (FRA) is the over-the-counter (OTC) agreement in which two parties agree to exchange periodic cash flows based on specific interest rates (fixed rate) determined at the initiation of contract and a floating rate prevailing at the commencement of the contract in the future and a specific notional principal. In a plain-vanilla FRA, the buyer of the FRA agrees at time (t_0) to pay a fixed rate, say 7 percent interest rate, at time (t_1) in nine months

EXHIBIT 7.2   Global Foreign Exchange and
Interest Rate Derivatives by Instrument
and Market Values (1998 and 2001)

Global notional amounts outstanding in OTC derivatives
markets by instrument[a]

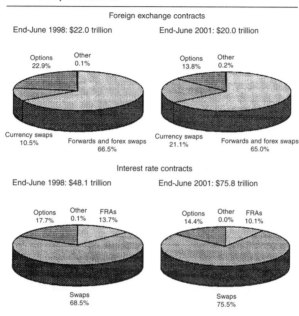

Foreign exchange contracts

End-June 1998: $22.0 trillion   End-June 2001: $20.0 trillion

Options 22.9%   Other 0.1%   Options 13.8%   Other 0.2%

Currency swaps 10.5%   Forwards and forex swaps 66.5%   Currency swaps 21.1%   Forwards and forex swaps 65.0%

Interest rate contracts

End-June 1998: $48.1 trillion   End-June 2001: $75.8 trillion

Options 17.7%   Other 0.1%   FRAs 13.7%   Options 14.4%   Other 0.0%   FRAs 10.1%

Swaps 68.5%   Swaps 75.5%

[a] Net of interdealer double-counting.
Source: Bank for International Settlement, Basle, June 2001.

on notional principal of $10 million to the seller of the FRA (the financial institution) for the periods between time (t_1 and t_2), 91 days.

t_0 t_1 t_2

The buyer of the FRA has essentially locked in the interest rate of 7 percent, thus eliminating interest rate risk. The FRA is an indirect guarantee, since in nine months the borrower pays the spot rate and receives or pays the differential in interest rates over the hedged horizon, as illustrated in Exhibit 7.3.

EXHIBIT 7.3   Structure of a Plain-Vanilla FRA

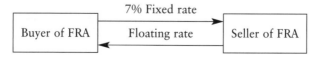

7% Fixed rate

Buyer of FRA   Floating rate   Seller of FRA

In nine months the buyer of the FRA borrows at the spot rate of, say, 10 percent, receiving the present value of the interest rate differentials of 3 percent over the hedged period of three months on notional principal of $10 million from the seller of FRA. The buyer of FRA borrows $10 million and pays principal and interest of:

$$10,000,000 \left(1 + .10 \left(\frac{91}{365}\right)\right) = \$10,249,315.06$$

The buyer of FRA receives the present value of:

$$\frac{\left[(.10 - .07)\left(\frac{91}{365}\right)(10,000,000)\right]}{\left(1 + .10\left(\frac{91}{365}\right)\right)} = \frac{74,794.52}{(1 + .0249)} = \$72,977.38$$

The buyer of the FRA can invest the $72,977.38 over a three-month period whose future value in three months depends on the rate at which the proceeds were invested. Assuming the proceeds from the swap dealer received are invested at a new higher rate of 10 percent, the future value will be equal to $74,794.52.

The effective cost of borrowing is equal to:

$$\frac{[\$10,249,315.06 - \$74,794.52]}{10,000,000} = .0175$$

The annualized effective borrowing rate $= .0175 \times \dfrac{365}{91}$
$$= .07$$

It turned out that the FRA effectively locked the borrower into the fixed rate of 7 percent. Had the rate in nine months decreased to 5 percent, the borrower in nine months will borrow at the interest rate of 5 percent. However, the buyer of the FRA will make compensation to the losing party, the seller of FRA, in nine months equal to the present value of interest rate differentials over the hedge period of three months:

$$\frac{\left[(.07 - .05)\left(\frac{91}{365}\right)(10,000,000)\right]}{\left(1 + .05\left(\frac{91}{365}\right)\right)} = \frac{\$49,863.01}{1.0125}$$

$$= \$49,247.41$$

The buyer of the FRA in nine months will borrow $10 million at 5 percent over the three-month period and will pay the interest and principal equal to:

$$10 \left(1 + .05 \left(\frac{91}{365}\right)\right) = \$10,124,657.53$$

Imputing the opportunity cost of $49,247.41 remitted by the buyer to the seller of the FRA at the new rate of 5 percent over the three months, the future value of this amount is equal to $49,863.01.

Adding this amount to the principal and interest of $10,124,657.53:

Total effective interest and principal: $10,174,520.54
The effective annualized rate = .07

The effective cost of borrowing turned out to be equal to the FRA rate of 7 percent that locked the borrower at the fixed rate no matter which interest rate scenario emerges in the future. It should be noted that interest paid and received is sensitive to the interest rate convention that is agreed to at the initiation of the FRA between the borrower and the lender. FRA is traded in the OTC market with a maturity of 1, 3, 6, 9, and 12 months. For example, a 3 × 6 FRA is a three-month FRA starting in three months that lasts for three months; likewise a 12 × 18 FRA is a six-month FRA starting in 12 months. In a plain-vanilla FRA, parties only exchange the interest rate deviations from the agreed fixed rate with that of floating rate prevailing in the future at the commencement of the contract. There is no exchange of principal.

INTEREST RATE CONVENTIONS

There are three accepted practices worldwide to calculate interest payments. Interest rate calculations differ depending on how many days per month are used as well as the number of days per year that are assumed:

	Day Counts in Period	**Days/Year**
International	Exact number of days	360
British	Exact number of days	365
Swiss	Assumed 30 days/month	360

Source: "Hedging Instruments for Foreign Exchange, Money Market and Precious Metals," Union Bank of Switzerland (1999), 41–2.

For example, the Bank of America employs the British convention for calculating interest payments owed to the bank by its clients on their lines of credit. The party that has invested in-the-money market instrument will be better off if its interest income is calculated using the exact number of days and 365 days per year as opposed to the Swiss practice, which uses 360 days per year and assumes 30 days per month.

STRIPES OF FORWARD RATE AGREEMENTS

To manage interest rate risk over multiperiods, borrowers can buy stripes of FRA, thereby insulating them from interest rate risks. FRAs also can be used to achieve a given interest rate in future investments, assuming that the seller of the FRA (the lender) is expecting interest rates to fall in the future. For example, a property casualty insurance company expects rent, royalties, and/or dividends of $2.5 million in six months and would like to invest this amount over 12 months.

The treasurer who wishes to invest and is concerned about falling interest rates in the next six months can sell stripes of three-month FRAs in six months:

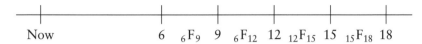

The treasurer can sell a series of three-month FRAs in six months—that is, 6×9 FRA or $_6F_9$ through $_{15}F_{18}$ (where $_{15}F_{18}$ is a 15×18 FRA starting in 15 months) that effectively locks the seller at the prevailing market forward rate today. Suppose the yield to maturity for off-the-run Treasury securities are as shown in Exhibit 7.4.[1]

The 6×9 is the FRA starting in six months and lasting for three months, and 15×18 is also a three-month forward rate prevailing between end of the 15th and 18th months.

The forward rates for the 6×9, 9×12, 12×15, and 15×18 can be estimated as:

$$_6F_9 = \frac{[9 \times 1.62 - 6 \times 1.52]}{9 - 6} = 1.82\%$$

$$_{15}F_{18} = \frac{[18 \times 2.50 - 15 \times 2.10]}{18 - 15} = 4.50\%$$

These forward rates are expected to be approximately equal to interest rates futures currently priced at the futures market for various maturities of up to 10 years in the future. There are differences between futures and forward contracts as addressed in Chapter 5. A futures contract is marked to market on a daily basis, however, a forward contract is only marked to market at the maturity of the forward contract, leading to a difference between forward and futures rates. Furthermore, the daily gains (losses) are invested (financed) at the prevailing interest rate in the futures market, while gains or losses in the forward contract are realized at maturity. Therefore, futures interest rates are expected to be higher than comparable maturity forward interest rates. The difference between futures and forward interest rates is known as *convexity bias;* this bias is more

EXHIBIT 7.4   Yield and Estimates of the Three-Month Forward Rates

	Yield %	Forward Rates %
3 month	1.50	
6 month	1.52	1.82
9 month	1.62	2.22
12 month	1.77	3.42
15 month	2.10	4.50
18 month	2.50	

pervasive in long-dated futures/forward, while it can be ignored in short-term futures/forward.

The seller of the stripes of FRA that wished to pay floating rate and to receive the forward rates in the future is not expected to receive the competitively priced FRA in Exhibit 7.4. Rather, the buyer of the FRA, in this case usually a financial institution, gives the forward rate to the seller at the bid rate that may be one-eighth of 1 percent lower than the forward rate estimated in the exhibit. Furthermore, the market maker of the FRA will usually find another party that wishes to buy the stripes of FRA by charging the buyer the offer rate of forward rates, which may be one-eighth of 1 percent higher than the competitively priced forward rates in the exhibit.

The extension of the stripes of FRA for managing interest rate risk produces the plain-vanilla interest rate swaps. To mitigate the counterparty risk, the parties to the swap pay a fee to a swap dealer by entering into a bilateral agreement with the dealer, who will pay float and receive fixed or pays fixed and receives float in an interest rate swaps.

MOTIVATIONS FOR SWAPS

Various economic reasons motivate swaps:

- To transform floating rate obligations synthetically to fixed rate
- To write off tax-loss carryforwards before they expire
- To manage interest rate risk at a lower cost relative to any other derivatives in its class as reflected in its enormous volume

For example, a construction company may borrow floating rates loans in building a shopping center when the yield curve is upward sloping, to find itself in a position to swap out of the floating rate and into the fixed rates loan market when the rates are likely to go up. The construction company therefore pays fixed rates and receives floating rates and synthetically has changed the structure of its debt obligations from floating to fixed rates without the usual substantial cost of refinancing its debt obligations. Exhibit 7.5 shows the foundation of floating for fixed rate swap.

The direction of the arrows in the exhibit shows the interest payments. The floating interest rate in swap is London Interbank Offer Rate (LIBOR), which is the ask rate on time deposits of varying maturities in the eurocurrency market.[2] The construction company is initially paying LIBOR plus 1 percent (pay LIBOR at offer rate) for its floating rate loan. By swapping the floating rate loan

EXHIBIT 7.5   Structure of Floating for Fixed Interest Rate Swaps

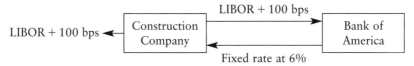

into fixed rate, the construction company is receiving LIBOR plus 1 percent (receives LIBOR at bid rate) and pays a fixed rate of 6 percent, which transforms its obligations synthetically to a fixed rate without refinancing parse. This repackaging is done by interest swaps in the OTC market, whose 1998 turnover had grown from $32.948 trillion to $57.229 trillion by the end of June 2001 (see Exhibit 7.2).

Some argue that all firms prefer to borrow long term to avoid interest rate risk.[3] However, good firm managers have inside information that their credit quality is likely to improve, and they will likely borrow short term and use interest rate swaps to hedge their interest rate risk. Good firms and financial institutions benefit in this case as the cost of borrowing for good firms is reduced initially and in the future if the credit quality is improved as expected. The financial institution is protected as long as the fortunes of the good firms improve; otherwise the bank may refuse to roll over the short-term loan.

In a plain-vanilla swap involving floating for fixed rate, the party that receives float and pays fixed pays nearly 70 basis points above the spread between LIBOR and the Treasury bond rate. Assuming the A- or BBB-rated firm can borrow at LIBOR plus 1.5 percent, then the cost of the borrowing after the swap would be at LIBOR plus 2.2 percent.

Illustration 7.1

Suppose Mercury Inc. enters into a three-year swap on February 11, 1999, to pay a fixed rate of 6 percent on notional principal of $25 million and receives a three-month LIBOR plus 1 percent with a semiannual reset date. Mercury will make six periodic payments of $750,000 interest every six months and will receive an unknown amount based on what the three-month LIBOR will be three months prior to date of receipt. For example, Mercury will pay $750,000 on August 11 and receive the three-month LIBOR prevailing on February 11. The next payment date will be February of the following year; at that time the firm pays $750,000 and receives three-month LIBOR prevailing on August of the previous year. In reality, one of the parties to the swap makes a net payment to the other party. Exhibit 7.6 presents the summary of the cash flows, assuming an interest rate for three-month LIBOR.

Assuming the interest rate scenarios for the three-month LIBOR in Exhibit 7.6, Mercury is expected to pay net amount of ($375,000), ($250,000), and ($125,000) on August 11, 2002, February 11, 2003, and August 11, 2003 to the swap dealer on the interest rate swap, while receiving $31,250, $93,750, and $15,625, respectively, on February 11, 2004, August 11, 2004, and February 11, 2005. The only cash flow that is being swapped is the periodic net coupon interest, not the principal, since the principal in both fixed and floating rates is identical and denominated in the same currency. Therefore, it is pointless to exchange principal.

EXHIBIT 7.6 Summary of Cash Flows on $25 Million Interest Rate Swap for Mercury, Inc. (6% Fixed Rate Paid and LIBOR + 1% Received)

Date	3-Month LIBOR Rate %	Fixed Rate Cash Flow Paid	Floating Rate Cash Flow Received	Net Cash Flow
February 11, 02	2			
August 11, 02	3	($750,000)	$375,000	−$375,000
February 11, 03	4	($750,000)	$500,000	−$250,000
August 11, 03	5.25	($750,000)	$625,000	−$125,000
February 11, 04	5.75	($750,000)	$781,250	+$ 31,250
August 11, 04	5.125	($750,000)	$843,750	+$ 93,750
February 11, 05	4.5	($750,000)	$765,625	+$ 15,625

The plain-vanilla interest rate swap in this example can be considered as a portfolio of long and short position in the fixed notional principal where the hedger in the example, Mercury, is short in fixed rate (pays fixed) and long in the floating rate (receives floating rate). However, the swap dealer is long in the fixed rate and short in the floating rate note over the swap period.

Swaps used in this way manage the interest rate risk exposure of the company and presumably are more effective and less costly than other derivatives in their class, as reflected in the enormous volume of swaps: in excess of $83.412 trillion annually in 2001.[4]

SWAPS DUE TO COMPARATIVE ADVANTAGE

Swap may be initiated due to asymmetric information and other imperfections in the market about the parties to an interest rate swap. For example, a party may enjoy an absolute advantage in securing debt at the fixed and floating rate over another party. However, the same party (which has absolute advantage in both rates market) enjoys only a relative or comparative advantage in one of the markets (fixed), while the party with an absolute disadvantage in both fixed and floating rate markets, is expected to enjoy a comparative advantage in the floating rate market.

Example: Two firms, A and B, have been quoted the rates in Exhibit 7.7 in the interbank markets.

EXHIBIT 7.7 Interest Rate Swap Quotes

Party	Fixed Rate %	Fixed Rate Differential	Floating Rate %	Floating Rate Differential
B	6	100 bps	LIBOR + 2%	50 bps
A	5		LIBOR + 1.5%	

The interest rate differential in the fixed rate market is 100 basis points, while it is only 50 basis points in the floating rate market. This asymmetric differential, for whatever reason, provides an opportunity for interest rates swaps that makes both parties better off without making any party worse off. The gain from the swap is the interest rate differential in the fixed and floating rate market:

Fixed rate differentials − Floating rate differentials = 50 basis points

Exhibit 7.8 assumes the gains are divided equally between A and B, and both parties borrow the notional principal of $10 million over a four-year period with semiannual exchange.

Company A has absolute advantage in both the fixed and floating rate market. However, A enjoys comparative advantage in the fixed rate market, where it pays 100 basis points less, while paying only 50 basis points less than B in the floating rate market. Company B has comparative advantage in the floating rate market, as it pays only .5 percent more compared to 1 percent more in the fixed rate market. According to the theory of the comparative advantage, the parties should borrow where they have comparative advantage and then swap with one another.

Company A borrows at the fixed rate of 5 percent and swaps the fixed rate for floating rate, paying LIBOR plus 2 percent, and receives 5.75 percent fixed. Company A nets 75 basis points in its outside borrowing; however, it pays 50 basis points more in its swap for a net gain of 25 basis points. Company B borrows in the floating rate market at LIBOR plus 2 percent and swaps floating rate for fixed rate, paying 5.75 percent and receiving LIBOR plus 2 percent for its outside borrowing. Company B is better off by 25 basis points, as it pays 5.75 percent for the fixed rate loan as compared to paying 6 percent without the swap.

The periodic cash flow exchanged assuming six-month LIBOR is equal to a December Eurodollar futures rate as of September 12, 2002. Subsequent LIBOR will be equal to the stripes of the Eurodollar futures for the next four years on the notional principal of $10 million, as shown in Exhibit 7.9.

This swap has net positive cash flow for the party that pays LIBOR plus 2 percent and receives a fixed rate of 5.75 percent in the early years and net negative cash flow in December 2004 through June 2007. This type of swap may be induced by Company A's tax-loss carryforward. It can use the profit in the early years of the swap to write off tax losses before they expire. Exhibit 7.10 shows the net cash flow exchanged on December 2002 through June 2007.

To mitigate the counterparty risk, the parties to the swap enter into a bilateral agreement with a financial intermediary that will take the offsetting position for a fee. The structure of the swap in Exhibit 7.10 assumes the swap dealer is

EXHIBIT 7.8   Interest Rate Swap Induced by
                   Comparative Advantage

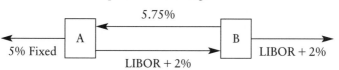

EXHIBIT 7.9   Fixed for Floating Rate Swap for Company A

Date	IMM Index	Implied Yield LIBOR %	Interest Paid %	Interest Received %	Net %	Net Cash Flow Swapped
Dec 02[a]	98.2	1.8	−3.8	5.75	1.95	97500
Jun 03	97.74	2.26	−4.26	5.75	1.49	74500
Dec 03	97.04	2.96	−4.96	5.75	0.79	39500
Jun 04	96.49	3.51	−5.51	5.75	0.24	12000
Dec 04	96.07	3.93	−5.93	5.75	−0.19	−9500
Jun 05	95.76	4.24	−6.24	5.75	−0.49	−24500
Dec 05	95.44	4.56	−6.56	5.75	−0.81	−40500
Jun 06	95.19	4.81	−6.81	5.75	−1.06	−53000
Dec 06	94.89	5.11	−7.11	5.75	−1.36	−68000
Jun 07	94.67	5.33	−7.33	5.75	−1.58	−79000

[a] The first two columns were adapted from the *Wall Street Journal,* September 12, 2002.

EXHIBIT 7.10   Net Cash Flows in Fixed for Floating Rate Swaps for Company A

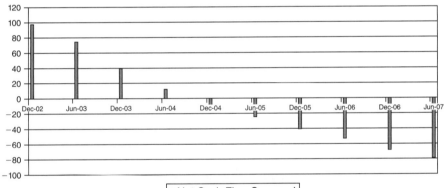

one of the parties to the swap where the gains from the swap, the 50 basis points, are divided so that the swap dealer receives 20 basis points and companies A and B receive 15 basis points (see Exhibit 7.11).

The swap dealer is long and short in both the fixed and floating rate markets. The swap dealer receives 5.85 percent from Company B and pays 5 percent

EXHIBIT 7.11   Structure of Plain-Vanilla Interest Rate Swap

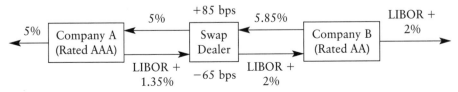

to Company A for providing a LIBOR-based loan to Company A at the spread of 135 basis points, which saves Company A 15 basis points in this swap. The swap dealer receives LIBOR plus 1.35 percent from Company A, while paying Company B LIBOR plus 2 percent. The swap dealer's overall gain in this swap is 20 basis points. Company B is also better off by 15 basis points, as it gets the fixed rate loan it wanted at 5.85 percent as compared to 6 percent without swap. The interest rate risk exposure to Company B is transferred to Company A indirectly through the swap dealer, as the debt structure of the firm is transformed from the floating rate to the fixed rate loan without the usual underwriting cost associated with refinancing.

A variety of options can be attached to plain-vanilla interest rate swaps, making them callable, putable, convertible, and/or extendable, as well as any other conceivable options, to cap the maximum interest rate the party has to pay in its floating rate loan or to impose floors on the minimum interest rate it can earn in investment in mitigating and transferring risk.

SWAP VALUATION

The value of an n-year swap (V_{swap}) to the party that receives floating rate and pays fixed rate will be equal to the value of the portfolio of n-FRAs, as defined in Equation 7.1, where the value of each FRA is equal to the present value of the fixed leg minus the present value of the floating leg.

V_{swap} = Present value of net cash flows exchanged excluding the principal that is not swapped discounted at the prevailing LIBOR rate.

$$= \frac{\sum_{i}^{n} c_i}{(1 + r_i)^i} - \frac{\sum_{i}^{n} c_F}{(1 + r_i)^i} \tag{7.1}$$

where

c_i = coupon interest on the floating rate bond
r_i = LIBOR rate prevailing on the respective dates in future
c_F = coupon interest on the fixed rate debt discounted at the LIBOR corresponding to the maturity of cash flow

The value of the swap in Illustration 7.1 for Mercury Inc., which pays fixed and receives floating rate, is:

$$V_{swap} = -\frac{\$375,000}{1.015} - \frac{\$250,000}{(1.02)^2} - \frac{\$125,000}{(1.02625)^3} + \frac{\$31,250}{(1.02875)^4}$$
$$+ \frac{\$93,750}{(1.025625)^5} + \frac{\$15,625}{(1.0225)^6}$$
$$= -\$601,227.15$$

The value of the swap to the financial institution that pays floating rate and receives fixed rate is positive by $601,227.15. The N-year interest rate swap can be regarded as the portfolio of $N - 1$ forward rate agreement, where the first

exchange of fixed rate for floating rate is known at the time the swap is initiated followed by the exchange of fixed rate with $N - 1$ unknown forward rates
(floating rate) that will be equal to the future LIBOR rates. The value of the first
FRA (V_{fra}) due on August 11, 2002, as of February 11, 2002, in Illustration 7.1
is defined in Equation 7.2.

$$V_{fra} = \text{Present value of net cash flow (fixed and floating) swapped}$$
$$\text{discounted at the prevailing LIBOR rate}$$
$$V_{fra} = PV \text{ of fixed leg} - PV \text{ of floating leg} \qquad (7.2)$$
$$V_{fra} = [\$750,000/(1.015)] - [\$375,000/(1.015)]$$
$$= \$369,458.12$$

The value of the first FRA is positive (negative) to the party that receives (pays)
fixed rate of 6 percent and pays (receives) three-month LIBOR plus 1 percent.

Illustration 7.2

Consider a four-year swap between a financial institution and a manufacturing company where the financial institution receives fixed rate of 5.5 percent
and pays floating interest rate based on the stripes of Eurodollar futures to
the counterparty on a semiannual basis. Exhibit 7.12 presents the cash flow
received and paid.

The floating interest rate is estimated from the Eurodollar futures IMM index
from March 2003 through September 2006.[5] The rates are 1.85, 2.48, 3.16,
3.67, 4.04, 4.44, 4.74, and 5 percent respectively from March 2003 through
September 2006.

The manufacturing firm hedged its interest rate exposure by swapping its
floating rate debt to fixed rate, thereby eliminating interest rate risk without
refinancing and restructuring the composition of its debt.

EXHIBIT 7.12 Fixed for Floating Interest Rate Swaps

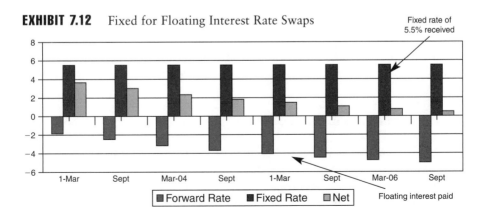

INTEREST RATE CAPS, FLOORS, COLLARS, AND CORRIDORS

These options-embedded derivatives are attached to plain-vanilla interest rate swaps to alter the cash flows of the interest-bearing instruments involving financing and investment. After the downfall of the savings and loan associations in the early 1980s and the introduction of the floating rate notes (FRNs), the cap market started in 1985 by the issuance of $2.75 billion FRNs by financial institutions in the U.S. capital market to transfer the interest rate risk to the ultimate borrower.

The introduction of FRNs prompted financial engineers to design new, innovative breeds of interest rate derivatives to make them more attractive to the market. Caps and floors in other currencies came to life as borrowers and lenders demanded protection from rising/falling interest rate conditions. The market responded by creating these derivative products. To fulfill the needs of various clientele financial institutions offer caps, floors, collars, and corridors to their clients to expand the range of possibilities in investment and financing decisions.

Interest Rate Caps

Interest rate caps are call options on interest rates where the buyer of the cap pays to the seller of the cap, usually an intermediary or insurance company, a fee up front so that the buyer gets protection from rising interest rates above the strike price (the cap rate) agreed to by both parties. The cap is intended to ensure the buyer that its interest rate over the life of the loan will not exceed the maximum rate (the cap rate or strike price) of 9 percent. Caps are activated when the interest rate exceeds the strike price of 9 percent, as the caps buyer receives compensation for the difference between the cap rate and interest rate (see Exhibit 7.13).

Illustration 7.3

Suppose Toledo Ltd. borrows $5 million for five years at the floating rate of six-month LIBOR plus 125 basis points. Furthermore, the company buys 8.25 percent caps from a financial institution and pays 250 basis points that protect it from a rising interest rate above the cap rate with a notional principal of $5 million. The interest payment is reset semiannually at the six-month LIBOR rate prevailing in the last three months. Exhibit 7.14 presents the behavior of the capped and uncapped interest rate paid.

The interest rates in the capped loan are higher than in the uncapped loan in the region where the float rate (R_f) is less than the cap rate (R_c) by the amount of the cap premium. The cap expires out-of-the-money as long as the floating interest rate remains below the cap rate. However, when the float rate is greater than the cap rate, the cap will be activated as a call option that is in-the-money. In this scenario, the cap buyer receives compensation from the cap writer that

EXHIBIT 7.13 Behavior of Caps Payment, Uncapped Market Rate for a 9% Cap over Time

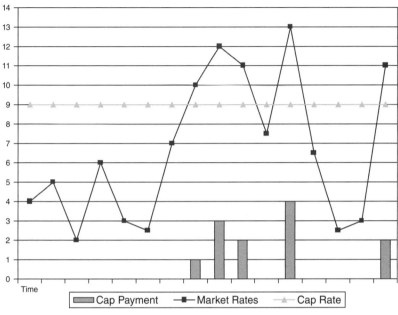

EXHIBIT 7.14 Behavior of Interest Rate Caps

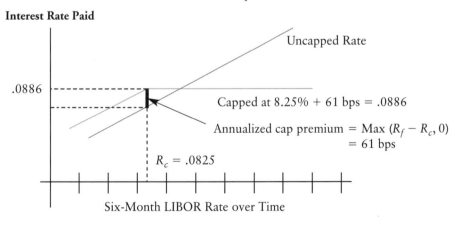

is equal to the difference between the float rate and cap rate weighted by the time the tenor of the cap and notional principal.

The amount of the first interest payment is known at the time the loan is taken. Suppose the six-month LIBOR was 4 percent. The borrower in six months pays:

$$(.0525) \times \tfrac{1}{2} \times \$5,000,000 = \$131,250$$

The amounts of nine interest payments are not known, and the cap can be considered as stripes of ten *caplets* in this example, where each caplet is a call option at the strike price of 8.25 percent. Assuming a given volatility of the interest rate, historical or implied, time to expiration, the float and the cap rate, the call option price (the cap premium) can be estimated using the standard option pricing formula. The cap premium is assumed to be 2.5 percent at the offer rate. This premium is paid up front to the financial institution and needs to be amortized over the life of the cap at the prevailing fixed rate for the five-year debt:

$$\text{Cap premium} = .025 \times \$5,000,000$$
$$= \$125,000$$

$$\text{Annualized premium amortized} = \cfrac{125,000}{\left[\left(1 + \dfrac{.075}{2}\right)^{10} - 1\right] \div \left[\left(1 + \dfrac{.075}{2}\right)^{10} + \dfrac{.075}{2}\right]}$$
$$= \$15,220.167$$

The amortized semiannual premium of \$15,220.167 is estimated assuming a five-year fixed rate of 7.5 percent.

Suppose six-month LIBOR is equal to 9.25 percent in the next reset date. The borrower pays the LIBOR plus 1.25 percent on the outstanding balance of \$5 million and receives 1 percent from the seller of the cap on scheduled semiannual payment dates:

Borrower pays: $(.1050) \times \frac{1}{2} \times \$5,000,000 = \$262,500$

Borrower receives: $(.01) \times \frac{1}{2} \times \$5,000,000 = \$25,000$

Borrower pays cap insurance premium of $= \$15,220.167$

All-in cost of cap $= \$252,720.16$

The cap guarantees that the maximum interest payments in any future period do not exceed \$252,720.16. This is equal to the annualized 10.108 percent, which is equal to a strike price of 8.25 percent (the cap rate) on the notional principal of \$5,000,000 every six months plus the annualized cap premium of 60.88 basis points as well as the credit spread of 1.25 percent over LIBOR. The cap also provides an opportunity to realize the benefits of lower interest rates in the future if rates remain below the cap rate.

This contrast with the interest rate swap in which the debt structure of the firm is transformed from floating to fixed rate of, say, 8.86 percent as the constant line in Exhibit 7.14, similar to the forward contract that locks the interest rate at the agreed FRA rate. The swap as demonstrated earlier is a portfolio of forward contracts.

Floors

Floors are put options that provide downside protection on the underlying instrument with an unknown payoff in the future. They provide insurance that the return will be no less than the minimum rate—floors rate—of, say, 5 percent over the life of the option. The behavior of floors over time against the floating market rate (index) is demonstrated in Exhibit 7.15, assuming a floor at a strike price of 5 percent. For example, the buyer of the floors is to receive compensation from the seller of the floors over the life of the option when the floating rate falls below the strike price of 5 percent. The put options underlying the floors are activated when the rates fall below the strike price of 5 percent as the put option provides the downside protection.

The N-period floors can be considered as the portfolio of N-put options. Each one is known as a *floorlet*. The price of each floorlet is defined in Equation 7.3.

$$\text{Floorlet premium} = \text{Max } (R_c - R_f, 0) \quad\quad (7.3)$$

where

R_c = the strike price of the floorlet
R_f = floating rate as proxy by LIBOR

Exhibit 7.16 shows the behavior of the hedged (floors) and the unhedged investment.

The buyer of the floors is guaranteed an interest rate equal to R_c less the premium for the put option that truncates the distribution of unhedged returns at the strike price of R_c. The floors provide an upside potential in the event rates go up in the future; the put option embedded in the contract is out-of-the-money at any rate above the strike price of R_c. However, at any rate below R_c, the put option is in-the-money, therefore, it will be exercised as the option is

EXHIBIT 7.15 Behavior of Floors Payments, Market Rate for a 5% Floor

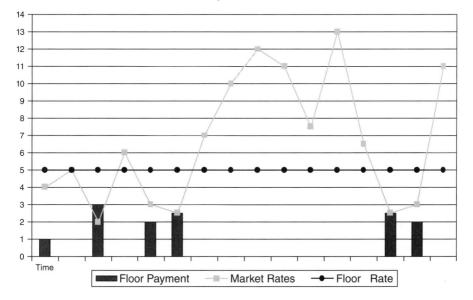

EXHIBIT 7.16   Interest Rate Floors

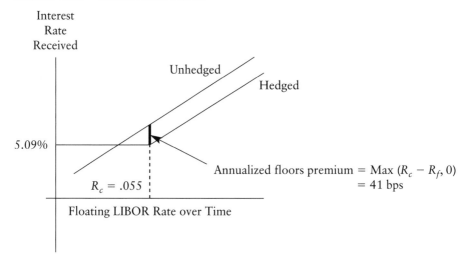

activated and the seller of the floors makes compensation to the buyer by the differential in the float and floors rates. Like the cap premium and any other insurance, the floors premium is paid in advance; therefore, it has to be amortized over the life of the hedge.

Illustration 7.4

Fabulous Fund has invested $10 million in a portfolio of bonds promising investors a minimum return of 5.5 percent guaranteed over a five-year investment horizon. The potential for high returns is tied to the performance of the Lehman Brothers government/credit index. The portfolio manager has purchased floors at the over-the-counter market for the life of the portfolio by paying an up-front fee at the offer rate of 1.75 percent to buy protection at the floors rate of 5.5 percent on the notional principal of $10 million. The portfolio manager has allocated the $10 million according to its benchmark: 38 percent to corporate, 25 percent to Treasuries, 25 percent to agencies, 10 percent to mortgage-backed securities, and 2 percent to cash. The fund is neutral its benchmark, the Lehman Brothers index (i.e., the fund and the benchmark have the same amount of exposure to the market risk).

A summary of the cash flows assuming the return in the portfolio is equal to the return in the benchmark of 4.5 percent in the first six months is as follows:

INTEREST RECEIVED

The interest received in the first six months is equal to:

$$\$10,000,000 \times \frac{.045}{2} = \$225,000$$

CASH FLOW RECEIVED ON FLOORS PROTECTION

Since the rate has fallen below the floors rate of 5.5 percent, the floors are activated and the buyer of the floors receives the interest rate differentials from the seller:

$$\$10,000,000 \times \frac{(.055 - .045)}{2} = \$50,000$$

AMORTIZED PREMIUM PAID FOR THE FLOORS

The semiannual premium paid for buying protection is equal to:

$$\text{Floors premium} = .0175 \times \$10,000,000 = \$175,000$$

$$\text{Amortized floors premium} = 175,000 \div \frac{\left[\left(1 + \frac{.06}{2}\right)^{10} - 1\right]}{\left[\left(1 + \frac{.06}{2}\right)^{10} \times \frac{.06}{2}\right]}$$

$$= \$20,515.33$$

The annualized floors premium is equal to $41,030.66, which translates to 41 basis points per year on the notional principal of $10 million assuming the fixed rate for a five-year debt is equal to 6 percent per annum.

Interest received: $225,000

Cash flow received on floors protection: $50,000

Amortized premium paid for the floors: $20,515.33

Total net semiannual cash flow: $254,484.67

$$\text{The annualized return} = \frac{\$508,969.34}{\$10,000,000}$$

$$= .0509$$

The return realized in the first six months is equal to the strike price of 5.5 percent less the 41 basis points for the annual premium on the floors, as is evidenced from this cash flow and also shown in Exhibit 7.17.

Guaranteed Investment Contracts (GICs) are wrapped products offered by insurance and other financial intermediaries that are embedded with floors, providing the investor a direct guarantee that the return realized over the life of GIC will be no less than the promised rate.

Interest Rate Collars

Buying put options, the floors, and simultaneously selling call options, the caps, creates collars. The motivation for such transactions is to finance some or all of the cost of the purchase of the floors by selling the caps and forgoing the potential of an increase in interest rates that could otherwise improve the performance

EXHIBIT 7.17   Interest Rate Cap and Floor Quotations

	U.S. Dollar Caps vs. 3m LIBOR		U.S. Dollar Floors vs. 3m LIBOR	
Maturity (Years)	Cap Rate (%)	Cap Premium Bid-Ask	Floor Rate (%)	Floor Premium Bid-Ask
2	5.00	42–46	4.00	42–47
	6.00	15–19	5.00	149–154
3	6.00	69–79	4.00	54–62
	7.00	35–42	5.00	190–200
5	7.00	147–165	5.00	245–261

	Deutsche Mark Caps vs. 6m LIBOR		Deutsche Mark Floors vs. 6m LIBOR	
Maturity (Years)	Cap Rate (%)	Cap Premium Bid-Ask	Floor Rate (%)	Floor Premium Bid-Ask
2	6.00	35–40	5.50	57–63
	6.50	19–24	6.00	101–107
3	6.00	93–99	5.50	89–96
	6.50	60–65	6.00	156–161
5	6.75	172–185	5.5	122–145

Source: International Financial Review, July 31, 1993, p. 83.

of the portfolio. Zero collars are created when the buyer of the collar simultaneously buys and sells floors and caps where the cost of purchasing floors is completely offset by selling the caps.

A U.S. firm buying three-year collars can finance the purchase of three-year 4 percent floors at the offer price of 62 basis points by selling 6 percent caps at the bid price of 69 basis points on a given notional principal (see Exhibit 7.17). Exhibit 7.18 demonstrates the interest rate collar behavior for this example.

The firm in Exhibit 7.18 has eliminated downside risk, the risk of falling rates, by buying a 4 percent floors on the three-month U.S. LIBOR financed by selling 6 percent caps on U.S. dollar three-month LIBOR. The caps sold obligate the firm to forgo potential higher rates in the future by truncating the returns at the strike price of 6 percent plus the amortized semiannual premium.

The amortized semiannual caps and floors premium is estimated over the life of the caps and floors assuming semiannual settlement and the three-year fixed rate of 5 percent to be equal to 12.5 and 11.25 basis points, respectively.[6]

$$\text{Cap premium} = 69 \text{ bps} / \left[\left(1 + \frac{.05}{2}\right)^6 - 1\right] / \left[\left(1 + \frac{.05}{2}\right)^6 \times \frac{.05}{2}\right] = 12.5 \text{ bps}$$

$$\text{Floor premium} = 62 \text{ bps} / \left[\left(1 + \frac{.05}{2}\right)^6 - 1\right] / \left[\left(1 + \frac{.05}{2}\right)^6 \times \frac{.05}{2}\right] = 11.25 \text{ bps}$$

Doubling the caps and floors premium results in an effective cap rate of 6.25 and an effective floor rate of 3.775 percent, as shown in Exhibit 7.18.

Illustration 7.5

J.P. Morgan issued 2.5 million shares of perpetual preferred stocks (PERPS) in February 1983 at $100 par value. PERPS granted the issuer the right to cap the dividend at 11.5 percent at the maximum, while simultaneously providing downside protection for the investor by having a floor rate of 5 percent as revealed in the company's prospectus.[7]

Interest Rate Corridors

A corridor is a portfolio of two caps; the borrower buys one cap at a certain strike price and simultaneously sells the second cap at a higher strike price to offset some of the cost of the cap purchased. Exhibit 7.19 shows the payoff for the corridor.

The borrower that buys a cap and simultaneously sells a cap at a higher strike price (higher rate) believes the interest rate will go down in the future. The cap purchased at x_1 provides protection from rising interest rates; however, the cap sold, in effect, obligates the borrower to pay when the second cap is activated at a rate above x_2, leaving the borrower exposed to a higher interest rate. For example, buying a three-year 6 percent cap against a three-month LIBOR for 79 basis points and simultaneously selling a three-year 7 percent cap and receiving 35 basis points partially defrays the cost of buying protection (see Exhibit 7.17).

EXHIBIT 7.18 Interest Rate Collars

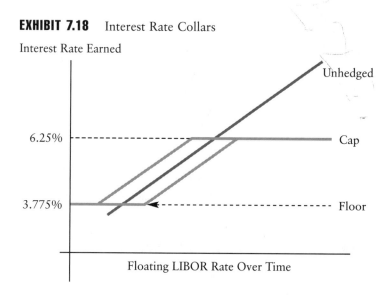

EXHIBIT 7.19   Interest Rate Corridor

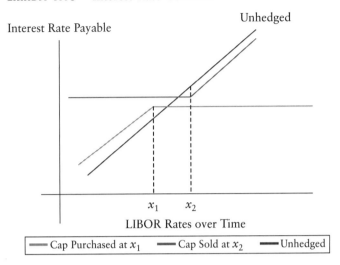

Assuming floating interest rates go up to 10 percent for the next payment date, the protection seller in the first cap will compensate the borrower by the difference between the floating rate and the cap rate, that is, 4 percent. However, the borrower is obligated to pay 3 percent as the difference between floating rate and the second cap rate of 7 percent. The borrower is better off by 1 percent and its effective cost of borrowing is equal to floating rate minus 1 percent plus 44 basis points (the difference between the premium paid and received) that need to be amortized over the life of the loan. However, if the rates fall below 6 percent, both caps will expire worthless.

VOLATILITY OF INTEREST RATES

The typical estimates of standard deviations of interest rates in the OTC market for pricing caps and floors are historical, implied spot, forward, and flat volatilities derived from the underlying historical LIBOR rates (historical volatility), caps/floors price (implied volatility), Eurodollar futures price (forward volatility), or using the same volatility estimate for all the caplets comprising the caps for a particular currency.

The estimates of volatility usually range from 18 to 25 percent for maturities ranging from 1 to 10 years with the bid-ask spread of nearly 100 to 200 basis points. The estimates or, rather, guesstimates are usually low in the near-term and long-term maturities and high in the midrange of maturities with hump. For example, the OTC quotes for percentage volatility per annum can be for 1, 5, and 10-year caps/floors, as shown in Exhibit 7.20.

EXHIBIT 7.20   Volatility Guesstimates for Caps Floors in the Over the Counter Percent per Annum

Maturity (Year)	Caps		Floors	
	Bid	Ask	Bid	Ask
1	19	21	19	21
5	23.75	25	24.25	25.25
10	0.50	21.75	21	22

Illustration 7.6

Suppose a German firm wishes to borrow for three years in the euro credit market at the six-month LIBOR rate. It wants to buy protection from rising interest rates above 6 percent. The firm buys in the OTC market three-year 6 percent caps at the offer price of 99 basis points, as in Exhibit 7.17. The firm would like to finance the purchase of the 6 percent caps by selling three-year 6.5 percent caps at the bid price of 60 basis points. The firm partially financed the purchase of the first cap by selling second caps; it believes that the rates are likely to fall. The premium in both ends of the transaction that is paid and received up front has to be amortized over the life of the loan, assuming a fixed rate interest of 5 percent. The borrower pays net premium of 39 basis points that is equal to 99 basis points paid for the first caps and 60 basis points received by selling 6.5 percent caps amortized at 5 percent over three years, assuming this semiannual reset date:

$$\text{Amortized semiannual net premium} = 39 / \left[\left(1 + \frac{.05}{2} \right)^6 - 1 \right) / \left[\left(1 + \frac{.05}{2} \right)^6 \times \frac{.05}{2} \right]$$

$$= 7.08 \text{ basis points}$$

The annualized net premium paid will be equal to 14.16 basis points over the life of the loan. Suppose the German firm borrows DM20 million or its euro equivalent. The annual net cost of buying corridor will be equal to DM28,320 or its euro equivalent:

$$20,000,000 \times .001416 = \text{DM } 28,320$$

The corridor is most effective when rates remain under the second cap. However, if the rates increase over 7 percent in the example, the borrower is obligated to pay to the cap buyer the difference between the float rate and the cap rate of 6.5 percent, while receiving the interest rate differential between the float rate and the first cap of 6 percent. By buying protection (buying cap) and selling protection (selling cap), the borrower is effectively exposed to a higher interest rate.

SWAPTIONS

A swaption provides the right, not an obligation, to enter into an *n*-year swap agreement, say in the next six months. For an up-front premium Mercury, Inc., in Illustration 7.1 can enter into a swaption (an option on the swap) to swap floating rate for fixed rate of 6 percent in the next six months over the swap period of, say, three years. If in the next six months the fixed interest rate on a three-year loan increases to 8 percent, Mercury exercises its right to enter into the swap agreement. However, if the interest rates on a three-year fixed rate loan drop to 5 percent, the swaption is worthless and expires without being exercised, and Mercury can secure better terms in the market.

The swaption in this example involves the right, not an obligation, to swap floating rate for fixed, that is, to pay fixed and receive float is a call option and is priced similarly using the standard Black-Scholes option pricing as defined in Equation 7.4.

$$\text{Swaption} = \text{Max} \ (R_{fl} - R_f, 0) \tag{7.4}$$

where

R_{fl} = floating interest rates
R_f = fixed interest rate

In the interest rate swap, the swap rate is the fixed rate that would be exchanged for LIBOR in a newly issued swap for the particular maturity at a specific time. The swaption involving the right, not an obligation, to swap a fixed interest rate for a floating rate—that is to pay float and receive fixed—is a put option and is priced similar to standard put options. A 2 × 4 put swaption is a two-year swap starting in two years to pay floating rate and receive fixed rate in every settlement period until the expiration. A 3 × 8 put swaption is a five-year swap starting in three years for five years where the buyer of the put swaption pays floating rate and receives fixed rate in an interest rate swap. The buyer of the put swaption is expecting the interest rate to drop in the future and wishes to realize a higher fixed rate for the portfolio if rates fall. However, if the rates go up, the buyer of the put swaption lets the option to enter into a swap to expire.

$$\text{Swaption} = \text{Max} \ (R_f - R_{fl}, 0)$$

Illustration 7.7

A construction company that finances the construction of a shopping mall in middle Tennessee at the floating rate of LIBOR plus 1 percent plans to enter into a five-year swap in nine months in a plain-vanilla swap involving a floating for fixed rate interest payment that guarantees a fixed rate of 6.5 percent.

The construction company buys a swaption from the Bank of America. The swaption is the option on swap that gives the right, not an obligation, to the

> construction company for a cost to enter into a swap where it pays 6.5 percent fixed rate and receives LIBOR plus 1 percent. If the five-year swap rate in nine months is 8 percent, the construction company will exercise its option to enter into the agreed swap; otherwise it will consider other options.

The call and put swaptions are usually European type, where the buyer forces the seller to pay floating (fixed) and receives fixed (floating) for the length of the swap. Exhibit 7.21 shows the typical OTC put swaptions quotations.

The buyer of the 2 × 4 put swaption pays 89 basis points on the notional principal of the swap to enter into a two-year swap at the end of two years. If in two years the rates fall below the strike price of 7 percent, the buyer forces the seller to pay 7 percent and receives the floating rate prevailing at the reset date on the exchange of cash flows for the length of the swap.

CALLABLE SWAP

A callable swap provides the party that makes fixed rate payments the option to terminate the swap prior to its maturity for a cost if interest rates fall in the future. The callable swap comes with a cost that is reflected in a higher fixed rate payment as compared to the plain-vanilla swap with no option attached. This option is similar to the option attached to the callable bonds, such as mortgage debt, where the borrower exercises the right to call the bond if interest rates fall. However, when rates continue to increase, the borrower finds its low fixed rate attractive. As long as the yield is upward sloping, the long-dated swap rate is higher than the short-dated swap rate and the callable swap will not be exercised. However, if the yield curve turns downward sloping, the fixed rate pay becomes unattractive and the callable swap is likely to be exercised, as it pays to terminate the swap.

Consider two interest rate scenarios: The falling rate induces the party that is making fixed rate payments to terminate the swap by paying a termination fee to the swap dealer; however, if rates increase, it makes sense not to terminate the swap.

EXHIBIT 7.21 Put Swaption Quotations[a]

Exercise Period	Length of Swap (Years)	Strike Price (Fixed Rate; %)	Premium in Basis Points
2 × 3	1	7	45–60
2 × 4	2	7	72–89
2 × 5	3	7	108–127

[a] The buyer of the put swaption has the right, not an obligation, to force the seller to pay fixed rate (strike price) and receives floating rate.

Scenario	Interest Rates	Action
I	Rising	Do nothing
II	Falling	Terminate the swap

In scenario I, the swap to the party that pays fixed and receives floating rate is likely to be a positive net present value. However, the value of the swap in scenario II is likely to be a negative net present value for the floating for fixed rate swap. The next example illustrates the swap termination.

Example: Consider the floating for fixed rate swap in Illustration 7.1 and assume the swap is callable by Mercury, which is making fixed rate payments and receiving float. Mercury plans to terminate the swap on December 2003, before the scheduled pay/receive date on February 11, 2004. The LIBOR rate has fallen to 4.5 percent. Therefore, the present value of the net cash flow for the remaining life of the swap has to be discounted at this rate in order to determine the amount paid or received.

$$\text{Net cash flows} = \frac{(-750,000)}{(1 + .045/2)} + \frac{(-750,000)}{(1 + .045/2)^2} + \frac{(-750,000)}{(1 + .045/2)^3}$$

$$+ \frac{(687,500)}{(1 + .045/2)} + \frac{(687,500)}{(1 + .045/2)^2} + \frac{(687,500)}{(1 + .045/2)^3}$$

$$= -\$179,368.54$$

The floating rate cash flow received is $687,500, which is equal to the LIBOR rate of 4.5 percent plus 100 basis points scaled by the semiannual schedule and principal of $25 million. Mercury pays $179,368.54 to terminate the swap before the scheduled exchange of cash flow on February 2004.

PUTABLE SWAP

A putable swap is an option that gives the party that pays floating rate and receives fixed rate the right, not an obligation, to terminate the swap. The motivation for this option is that the party that pays floating rate is concerned about rising interest rates in the future and therefore wishes to protect itself from interest rate risk. This option is not free. The party provided with this feature in the interest rate swap pays either directly or indirectly through a higher floating rate compared with the plain-vanilla swap with no such option. Assuming the following interest rate scenarios, the party that pays fixed rate and receives floating rate in a fixed for floating rate swap will terminate the swap in scenario I and do nothing in scenario II.

Scenario	Interest Rates	Action
I	Rising	Terminate the swap
II	Falling	Do nothing

WAREHOUSING SWAP

It is highly unlikely that two parties to interest rate or currency swaps would take an offsetting position in exactly the same notional principal and over the same time horizon. In practice, the market maker in the swap or the swap bank (the financial institution) may not be able to find a party willing to take the offsetting position in the swap. Therefore, financial institutions are likely to warehouse the swap and use a forward rate agreement or futures contract to manage their exposure until a suitable party is located that is willing to take the offsetting position but may not wish to swap for exactly the same amount of notional principal and the same maturity that the financial institution has entered in its first swap transaction. In this case, the financial institution may have residual and basis exposure as the small bid-ask spread of 3 to 5 basis points in the interest rate swap reduces the profitability of such a transaction unless basis and residual exposure are properly mitigated.

SWAPS RISKS

Several risks need to be considered in interest rate and currency swaps. These risks include basis risk due to the mismatch of the cash flow created, the counterparty or credit exposure, and sovereign risk.[8]

Basis Risk

Basis risk stems from the mismatch of the cash flows in the interest rate or currency swaps. The interest rate index used may not be perfectly correlated with the floating rate interest rate in the swap. For example, the LIBOR index used in floating rate notes may go up by 0.8 percent, while the cost of borrowing by a financial institution pegged to an index of money market funds increases by 1 percent over the same period. The swap cash flow for the financial institution receiving LIBOR and paying based on money market index would be adversely affected as a result of basis risk as the financial institution exposure to interest rate risk would not be completely eliminated.[9]

Counterparty Risk

This risk is due to the failure of one of the parties to the swap to meet its financial obligations; therefore, the financial institution has to pick up the offsetting position of the party that failed to make a payment. The financial institution assumes the counterparty risk by charging a fee directly or indirectly to both parties in the swap; the swap dealer takes the offsetting position in both fixed for floating and floating for fixed interest rate swaps.

Example: The local government in the London community of Hammersmith and Fulham was reported to have entered into a fixed for floating rate swap with a notional principal over $9.5 billion. The floating rate "euro pound" rose from 8.1 percent in 1988 to 15.2 percent in December 1989, causing the local community a loss of nearly $600 million as floating rate payments ballooned due to rising short-term interest rates.

The House of Lords ruled that the local community lacked the authority to enter into interest rate swaps; thus it was not responsible to make payments to the banks. The loss resulting from interest rate swaps spread over 78 banks.[10]

To mitigate the counterparty risk to the financial institution engaged in derivative transactions such as swaps, the Bank for International Settlement has imposed a minimum capital requirement to provide a buffer against large unexpected losses. The amount of capital for financial institutions exposed to interest rate and currency risks has to be equal to three times the 10-day value at risk with 99 percent confidence interval.

Exhibit 7.22 presents the amount of credit risk exposure for various interest rates swaps maturing in 1 to 15 years. For example, the amount of credit exposure on a five-year swap reaches $9.24 million by the two-year per $100 million notional principal in which a bank pays floating rates and receives fixed rate and vice versa. The credit exposure in the 15-year swap reaches a maximum of $46.05 million in 8.5 years, where a bank pays a fixed rate and receives a floating rate per $100 million notional principal.

The credit risk exposure is due to an *amortization process*, that is, the credit exposure is a decreasing function of time (as time increases, the swap is amortized over time) as well as due to a *diffusion process* (the exposure increases over time in a long-dated swap). The combination of these two processes produces a hump-shaped credit exposure, which is demonstrated in Exhibit 7.23 for the floating rate leg of the swap.

The amount of credit exposure is significantly higher for the fixed leg of the interest rate swap as it increases to a maximum of $14.4 million in 2.5 years per $100 million notional principal on the five-year swap and gradually falls to $4.27 million by the end of five years. The amount of credit exposure is also directly related to the term structure of interest rates, as interest rates increase/decrease as the amount of credit exposure increases/decreases.

Sovereign Risk

This risk reflects the political fallout and its impact on the stability of the sovereign nation in meeting its financial obligations in a swap transaction. The sovereign country may impose exchange controls and block access by the counterparty to foreign exchange, causing the counterparty to default in its financial obligations.

For example, Credit Suisse First Boston (CSFB) counterparty to forward ruble/dollar contract failed to deliver dollars when the Russian government froze access to dollars in August 1997, preceding the Russian ruble currency crisis of August 1998. While CSFB had insignificant credit or counterparty risk, it presumably had high sovereign risk because of the Russian government.

EXHIBIT 7.22 Credit Exposure for U.S. Dollar Interest Rate Swaps as of July 1997

Maturity	1 Year		5 Years		10 Years		15 Years	
Time	Fixed	Floating	Fixed	Floating	Fixed	Floating	Fixed	Floating
0	0.00	0.00	0.00	0.00	0.00	0.00	0.00	0.00
2 weeks	0.32	0.30	1.85	1.79	2.95	2.92	3.89	3.92
1 month	0.47	0.43	2.74	2.62	4.35	4.29	5.70	5.77
2 months	0.68	0.59	3.99	3.72	6.28	6.13	8.17	8.29
3 months	0.84	0.71	4.99	4.57	7.79	7.56	10.77	10.24
4 months	0.96	0.79	5.83	5.27	9.07	8.74	11.67	11.85
5 months	1.08	0.87	6.63	5.90	10.27	9.82	13.15	13.34
6 months	1.18	0.93	7.37	6.46	11.35	10.77	14.48	14.66
9 months	1.30	0.84	9.52	7.39	14.57	12.65	18.44	17.36
1.0 year	1.33	0.85	11.24	8.51	17.16	14.73	21.55	20.28
1.5 years			13.22	9.18	20.82	16.92	26.22	23.77
2.0 years			14.23	9.24	23.47	18.29	29.79	26.26
2.5 years			14.44	8.88	25.39	19.16	32.60	28.14
3.0 years			14.20	8.23	26.98	19.66	35.12	29.62
3.5 years			13.15	7.19	28.09	19.80	37.21	30.68
4.0 years			11.11	5.77	28.94	19.62	38.88	31.36
4.5 years			8.04	4.06	28.29	19.20	40.30	31.76
5.0 years			4.27	2.05	27.32	18.40	41.57	31.76
5.5 years					26.01	17.47	42.83	31.63
6.0 years					24.11	16.36	43.76	31.30
6.5 years					22.24	15.15	44.54	30.89
7.0 years					19.46	13.80	45.21	30.36
7.5 years					15.97	12.26	45.57	29.63
8.0 years					11.53	10.69	45.98	28.75
8.5 years					6.03	8.87	46.05	27.71
9.0 years						6.86	46.00	26.54
9.5 years						4.69	45.75	25.24
10.0 years						2.34	45.42	23.79
11.0 years							43.34	20.76
12.0 years							35.44	17.29
13.0 years							26.85	12.97
14.0 years							18.75	7.92
15.0 years							7.24	2.67

Source: J. Tavakoli *Credit Derivatives and Synthetic Structure* (Hoboken, NJ: John Wiley & Sons, 2001, p. 151.

EXHIBIT 7.23   Credit Risk Exposure for U.S. Dollars Interest Rate Swaps

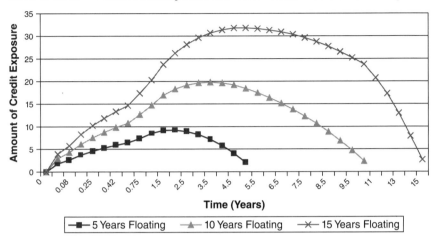

EXOTIC SWAPS

Exotic swaps are designed to provide protection against interest rate or currency exchange rate risk as well as to enhance risk return in speculative transactions. The cash flow in a simple plain-vanilla swap is tied to fixed for floating or floating for fixed as well as floating for floating, where one of the floating rates is pegged to LIBOR and the other float is pegged to U.S. Treasury bills. The cash flow in an exotic swap could be tied to an algorithm that defines the relationship between a few parameters, such as price, yield, as well as an arbitrary constant or term involving square or cubic root and any other numbers that the party that is likely to receive fixed and pay floating based on the algorithm that it may not fully comprehend.

Gibson Greetings and Procter and Gamble Swaps

Two companies, Gibson Greetings (GG) and Procter and Gamble (P&G), entered into an exotic interest rate swap with Bankers Trust that resulted in significant losses to both companies. GG lost nearly $20 million in an interest rate swap involving fixed for floating, where the floating payment was pegged to the square of LIBOR rate.[11]

P&G and Bankers Trust entered into a fixed for floating swap where Bankers Trust agreed to pay 5.3 percent to P&G and receive a 30-day commercial paper rate less 75 basis points.[12] However, if the payment formula that P&G was required to make to Bankers Trust was zero or negative, Bankers Trust received a 30-day commercial paper rate minus 75 basis points. This requirement amounted to imposing a floor rate on the floating rate leg of the swap, insulating the swap dealer from adverse scenario. P&G lost $157 million in an exotic interest rate swap with notional principal of $200 million with Bankers Trust whose payments were defined by this formula:

Max [(17.0415 × (5-year T-note rate) − (Price of 6.25% T-bond due 8/2023), 30-day commercial paper rate − .75 %]

Exhibit 7.24 provides various interest rate scenarios for five-year rates and corresponding yields and prices for the 30-year Treasury bond embedded in the formula for the floating rate payments. According to the formula, the float payment is −51.15 percent where the five-year rate is 4 percent and a 30-year bond is rated to yield 5 percent. To prevent negative float payments by P&G, the 30-day commercial paper rate at the time of the exchange of cash flow minus 75 basis points provided the minimum floors.

Bankers Trust in effect did get protection in the event the rates fell; however, P&G was not afforded the same protection if rates rose substantially, as maximum interest payments by P&G to Bankers Trust were not capped. The float payment increases as the rates increases. For example, assuming five-year Treasury rate is 7 percent and the yield on the 30-year is 8 percent, the float payment will be equal to 39.07 percent. In essence, the Bankers Trust swap agreement with P&G was a game with the payoff of tails, I win, heads, you lose.

Both GG and P&G closed out their swap positions and filed lawsuits against Bankers Trust. The GG case was settled out of court. Bankers Trust agreed to accept $6 million out of $20 million owed to it in November 1994 and to pay $10 million in fines to federal securities regulators to settle charges for providing misleading information to GG.[13] The P&G lawsuit against Bankers Trust settled out of court. Bankers Trust agreed to absorb $150 million out of $157 million loss in May 1996.[14] Other banks reportedly absorb losses on swaps to their clients to prevent bad publicity and lengthy litigation.[15]

CURRENCY SWAPS

In a simple plain-vanilla currency swap, two parties agree to exchange periodic interest in two different currencies over specific periods of time and to exchange the notional principal at the maturity at the agreed rate. For example, IBM and

EXHIBIT 7.24   Floating Rate Payments under Various Interest Rate Scenarios on P&G and Bankers Trust Swaps Based on the Formula

	30-year rate (%)			
5-year rate (%)	5	6	7	8
4	−51.1594	−35.3009	−22.4872	−12.0459
5	−34.1179	−18.2594	−5.4457	4.9956
6	−17.0764	−1.2179	11.5958	22.0371
7	−0.0349	15.8236	28.6373	39.0786

British Petroleum agree to exchange periodic interest denominated in their respective currencies, that is, dollars for pounds, on a notional principal of $150 million and £100 million at the current exchange of $1.50/£ over the five-year swap period with semiannual compounding. Exhibit 7.25 presents the structure of the currency swap.

IBM borrows in the U.S. capital market at a fixed rate of 6 percent and swaps this loan with British Petroleum's loan denominated in pounds. IBM borrows and lends dollar debt at 6 percent and pays 7.5 percent for a pound-denominated loan, thereby transforming its dollar-based loan to pound-based debt without the underwriting cost of borrowing in the pound market. British Petroleum follows the same principle as its debt transforms from pounds to dollars.

The motivation for IBM to engage in currency swaps stems from its desire to hedge its pound cash flows derived from the Commonwealth of the United Kingdom over the next five years by assuming pounds-denominated debt, while British Petroleum is interested in managing its dollar-denominated cash flow derived in North America for the next five years by borrowing dollar-denominated debt. IBM and British Petroleum will borrow in their respective markets on a notional principal of $150 and £100 million, respectively.

Suppose IBM will take a five-year fixed rate balloon debt with semiannual compounding at 6 percent on notional principal of $150 million. British Petroleum, however, will take £100 million over the five years at a fixed rate of 7.5 percent. Exhibit 7.26 presents the proceeds and coupons for both loans.

IBM and British Petroleum may commence the currency swaps without an intermediary and taking the counterparty risk by swapping the initial principal

EXHIBIT 7.25   Plain-Vanilla Currency Swap

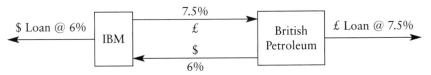

EXHIBIT 7.26   Cash Flows on Dollar and Pound
Loans for IBM and British Petroleum

Period	IBM	British Petroleum
0	$150 million	£100 million
1	(4.5)	(3.75)
2	(4.5)	(3.75)
3	(4.5)	(3.75)
4	(4.5)	(3.75)
.	.	.
.	.	.
10	(154.5)	(£103.75)

and every scheduled coupon and the final principal at the maturity of the swap, as seen in Exhibit 7.27.

Both companies restructured their balance sheets in the currency in which they wished to have exposure—that is, in pounds for IBM and dollars for British Petroleum—without actually going to the euro credit market to secure debt denominated in other than their own currency. The cash flows IBM derives from its operation in the United Kingdom is used to service the debt denominated in pounds. Similarly British Petroleum's dollar-denominated cash flows in the U.S. markets is used to pay the dollar-denominated debt. In this way both companies hedge their currency exposure to exchange rate risk.

IBM would like to enter into a currency swap with British Petroleum; however, neither party is interested in taking counterparty risk. This is where a financial institution comes in; it takes an offsetting position in both currencies for a fee (spread) where it simultaneously borrows and lends in dollars and pounds. The structure of the swap will be as shown in Exhibit 7.28, assuming there is a swap dealer to mitigate counterparty risk. The rates have been quoted to IBM and British Petroleum in the dollar and pound markets.

The asymmetric interest rate differentials in the dollar and pound markets for the two parties provide an incentive to engage in a swap based on comparative

EXHIBIT 7.27 Currency Swaps Between IBM and British Petroleum

Period	IBM	British Petroleum
0	$150 million	£100 million
Swap fee	$1.25 million	
1	(£3.75)	($4.5)
2	(£3.75)	($4.5)
3	(£3.75)	($4.5)
4	(£3.75)	($4.5)
.	.	.
.	.	.
10	(£103.75)	($154.5)
All-in cost of swap	7.70%	
IRR	7.70%	

EXHIBIT 7.28 Currency Swap Quotes

	$-rate	$-rate differential	£-rate	£-rate differential
IBM	6		7	
British Petroleum	7.25	**1.25**	7.5	$\frac{1}{2}$
Swap gain				$\left(1.25 - \frac{1}{2}\right) = 75$ bps

advantage. The interest rates differentials (in dollars and pounds) are 75 basis points, that is, the gains from the currency and interest rate swaps, assuming the gains are divided equally among the parties to the swap, IBM, British Petroleum, and the swap dealer. Exhibit 7.29 shows the structure of this currency swap.

According to Exhibit 7.29, IBM and British Petroleum borrow in the market where they have comparative advantage. IBM, despite having absolute advantage in both markets, has a relative or comparative advantage in the dollar market where it borrows at 6 percent per annum in its outside borrowing. British Petroleum, having absolute disadvantage in both the dollar and pound markets, has relative or comparative advantage in the pound market and therefore borrows in the pound market at the rate of 7.5 percent.

By swapping dollars for pounds, IBM secures pound-denominated debt at the rate 6.75 percent, which is better than the 7 percent rate in the pound market without the swap. Therefore, IBM saves 25 basis points and transforms dollar debt for pound debt for managing its currency exposure to foreign exchange risk. British Petroleum also swaps its pound debt for dollar-denominated debt at the rate of 7 percent per annum, which is better than the 7.25 percent rate without the swap, saving 25 basis points and restructuring its pound debt to dollar debt for managing its exposure to foreign exchange risk. The swap dealer, having long and short positions in dollars and pounds, makes 100 basis points in dollars, while losing 75 basis points in the pound market, for a net gain of 25 basis points.

This analysis is predicated on the assumption that basis points in dollars and pounds are equal, assuming interest parity holds the basis points in dollars and foreign currency can be treated as if they are identical. However, in reality the parity is violated for various reasons; therefore, the basis points in dollars and foreign currency are not identical. The method of conversion of basis points procedure is used to convert the basis points in one currency to another.

Method of Conversion of Basis Points

In Exhibit 7.29 the swap dealer is expected to lose 75 basis points in pound-denominated debt over the five-year length of the swap, while making 100 basis

EXHIBIT 7.29   Currency Swap

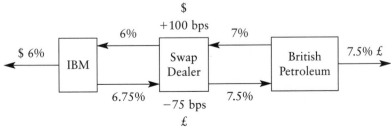

points in dollar-denominated debt. Using the following procedure, the basis points can be converted from pounds into dollars:

Step 1. Estimate the present value of the basis points in foreign currency (pounds) over the length of swap, assuming the foreign interest rate of 7.5 percent from Exhibit 7.29.

$$37.5 \times \frac{\left[\left(1 + \frac{.075}{2}\right)^{10} - 1\right]}{\left[\left(1 + \frac{.075}{2}\right)^{10} \times \frac{.075}{2}\right]} = 307.98$$

Step 2. Set the 307.98 as the present value of the annuity and solve for the annuity payment X discounted at the U.S. interest rate of 6 percent over the length of swap with semiannual compounding.

$$307.98 = X \frac{\left[\left(1 + \frac{.06}{2}\right)^{10} - 1\right]}{\left[\left(1 + \frac{.06}{2}\right)^{10} \times \left(\frac{.06}{2}\right)\right]}$$

$$X = 36.10$$

Double the 36.10 to arrive at the 72.20 basis points. It turns out that the 75 basis points in pounds are equal to 72.20 basis points in dollars. The higher the foreign interest rate, the lower is the value of one basis point.

BREAK-EVEN ANALYSIS OF SWAP AND REFINANCING

The intermediary is always present in a swap transaction for mitigating counterparty risk; the party swapping dollars for pounds or pounds for dollars pays fees either directly or indirectly to a swap dealer for the dealer's services. This cost and any other cost—the all-in cost of swaps—is the effective cost of borrowing in foreign currency interest rates net of transaction costs that a firm pays on the proceeds from a swap transaction. Suppose IBM pays $1.25 million to a swap dealer for intermediation and risk taking in the swap transaction in Exhibit 7.29. The break-even swap rate r is the interest rate that equates the present value of the swap payment denominated in foreign currency with swap proceeds net of all-in cost as defined in Equation 7.5.

$$\frac{\text{(Swap principal} - \text{Swap fees)}}{S_0} = \frac{C_1}{(1 + r)} + \frac{C_2}{(1 + r)^2} + \cdots + \frac{(F + C_n)}{(1 + r)^n} \quad (7.5)$$

where

C_1, C_2, C_n = coupon interest payments from debt denominated in foreign currency

F = the principal amount of foreign currency debt

S = spot exchange rate

$$\frac{(150 - 1.25)}{\$1.50/£} = \frac{3.75}{(1 + r)} + \frac{3.75}{(1 + r)^2} + \cdots \frac{103.75}{(1 + r)^{10}}$$

The annualized swap rate is estimated from the equation to be 7.7039 percent. This is the rate that IBM's treasurer uses as a benchmark to compare the rate on the pound-denominated loan in the Eurocredit market. If the rate in the Europound (pound loan offshore) for a five-year loan is greater than 7.7039 percent, then swapping dollars with pounds in the example makes economic sense. Otherwise IBM may be better off directly borrowing in the Europound market.

OPTIONS EMBEDDED IN CURRENCY SWAPS

The plain-vanilla currency swap just described can be structured to provide the same type of options attached to interest rate swaps, namely, call, put, and so forth. For example, the currency swap may be terminated by one of the parties to the swap by attaching call or put options to the plain-vanilla swap.

Unwinding Currency Swaps

In the currency swap in Exhibit 7.29, British Petroleum decides to terminate the swap at the end of the third year. The pound has depreciated to $1.42/pound, and the two-year debt in dollars and pounds is rated to yield 4 and 5 percent, respectively.

The present value of the cash flow paid by British Petroleum to the swap dealer and received from the swap dealer for the remaining life of the swap is:

$$PV \text{ (Paid \$)} = \frac{\$5.25}{\left(1 + \frac{.04}{2}\right)} + \frac{\$5.25}{\left(1 + \frac{.04}{2}\right)^2} + \frac{\$5.25}{\left(1 + \frac{.04}{2}\right)^3} + \frac{\$155.25}{(1 + \frac{.04}{2})^4}$$

$$= \$158.5674 \text{ million}$$

$$PV \text{ (Rec £)} = \frac{£3.75}{\left(1 + \frac{.05}{2}\right)} + \frac{£3.75}{\left(1 + \frac{.05}{2}\right)^2} + \frac{£3.75}{\left(1 + \frac{.05}{2}\right)^3} + \frac{£103.75}{\left(1 + \frac{.05}{2}\right)^4}$$

$$= £104.7025$$

The present value of the amount received from the swap dealer is valued at the current exchange rate of $1.42/pound, which converts to $148.6776 million. British Petroleum pays an out-of-pocket cost of $9.8899 million to terminate the swap.

$$\text{Termination fee} = -\$158.5674 + 148.6776$$
$$= -\$9.8899 \text{ million}$$

After the termination of one of the parties to the swap—in this case, British Petroleum—the swap dealer uses a forward or futures contract to manage its exposure to interest rate and currency exchange rate risk by warehousing the swap until a suitable party is identified who is willing to take the offsetting position. The swap dealer may provide an incentive in the form of lower interest rate to mitigate its own exposure.

What Happened to Currency Exchange Rate Risk?

This risk did not disappear; it was transferred to someone else. In Exhibit 7.29, the swap dealer is expected to receive net 100 basis points in dollars, which translates to $750,000 every six months; however, the swap dealer is expected to make net payment in pounds of 75 basis points, which converts to £375,000 every six months. The swap dealer is net long in dollar and net short in pounds; therefore, it is exposed to foreign exchange rate risk for which it can buy stripes of six-month forward with the notional amount of £375,000.

The swap rates for various currencies are derived from the underlying government Treasury securities yield curve plus the spread attributed to the borrower in the respective Eurocredit markets. For example, the 30-year U.S. Treasury constant maturity rate as of March 30, 1999, was 5.59 percent; therefore the 30-year swap rate of 6.28–6.31 percent in Exhibit 7.30 reflects a credit spread of 69–72 basis points at bid/ask.

For example, in a five-year fixed for floating rate swap in the U.S. dollar, the party to an interest rate swap receives a fixed rate of 5.73 percent (bid rate) and pays a three-month LIBOR rate of 5.0626 (offer rate) as of March 30, 1999, as seen in Exhibit 7.30. Alternatively, in a seven-year floating for fixed interest rate in Swiss francs, a Swiss borrower pays 2.81 percent (ask rate) and receives six-month Swiss franc LIBOR of 1.3125 percent (bid rate) as of March 30, 1999, as can be verified from Exhibit 7.30.

Cross-currency swap quotes in Exhibit 7.30 reveal that a seven-year swap in U.S. dollars at 5.89 percent may be swapped with 1.58 percent interest rate in Japanese yen, 2.81 percent rate in Swiss francs, and 4.05 percent interest rate in euros. For example, a U.S. multinational company can swap seven-year $100 million denominated debt for Swiss francs paying 2.81 percent (ask rate) and receiving 5.86 percent (bid rate) in U.S. dollars. The Swiss counterparty in the swap pays 5.89 percent in dollars and receives 2.73 percent (bid rate) in Swiss francs.

THREE-WAY SWAPS

There are four parties to three-way swaps, the swap dealer and the three parties. The swap dealer has a bilateral agreement with each party, paying (bid rate) and receiving (ask rate) in a given currency.

Example: Consider Nissan, a Japanese manufacturing firm, which is borrowing 20 billion yen for five years at the fixed offer rate of 1.12 percent to swap with 172 million euro debt issued by MG, a German firm, at fixed offer rate of 3.67

EXHIBIT 7.30 Interest Rate and Currency Swap Quotes

Years	Euro Bid	Euro Ask	Swiss Franc Bid	Swiss Franc Ask	U.S. Dollar Bid	U.S. Dollar Ask	Japanese Yen Bid	Japanese Yen Ask
1	2.99	3.02	1.43	1.47	5.24	5.26	0.23	0.26
2	3.08	3.12	1.68	1.76	5.43	5.46	0.36	0.39
3	3.24	3.28	1.93	2.01	5.56	5.59	0.56	0.59
4	3.44	3.48	2.15	2.23	5.65	5.68	0.82	0.85
5	3.63	3.67	2.35	2.43	5.73	5.76	1.09	1.12
6	3.83	3.87	2.54	2.62	5.80	5.83	1.33	1.36
7	**4.01**	**4.05**	**2.73**	**2.81**	**5.86**	**5.89**	**1.55**	**1.58**
8	4.18	4.22	2.91	2.99	5.92	5.95	1.75	1.78
9	4.32	4.36	3.08	3.16	5.96	5.99	1.90	1.93
10	4.42	4.46	3.22	3.30	6.01	6.04	2.04	2.07
12	4.58	4.62	3.45	3.55	6.10	6.13	2.28	2.32
15	4.78	4.82	3.71	3.81	6.20	6.23	2.51	2.56
20	5.00	5.04	3.96	4.06	6.29	6.32	2.71	2.76
25	5.13	5.17	4.07	4.17	6.29	6.32	2.77	2.82
30	5.19	5.23	4.16	4.26	6.28	6.31	2.82	2.88
LIBOR	3.0313	3.0938	1.3125	1.4375	4.9375	5.0625	0.1250	0.2188

Source: The Financial Times, March 30, 1999, p. 27. Bid and ask spreads as of close of London business. U.S.$ is quoted against three-month LIBOR; Japanese yen against six-month LIBOR; euro and Swiss franc against six-month LIBOR.

percent (see Exhibit 7.30), which will swap 328 million of its 500 million euro-based debt borrowed at the offer rate of 3.67 percent with 468.5 million Swiss franc-denominated debt of a Swiss firm paying offer rate of 2.43 percent to swap dealer with semiannual pay/receive schedule.

Nissan swaps yen for Swiss francs, paying 1.12 percent at the offer, and receives 1.09 percent at the bid for its yen-denominated debt, thereby losing 3 basis points in a yen loan (the swap dealer picks up 3 basis points). MG borrows at the fixed offer rate of 3.67 percent and swaps parts of its euro debt with Nissan, paying 1.12 for yen debt and receiving 3.63 percent for its euro-based loan from the swap dealer, thereby losing 4 basis points in its euro-based loans (the swap dealer picks up 4 basis points).

MG swaps 328 million euro for a 476.5 million Swiss franc loan, receiving 3.63 percent on euro debt from the swap dealer and paying 2.43 percent for the Swiss franc debt, losing 4 basis points on the euro loan (the swap dealer picks up 4 basis points). The Swiss firm swaps its debt with euros, paying 2.43 percent at the offer and receiving 2.35 percent at the bid, losing 8 basis points in its Swiss franc loan (the swap dealer picks up 8 basis points); however, the

EXHIBIT 7.31   Three-way Swaps

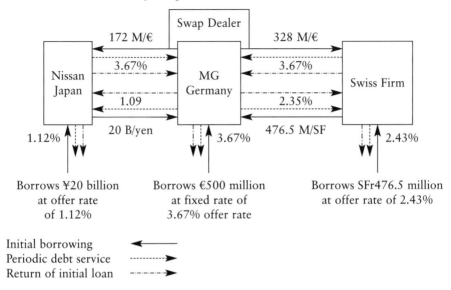

Initial borrowing	←
Periodic debt service	╌╌╌╌►
Return of initial loan	╌ ╌ ╌►

Swiss firm pays for the euro debt at the ask rate of 3.67 percent. Exhibit 7.31 shows the structure of this three-way swap.

The swap is initiated where parties borrowed in the market in which they are able to acquire the capital at a competitive rate. The capital essentially is acquired in the market where the parties enjoyed comparative advantage and swapped for the desired currency in which they wished to have exposure. The three-way swaps in Exhibit 7.31 are executed assuming 116.279 yen/euro, as 20 billion yen (20 B) swapped for 172 million euro (172 M), as well as 1.4527 Swiss franc/euro, as MG swapped 328 million euro for 476.5 million Swiss franc.

NOTES:

1. These rates are approximately equal to the off-the-run Treasury securities as of October 30, 2002.
2. LIBOR is the average of the offer rate in the interbank market of 16 largest banks in London at 11 A.M. London time. LIBOR is used as a reference rate for making loans to corporations in the international financial markets.
3. Titman (1992).
4. This figure is calculated from the average daily turnover of $331 billion as reported by the Bank for International Settlement × 252 trading per year.
5. The Eurodollar futures interest rates are obtained from the stripes of the six-month futures from March 2003 through September 2006 from the *Wall Street Journal* of September 9, 2002.

6. Using Black option pricing, the caps and floors are estimated as:

$$\text{Caps} = \text{Max} \ (R_f - R_c, \ 0)$$
$$= e^{-R_f \times T} [R_f N(d_1) - e^{-R_f \times T} R_c (N(d_2)]$$
$$d_1 = [1n \ (R_f/R_c) + \sigma^2 T/2]/\sigma \sqrt{T}$$
$$d_2 = d_1 - \sigma \sqrt{T}$$

where

R_f = float rate
R_c = caps rate
σ = volatility estimate implied or flat
T = maturity of the cap

7. See Prospectus, Merrill Lynch, February 23, 1983.
8. See Marshall and Kapner (1993) for detailed discussion of risks to swap dealers.
9. State of Wisconsin Investment Board lost nearly $95 million in March 1995 in an interest rate and currency swap involving U.S dollar and Mexican peso when the peso devalued and the interest rate spread widened. This is an example of basis risk where the Investment Board paid more in dollars and received pesos not worth as much as they used to be worth.
10. "U.K. Court Rules Borough, Banks' Swaps Illegal," *The Wall Street Journal,* November 6, 1989.
11. J. Neu, "Gibson Greetings Goes for It," *International Treasure,* September 19, 1994.
12. F. Norris, "Procter's Tale: Gambling in Ignorance," *New York Times,* October 30, 1994.
13. Lippinn and Taylor, "Bankers Trust Settles Charges on Derivatives," *Wall Street Journal,* December 23, 1994.
14. L. Hays, "Bankers Trust Settles Dispute with P&G," *Wall Street Journal,* May 10, 1996.
15. A. Sikri, "Quietly Bankers Eat Clients' Losses Tied to Derivatives," *Wall Street Journal,* April 29, 1996.

CHAPTER 8

Translation, Transaction, and Operating Exposure

Firms in increasingly integrated global economies face exchange rate risk in the course of the exchange of goods and services to one another. This risk is relevant, material, affects their cash flows, and needs to be managed properly. This chapter outlines the translation, transaction, and operating-induced exposure to foreign exchange risk and provides remedies that are available in terms of hedging instruments to manage such exposure.[1]

TRANSLATION EXPOSURE

Translation exposure defines the unexpected change in exchange rates on the balance sheet of the subsidiary as translated for consolidation purposes into the parent company's currency. The translation of the subsidiary's balance sheet and income statements from the currency of the operating units offshore to that of the parent potentially changes stockholders' equity. Multinational corporations with various overseas subsidiaries must translate the subsidiaries' balance sheet and income statements into the functional currency of the parent for consolidation and to report to regulatory agencies and shareholders. The change in exchange rate for the currency of the subsidiary from the last translation produces accounting gains or losses that are posted to the stockholders' equity and produce accounting exposure.

Translation exposure measures the change in the book value of the assets and liabilities, excluding stockholders' equity as residuals, due to changes in the exchange rate from the last translation. In the past, corporation accounting conventions used these translation methods:

- Current noncurrent
- Monetary nonmonetary
- Temporal
- Current rate

Depending on the method employed, the accounting standard for classifying assets and liabilities as exposed/unexposed to exchange rate risk produced an overwhelming support for reform to remedy the problem. That is, the distortion caused by the application of one or the other method prompted the Financial Accounting Standards Board (FASB) to issue a new ruling in 1981, FASB No. 52. This statement required firms to use the *all-current rate method* approach for translation purposes. Exhibit 8.1 presents the exposed assets and liabilities under various translation methods.

Exposed assets net of exposed liabilities times the change in exchange rate $(S_t - S_{t-1})$ produces net translation exposure, which is reflected in the stockholders' equity account as a separate item known as cumulative translation adjustment (CTA). For example, suppose the balance sheet of Coca-Cola's subsidiary in the United Kingdom is translated to U.S. dollars for consolidation purposes and the pound has appreciated to $1.60/£ from $1.52/£ since the last translation. As seen in Exhibit 8.1, under the temporal method, all of the components of the balance sheet will be translated at the new exchange rate with the exception of the inventory and long-term assets, which are translated at the historic rate, as they are treated as unexposed.

The difference between temporal and monetary/nonmonetary methods is that the historic cost of the marketable securities is translated at the historic rate under the temporal method and at the current spot rate under the monetary/nonmonetary method. Suppose the pound value of the exposed assets net of exposed liabilities under the monetary/nonmonetary method is £1.2 million. The translation exposure is therefore equal to

$$1,200,000 \times (\$1.60 - \$1.52/\pounds) = \$96,000$$

Coca-Cola's stockholders' equity increases by $96,000 due to a favorable exchange rate scenario as the pound revalues from $1.52/£ to $1.60/£. This increase is a paper gain as reflected in the CTA to the stockholders' equity account.

EXHIBIT 8.1   Balance Sheet Translations under Various Methods

	Current Noncurrent	Monetary Nonmonetary	Temporal	All-Current Rate
Cash	S	S	S	S
Marketable securities	S	S	S	S
Receivables	S	S	S	S
Inventory	S	S_h	S_h	S
Long-term assets	S_h	S_h	S_h	S
Payables	S	S	S	S
Long-term debt	S_h	S	S	S
Equity	Residual	Residual	Residual	Residual

S: Spot exchange rate S_h: Historic exchange rate

Under all translation methods except the all-current rate method, the income statement is translated at the weighted average of the exchange rate during the reporting period. Under the all-current rate method, the income statement is translated at the spot exchange rate at the time revenue and expense are recognized. However, revenue and expense associated with noncurrent, nonmonetary assets or liabilities, such as depreciations and cost of goods sold, are translated at the historic rate.

Example: Consider a U.S. multinational company's subsidiary in Great Britain whose balance sheet and income statement are translated to the parent's functional currency—the U.S. dollar. The pound has devalued from $1.50/£ to $1.40/£ since the last translation. Exhibit 8.2 presents the impact of the pound devaluation under various translation methods as reflected in the stockholders' equity of the parent.

EXHIBIT 8.2 Impact of Translation Methods on U.K. Subsidiary of U.S. Firm Assuming Pound Devalues from $1.50/£ to $1.40/£

In Millions	Current Noncurrent		Monetary Nonmonetary		Temporal		All-Current Rate	
	£	$	£	$	£	$	£	$
Cash	15[a]	21	15	21	15	21	15	21
Marketable securities	30	42	30	42	30	42	30	42
Receivables	40	56	40	56	40	56	40	56
Inventory	60	84	60	90	90	90	60	84
Long-term assets	250	375	250	375	250	375	250	350
Total assets	395	578	395	584	395	584	395	553
Payables	100	140	100	140	100	140	100	140
Long-term debt	145	217.5	145	203	145	203	145	203
Equity	150	220.5[b]	150	241[b]	150	241[b]	150	210[b]
Total liabilities	395	578	395	584	395	584	395	553
Exposed assets	145		85		85		395	
Exposed liabilities	100		245		245		245	
Net exposure[c]	£45		−£160		−£160		£150	
CTA[d]	−$4.5		+$16		+$16		−$15	

[a] Items highlighted are exposed.

[b] Stockholders' equity adjusted to the new level after translation. For example, the net worth translated to dollar under the old exchange rate of $1.50/£ produces $225 million. However, the adjusted net worth after translation to dollars of $220.5 million under the monetary nonmonetary method shows a decline of $4.5 million, which is reflected in the CTA of the same magnitude. However, the stockholders' equity under the temporal method is $241 million after translation at the new exchange rate, an increase of $16 million, as is evidenced by a CTA of the same magnitude.

[c] Exposed assets minus exposed liabilities.

[d] Cumulative Translation Adjustment = (Net Exposure) $(S_t - S_{t-1})$.

Case Study

ACCOUNTING EXPOSURE

*Jeannie Johnson Harrington**

ILLUSTRATION OF THE CURRENT RATE METHOD

Under the current rate method, the income statement is translated at the average conversion rate and the assets and liabilities are converted at the balance sheet rate (current or closing rate). The shareholders' equity items are translated at the rate in effect when the transactions occurred (historical rate).

A U.S. company has a German subsidiary that reports and operates using the euro. Financial statements for the German subsidiary are:

Balance Sheet 12/31/02

Assets		Liabilities and Shareholders' Equity	
Cash	€ 10,000	Accounts payable	€ 50,000
Inventory	100,000	Capital stock	500,000
Property, plant, and equipment	600,000	Retained earnings	160,000
	€710,000		€710,000

Income Statement for the Year Ended 12/31/02

Revenues	€300,000
Cost of goods sold	(140,000)
Operating expenses	(120,000)
Net income	€ 40,000

Foreign currency exchange rates for euro €/U.S. $:

12/31/01	.8898
12/31/02	1.0487
Average 2002	.9428
Historical rate	1.0071

Translation of income statement:

Revenues	€300,000	×	.9428	=	$282,840
Cost of goods sold	(140,000)	×	.9428	=	(131,992)
Operating expenses	(120,000)	×	.9428	=	(113,136)
Net income	€ 40,000				$ 37,712

*Associate professor of accounting, Middle Tennessee State University

Translation of balance sheet:

Assets

Cash	€ 10,000	× 1.0487 =	$ 10,487
Inventory	100,000	× 1.0487 =	104,870
Property, plant, and equipment	600,000	× 1.0487 =	629,220
	€710,000		$744,577

Liabilities and Shareholders' Equity

Accounts payable	€ 50,000	× 1.0487	$ 52,435
Capital stock	500,000	× 1.0071	503,550
Retained earnings	160,000		85,838*
Accumulated foreign currency translation adjustment			102,754†
	€710,000		$744,577

* Balance consists of earlier translated retained earnings balance of $48,126 plus translated 2002 net income.

† Balance in the account accumulates from year to year with a positive balance reflecting net foreign currency translation gains.

Large differences in foreign currency rates from one fiscal year to the next can result in substantial accounting exposure. The U.S. dollar was strong against most foreign currencies from 1999 through 2001. Beginning in 2002, several currencies rebounded, with the dollar weakening. Listed below are some examples of how the currency market has affected two international companies.

PepsiCo Inc., USA, reported the following foreign currency translation changes for the respective fiscal years in its shareholders' equity:

Fiscal Year End	Net Earnings	Foreign Currency Translation
December 31, 1999	€2,505,000,000	($136,000,000)
December 31, 2000	2,543,000,000	(289,000,000)
December 31, 2001	2,662,000,000	(218,000,000)
December 31, 2002	3,313,000,000	56,000,000

Operations outside of the United States represent 34 percent of net sales, of which Mexico, the United Kingdom, and Canada contribute 19 percent.

(continues)

DaimlerChrysler, AG, Germany, reported the following foreign currency translation changes for the respective fiscal years in its shareholders' equity:

Fiscal Year End	Net Earnings	Foreign Currency Translation
December 31, 1999	€2,505,000,000	($136,000,000)
December 31, 1999	€5,746,000,000	€2,431,000,000
December 31, 2000	7,894,000,000	1,363,000,000
December 31, 2001	(662,000,000)	565,000,000
December 31, 2002	4,718,000,000	(3,250,000,000)

Net sales to the U.S. represent 52 percent of total net sales, with 15 percent going to Germany and 16 percent to other countries in the European Union.

Analysts should not be fooled by these foreign currency translation adjustments. All the adjustments reported were paper adjustments only. The real cash effect of the currency changes was much less, as the international affiliates all operated within their local territories and were not as affected by the foreign exchange rate changes.

FUNCTIONAL CURRENCY

FASB No. 52 defines functional currency as "the currency of the primary economic environment in which the entity operates," that is, the currency in which the entity derives most of its revenue and expenses its cost. The FASB has established the following criteria for the determination of the functional currency.[2]

Accounting for Hyperinflationary Economy

Depreciation tends to inflate the earnings before interest and taxes as the all-current rate method underestimates depreciation relative to the replacement cost of the assets under inflationary environments and overestimates profit as the currency of the operating units significantly devalues. A hyperinflationary economy is defined as a country with 100 percent or more cumulative inflations during a span of three years. The inflation leads to significant devaluation of the currency, making translation of depreciation in the all-current rate method trivial and leading to the problem of disappearing assets.

To remedy the problem of disappearing assets, the FASB requires translating the balance sheet of the unit besieged by hyperinflation using the temporal method; translating plant, equipment, and depreciation at historic cost will result in higher values and will lead to less distortion of earnings of the operating unit. The FASB in essence has mandated that the functional currency of U.S. firms operating in hyperinflationary environment must be the U.S. dollar.

MANAGING TRANSLATION EXPOSURE

Accounting exposure stems from the mismatch of exposed assets and liabilities as the source of exposure. Balance sheet hedging can be effective as the company reduces the exposed assets by selling some of its assets for cash or by increasing its liabilities by borrowing additional amounts to incur transaction exposure. For example, if the exposed assets are $100 million and exposed liabilities are $80 million, the net exposure is $20 million that can be mitigated as:

- Sell $20 million worth of assets for cash, or
- Borrow $20 million to match the exposed assets equal to exposed liabilities of $100 million.

The $20 million borrowed raises the liabilities by $20 million, while simultaneously increasing cash by $20 million that could be invested in money market or long-term projects that will create transaction or economic exposure for the firm.

At times firms attempt to use the forward contract to manage accounting-induced exposure to foreign exchange.

BALANCE SHEET HEDGING

In the previous example of a firm having $20 million more exposed assets than liabilities, the firm may sell a $20 million forward contract to hedge its accounting exposure. If the functional currency devalues, the loss (paper loss due to accounting translation) is offset by the gain in the forward contract. The paper loss and actual real gains are offset against one another.

However, had the functional currency revalued, the paper gains due to a favorable exchange rate translation and the real loss in the forward contract offset one another only on paper. The firm, in reality, realizes real loss in dollars and cents, rendering hedging balance sheet exposure with the forward contract a speculation. At the expiration of the forward contract, the seller is obligated to sell at the rate agreed despite the fact that not selling forward the contract would have been the best course of action for the company.

Example: Consider the U.K. subsidiary of the U.S. firm in Exhibit 8.2. Using the temporal method for translation, the firm has £85 million exposed assets while having £245 million exposed liabilities. Balance sheet hedging requires eliminating the source of exposure that is rooted in the mismatch of exposed assets and liabilities. The firm can buy a £160 million three-month forward at $1.50/£ to match the exposed assets with liabilities. The pound devalues to $1.40/£ for the next translation period. The real loss of $16 million will be realized in the forward purchase of pounds, offset by the paper gains of $16 million in the translation from pounds to functional currency the U.S. dollar.[3]

A U.S. subsidiary in the United Kingdom believes that it will have a net translation exposure of $-£160$ million for the next translation period.

STRATEGY

The subsidiary buys £160 million three-month forward at $1.50/£.

The pound devalues to $1.40/£ for the next translation period.

Forward loss: ($1.40/£ $-$ $1.50/£) (£160 million) = $-$16 million

Translation gains: ($1.40/£ $-$ $1.50/£) ($-£160$ million) = $+$16 million

Results

Paper gains are equal to real losses of $16 million.

This strategy appears to have neutralized the firm's translation exposure to foreign exchange, as the firm substitutes paper gains for real losses and vice versa. The strategy is speculative in nature. Value-maximizing firms will be better off to avoid such a strategy.

TRANSACTION EXPOSURE

Transaction exposure is defined as the impact of the unexpected change in the exchange rate on the cash flow arising from all the contractual relationships entered prior to the change in exchange rate at time (t_1) to be settled after the change in exchange rate at time (t_2).

The contractual relationship is entered at time t_1 between two parties for exchange of goods or services at a price denominated in foreign currency for delivery and settlement at time t_2. The exchange rate is likely to change between t_1 and t_2, producing exposure to the party that is expected to make or receive cash flow denominated in foreign currency.

OPERATING EXPOSURE

The exposure to the multiperiod future cash flows arising due to an unexpected change in exchange rate is referred to as an economic or operating exposure. In this scenario the present value of the future cash flows is affected as a result of an unexpected change in the exchange rate. The transaction exposure is the effect of unexpected change in the nominal exchange rate on the cash flow associated with the monetary assets and liabilities and is usually short term and hedged with financial derivatives traded over the counter or on organized exchanges. The operating exposure, however, is related to the impact of the unexpected change in the exchange rate on future cash flows associated with the real assets and liabilities. Therefore, it is long term in nature.

The party with exposure to foreign exchange rate risk may wish to manage its exposure using:

- Exchange-traded financial derivatives such as futures or options
- Forward contracts, money market hedges, caps, floors, collars, and swaps in the over-the-counter (OTC) market

A multinational corporation (MNC) identifies its exposure to foreign exchange risk on a particular transaction on a currency-by-currency basis and nets out its aggregate inflows and outflows from various subsidiaries for a particular currency and time. Next the MNC determines how much of the exposure to manage—that is, whether to hedge or not to hedge. Finally, it identifies which hedging instrument is to be used based on cost/benefit analysis for managing and mitigating risk.

HEDGING IN PRACTICE: NIKE AND DUPONT

Nike markets its products in over 140 countries with foreign sales revenue accounting for 46 percent of its total revenue in fiscal 2001.[4] Given its huge presence in the foreign market, Nike's annual report states:

> It is the company's policy to utilize derivative financial instruments to reduce foreign exchange risks where internal netting strategies cannot be effectively employed. Fluctuation in the value of the hedging instruments are offset by fluctuations in the value of the underlying exposures being hedged.[5]

Nike uses forward contracts for firm commitments to hedge receivables and payables as well as intercompany foreign currency transactions, while using currency options to hedge certain anticipated but not yet firmly committed export sales and purchase transactions expected in futures denominated in foreign currency. Cross-currency swaps are employed to hedge foreign currency-denominated payments related to intercompany loan agreements.[6]

DuPont enters forward contracts involving firm commitments denominated in foreign currency. The decision to hedge or not to hedge a particular exposure is made case by case by taking into account the amount and duration of the exposure and economic outlook.[7]

In December 1998 DuPont entered into a forward contract in the acquisition of the performance coating business of Hoechst AG for 3.1 billion deutsche marks (DM) at $1.9 billion. The forward contract effectively locked the company at the forward exchange rate of DM 1.6316/$, insulating DuPont from adverse exchange rate movements that would likely have increased the dollar price of the acquisition. Note that the forward contract also eliminated any potential gains from a favorable exchange rate scenario, such as appreciation of the

U.S. dollar from the inception of the contract to the date of settlement. The change in the value of the contract was included in the income statement in the period in which the change occurred. The forward contract expired in August 1999.[8]

EXPOSURE NETTING

Netting inflows and outflows produces a natural hedge for MNCs. For example, consider Lufthansa Airlines, which derives revenue in dollars and deutsche marks (euros). Suppose the airline has a payable in dollars for $700 million in one year and is expected to derive $610 million over the same period in U.S. dollars. The dollars payable as exposed liabilities are naturally hedged by dollars receivable as exposed assets. The netting of inflows and outflows reduces the net exposure in the dollar to only $90 million. The airline may wish to hedge using one or another hedging instrument. Exhibit 8.3 shows the distribution of the unhedged and hedged cash flows.

The unhedged cash flows have a higher variance and higher expected cash flows, while the hedged cash flow with zero or smaller variance (due to the choice of hedging instruments) may have a lower expected cash flow compared to the unhedged cash flow. The insurance to buy protection (hedging) is likely to lead to a smaller hedged cash flow, as seen in Exhibit 8.3. However, the ex-post hedged cash flow may be higher or lower than the unhedged cash flows.

FORWARD HEDGING: EXAMPLE

Consider a U.S. firm that has entered into a contractual relationship with a U.K. company to sell precision drilling equipment valued at £3.5 million, receivable in 120 days. The U.S. firm has assets denominated in foreign currency whose value in 120 days is uncertain and is likely to be converted to more or less U.S. dollars.

EXHIBIT 8.3   Payoff and Variance of Hedged and
Unhedged Cash Flow

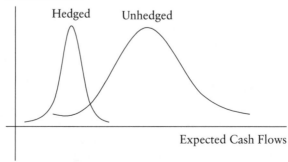

Frequency of Distributions

Hedged   Unhedged

Expected Cash Flows

Exhibit 8.4 shows the payoffs from forward hedging and an unhedged position, assuming exchange rates in the listed ranges over the hedged horizon.

Assuming the 120-day forward rate is $1.61/£ provided that the bid-ask spread is ignored. The hedger is likely to pay a higher ask rate in the interbank market in securing the forward contract in the OTC market. As seen in Exhibit 8.4, the forward contract eliminates the exchange rate uncertainty by locking the hedger at the contractually fixed exchange rate. Therefore, it also eliminates any potential for favorable exchange rate movements. The forward contract has a fixed payoff in a priori agreed price by both parties with zero variance, as evidenced in Exhibit 8.5.

The unhedged payoff is greater than the hedged payoff at an exchange rate over and above the 120-day forward rate of $1.61/£; this is the area of exchange loss attributed to hedge. However, the hedge payoff is greater than the unhedged payoffs at an exchange rate below the forward rate of $1.61/£, this is the area of the exchange gains due to hedge, as illustrated in Exhibit 8.6.

The exchange gains and losses are symmetrical, as can be verified from Exhibit 8.6. Only when the expected future exchange rate (S_t) is equal to forward rate are the gains and losses equal to zero.

EXHIBIT 8.4   Payoff on Hedged and Exposed Position

Expected Spot Rate $/£	Forward Hedge $ (in millions)	Unhedged $ (in millions)	Exchange Gains (losses) $
1.58	5.6350	5.53	$105,000
1.59	5.6350	5.565	70,000
1.60	5.6350	5.60	35,000
1.61	5.6350	5.6350	0.0
1.62	5.6350	5.67	−35,000
1.63	5.6350	5.7050	−70,000
1.64	5.6350	5.74	−105,000

EXHIBIT 8.5   Hedged and Unhedged Payoffs

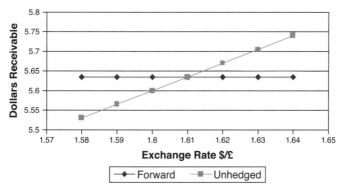

EXHIBIT 8.6   Exchange Gains and Losses

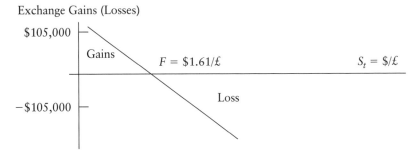

Exchange Gains (Losses)

MONEY MARKET HEDGE

Short Hedge

The short hedge requires taking an offsetting position like any other hedge to the exposure that the firm has. In Exhibit 8.4 the hedger, who has receivables denominated in pounds, is long in pounds and will borrow in British pounds (short pounds) using the receivable as collateral. The firm's objective is to maximize the dollar value of the receivables denominated in the foreign currency. The exporter borrows pounds with a small haircut for the face value of its receivable discounted at the 120-day British borrowing rates. The exporter immediately converts the pounds to dollars at the current spot and invests the proceeds into T-bills or the alternative at the firm's cost of capital. At the end of the 120 days, the pound loan is paid off with the receivable denominated in British pounds. Exhibit 8.7 present the structure of the money market hedge.

Suppose the borrowing and investment rates in the United States and United Kingdom are:

	Borrowing %	Lending %
U.S.	5	4.5
U.K.	6	5.60

EXHIBIT 8.7   Structure of Money Market Hedge of Receivables

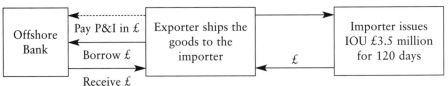

P&I refers to principal and interest.

The exporter is likely to borrow the present value of the £3,500,000 discounted at the annualized rate of 6 percent for 120 days.

- Borrow: £3,500,000/(1 + .06 × 120/365) = £3,432,294.46.

  This borrowing (short pound) in the currency of the receivable is the offsetting transaction required to hedge in order to insulate the exposure to foreign exchange risk.

- Convert £3,432,294.46 into dollars at the current spot rate (bid rate) of $1.60/£.

- Invest the proceeds of $5,491,671.14 at the annualized rate of 4.5 percent over 120 days.

- In 120 days, the proceeds are equal to $5,572,917.78.

The ratio of the receivables denominated in dollars and pounds in 120 days is the implied forward rate (F) derived from the law of one price:

$$F = \frac{\$5,572,917.78}{£3,500,000}$$
$$= \$1.5922/£$$

If the quoted forward rate is identical to the implied forward rate, then interest parity does hold and the payoff from the forward hedge will be identical to the payoff from the money market hedge requiring borrowing in foreign currency and investing in dollars. Had the forward rate (direct quote) been greater (less) than the implied forward rate, the forward hedge will be more (less) desirable than the money market hedge in this example.

The exporter following this procedure has effectively eliminated exposure to foreign exchange risk.

Long Hedge

DuPont has €12 million payable in 90 days for the supplies it purchased from a Finnish company on August 13. To hedge against unfavorable exchange rate movements, the treasurer is contemplating using a money market hedge to manage the exchange rate risk. The treasurer is concerned about the likelihood of euro's revaluation against the U.S. dollar that will increase the dollars payable in 90 days. DuPont's objective is to minimize the dollar outflows associated with the foreign currency-denominated payables. In the analysis DuPont is short in euros, and hedging requires taking an offsetting position (long). Exhibit 8.8 shows the structure of the money market hedge in this scenario.

EXHIBIT 8.8 Structure of Money Market Hedge of Payables

DuPont can use either excess cash or borrow dollars to buy euros. The euro proceeds are invested for 90 days at the euro-denominated short-term investment asset. In this scenario, assume these borrowing and lending rates:

		Borrowing %	Lending %
U.S.		5.5	5
Euro		5.125	4.70
Spot rate	$.96/€		
Forward rate	$.9675/€		

The process of hedging payables with money market hedges requires figuring out the amount of euros DuPont needs to purchase (long) to hedge the payables (short).

- Buy €11,862,524.72 at the current spot ask rate (offer rate) of $.96/€.

$$\frac{€12,000,000}{1 + \left(.047 \times \frac{90}{365}\right)} = €11,862,524.72$$

This is the present value of €12 million discounted at the annualized rate of 4.7 percent for 90 days.

- Borrow $11,388,023.73 = €11,862,524.72 × $.96/€ at 5.5 percent annualized rate for 90 days and pay the interest and principal in 90 days:

$$\$11,388,023.73 \left(1 + \left(.055 \times \frac{90}{365}\right)\right) = \$11,542,464.51$$

The payables denominated in euros are hedged at the cost of $11,542,464.51 to DuPont.

The ratio of the payables denominated in dollars and euros in 90 days is the implied forward rate (F) derived from the law of one price.

$$F = \frac{\$11,542,464.51}{12,000,000}$$

$$= \$.96187/€$$

If the actual quoted forward rate is equal to the implied forward rate, then interest parity is maintained and the payoff from a money market hedge requiring borrowing in dollars and investing in foreign currency has to be identical to the forward hedge. In this case, the implied 90-day forward rate is equal to $.96187/€. Had the 90-day forward rate been below $.9619/€, the forward hedge would have been more desirable than the money market hedge. However, had the forward rate been above the $.96187/€, the money market hedge would have been less costly than the forward hedge.

The actual forward rate is $.9675/€ and the cost of the money market hedge and forward hedge will be:

Cost of forward hedge: €12,000,000 × $.9675/€ = $11,610,000
Cost of money market hedge: $11,542,464.51

HEDGING WITH FUTURES

The money market hedge and forward hedge will be identical assuming covered interest parity holds. Hedging with futures contracts as opposed to forward contracts does not completely eliminate risk, as basis risk must be considered. DuPont can hedge its exposure with futures by buying 96 December futures contracts at the Chicago Mercantile Exchange (CME) at $.9735/€. Each futures contract at CME is for delivery of 125,000 units of euro. The euro futures have to be closed out on November 13, the date that payables denominated in euros have to be settled. The futures contracts are closed out at $.9858/€ on November 13. Exhibit 8.9 summarizes the results of the hedge.

EXHIBIT 8.9   Hedging with Futures

DuPont has €12 million payable in 90 days for the supplies it purchased from a Finnish company on August 13.

August 13
Spot rate: $.97/€
December futures: $.9735/€
Buy 96 December futures at $.9735/€
Proceeds per one contract: 125,000 × $.9735/€ = $121687.50
Total proceeds: 96 × $121687.50 = $11,682,000

November 13
Spot market: Buy €12,000,000 @ $.9845/€
Close out futures by selling 96 December contracts @ $.9858/€
Proceeds per one contract: 125,000 × $.9858/€ = $123,225

Results
Spot market: Pay $11,814,000 to settle the €12 million payable to Finnish firm
Futures market: Gains per contract: $123,225 − $121687.50 = $1,537.50
Total gains: $1,537.50 × 96 = $147,600
Effective cost: $11,814,000 − $147,600 = $11,666,400
Effective rate: $11,666,400/€12,000,000 = $.9722/€

The difference in the cost of hedge as related to the forward and futures hedge can be attributed to the basis risk present in the futures contract but absent in the forward market. The forward hedge resulted in the cash outlay of $11,610,000, effectively locking the hedger at the forward exchange rate. However, the futures hedging resulted in a cash outlay of $11,666,400.

Hedging in the futures market as opposed to the OTC market requires posting a margin as well as margin maintenance for marking to market the value of the short or long position on a daily basis, as discussed in Chapter 5. The gains/losses in the futures market at the settlement are the cumulative gains/losses for the futures contract over the hedge period. Exhibit 8.10 shows the distribution of hedged and unhedged positions for expected payables for DuPont.

EXHIBIT 8.10 Distribution of DuPont Forward, Futures, and Unhedged Payables

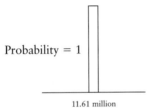

11.61 million
Forward Hedge

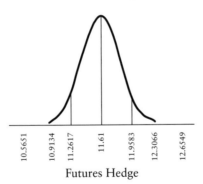

Futures Hedge

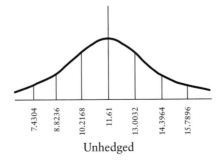

Unhedged

The standard deviation of the forward hedge is equal to zero; there is no uncertainty about the future cash flow. However, futures hedge and unhedged cash flows are risky and, therefore, are assumed to have a standard deviation respectively equal to 3 and 12 percent. The standard deviation of the exposed position as denoted by σ can be estimated as the product of the amount of exposed assets or liabilities as q, the expected exchange rate denoted as E_s, and standard deviation of the change in exchange rate denoted as σ_s (estimated from the time series of observations from the inception of the contract to the settlement or delivery date) as defined in Equation 8.1.

$$\sigma \text{ (Exposed)} = q \times E_s \times \sigma_s \quad (8.1)$$

The standard deviation of the futures hedge and unhedged position assuming an expected exchange rate of \$.9675/€ and normal underlying distribution will be:

$$\sigma \text{ (futures hedge)} = €12,000,000 \times \$.9675/€ \times .03$$
$$= \$348,300$$
$$\sigma \text{ (unhedged)} = €12,000,000 \times \$.9675/€ \times .12$$
$$= \$1,393,200$$

The payoff of futures hedge is expected to be with a probability of 68 percent within one standard deviation at \$11.61 million +/− \$348,300, that is, \$11.9583 or \$11.2617 million. Likewise, the payoff of futures hedge is expected to be with in two standard deviations at \$12.3066 million or \$10.9134 million with a probability of 95 percent and within three standard deviations at \$12.6549 million or \$10.5651 million with the probability of 99.7 percent, as seen in Exhibit 8.10.

OPTION HEDGING

Options provide protection against unexpected losses below certain exchange rates designated by the hedger. The hedger may wish to buy protection at the currently prevailing exchange rate—at-the-money (ATM) option—for which a higher premium is expected upfront. The hedger may wish to buy insurance at the exchange rate below the current spot rate—out-of-the-money (OTM) option— for which a smaller premium is expected up front. Finally, the hedger may buy protection at the strike prices over and above the current exchange rate—in-the-money (ITM) option—for which the highest premium is expected upfront.

The decision to buy ITM, ATM, or OTM depends on the individual decision maker's attitude toward risk and degree of aversion and/or tolerance for risk. Furthermore, the cost of buying protection progressively is highest for the ITM, followed by ATM, and lowest for the OTM. This is the case when people buy protection on property requiring no deductibles, some deductible, or a large deductible. The premium will be the highest in no deductible and lowest in the large deductible and may be some where in the middle of the range of the highest and the lowest deductible. The options premium, assuming it is efficiently priced in the market, is very sensitive to the amount of volatility (historical or implied) estimates or correctly calling it guesstimate.

Example: Consider the call option in Euro FX November futures at strike price of 98 cents. The quoted premium is 1.27 cents per euro as of August 23, 2002, in the CME. Each contract is for delivery of 125,000 units of euro. The spot euro is \$.9731/£. The DuPont treasurer in Exhibit 8.9 can buy 96 call options to hedge against the possible appreciation of the euro in the next three months. The premium for one call option will be equal to \$1,587.50. Hedging the entire exposure requires an up-front premium of \$152,400. The call option provides protection by imposing a ceiling on the exchange rate that is equal to the strike price plus the premium for the call:

$$\$.98/€ + \$.0127/€ = \$.9927/€$$

The ceiling on the exchange rate indirectly guarantees that the maximum payables for DuPont will be no more than \$11,912,400, as seen in Exhibit 8.11, that is, equal to the product of €12 million payable and \$.9927/€.

$$€12,000,000 \times \$.9927/€ = \$11,912,400$$

The minimum payables will be greater than the payoff from the unhedged position by the amount of premium paid up front. The option protects the hedger in case the exchange rate appreciates, as the hedger expects; however, the option provides the hedger the opportunity to enjoy benefits of being unhedged, as the hedged payoff is parallel to the unhedged (the call options will expire worthless)

EXHIBIT 8.11　　Hedging Payables with Call Options

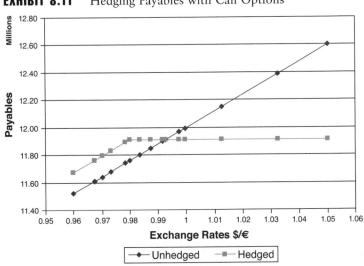

when the exchange rate remains below the strike price of 98 cents, as seen in Exhibit 8.11, and DuPont lets the call option expire.

VALUE AT RISK

Value at risk (VAR) provides a framework for analysis of the maximum potential loss in the fair value of an exposed position over a specific period assuming normal market conditions and a given confidence interval. MNCs have various exposures due to interest rate changes, foreign exchange rate changes, and changes in commodity prices that could adversely affect firm value. VAR analysis uses simulation models by assuming various scenarios to generate the amount of maximum loss that could be realized in a given period for a given confidence interval.

For example, a bond portfolio with market value of $250 million might have VAR at 95 percent confidence interval of $15.6176 million over the next 10 days assuming standard deviation of the exposed portfolio is equal to 16 percent per annum. The volatility is usually quoted in years; however, for the purpose of estimating the VAR of an asset, the volatility of the asset is quoted on a daily basis as volatility per day:

$$\sigma_d = \frac{\sigma_y}{(252)^{1/2}}$$

where

σ_y = yearly standard deviation
σ_d = daily standard deviation assuming 252 trading days per year

The daily standard deviation of the portfolio therefore will be equal to:

$$\sigma_d = .16/15.8745$$
$$= .010079$$

The VAR can be estimated as the product of the standard deviation, the confidence interval imposed, and the value of the exposed portfolio. Assuming a 95 percent confidence interval, 95 percent of the time the actual outcome will fall within 1.96 standard deviations of the all outcomes and $250 million exposed portfolio, the one-day VAR can be estimated as:

$$\text{One-day VAR} = .010079 \times 1.96 \times \$250$$
$$= \$4.9387 \text{ million}$$
$$\text{10-day VAR} = \text{One-day VAR} \times \sqrt{10}$$
$$\text{10-day VAR} = \$4.9387 \sqrt{10}$$
$$= \$15.6176 \text{ million}$$

This is the estimate of the maximum amount that the firm is likely to lose in this portfolio over the 10-day horizon with a probability of 5 percent or less.

VAR provides senior management in a single statistic what can be summarized as: "We are 95 percent confident that our maximum loss within the next n-day to be no larger than q dollars in our portfolio."

Exhibit 8.12 presents the results of the VAR analysis for each of the significant risk management portfolio as of December 31, 2000, and 2001 for DuPont.

For example, the overall VAR in 2001 is $84 million: the sum of the individual VAR for interest rates, foreign exchange, agriculture, and energy. The VAR of each component, such as interest rate, is correlated positively or negatively to the foreign exchange, agriculture, and energy. The actual total VAR, therefore, is likely to be smaller than $84 million for DuPont, due to diversification of various risk factors in the context of a portfolio. VAR is an important risk measurement parameter that is applicable in the private sector as well as government agencies.

Supervisory and regulatory agencies of U.S. banks require them to use VAR to determine the amount of capital needed to cover their market exposure in their various derivative trading activities.[9] The regulatory oversight and central bank requires banks to have capital of three times the 10-day VAR with 99 percent confidence interval on their derivatives transactions.

Example: Assume a bank has a $750 million exposure to market risk in its foreign exchange portfolio with implied volatility of 18 percent per annum. The amount of capital the bank should maintain to meet the capital requirement would be as depicted in Exhibit 8.13.

EXHIBIT 8.12   Value at Risk on Various Exposures for DuPont

	2000	2001 (Dollars in millions)
Interest rates	(7)	(30)
Foreign exchange	(29)	(20)
Agricultural commodities	(20)	(20)
Energy feedstock commodities	—	(14)

Source: DuPont annual report, 2001.

EXHIBIT 8.13   Standard Normal Distribution

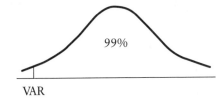

Assuming normal distribution, 99 percent of the outcome is within 2.33 standard deviation, as shown in Exhibit 8.13.

$$N(-2.33) = 1\%$$

$$\sigma_d = \frac{\sigma_y}{\sqrt{252}}$$

$$\frac{.18}{15.8745} = .0113$$

$$\text{10-day VAR} = \sqrt{10} \times .0113 \times 2.33 \times \$750$$
$$= \$62.4447 \text{ million}$$

When conveyed to senior management, this figure indicates that the maximum expected loss in the portfolio is $62.4447 million with a probability of 1 percent or less.

The capital requirement is $3 \times$ 10-day VAR at 99 percent confidence interval, or $187.3341 million.

The Securities and Exchange Commission requires disclosure of the trading activities in the derivative markets involving VAR for nonfinancial corporations.[10] The VAR analysis uses historical time series observations in the composition of the portfolio as well as the various risk factors as they relate to interest rates, foreign exchange, and commodity and equity price changes to generate a variance-covariance matrix for estimating historical volatilities and correlations. The market risk factors can be obtained from the Web site *www.riskmetrics.com:*

> The data sets contain consistently calculated volatilities and correlation forecasts for use in estimating market risk. The asset classes covered are government bonds, money markets, swaps, foreign exchange, and equity indices (where applicable) for 31 currencies and commodities. Data sets are provided for a one day and one month horizon.[11]

TWO ASSETS PORTFOLIO

Consider a financial institution having a portfolio of stocks and foreign currencies worth $120 and $180 million, respectively. The daily standard deviation of the stock portfolio is 1.125 percent, while the daily standard deviation of the portfolio of foreign currencies is 0.8 percent. The correlation of daily percentage change of the two portfolios is 10 percent. The portfolio of the two assets has the following amount of daily volatility[12]:

$$\sigma_p = \sqrt{0.4^2 \times 0.01125^2 + 0.6^2 \times 0.008^2 + 2 \times 0.4 \times 0.6 \times 0.01125 \times 0.008 \times 0.1}$$
$$= .0069$$

One-day VAR of this portfolio is therefore equal to $4.0572 million, assuming 95 percent confidence interval:

$$\text{VAR} = .0069 \times 1.96 \times 300 = \$4.0572$$

The one-day VAR of the individual portfolio of the stocks and currencies, assuming a 95 percent confidence interval, is:

VAR = .01125 × 1.96 × 120 = $2.646 million for the portfolio of stocks

VAR = .008 × 1.96 × 180 = $2.8224 million for the portfolio of currencies

The VAR of the individual portfolio combined is equal to:

$$\$2.646 + \$2.8224 = \$5.4684$$

The benefits of diversification in dollar is:

$$\$5.4684 - \$4.0572 = \$1.4112 \text{ million}$$

LUFTHANSA BUYS AIRCRAFT FROM BOEING13

Lufthansa purchased 20 aircraft from Boeing at the cost of $500 million payable in one year in January 1986. The spot and one-year forward exchange rates at the time the contract was entered into was $.3125/DM. By agreeing to pay dollars for the aircraft, Lufthansa accepted all the exchange rate risk and reward for the contract. To manage exposure to dollar appreciation, the company decided to leave half of the liability exposed to foreign exchange risk and purchased the other half, $250 million, in the forward market at the forward rate of $.3125/DM. By hedging half of the exposure, the company effectively locked at the forward rate of $.3125/DM, to pay DM800 million for buying $250 million forward.

Hedged $250 million at $.3125 for DM800 million.

Exposed $250 million at the prevailing exchange rate in January 1986.

By January 1986 the deutsche mark appreciated and the dollar weakened to $.45/DM. The forward hedging turned out to be very costly ex-post.

Hedging Alternatives

- Remain unhedged
- Fully cover the exposure: Buy dollars forward
- Manage some of the exposure, leaving some exposed
- Use call options in dollar/deutsche mark or its equivalent, put options in deutsche mark/dollar
- Buy caps in dollars or floors in deutsche marks (in the OTC market from a bank or insurance company)
- Money market hedge of payables

Ex-post, remaining unhedged would have been the best course of action for the airline as the dollar weakened and the deutsche mark appreciated to over $.45/DM. However, management did not predict well, nor has anyone else. The question is, what was the best course of action for management to take under the conditions prevailing at the time Lufthansa entered into such a contract for managing its exposure. Did Lufthansa really have exposure to the dollar?

On the surface, the answer is yes; however, Lufthansa actually derives revenue denominated in dollars for tickets sold to passengers traveling to and from the United States, rendering hedging dollar exposure unnecessary. The revenue derived in dollars naturally hedges payables denominated in dollars. However, the dollar-denominated revenue was far less than the dollar-denominated payables. Why did management not try to hedge the net exposure to dollar? Did it carefully analyze all the alternatives available in exchange-traded derivatives and in the OTC market? These questions are difficult to answer now. However, it appears that management did not do its homework right before committing to forward hedging.

Exhibit 8.14 demonstrates the payoff of hedging with the forward as well as hedging with two call options in dollar/DM. The ATM option at the strike price of $.3125/DM (DM3.2/$) is equal to $.01875/DM, assuming a volatility of 10 percent for a European option with a maturity of one year. The premium for the OTM call option at strike price of $.30/DM (DM3.33/$) is estimated to be equal to $.009/DM.[14]

Let us now consider Lufthansa's six options.

1. Remain Unhedged

This scenario has the highest dispersion around the average outcome. Had the exchange rate been at $.25/DM or DM4/$ by the end of the contract period, management would have been blamed for not hedging the entire exposure as opposed to 50 percent of the exposure. The cost to the airline would have been DM2 billion. Newspaper headlines would have scorned management for speculating and hedging too little. There is no reason to believe that this would have

EXHIBIT 8.14 Lufthansa's Payables with Various Hedging Alternatives

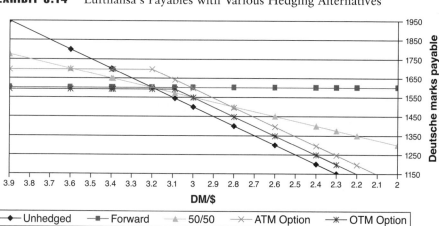

been the best course of action simply speculating before the fact (a priori) and leaving the entire exposed position unprotected. After the fact, the outcome favored no hedging.

2. Fully Cover the Exposure

Certainly this scenario leaves nothing to chance as the entire exposure is locked at the forward rate, eliminating for all practical purposes the exchange rate risk due to an unfavorable rate scenario as well as any potential windfall gains due to favorable exchange movements. The cost of hedging 100 percent of the exposure by buying dollars forward at the rate of DM3.2/$ (DM3.2/$ × $500 million) is DM1.6 billion, as evidenced in Exhibit 8.14. This hedging made headlines, as the forward hedge turned out to be expensive ex-post. DuPont's acquisition of the performance coating from Hoechst AG for $1.9 billion hedged with the forward contract at the cost of DM3.1 billion did not make headlines as hedging with the forward contract did not turn out to be costly.

3. Manage Some of the Exposure

This scenario provides management with the opportunity to have some of its exposure unprotected, as it may or may not be in the interest of the firm ex-post. It runs the risk of speculating with stockholders' money if the decision to remain fully hedged would have been the right course of action; the decision maker also may be praised for leaving some of the position exposed. The cost of a 50 percent forward hedge and 50 percent exposed ($250 million × DM3.2/$ + $250 million × DM2.3/$) adds up to DM1.375 billion, as the exchange rate turned out to be DM2.3/$ by January 1986.

4. Use Call Options in Dollars or Put Options in Deutsche Marks

The payables denominated in dollars are hedged by buying a call option on $/DM or a put option in DM/$. The call option in $/DM (dollar appreciating) is identical to the put option in DM/$ (DM devalues), as the exchange rates are the ratio of one currency over another. The call in $/DM and the put in DM/$ is used interchangeably throughout this section. The hedger's objective is to buy protection against a rising dollar (falling DM); buying put options in deutsche marks can accommodate the hedger's concern. The ATM call option with the strike price of $.3125/DM would have cost 6 percent, while an OTM call at strike price of $.33/DM nearly cost 3 percent per annum.

Exhibit 8.14 shows that the payoff on the call/put option is above the unhedged position by the amount of option premium of DM96 million (.06 × DM1.6 billion payable at DM3.2/$). The ATM put is providing protection against falling DM value at the exchange rate of DM3.392/$ (i.e., DM3.2/$ strike price plus 6 percent premium). This is the maximum rate, the cap in the deutsche mark that the hedger is likely to pay, and is equal to DM1.696 billion ($500 million × DM3.392/$).

For example, if the exchange rate at the expiration is DM3.6/$, the hedger buys the dollar in spot by paying DM1.8 billion for the $500 million payable to Boeing. However, the put options provide some relief in the form of profit. The profit in the put option will be equal to DM104 million (i.e., equal to unit profit of DM.208/$ (DM3.6 − 3.392/$) times $500 million. The effective cost of the payable is exactly equal to DM1.696 billion at any exchange rate above the DM3.392/$. However, if the deutsche mark revalues, the put option expires worthless and hedged payoffs will be above the unhedged position by the cost of insurance, as can be seen from Exhibit 8.14.

The payables in deutsche marks with put options in Exhibit 8.14 are parallel, albeit higher than that of the unhedged position at any exchange rate below the strike price of DM3.2/$. The put option is out of money and will not be exercised. However, the payoff on a hedged position with put options is truncated at the strike price plus the premium at any exchange rate above the strike price of DM3.2/$ in which the put option is in the money and will be exercised. Unlike forward contracts, call/put options involve up-front premiums. The premium in the Lufthansa case would have been nearly $32 million, a substantial amount of capital commitment that management would likely oppose. However, there was a possibility of financing the purchase of the call/put option for hedging payables denominated in dollars by selling DM/$ puts at the strike price of DM3.2/$ for 6 percent premium, which pays the cost of buying protection. This could have been accomplished through buying a zero collar, requiring Lufthansa to sell deutsche marks at $.3125/DM, which would have been very costly ex-post as the exchange rate turned out to be nearly $.45/DM at the settlement of the contract in January 1986.

5. Buy Caps in Dollars or Floors in Deutsche Marks

Lufthansa had the option of buying caps in dollars or buying floors in deutsche marks in the OTC market from a bank or insurance company. Caps in the foreign currency exchange market are similar to buying caps in the floating rate notes for a cost, where the caps provide protection against rising interest rates above the cap rate. In the event the dollar appreciates over the strike price (cap rate of, say, $.32/DM), the cap buyer is compensated, that is, equal to the difference between the spot rate and the cap rate. In the event the exchange rates remain below the cap rate by the maturity of the cap, the buyer of the cap will buy the dollar at the spot rate to fulfill its financial obligation.

For example, Lufthansa had an option to buy floors on deutsche marks below DM3.2/$. If the currency devalues to DM3.4/$, the floors seller compensates the buyer for the difference between the exchange rate and the floors rate. In this scenario, Lufthansa pays DM1.7 billion in the spot market to settle $500 million payables to Boeing; however, it receives DM100 million from the seller as the floors are activated. The behavior of floors is similar to the put option and is priced similarly.

6. Make a Money Market Hedge of Payables

This alternative will be similar to forward hedging provided that the covered interest parity between dollar– and deutsche mark–denominated interest rates is in line and forward premium or discount is equal to interest rate differentials. The forward premium was equal to zero for the one-year forward rate, as this rate was the same as the prevailing spot rate of DM3.2/$ at the inception of the contract. Exhibit 8.15 shows the quarterly money market interest rates in the United States and Germany in 1985 and 1986.

Clearly, interest rate differentials of nearly 300 basis points showed that the U.S. dollar is overpriced against the deutsche mark and interest parity does not hold. The interest rate differentials of 300 basis points were indicative of an approximate 3 percent devaluation of the dollar against the deutsche mark in the first quarter of 1985. The three-month forward rates as opposed to one-year forward rate were in line with the behavior of the spot rates, as seen in the exhibit.

Hedging with money markets would have necessitated tying up deutsche marks in 1985 to buy the present value of the $500 million payables discounted at the U.S. lending rate for one year. This option was very similar to hedging with forward rates the entire amount of exposure to foreign exchange risk.

However, hedging with the three-month forward contract as opposed to the one-year forward contract would have provided protection over the three-month period and afforded management the opportunity to revisit its exposure for the remainder of the exposure horizon by rolling over into another three-month forward contract at a preferential rate that would have brought Lufthansa closer to the spot rate. Rolling over the forward contracts as stripes of forwards as opposed to simply locking in at the one-year forward rate produces lower costs

EXHIBIT 8.15   Interest Rates, Forward/Spot Exchange Rates for Germany and the United States

	Germany %	U.S. %	3-Month Forward $/DM	Spot Rate $/DM
1985.1	6.10	9.02	$.32717	$.3233
1985.2	5.80	7.44	.32848	.3267
1985.3	4.90	7.93	.37781	.3746
1985.4	4.80	7.80	.40932	.4063
1986.1	4.60	7.24	.43439	.4315
1986.2	4.60	6.73	.45720	.4548
1986.3	4.60	5.71	.49655	.4949

Source: Bundesbank and Federal Reserve Bank of St. Louis.

to the hedger when the yield is inverted, as it was in 1985–1986, and when interest rate differentials remain roughly the same over the hedge period. For example, consider the stripes of forward contracts on foreign exchange rates \$/DM from January 1985 through January 1986, as shown in Exhibit 8.16. The one-year forward rate ($F_{12} \neq \Pi F_3$) is not equal to the geometric average of the three-month forward rates in the inverted market as experienced in 1985–1986 of Exhibit 8.15.

When the exchange rate is at a nearly historic high, as the dollar was in 1985, hedgers need to be aware of the tendency of the exchange rate to revert toward the mean. This is known as mean reversion. Mean reversion refers to the tendency of market parameters to fall when they are at historic highs and to go up when they are at or closer to historic lows. Exhibit 8.17 summarizes Lufthansa's payables under various alternatives ex-post.

MANAGING OPERATING EXPOSURE

Operating exposure arises due to the impact of unexpected changes in the exchange rate on the firm's input price. Input prices consist of raw materials and labor costs; output prices are prices of the goods and services produced. To the

EXHIBIT 8.16   Stripes of Forward Exchange Rates on Dollar/Deutsche Mark

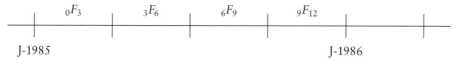

EXHIBIT 8.17   Summary of the Lufthansa's Payable under Various Alternatives Ex-Post

Uncovered	2.3 DM/\$ × \$500 M = 1.15 billion DM
Forward hedging 100% of exposure	3.2 DM/\$ × \$500 M = 1.6 billion DM
Partial hedging 50% of exposure	3.2 × \$250 + 2.3 × \$250 M = 1.375 billion DM
Options hedging	1.15 billion DM + 96 million DM = 1.246 billion DM
Partial hedging 50% of exposure via rollover	1.275 billion DM[a]

[a] This scenario assumes that Lufthansa hedged half of the exposure with 3-month forward rates prevailing at the inception of the contract and rolled over into another 3-month forward contract at the end of the first three months at the rates prevailing at that time. Following this procedure and assuming the forward rates used are the rates shown in Exhibit 8.15 from the first quarter of 1985 through fourth quarter of 1985, on average cost Lufthansa 1.275 billion DM to pay for \$500 million to Boeing.

extent that the correlation between exchange rate changes and changes in prices is determined by the degree of market segmentation, operating exposure depends on whether the output prices and input costs are determined locally or globally. Operating exposure is long term in nature and therefore can be managed only through operating hedges.[15] There are several ways to achieve operating hedges.

1. Increase Flexibility of Operating Networks

Provide MNCs the flexibility to arbitrage institutional restrictions, such as regulatory impediments and various requirements by regulatory agencies, as well as to arbitrage taxes and factors of productions across international boundaries by transferring such resources as production, marketing, and research and development across their global networks.[16]

The increased flexibility of operating networks provides MNCs the real options, which are the right, not an obligation, to: expand, contract (shrink), alter, and convert the existing operation with other operations worldwide as market conditions and demands change.

2. Diversify Operations

Diversification naturally hedges cash flow derived from various operations overseas; however, it is expensive in terms of cost and lengthy to implement. The operation exposure is related to the breath and depth of the MNC's involvement in the number of different countries (the breadth) as well as concentration of the MNC's foreign subsidiary in selected countries (the depth). MNCs with greater breadth are less prone to currency exchange rate risk, whereas firms with concentrated networks (greater depth) are more exposed to foreign exchange rate risk.[17]

3. Diversify Financing with Matching Cash Flows

This approach is similar to money market hedging discussed earlier in the chapter. The exporter selling goods and services overseas in this scenario has accepted foreign currency for the receivables and therefore is exposed to foreign exchange risk. The exporter ships the goods, say, to Norway and accepts Norwegian kron for payments in 180 days. The exporter has receivables denominated in foreign currency and borrows in the offshore banking facility Norwegian kron that matches the assets of the exporter (the receivables) with the liability created by taking the loan denominated in the foreign currency. Exhibit 8.18 shows the structure of diversifying financing by matching cash flow denominated in foreign currency.

The exporter borrows in the currency of the receivable, thereby hedging its exposure to foreign exchange risk. The receivable in foreign currency is used as collateral to secure a loan denominated in a foreign currency. The loan is paid off using the receivable denominated in the foreign currency.

EXHIBIT 8.18   Matching Cash Flow

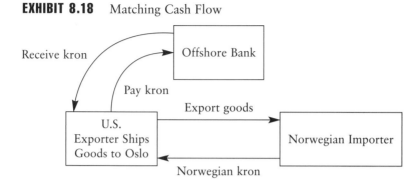

4. Parallel Loans

The parallel loan was originally created as a result of exchange control the British government imposed in the early 1970s on British companies, making it less attractive for British firms to invest in the overseas market. Parallel loans were designed to legally circumvent the exchange control and the higher tax associated with such transactions. Parallel loan are generic swaps where two parties borrow where they can secure better terms and pass the borrowing to one another through their respective subsidiary. There are four parties to the parallel loans.

For example, MMM wishes to borrow £100 million to expand its subsidiary's operation in the United Kingdom, while Allied Lyon contemplates extending $152 million to its subsidiary in New York. However, the exchange control could make such financing very expensive for the parent company. The parallel loan mitigates this problem, where MMM borrows at the U.S. LIBOR plus 1 percent over a seven-year period and passes this amount on to the Allied Lyon subsidiary in New York. Allied Lyon borrows £100 million in the euro-sterling market at 6.75 percent fixed rate over a seven-year period and passes on this amount to the U.S. subsidiary in London. Exhibit 8.19 shows the structure of the parallel loan.

The principal is transferred from the parent company to the subsidiary of the other firm, as shown in the exhibit. The Allied Lyon subsidiary in New York receives the principal and makes periodic interest payments to MMM. At the end of the seven-year period, it repays the principal, $152 million, to the MMM parent company. Likewise, the MMM subsidiary in London, having received the principal loan, makes periodic interest payments and pays the final principal at the end of seven years to the Allied Lyon parent company.

The advantage of the parallel loan is that the cost of the fund secured and transferred by both parties to each other's subsidiary would be less than the all in cost of financing (interest, underwriting, legal, etc.) by the subsidiary directly had the subsidiary tried to borrow in the country of domicile. For example, it would have been more costly for the Allied Lyon subsidiary in New York to raise

EXHIBIT 8.19 Parallel Loans

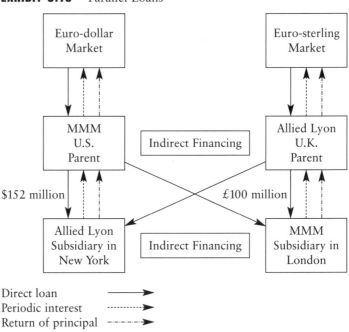

$152 million in the United States. Similarly, the cost of borrowing £100 million in the U.K. market would have been higher for the MMM subsidiary in London because the subsidiary is not well known and its credit rating may not be as high as its parent.

5. Back-to-Back Loans

This loan arrangement involves two parties, where each party borrows in its own capital market and passes on the principal and periodic interest to the another. For example, MMM borrows in the U.S. capital market, while Allied Lyon borrows in the British pounds market. Subsequently they pass the principal, periodic interest, and return of the principal to one another. Each company in essence is borrowing in its own currency and lending it to the other company at cost. For example, MMM borrows at 6.5 percent seven-year loan and lends this to Allied Lyon at 6.5 percent. However, Allied Lyons borrows at pound sterling at LIBOR plus 1 percent and lends the principal to MMM at cost.

MMM and Allied Lyons will use the proceeds of the loans in any way they deem appropriate, including lending the proceeds to their own subsidiaries in a foreign country. This type of OTC loan arrangement is difficult to establish, as it is highly unlikely for a firm to find another firm with the same needs and over the same time horizon to take a loan in its own currency. This arrangement also faces the likelihood of counterparty risk, the risk that one of the parties to the transaction will fail to fulfill its financial obligations. Exhibit 8.20 shows the structure of the back-to-back loans.

6. Share Risks

Risk sharing is a conventional approach to risk management by two parties that have established a long-term business relationship. The parties agree a priori that if the exchange rate is within a certain range, the importer pays the exporter the actual exchange rate prevailing at the time. However, if the exchange rate deviates from the range, the parties agree to split the difference no matter which direction the exchange rate is destined. In this scenario, the two parties to the transaction share the exchange rate risks. For example, the contract between a U.S. exporter of lumber to Japanese Construction Company may contain the following risk-sharing clause:

> If the exchange rate remains in the range of 125 to140 yen/dollar, the Japanese Construction Company will pay exactly the amount of yen in effect on the date the payables to the U.S. company is due. However, if the yen devalues say to 160 yen/dollar, the 20 yen will be split in half and the Japanese firm pays 150 yen/dollar to settle its outstanding obligations to the U.S. exporter.

Assuming the U.S. exporter sold lumber valued at $30 million receivable in Japanese yen, the importer under a risk-sharing clause will pay 4.5 billion yen at the maturity of the contract. In effect, the U.S. exporter has 4.5 billion yen worth only $28.125 million at the current exchange rate of ¥160/$. However, if the

EXHIBIT 8.20   Back-to-Back Loans

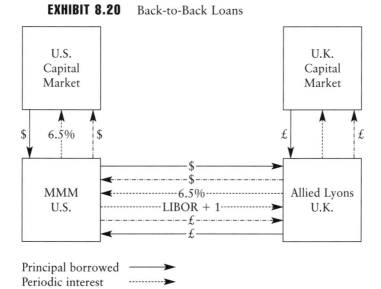

Principal borrowed ⟶
Periodic interest ⟶
Return of principal ⟶

yen revalues to ¥110/$, under the risk-sharing clause the difference of 15 yen will be split between the two parties as the importer pays 117.5 yen for its dollar obligations. Under this scenario, the importer pays 3.525 billion yen to settle its $30 million obligations to the U.S. exporter. The exporter in effect has 3.525 billion yen valued at $32.0455 million at the current exchange rate of ¥110/$.

7. Currency and Interest Rate Swaps

Swaps are a low-cost means of refinancing by two parties in which the parties agree to exchange periodic interest (cash flow) on one or two currencies, fixed for floating or floating for floating, based on different indices as currency/interest rate swaps in the future. The parties to the swap borrow in the market in which they have comparative advantage. In mid-1981 IBM and the World Bank became involved in a seven-year currency swap.[18] Exhibit 8.21 shows the interest rates quoted to IBM and the World Bank.

Neither of the parties to the swap has absolute advantage in both markets. IBM has absolute and comparative advantage in the Swiss market, where it can borrow at the Swiss Treasury rate. The World Bank, however, has absolute and comparative advantage in the U.S. capital market, where it can borrow at the U.S. Treasury rate plus 40 basis points.

The gains from this swap are equal to the rate differentials in the dollar and Swiss franc markets of 25 basis points. Although details of the swaps worked out were not revealed, Exhibit 8.22 shows the structure of the basic swap, assuming the gains in the swap are divided by 15 to 10 basis points, respectively, for IBM and the World Bank.

The World Bank borrows in the U.S. market at Treasury plus 40 basis points and lends this amount to IBM at Treasury plus 30 basis points, losing 10 basis points in its outside borrowing/lending. However, the World Bank only pays Swiss Treasury for the desired currency in which it wants exposure, saving 20 basis points in Swiss francs borrowing, at a net saving of 10 basis points.

EXHIBIT 8.21   Rates Quoted to IBM and the World Bank

	U.S. Rate	**Swiss Rate**	**Gains in Swap**
IBM	U.S. Treasury + 45 bps	Swiss Treasury	
World Bank	U.S. Treasury + 40 bps	Swiss Treasury +20 bps	
Rate differentials	5 bps	−20 bps	25 bps

EXHIBIT 8.22   Currency Swap between IBM and the World Bank

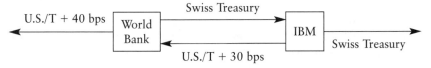

IBM borrows and lends in Swiss francs at the Swiss Treasury rate; however, it pays only the U.S. Treasury rate plus 30 basis points, for a net savings of 15 basis points. The currency swaps have made both parties better off without making any party worse off, thereby creating value for the parties involved in the swap.

The swap structured in Exhibit 8.22 favors IBM, as it pays and receives Swiss-denominated interest rates with no exposure to foreign exchange risk. The World Bank, however, has net exposure to the U.S. dollar, as it pays 10 basis points more than it receives. This exposure needs to be managed by buying stripes of forward, or futures, contracts.

FIXED FOR FIXED CURRENCY AND INTEREST RATE SWAPS

Consider the fixed for fixed seven-year currency and interest rate swaps quotes in Exhibit 8.23, involving a U.S. firm and a Swiss conglomerate. The U.S. firm borrows dollars at the offer rate of 7.26 percent and swaps for Swiss francs,

EXHIBIT 8.23   Interest Rate Swaps Quotes

June 20 (Year)	Euro Bid	Euro Ask	£Stlg Bid	£Stlg Ask	SFr Bid	SFr Ask	US$ Bid	US$ Ask	Yen Bid	Yen Ask
1	4.98	5.02	6.50	6.53	3.95	3.98	7.16	7.19	0.30	0.33
2	5.20	5.24	6.50	6.54	4.13	4.21	7.22	7.25	0.53	0.56
3	5.30	5.34	6.54	6.58	4.21	4.29	7.22	7.25	0.75	0.78
4	5.39	5.43	6.50	6.55	4.26	4.34	7.22	7.25	0.97	1.00
5	5.47	5.51	6.48	6.53	4.30	4.38	7.22	7.25	1.19	1.22
6	5.54	5.58	6.46	6.51	4.35	4.43	7.23	7.26	1.39	1.42
7	**5.61**	**5.65**	**6.44**	**6.49**	**4.40**	**4.48**	**7.23**	**7.26**	**1.57**	**1.60**
8	5.66	5.70	6.41	6.46	4.45	4.53	7.23	7.26	1.71	1.74
9	5.71	5.75	6.40	6.45	4.50	4.58	7.23	7.26	1.83	1.86
10	5.74	5.78	6.39	6.44	4.54	4.62	7.23	7.26	1.93	1.96
12	5.81	5.85	6.35	6.42	4.60	4.70	7.25	7.28	2.10	2.13
15	5.90	5.94	6.27	6.36	4.67	4.77	7.25	7.28	2.28	2.31
20	5.95	5.99	6.11	6.24	4.73	4.83	7.25	7.28	2.39	2.42
25	5.96	6.00	6.00	6.13	4.75	4.85	7.24	7.27	2.41	2.44
30	5.95	5.99	5.93	6.06	4.76	4.86	7.23	7.26	2.42	2.45

Source: Financial Times, June 21, 2000.

Bid and ask rates as of close of London business. U.S.$ is quoted annual money actual/360 basis against 3-month LIBOR; £ and yen quoted on semiannual actual/365 basis against 6-month LIBOR; Euro/Swiss franc quoted on annual bond 30/360 basis against 6-month EURIBOR/LIBOR with the exception of the 1-year rate, which is quoted against 3-month EURIBOR/LIBOR.

EXHIBIT 8.24   Currency and Interest Rate Swaps

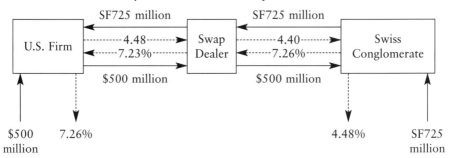

receiving 7.23 percent at the bid and paying 4.48 percent at the offer, as shown in the exhibit. The Swiss conglomerate borrows in the Swiss franc market at the offer rate of 4.48 percent to swap with the swap dealer, receiving 4.40 and paying 7.26 percent at the offer rate for dollar-denominated debt. Both companies' debt structures have been transformed to the currency in which they wished to have exposure. This swap is callable in four years, and the parties can exercise this option to terminate the swap. Exhibit 8.24 presents the structure of this swap.

For arranging the swap and taking counterparty risk, the swap dealer makes the spread of 8 basis points in SF725 million loans as well as 3 basis points in $500 million denominated debt over the swap period of seven years. The currency swaps are embedded with the *right of offset,* which provides the party an option for nonpayment of any interest or principal to offset with a comparable nonpayment.

Assuming semiannual exchange, the U.S. firm will make a semiannual payment of SF16,307,200, that is, 725,000,000 × 1/2 × .0448, and will receive $18,150,000, that is, $500,000,000 × 1/2 × .0726.

NOTES

1. See K. Jesswein, C. Y. Kwok, and W. R. Folks, "Corporate Use of Innovative Foreign Exchange Risk Management Products," *Columbia Journal of World Business* (Fall 1995): 70–82.
2. Excerpted from Financial Accounting Standards Board, *Foreign Currency Translation, Statement of Financial Accounting Records No. 52,* Stamford, CT: FASB, (October 1981), para. 42.
3. The Financial Accounting Standard Board in June 1998 issued statement No. 133 requiring counterparties to treat derivatives as assets and liabilities and the changes in the fair value of the position as gains or losses.
4. See Nike 2001 annual report.
5. Ibid.
6. Ibid.
7. See DuPont 2001 annual report.

8. Ibid.
9. See Jackson et al. (1997).
10. For an introduction to VAR, see Simons (1989). For the comprehensive analysis of the VAR, see Jorion (1997).
11. See *www.riskmetrics.com.*
12. The standard deviation of the portfolio of two assets σ_p is:

$$\sigma_p = \sqrt{w_i^2 \times \sigma_i^2 + w_j^2 + \sigma_j^2 + 2 \times w_i \times w_j \times \sigma_i \times \sigma_j \times \rho_{ij}}$$

where

w_i and w_j = proportion of investment in the i and j asset
σ_i and σ_j = standard deviation of the asset i and j respectively
ρ_{ij} = correlation coefficient of the assets i and j

For n-assets portfolio, σ_p is:

$$\sigma_p = \sqrt{\sum w_i \times \sigma_i^2 + 2 \times \sum_{i \neq j} \sum_j w_i \times w_j \times \sigma_i \times \sigma_j \times \rho_{ij}}$$

13. Neil McGeown, "Lufthansa: A Case Study in Options," *Market Perspectives: Topics in Options and Financial* (September 1986).
14. These premiums are estimated from the standard options pricing formula assuming implied volatility of 10 percent, strike price of $.3125/DM for the ATM, and $.30/DM for OTM and the prevailing one-year interest rates in the United States and Germany in 1985.
15. See E. Flood and D. R. Lessard, "On the Measurement of Operating Exposure to Exchange Rates: A Conceptual Approach," *Financial Management* (Spring 1986): 25–36.
16. See Allen and Pantzalis (1996); Buckley and Casson (1998).
17. See J. Doukas, C. Pantzalis, and S. Kim, "Intangible Assets and the Network Structure of MNCs," *Journal of International Financial Management and Accounting* 10 (1): 1–23.
18. See D. Bock, "Exchange of Borrowings," B. Antl., ed., in *Swap Financing Techniques* (London: Euromoney Publications, 1983).

CHAPTER 9

Debt, Equity, and Other Synthetic Structures

This chapter outlines the nonstandard debt derivatives developed in the over-the-counter (OTC) market to shift risk, mitigate reinvestment rate risk, transfer the prepayment risk from one class of bond to other classes, manage default risk, mitigate price and exchange rate risks, increase liquidity, reduce agency costs, reduce transaction costs, and reduce the tax burden by circumventing regulatory restrictions. The nonstandard derivative products offer opportunities in the financial market to enhance yield and reduce risk if they are properly combined by other assets in the portfolio. Therefore, these products demand an understanding of the underlying factors that determine its value. The reward is higher, as is the risk of the individual derivative product. Careful analysis of price, yield, and volatility must be performed. It is imperative to fully understand pricing mechanisms before committing capital.

INVERSE FLOATER

The inverse floater is a derivative security synthetically created with the fixed rate debt instrument as the underlying collateral. The many variations of inverse floaters are known as reverse floater, bull floaters, yield curve notes, and maximum rate notes. They were created in 1986. The incentive to create synthetic security is to create value and reduce risk. Consider collateral is a 6.5 percent par bond with 25 years to maturity and market value P_c of $250 million. From the collateral, two distinct securities are created: a floater (P_f) with market value of $200 million, and inverse floater (P_{if}) with market value of $50 million, as defined in Equation 9.1.

$$P_c = P_f + P_{if} \tag{9.1}$$

The floater coupon is capped and zero floors are imposed on the coupon of the inverse floater to prevent this bond from having a negative coupon. The floater coupon is pegged to an index, such as the yield on Treasury or LIBOR. Suppose the coupon of the floater is set as:

$$\text{LIBOR} + 1\tfrac{1}{2}\%$$

The coupon of inverse floater is set to take into account the amount of floater relative to an inverse floater known as leverage factor (L), the index (LIBOR) as well as a constant term (q) is defined in Equation 9.2.

$$q - L \text{ (Index)} \qquad (9.2)$$

The weighted average of coupon (WAC) of the two bonds created has to be equal to 6.5 percent fixed coupon rate of the collateral. The leverage factor is equal to 4, as there is $4 of floater for every $1 of inverse, as shown in Equation 9.3.

$$\text{WAC} = .80 \left[\text{LIBOR} + 1\tfrac{1}{2}\% \right] + .20[q - 4 \text{ (LIBOR)}]$$
$$.065 = .80 \left[\text{LIBOR} + 1\tfrac{1}{2}\% \right] + .20[q - 4 \text{ (LIBOR)}] \qquad (9.3)$$

The relationship expressed in Equation 9.3 assuming WAC of 6.5 percent does not have a solution, as there is one equation with two unknowns; therefore, we need to impose a minimum coupon of zero on the inverse floater to solve the problem. A cap in the floater is determined by setting the coupon on the floater equal to 6.5 percent in Equation 9.3, assuming the inverse floater coupon is zero.

$$.065 = .80 \left[\text{LIBOR} + 1\tfrac{1}{2}\% \right], \text{ solving for LIBOR}$$
$$\text{LIBOR} = 6.625 \text{ percent}$$

LIBOR is capped at 6.625 percent. The constant on the inverse floater is determined by setting the coupon for the inverse floater equal to zero when the index is at the maximum cap rate:

$$q - 4 \ (6.625\%) = 0$$
$$q = .2652$$

The WAC is reset in Equation 9.3 as:

$$\text{WAC} = .80 \left[\text{LIBOR} + 1\tfrac{1}{2}\% \right] + .20 \ [.2652 - 4 \text{ (LIBOR)}]$$

Suppose LIBOR is equal to 3.5 percent; the WAC would be equal to 6.5 percent.

$$.80 \left[3.5\% + 1\tfrac{1}{2}\% \right] + .20 \ [.2650 - .14] = .065$$

The price of the floater will trade close to par as long as the spread that depends on the credit quality of the issuer remains the same and neither the floor nor the cap is activated. The price of the inverse, however, is inversely related to the interest rate. When rates fall, the floater will get a smaller share of the coupon interest rate, and the inverse floater will receive the larger share of the fixed coupon interest underlying the collateral. The price sensitivity of the floater and the inverse floater can be analyzed assuming the interest rate scenarios shown in Exhibit 9.1.

EXHIBIT 9.1   Share of Floater and Inverse Floater Coupons Interest from the 6.5 Percent Collateral under Various Interest Rates

	Value of LIBOR						
	0.01	0.02	0.03	0.04	0.05	0.06	0.06625
Floater	0.02	0.028	0.036	0.044	0.052	0.06	0.065
Inverse	0.045	0.037	0.029	0.021	0.013	0.005	0
Collateral	0.065	0.065	0.065	0.065	0.065	0.065	0.065

Note: LIBOR is capped at 6.625% on the floater, and zero is set as floors on the inverse floater.

As interest rates fall, the floater is receiving a smaller share of the 6.5 percent coupon underlying the collateral; the inverse floater is receiving the lion's share of the coupon, not proportional to its share. The floater is expected to trade below its par while the inverse is expected to trade at premium. However, as interest rates rise above 5 percent, the inverse floater will receive a smaller share of the coupon. At the limit, when the LIBOR reaches the cap rate of 6.625 percent, all of the coupon will accrue to the floater and the investors with the inverse floater will get nothing.

When the LIBOR reaches 5 percent, the floater and inverse floater price are at par, because both debt instruments are receiving their proportional share of the underlying collateral. The inverse floater is receiving 20 percent of the 6.5 percent coupon, or 1.3 percent, and the floater is garnering the remaining 5.2 percent, which is 80 percent of the coupon.

Example: Orange County Retirement Fund invested in interest rates futures, betting that the rates would go down. It also invested heavily in the highly leveraged inverse floater. The rates continued to go up, forcing significant margin calls as the interest rate futures plummeted due to rising interest rates in 1994. The fallout resulted in a loss of $1.7 billion. Having an inverse floater in the portfolio at times of rising interest rates aggravated the retirement fund's cash flow, as the coupon interest accrued to the floating rate notes and the inverse floater coupon is inversely related to the market interest rate (as can be verified from Exhibit 9.1). The inverse floater is structured to help an active portfolio manager bet in the direction of interest rates, particularly those with greater price sensitivity with a higher leverage factor.

Having floating rate notes would have been a hedge, as the loss in futures due to rising interest rates would have been offset somewhat by higher coupon interest rates. Had the rate fallen, the retirement fund would have liquidated the long futures for a profit as well as receiving the higher coupon from the inverse floater. There is no justification to buy interest futures expecting rates to fall when the portfolio manager has invested in the inverse floater that can pay off only if the floating interest rate goes down. The portfolio manager presumably wished to have a double exposure to a long position in the interest rate futures as well as a long position to the inverse floater.

CREATING A SYNTHETIC FIXED RATE

Portfolio managers can buy the floater and inverse floater underlying the collateral in proportion in which the two derivatives are created to produce a synthetic fixed rate rather than buying a fixed rate bond parse. For example, in the Orange County Retirement Fund case, a portfolio manager wishes to use $10 million to create a synthetic fixed rate of 6.5 percent. The portfolio manager has to buy an $8 million floater and a $2 million inverse floater to realize a fixed rate of 6.5 percent in the example, no matter which direction interest rates go.

The portfolio underlying the fixed rate is considered a bullet, while the derivative portfolio of the floater and the inverse floater is known as *barbell*. The barbell portfolio is embedded with options and possesses a positive convexity that is highly valuable in active bond portfolio management.

Consider that collateral has duration (D_c) of 12.35 years.[1] Suppose interest rates increase by 100 basis points. The underlying collateral price is actually reduced to 88.78 per $100 face value, a drop of 11.22 percent. Assuming zero curvature, the market value of the collateral is expected to drop by 12.35 percent, as can be derived from Equation 6.6.

$$\Delta P = -D_c \times P \times \Delta y$$
$$= -12.35 \times 250,000,000 \times .01$$
$$= -\$30,875,000$$

The duration of the inverse floater (D_{if}) is defined in Equation 9.4 assuming the collateral and inverse is priced at par $(P_c = P_{if})$:

$$D_{if} = (L + 1) D_c \times \frac{P_c}{P_{if}}$$
$$= (4 + 1) \, 12.35 \qquad\qquad (9.4)$$
$$= 61.75$$

The duration of the inverse floater is estimated to be 61.75 years, assuming collateral and inverse prices are equal to $100 per $100 par value. This inverse floater is extremely sensitive to interest rate changes, as 1 percent change in interest rates is expected to change the inverse floater price by approximately 61.75 percent in the opposite direction. The market value of the inverse floater with the duration of 61.75 is expected to drop:

$$-61.75 \times \$50,000,000 \times (+ .01) = -\$30,875,000$$

The inverse floater is expected to absorb the entire drop in the market value of the underlying collateral, as seen in this example.

Suppose the duration of the floater created from the collateral is six months and the duration of the inverse and the collateral is:

	Duration
Inverse	61.75
Floater	$\frac{1}{2}$
Collateral	12.35

Combining the floater and inverse floater in the following proportion creates the barbell portfolio:

$$W_{if}(D_{if}) + W_f(D_f) = D_{c,}\ W_{if}(61.75) + W_f\left(\tfrac{1}{2}\right) = 12.35$$
$$W_{if} + W_f = 1$$

where

W_{if} = proportion of the inverse floater
W_f = floater in the barbell portfolio

The proportions are estimated to be .1935 and .8065, respectively, for the inverse floater and the floater. The convexity of the barbell portfolio is greater than the bullet, as nonlinearity in the barbell portfolio provides the opportunity to gain convexity without sacrificing the yield.

Example: Brandywine Asset Management fund has invested 5 percent of its portfolio of $1.8 billion in the inverse floater with a current yield of 18 percent. The higher yield in the inverse floater is due to falling interest rates, which make the inverse floater such an attractive issue at this time. The portfolio manager, betting that interest rates will go down, presumably has acquired the inverse floater, and it appears that his bets have paid off. However, the earlier example of Orange County reveals the other side of the bet, where rates move in the direction opposite to the bet.

> Wilmington, Del.-based Brandywine Asset Management. While the fund is global in scope, Smith says it can invest in corporate credits, mortgage- and asset-backed bonds and government bonds with no rating or country specific allocation issues. An 11-year veteran of Brandywine, Smith has been in the portfolio management business since 1967. "We have a good size position in inverse floater mortgage-backed bonds, more than 5% of our total portfolio. These bonds yield 18% on average. Even if U.S. rates doubled—and I do believe that we have clearly hit the bottom of this rate cycle—they will return 14% and give us three times the cash flow of long Treasuries."[2]

The portfolio manager can add floater to the portfolio in the future to replicate the fixed rate payoff of the underlying collateral from which the inverse was created, provided that the floater and the inverse floater in the portfolio are in the same proportion that they were in producing the underlying derivatives.

SYNTHETIC STRUCTURES

Investors synthetically create a fixed rate by buying a floating rate note and simultaneously selling a swap that pays floating and receives a fixed rate, as shown in Exhibit 9.2, with the payoff equal to the fixed rate of 6.5 percent. The synthetic fixed rate enables investors to adjust their portfolio positions by terminating (unwinding swap) without the cost of selling and repurchasing the entire amount of the principal. Investors achieve the desired position at reduced transaction costs and gain a potential for higher returns if rates continue to go up.

The inverse floating rate notes (FRN) from Equation 9.1 can be restated in Equation 9.5 as a portfolio of long fixed rate, short a swap to pay floating and receive fixed, and buying an interest rate floor at zero rate for the inverse floater and simultaneously buying a cap on the floater, as shown in Exhibit 9.3.

$$P_c - P_f = P_{if} \qquad (9.5)$$

Buy fixed rate bond + short a swap to pay floating and receive fixed = Synthetic inverse

An inverse FRN with a leverage factor as high as 3, 4, 5, and 6 or more can be designed to be extremely sensitive to interest rate changes. The structure of the inverse FRN with the leverage factor of 4 in Exhibit 9.3 is similar to the structure in Exhibit 9.2, where the investor is synthetically long in the fixed rate note, short a swap in notional principal that is equal to the amount of floater in the structure of the underlying fixed rate, (i.e., $4 per $1 of inverse floater), paying/receiving four times (floating rate and receiving fixed rate) with the cap and floors in place.

EXHIBIT 9.2 Creating Synthetic Fixed Rate

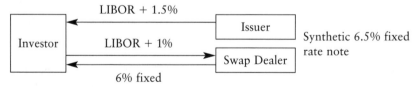

EXHIBIT 9.3 Creating Inverse Floater with Leverage Factor of 4

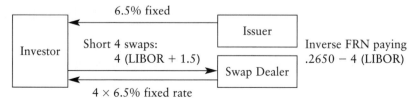

The synthetic inverse created in Exhibit 9.3 bears credit risk on the fixed rate as well as on the underlying four swaps and on the caps. Therefore, investors find it more convenient and less risky to buy the inverse rather than synthetically creating one.[3]

MORTGAGE- AND ASSET-BACKED DERIVATIVES

Pooling single- or multifamily mortgages creates the pass-through security in a portfolio by repackaging their cash flows into new securities and selling the new securities to broader classes of investors. The objective of repackaging an ordinary coupon-paying instrument into shares or participation certificates through securitization is to increase liquidity and marketability as well as to realize economic rent, as the investment banking firm realizes the difference between what it pays for the securities in the pool and what it receives from the shares when the shares are sold in the secondary market.

By separating coupons from principal, stripped Treasury and municipal securities are created that prove successful, as the sums of the parts exceed the whole.[4]

Most mortgage debt instruments are embedded with the call option, providing the issuer the opportunity to prepay part or all of the issue at par, if the issuer deems doing so to be appropriate. The pass-through created from pooling the mortgages also entails prepayment risk, which investors in the pass-through find troubling.[5]

From the pass-throughs, two distinctive derivatives are created—collateralized mortgage obligations (CMOs) and stripped mortgage-backed securities (SMBS)—that address prepayment risk. Investors in the bond market make investment decisions based on the nature of their assets and liabilities that lead to segmentation of the debt market. For example, money market funds invest in the short end of the market, and prepayment risk is not a primary concern. However, long-term investors, such as insurance companies and pension funds, find prepayment risk of significant importance. Derivatives that provide protection against prepayment risk afford these investors the opportunity to mitigate reinvestment rate risk embedded in the prepayment options.

PREPAYMENT RISKS

Prepayments expose investors into two types of risk:

1. Extension risk
2. Contraction risk

Extension risk arises as the pass-through underlying mortgage pays slowly as interest rates rise. When interest rates rise, prepayments decline, as prepaying mortgages does not pay off. Rather, mortgagors find it more attractive to invest their funds rather than prepay. In this scenario, as the underlying mortgage debt price falls due to rising interest rates, the price of the pass-through securities falls even more as prepayment slows. Pass-through investors would prefer to see prepayment accelerated so that they could reinvest the proceeds at the prevailing higher rates. The slower prepayment under a rising interest rate scenario contributes to extension risk that is undesirable to the pass-through class of securities (negative convexity).

For example, investor classes that wish to avoid the extension risk are banks and other financial intermediaries that raise capital in the short end of the market and invest in long-term debt. The assets are long term, and their liabilities are short term, creating a mismatch. The pass-through security is long term in nature and exposes financial institutions to extension risk, as they are far more sensitive to interest rate changes than the capital (liabilities) used to finance the investment.

Insurance companies find pass-through securities unattractive, as they expose them to extension risk in the event rates increase and prepayment slows. The cash flows from the pass-through securities are uncertain, making them undesirable from assets liability management for institutions such as insurance companies. Individual investors and corporations with a given investment horizon, say 5 to 10 years, may find pass-throughs undesirable as they expose investors to extension risk, since slow prepayments lengthen the investment maturity beyond their horizon and the pass-through has to be liquidated at a discount to meet financial obligations.

Contraction risk arises in the event of falling interest rates, as prepayments speed up. The fall in interest rates makes refinancing attractive for mortgagors or individuals relocating and selling property. The pass-through life therefore shortens and subjects investors to contraction risk. When the rates fall, the price of the plain-vanilla bonds increases; however, the price of the callable pass-through is not expected to go up as much, as the upside potential is truncated due to *negative convexity* as the prepayment shortens the duration of the bond similar to a callable bond.

Pension funds are exposed to contraction risk, as the nature of their liabilities is generally long term. The pass-through exposes long-term investors to reinvestment rate risk, as falling interest rates increase the likelihood of prepayments, therefore shortening the duration of the issue. Furthermore, the proceeds from the issue are invested at a lower interest rates.

Collateralized mortgage obligations and stripped mortgage-backed securities are derivatives created by redistributing cash flow underlying pass-through (the collateral) to transfer and mitigate the prepayment risk from some classes of bonds to other classes based on established payment rules for disbursing the coupon interest payments, prepayments, and principal repayments to different classes. The innovative new derivatives designed to transfer the contraction and extension risks have not eliminated these risks; they have simply reallocated these risks to the classes of bonds with risk-return characteristics different from that of the underlying mortgages, appealing to the needs and expectations of certain segments of investors.

SEQUENTIAL-PAY COLLATERALIZED MORTGAGE OBLIGATIONS

This class of CMO was created in 1983. The principal payment accrues sequentially to the first class until it is paid off, while the coupon is paid to all of the classes. Once the first class is retired, the next class receives all of the principal and prepayments until it is paid off. Other classes receive only coupon interest based on their outstanding principal in the underlying collateral at the beginning of the period.

The Planned Amortization Class (PAC) and Targeted Amortization Class (TAC) are CMO structures with greater predictability of cash flow and offer more protection than sequential-pay variety.[6] The PAC class has priority over all other classes in receiving principal payments from the underlying collateral. The PAC bonds have protection from the contraction and extension risk over a wide range of prepayment schedules due to the existence of companion bonds known as *support bonds* in the underlying collateral.

The TAC bonds are similar to the PAC bonds, but they provide protection against prepayment risk targeted to a narrower range of prepayment rates. The TAC bonds are targeted to provide protection only against contraction risk, not extension risk; therefore, the TAC bonds appeal to investors concerned about contraction risk without too much concern about the extension risk.

INTEREST ONLY AND PRINCIPAL ONLY

Stripped mortgage-backed securities issued in early 1987 separated coupons from the corpus of the underlying pool of mortgages into a class of securities known as interest-only (IO) securities, with all of the principal going to another class known as principal-only (PO) securities. The IO class therefore receives no principal. The PO class receives no interest, and its price behavior depends entirely on the rate at which prepayments are made. The PO class can be considered as deep-discount zero coupon bonds with high duration and interest rate volatility. When interest rates are at historic lows, prepayments accelerate, the duration of POs is reduced, and their price is positively affected.

Example: Suppose the pass-through underlying the collateral is $200 million mortgage securities with 6.5 percent coupon and priced at par with maturity of 25 years. The PO backed by this pass-through is worth $50 million, since it is a deep-discount bond. The PO investors (who receive no coupon interest) will receive a dollar return of $150 million ($200 million principal less initial investment of $50 million) over 25 years, or 5.7 percent annualized return, assuming zero prepayment and annual compounding. The higher the speed of the prepayments, the sooner the PO class of bondholders receive the $150 million interest income and the greater their realized returns in excess of 5.7 percent. Therefore, the price/yield relationship is inverse for this bond, similar to the underlying pass-through. This bond possesses negative convexity; as the yield declines the price does not increase, and as prepayments accelerate the bond is likely to be called.

The 6.5 percent 25-year collateral is used to create tranches in a sequential-pay structure, as shown in Exhibit 9.4.

The structure in Exhibit 9.4 contains $90 million support bonds to absorb the prepayment risk for the classes of bonds in tranches A, B, and C. The coupon rates in the various tranches are smaller than the coupon rates underlying the pass-through, as the average life is progressively higher in tranches B, C, S, and IO class.

The IO stripes of $21,923,076.91 notional amount are receiving all the interest and none of the principal. The IO bonds have large volatility and are exposed to contraction risk. When prepayments accelerate (falling interest rates), the price of IO stripes declines, because total interest paid is reduced as principal goes down. However, when prepayment slows (rising interest rate), the total interest received increases and the price of the IO stripes increases. The price and yield for the IO stripes are positively related at the low interest rates range below the mortgage contract rates underlying the pass-through. The investors in the IO stripes are averse to contraction risk, however, preferring extension risk. The notional amount of IO stripes is estimated using Equation 9.6.

$$\frac{(\text{tranche par value} \times \text{excess interest rate})}{(.065)} = \text{notional amount of 6.5\% IO} \quad (9.6)$$

For example, from tranche A, IO stripes of $10,384,615.38 are created using Equation 9.6. Likewise, tranche B produces IO stripes of $6,153,846.15. The total amount of IO stripes from all four tranches is estimated to be $21,923,076.91 of notional amount with 6.5 percent coupon. Exhibit 9.5 presents the price/yield relationship for the 25-year 6.5 percent pass-through, 6.5 percent PO, and 6.5 percent IO securities.

The price/yield relationship is convex, exhibiting an inverse relation at the yields over 6.5 percent. However, when the yield drops, prepayment speeds up as underlying mortgage bonds are called. As generic bonds, PO bonds behave like

EXHIBIT 9.4   Five Hypothetical Sequential-Pay Tranches Underlying the $200 Million Pass-Through with a Coupon of 6.5 Percent and 25 Years to Maturity

Tranche	Par Amount	IO	Coupon Rate (%)
A	$ 45,000,000	$10,384,615.38	5
B	$ 40,000,000	$ 6,153,846.15	5.5
C	$ 25,000,000	$ 1,923,076.92	6
S	$ 90,000,000	$ 3,461,538.46	6.25
	$200,000,000		
IO		$21,923,076.91 notional	6.5

EXHIBIT 9.5   Price Yield Relationship for 6.5 Percent Pass-Through (PO and IO)

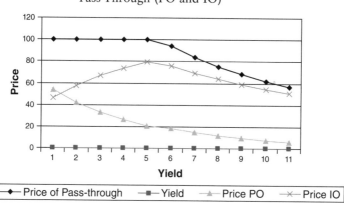

the pass-throughs, as there is an inverse relationship between the yield and the price. The IO debts exhibit both convexity and concavity in certain interest rate ranges. For example, at mortgage rates below 5 percent, where prepayments accelerate, the relationship between the yield and the price is direct; however, as mortgage rates increase, the prepayments fall and the price of the IO securities fall as interest rates increase.

The PO stripes provide investors with the opportunity to increase the convexity of the portfolio of mortgage debts in rate anticipation swaps where the POs are acquired by liquidating IOs in anticipation of the interest rate decline as prepayments speed up and the price of the POs and the price of the underlying portfolio increase. The PO stripes can also be used to hedge a portfolio of high-coupon mortgages against rising prepayments when rates fall. The PO stripes in this scenario with high duration and convexity are expected to increase in value as investors realize the principal faster.

The IO stripes, however, are considered bearish investments: As rates decline, the price of the IOs decrease. The IO stripes have been used to hedge the slower prepayment rate (due to rising interest rates) that will reduce the value of the mortgage portfolio, resulting in large losses trading in these instruments.[7] As can be verified from Exhibit 9.5, the price of IO stripes is positively related to interest rates only in interest rate ranges below the contract rates on the underlying mortgage portfolio. It is important to recognize that when rates increase, the market value of the portfolio of mortgage declines. The IO stripes are not immune from this phenomenon, as the price yield for the IO, PO, and pass-through is similar in certain interest rates range.

EQUITY-LINKED DEBT

Commodity-linked debt or equity instruments provide the issuer the opportunity to hedge against the volatility of the price of its input and reduce and stabilize the volatility of its earnings. The coupon or dividend and principal repayments are pegged to the price of commodities, such as gold, silver, platinum, agricultural products, oil prices, or any other price index. Revenue and profit of the producer of the underlying commodity tends to go up or down as the commodity price goes up or down worldwide in good economic time or periods of recession. The events, such as drought, frost, or hurricanes, tend to adversely affect the supply.

For example, orange producers can hedge the volatility of their operating profit by issuing debt linked to the price of orange juice. The coupon on the debt may offer a base coupon plus or minus spread as a percentage of the orange juice spot price at the end of each harvest period. As the price goes up, the coupon on the debt offers investors step-up coupons/dividends returns; however, as the price falls, the company's operation profit is not as adversely affected since its debt service falls as investors receive smaller coupon interest by accepting the price risk.

Example: Freeport-McMoran Copper and Gold Inc. raised $230 million in 1993 by issuing gold-denominated preferred stocks for $37.8 per share in exchange for one-tenth of an ounce of gold in funding the expansion of its gold mining operation. To manage its exposure to commodity price changes, the firm essentially sold forward 600,000 ounces of its gold at the current price of $37.80/ounce for delivery at the maturity of the preferred stock. At the inception of the contract, Freeport-McMoran issued 6 million shares of preferred stock at $37.80; that amounts to forward sale of 600,000 ounces of gold for $230 million net of underwriting cost, as shown in Exhibit 9.6.

Each share of the preferred stock is redeemable by the issuer for .10 ounce of gold at maturity. Investors basically have accepted the price volatility, since at maturity of the preferred stock one share may be worth more or less than $37.80 if the gold price is greater or less than $378 per ounce.

ZERO COUPON BOND LINKED TO GOLDMAN SACHS COMMODITY INDEX

In 1991 Swedish Export Credit Corporation, an AAA rated firm, issued a $100 million three-year zero coupon bond. The three-year zeros were sold to institutional investors at par in denominations of $50,000 and $100,000. The yield

EXHIBIT 9.6   Equity-Linked Preferred Stocks

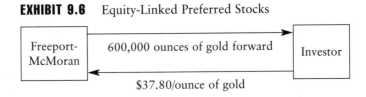

on this issue was tied to the future value of the Goldman Sachs Commodity Index (GSCI) futures, as shown in Equation 9.7.

$$\text{Par} \times .9557 \times \text{GSCI (as of 11/7/94)}/\text{GSCI (as of 11/7/91)} \qquad (9.7)$$

The GSCI was 2,590.81 as of November 7, 1991. The yield to be realized by investors depended on the value of the index at the maturity of the issue on November 7, 1994. The GSCI measured the total return realized by investors investing in a basket of collateralized commodity futures in livestock, agricultural, energy, industrial metals, and precious metals. In January 1992 the GSCI futures were weighted 23.3 percent livestock, 21 percent agricultural, 47.6 percent energy, 5.8 percent industrial metals, and 2.3 percent precious metals.

The commodity-linked notes issued by the Swedish firm were noncallable and nonredeemable prior to maturity. However, the notes traded in the secondary market. Setting Equation 9.7 equal to 1 provides the break-even point for investors at the GSCI value of 2710.90 at maturity. This index value represents zero return to the investor and zero interest cost to the issuer.

The value of the GSCI as of October 31, 1994, and November 30 1994, respectively, was 2,209.26 and 2,136.92. It appears that the $100 million funding for the Swedish Export Credit Corporation at zero marginal cost to the issuer was a sobering experience for the provider of the capital; as the value of the index at the maturity of the issue was well below the break-even GSCI value of 2,710.90.

The underwriter of the issue would have been able to embed an option to limit investors' exposure to commodity price risks in the GSCI. For example, ideally the $100 million note would have a minimum floor interest rate of, say, 5 percent per annum, payable to the investor in the event the GSCI value at maturity was below its value at inception. Furthermore, investors should have required the issuer to pay a minimum of, say, 5 percent per annum on the formula set by the underwriter.

GLOBAL DIVERSIFICATION WITH SWAPS

Emerging market economies provide fertile ground for diversification for investors on both sides of the Atlantic. The process of actually buying shares in these economies raises few problems for investors and portfolio managers. For example, the bid-ask spreads are usually much higher for shares of stocks/bonds in smaller, newly developing economies, which renders the gains from global diversification minimal. Furthermore, foreign exchange rate risk adds an additional element of uncertainty. Host countries also may impose capital control to mitigate the flight of capital that hinders asset allocation decisions.

To mitigate all of these problems, swaps can be structured in the underlying stock returns, that is, return on S&P 500 with return on the index of the emerge market economies.

Example: Suppose the College Retirement Equity Funds (CREF) portfolio manager wishes to allocate and diversify $5 billion into stocks of emerging market economies. CREF may swap total return on its growth portfolio with that of the return on the Morgan Stanley International Index (MSII) for the emerging market over the next two years with semiannual settlement. CREF and its counterparty only exchange the difference in the return from the respective indices. For example, if the annualized return on NASDAQ is equal to 11 percent and the corresponding return on the MSII is equal to 14 percent, the CREF portfolio manager will receive $75 million from the counterparty, as shown in Exhibit 9.7.

The strategy in Exhibit 9.7 is far more efficient than physically diversifying by tying up $5 billion in the portfolio of foreign stocks whose payoffs are subject to foreign exchange gains (losses), capital control, withholding tax, and higher bid/ask spread.

CATASTROPHE BONDS

Property casualty companies issue catastrophe bonds by shifting and reallocating business risk to large classes of investors. The yield on these bonds is slightly higher than on comparable bonds, and the bonds are embedded with an option that reduces the coupon interest or principal payments to investors should the issuer suffer large losses due to earthquake or hurricane. Investors find these bonds attractive because the correlation between catastrophic risk and financial risks is relatively low, thus providing diversification benefits to investors. The issuer's business risk is reduced as the cost of servicing the debt falls when the issuer is hit with large claims due to the events for which catastrophic debt is issued in lieu of reinsurance.

LIABILITY MANAGEMENT WITH DERIVATIVES

For most corporations in the United States and for multinationals, liability management is intended to reduce the cost of borrowing through innovative derivatives. The objectives of liability management are to organize the firm's financing activities by blending various classes to securities to achieve the lowest cost of

EXHIBIT 9.7   Total Return Swap Induced
by Diversification

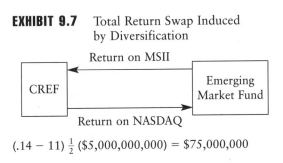

$$(.14 - 11) \tfrac{1}{2} (\$5,000,000,000) = \$75,000,000$$

short- and long-term capital and to minimize interest rate volatility that may adversely affect the operating cash flows. Firms in an increasingly global environment strive to achieve economies of scale and scope in their financing.

ILLUSTRATION 9.1

Consider Gregory Archer, the treasurer of a multinational company in charge of liability management. Archer is contemplating raising $350 million by issuing a seven-year debt noncallable and nonextendable at the fixed rate of 3.85 percent. This issue will be placed privately. Archer believes it will get an AAA rating by Fitch and Moody's. The company will receive $99.7 per $100 face value and pay $1.05 million for the underwriting cost. To manage the firm's exposure to interest rate risk and to reduce the overall cost of financing, Archer has received several bids from vendors rated AAA on derivative products. The derivative products are so numerous, however, that Archer has classified them into six categories:

1. Swaps
2. FRA
3. Caps, floors, and collars
4. Swaptions
5. Interest rate futures (spread transactions)

The seven-year swap can be structured with a AAA-rated counterparty where the firm receives fixed rate and pays floating rate based on U.S. six-month LIBOR that transforms Archer's fixed rate borrowing at 3.50 percent with that of the floating rate. By borrowing and lending at fixed rate, Archer is losing 4 basis points. The cost of borrowing for Archer is equal to six-month LIBOR plus 4 basis points. Archer has accepted the interest rate exposure of the floating rate. Exhibit 9.8 shows the structure of this swap.

EXHIBIT 9.8   Structure of Interest Rate Swap for Archer

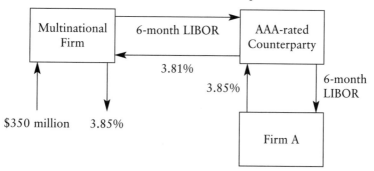

The swap in Exhibit 9.8 is structured using swap quotes from Exhibit 9.9 that represent the midpoints of bid-ask spread. The spread is 4 basis points. For example, the seven-year swap rate of 3.83 is 3.81–3.85 at bid-ask. The swap rates approximate the yield on AA-rated bonds. The spread of swap rates over the Treasuries reflects market-required credit risk premium, where the spread has a tendency to widen during recession and tighten during times of prosperity. The swap dealer selling seven-year swaps on October 10, 2002, receives fixed rate plus spread of 55 basis points on the seven-year Treasury note of 3.3 percent prevailing at the time of sell and pays LIBOR. The swap dealer buying seven-year swaps pays a fixed rate of 3.3 percent on a seven-year Treasury prevailing on the same date plus a spread of 51 basis points and receives LIBOR.

Exhibit 9.10 presents over-the-counter interest rate swap indications by Morgan Guaranty Bank for 3-, 5-, 7-, and 10-year swaps from the bank's perspective. The spread over the U.S. Treasury is the largest for the three-year swap, indicating greater demand by firms and other institutions where the bank pays bid rate of 8.79 percent on a semiannual basis and receives six-month U.S.

EXHIBIT 9.9 Swap Rates, Treasury Rates

Maturity (Tenor)	Swap Rates (%)	U.S. Treasury (%)	Spread over Treasury in Basis Points
1 year	1.75	1.6	15
2 year	2.17	1.75	42
3 year	2.63	2.06	57
5 year	3.32	2.68	64
7 year	3.83	3.3	53

Source: Board of Governors, October 10, 2002.

EXHIBIT 9.10 Interest Rate Swap Indications: Fixed U.S. Dollar Payments against Six-Month U.S. Dollar LIBOR

Year	Semiannual Quotations Bid	Offer	Benchmark U.S. Treas. (%)	Semiannual Rates (%) Bid	Offer	Annual Rate (%) Bid	Offer
3	T+55	T+73	8.24	8.79	8.97	8.98	9.17
5	T+55	T+70	8.66	9.21	9.36	9.42	9.58
7	T+45	T+60	9.03	9.48	9.63	9.70	9.86
10	T+45	T+60	9.21	9.66	9.81	9.89	10.05

Semiannual basis point spread over benchmark Treasuries.

Rates are quoted from the bank's perspective; the bank will pay annual US$ 8.98% against receiving 6-month US$ LIBOR, or the bank will receive annual US$ 9.17% against paying six-month US$ LIBOR.

LIBOR, or pays LIBOR and receives an offer rate of 8.97 percent on semiannual basis in a three-year swap.

Exhibit 9.11 shows the currency swap indications for various currencies against six-month U.S. LIBOR as quoted by the Morgan Guaranty Bank in the OTC market. For example, a Canadian firm pays 10.26 percent interest rate in a five-year swap in a Canadian dollar–for–U.S. dollar swap, receiving six-month U.S. LIBOR. The Canadian firm and swap market maker exchange 5 annual net cash flows in which the Canadian firm pays 10.26 percent and receives six-month U.S. LIBOR on the notional principal of swap. Likewise, a U.S. company pays six-month U.S. LIBOR and receives 10.05 percent interest rate denominated in Canadian dollars on an annual basis in a five-year swap.

The swap rates quoted are on a bond-equivalent basis, where the counterparty receives the midmarket semiannual swap rate and pays floating six-month LIBOR.

Forward Rate Agreements

Archer can sell stripes of FRAs where each FRA is an OTC contract where the seller agrees to a single-pay floating rate of LIBOR and receives fixed rate on a

EXHIBIT 9.11 Currency Swap Indications on December 16: All Rates Are against Six-Month U.S. Dollar LIBOR

Currency	3 years Pay (%)	3 years Receive (%)	5 years Pay (%)	5 years Receive (%)	7 years Pay (%)	7 years Receive (%)	10 years Pay (%)	10 years Receive (%)
Semiannual								
U.S. dollars	8.79	8.97	9.21	9.36	9.48	9.63	9.66	9.81
British sterling	11.18	11.38	11.14	11.34	11.08	11.28	11.20	11.40
Canadian dollars	9.46	9.66	9.81	10.01	9.97	10.07	10.13	10.33
Japanese yen	7.00	7.15	6.90	7.05	7.00	7.15	7.00	7.15
Swiss francs	5.04	5.28	5.28	5.52	5.48	5.72	5.57	5.82
Deutsche marks	5.72	6.01	6.35	6.64	6.59	6.88	6.83	7.07
Annual								
U.S. dollars	8.98	9.17	9.42	9.58	9.70	9.86	9.89	10.05
British sterling	11.49	11.70	11.45	11.66	11.39	11.60	11.51	11.72
Canadian dollars	9.68	9.89	10.05	10.26	10.22	10.43	10.39	10.60
Japanese yen	7.12	7.28	7.02	7.17	7.12	7.28	7.12	7.28
Swiss francs	5.10	5.35	5.35	5.60	5.56	5.80	5.65	5.90
Deutsche marks	5.80	6.10	6.45	6.75	6.70	7.00	6.95	7.19

Source: Morgan Guaranty Ltd., London.

Rates are quoted from the bank's perspective; the bank will pay semiannual US$ 8.79% against receiving 6-month US$ LIBOR, or the bank will receive semiannual US$ 8.97% against paying 6-month US$ LIBOR.

notional principal to commence sometime in the future for a given interval. For example, a 6 × 12 FRA requires the parties to exchange the present value of the pay/receive starting six months from today for six months on notional principal of $350 million. The swaps last only six months.

A 12 × 24 FRA is a one-year swap that begins one year from today and lasts for one year. The seller agrees to pay floating rate three-month LIBOR and receives a fixed rate of 2.57 percent at bid rate. The one-year forward (F_{12}) rate is estimated from Exhibit 9.9 at the midpoint as:

$$F_{12} = \frac{(24 \times 2.17 - 12 \times 1.75)}{12}$$
$$= 2.59 \text{ percent or } 2.57 - 2.61 \text{ at the bid-ask}$$

Assuming Archer sells the 12 × 24 FRA, the firm is expected to pay/receive the cash flow shown in Exhibit 9.12.

Suppose the six-month LIBOR one year from today is 2.71–2.75 percent at the bid-ask rate. The treasurer will receive the present value of $8,995,000 discounted at 2.73 percent (midpoint), equal to $8,755,962.23, and pays the present value of $9,625,000 discounted at 2.73 percent, equal to $9,369,220.28. The net cash flow paid by Archer on the sale of the 12 × 24 FRA is equal to $255,779.71.

The market maker (the bank) fixed its interest expense on the variable rate deposit or anticipated deposit by locking in the fixed interest rate (the FRA) in the above example offered to the buyer. Now consider the bank that has variable rate loans to be reset in the next six months. The stream of future revenues on the variable rate loans is not known in advance. By selling 6 × 12 FRA with the notional principal equal to the principal balance on its variable rate loans and anticipated portfolio of loans, the financial intermediary can effectively lock in advance the fixed interest rate revenues. The intermediary in six months receiving the fixed forward rate over six-month period pays the prevailing floating market interest on the notional principal of the FRA, which would exactly offset the revenue it received on the variable rate loans once it also reset to the prevailing floating rate index.

Example: Bank B has $200 million variable rate loan in its assets portfolio; the rate is to be reset in the next three months. The revenue is exposed to interest rate risk. Bank B wishes to manage its exposure by selling 3 × 6 FRA with

EXHIBIT 9.12   Plain-Vanilla FRA

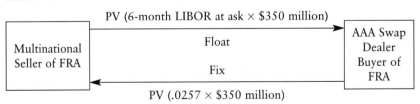

notional principal of $200 million. Exhibit 9.13 presents the cash flow stream that is exchanged.

Bank B, paying a three-month LIBOR rate to be determined in three months, is expected to receive the fixed forward rate and a floating rate revenue from its portfolio of variable rate loans. What Bank B pays and receives on its variable rate loans would be offsetting transactions that transform the variable rate revenue to fixed rate revenue once the FRA shown in Exhibit 9.13 is consummated in three months.

Caps

Archer contemplates selling caps in the over-the-counter market. For receiving an up-front fee, this strategy obligates the firm to pay the interest differential between the cap rate and floating interest rates that reduces the all-in cost of financing for the company, assuming the caps are not activated over its life. In the event the rates rise over and above the cap rate, the cap is activated, obligating the firm to pay, thereby increasing the all in cost of its financing. Caps are call options and are priced accordingly. The firm can also sell floors for a premium that obligates it to pay the interest differential between the floors rate and the floating rate in the event rates fall.

Collars are created when caps are purchased by selling floors where the cost of the caps are financed by selling floors, or buying floors financed by selling caps. For example, consider buying five-year deutsche mark floors at 5.5 percent strike price for 145 basis points financed by selling 6.75 percent caps for a premium of 172 basis points, as shown in Exhibit 7.12. The collars created produce +27 basis points, assuming that an interest rate tied to six-month U.S. LIBOR remains in the 5.5 to 6.75 percent range over the five-year life of the collars.

As shown in Exhibit 9.14, the caps are activated when the floating rate index exceeds the cap rate of 6.75 percent as the buyer of the caps receives interest rate differentials. The cap payment is 5.25 percent when the index is at 12 percent, as can be verified from the exhibit.

Exhibit 9.15 shows the behavior of the 5.5 percent floors. The floors are activated when the rates fall below the strike price of 5.5 percent as the underlying put options provide downside protection as the floors buyer receives compensation that is equal to the interest rate differentials shown in the exhibit. For example, if the floating rate falls to 2 percent, the floors buyer receives 3.5 percent from the seller of the floors as the put option underlying the floors provides relief. The put options will be out-of-the-money for rates over the strike price of 5.5 percent.

EXHIBIT 9.13   Cash Flow of 3 × 6 FRA

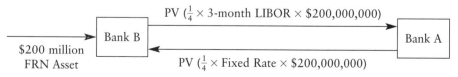

EXHIBIT 9.14   Behavior of the Floating Rate and the Cap Payment

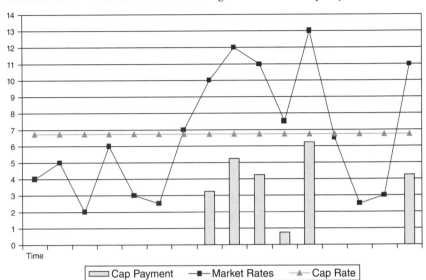

EXHIBIT 9.15   Floors Payment, Floating Rates

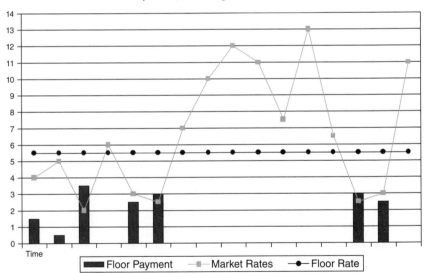

Swaptions

Swaptions are a right, not an obligation, to enter into interest rate swaps sometime in the future over a given period. For example, a 2 × 3 swaption at a strike price of 6.75 percent is a one-year swap starting in two years, where the buyer is expecting interest rates to go up in two years. Assuming the interest rate in two years is 10 percent on the one-year swap, the seller of the swaptions is obligated to receive a 6.75 percent strike price and pay a floating rate of 10 percent over the one-year *tenor* of the swap. The seller of the swaption receives an up-front fee from the buyer for writing the swaption. In the foregoing analysis, the swaption buyer is buying the put swaption, as it is expecting interest rates to go up in the future and will force the seller to pay the floating rates and receive the strike price plus the premium.

Call swaptions obligate the seller to pay fixed and to receive float in the event the rates go down. The buyer of call swaptions, however, has the right, not an obligation, to enter into an interest rate swap to pay floating and receive fixed where the buyer is expecting rates in the future to fall below the strike price, forcing the seller to pay the strike price and receive the floating rate.

Archer contemplates selling 2 × 5 put swaptions at strike price that is 200 basis points over the fixed rate of its seven-year note of 3.85 percent. This swaption will obligate Archer to enter into a three-year interest rate swap in two years to receive the strike price of 5.85 percent plus the premium on the swaptions and to pay floating rates over three years. The buyer of the swaptions will exercise its right when it pays off to do so, that is, when the interest rate goes up over the strike price of 5.85 percent. However, if the rates remain below the strike price, the buyer of the swaption lets the option expire, and the seller effectively reduces its cost of borrowing by keeping the entire premium received.

The multinational firm borrows the capital in the fixed rate market where it enjoys a comparative advantage to swap for floating rates. Firms with good credit borrow fixed rate and swap for floating rates to transform their debt structure to short term. This strategy pays off as long as the yield curve for the swap rate is upward sloping. Firms effectively can reduce their cost of borrowing to be equal to the floating rate. The swap market maker reduces its exposure by entering an offsetting swap with firm A where the dealer pays LIBOR and receives 3.85 percent, as demonstrated in Exhibit 9.8.

Exhibit 9.16 presents the behavior of the spread of the three-month AA-rated commercial paper for nonfinancial corporations; the benchmark for short-term corporate borrowing against Overnight Federal Funds; and the rate member banks could borrow from one another between 1982 and 2002.

The spread appears to be highly volatile and mostly negative in the early 1980s, reflecting the extreme volatility of the Overnight Federal Fund rate, which at times was greater than the AA-rated three-month commercial paper offer rate for nonfinancial corporations. The spread appears to be less volatile

EXHIBIT 9.16   Spread of AA 3-M Commercial Paper against
Overnight Federal Funds Rate

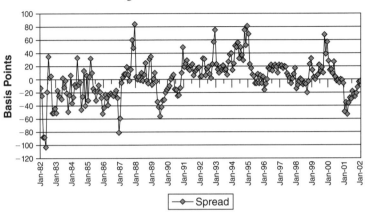

in the 1990s, despite a few spikes in 1993 and 1995, reflecting the market consensus of a prosperous U.S. economy and reduced corporate exposure to bankruptcy.[8]

Exhibit 9.17 presents the spread of the AA commercial paper against the
three-month Treasury bills rate over the period from 1982 to 2002. The spread
in the 1990s appears to be under 50 basis points, reflecting the overall market
consensus of a healthy economy. The tightening of the spread in late 2001 and
2002 was due to the nine interest rate cuts by the Federal Reserve Board and
the reduced appetite of corporate borrowers to borrow in a weak economic
environment.

EXHIBIT 9.17   Spread of AA Commercial Paper against
3-Month Treasury Bill Rate

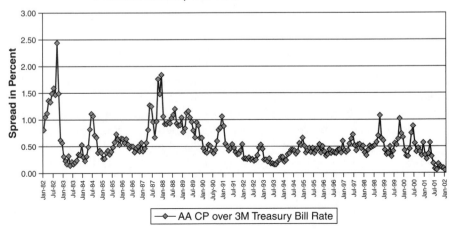

SPREAD ON TREASURY YIELD CURVE

The yield spread on the Treasury bonds and Treasury notes is expected to flatten in the next three months. A portfolio manager buys Treasury bonds March 2003 futures and simultaneously sells Treasury notes futures for delivery in March 2003. The ratio spread or the hedge ratio has to be estimated, as the underlying futures respond differently to changes in interest rates, and as the volatility of the Treasury bonds is greater than that of its Treasury notes.

The portfolio manager buys Treasury bonds March 2003 futures at 111–19, or $111.59375, and simultaneously sells Treasury notes March 2003 for 113–29, or $113.90625, as quoted by the *Wall Street Journal* on October 12. To estimate the ratio spread, dollar value of 1 basis point (DVO1) needs to be calculated for both futures and weighted by the respective cheapest to deliver (CTD) conversion factors for 10- and 30-year bonds. The conversion factor for the 10- and 30-year CTD bonds, respectively, is equal to .8568 and .9353 for March 2003. The DVO1 is estimated:

DVO1: Treasury bonds	
P = $111,430.82	Yield = 5.24
P = $111,758.01	Yield = 5.22
ΔP = 327.19	327.19/2 = $163.59
DVO1: Treasury bonds:	$163.59/.9353 = $174.91

DVO1: Treasury notes	
P = $114,048.88	Yield = 4.26
P = $114,224	Yield = $4.24
ΔP = $175.12	$175.12/2 = $87.56
DVO1: Treasury notes:	$87.56/.8568 = $102.19

The ratio spread or hedge ratio is estimated using Equation 9.8.

$$h = \frac{\text{DVO1: Treasury bonds}}{\text{DVO1: Treasury notes}} \qquad (9.8)$$

$$\frac{\$174.91}{\$102.19} = 1.71$$

The portfolio manager needs to sell 171 Treasury notes futures short and buy 100 Treasury bonds to neutralize the sensitivities of the futures to the direction of the interest rate changes. In other words, the portfolio manager is expected to have the same amount of exposure in the short and long positions. The price change for the 171 contracts shorted on the Treasury notes futures is identical to the price change for the 100 contracts on Treasury bonds futures purchased.

As shown in Exhibit 9.18, as the yield changes are symmetric (parallel shift in the yield curve), the spread produces nearly zero profit (loss). The loss of

EXHIBIT 9.18   Parallel Shift in the Yield

	DVO1	ΔY^a	# of Contracts	Profit (Loss)
Treasury bonds	$174.91	+5	100	−$87,455
Treasury notes	$102.19	+5	−171	+$87,372.45
Spread profit (loss)				−$82.55

^{a} Change in the yield.

$82.55 is attributed to the rounding error. The DVO1 of the one long position is identical to DVO1 of 1.71 contract shorted. Exhibit 9.19 presents the outcome of the spread when the Treasury yield curve tightens (when the spread between the Treasury bonds and Treasury notes is reduced). This scenario is likely to happen as the yield on the long bonds remain virtually the same or rising marginally; however, the yield on the Treasury notes rises by larger increments. For example, suppose the yield on the long bond rises by 5 basis points while the yield on Treasury notes increases by 25 basis points. As shown in the exhibit, this scenario produces the largest profit for the spread as yield differentials between the two sectors narrows.

As the yield spread tightens, the loss of $87,455 in the long bond is far more than offset by the gains in the Treasury notes as short position produces a profit of $436,862.25.

Assume the yield curve for Treasury securities steepened as the yield in the long bond increased by 30 basis points, while the yield in the Treasury notes rises by 10 basis points producing a significant loss for the spread. Exhibit 9.20

EXHIBIT 9.19   Yield Spread Tightens (Yield Curve Flattens)

	DVO1	ΔY^a	# of Contracts	Profit (Loss)
Treasury bonds	$174.91	+5	100	−$87,455
Treasury notes	$102.19	+25	−171	+$436,862.25
Spread profit (loss)				+$349,407.25

^{a} Change in the yield.

EXHIBIT 9.20   Yield Curve Steepens

	DVO1	ΔY^a	# of Contracts	Profit (Loss)
Treasury bonds	$174.91	+30	100	−$524,730
Treasury notes	$102.19	+10	−171	+$174,744.90
Spread profit (loss)				−$349,985.10

^{a} Change in the yield.

presents the result of the spread under this scenario. As expected, the spread produces the largest losses as the yield curve steepened rather than flattening, as the portfolio manager was anticipating. When the yield curve steepens, the long end of the yield is likely to rise more than the short end. As Murphy's Law implies, everything that could go wrong can go wrong.

These scenarios provide the basic principles of spread transactions. Actual outcomes might be different from the one analyzed, as underlying yields for a particular sector may respond differently due to changes in supply and demand.

NOTES

1. The duration of the collateral is estimated using approximate duration.
2. *Bond Week,* March 10, 2002.
3. See Finnerty and Emery (2002).
4. The stripping of the U.S. Treasury Securities revealed huge profits early on as Wall Street investment banks acquired the coupon-paying instruments and deposited the bonds in the Federal Reserve Bank, while issuing certificates in the amount of the coupon underlying the bond as the sums of the pieces sold separately for higher than the whole that came to be known as coupon stripping. The Treasury responded by issuing registered Treasury STRIPS (Separate Trading of Registered Interest and Principal) in the hope of realizing the benefits of stripping coupon on its own.
5. See F. Fabozzi and C. Ramsey, *Collateralized Mortgage Obligations: Structure and Analysis,* 3rd ed. (New Hope, PA: Frank J. Fabozzi Associates, 1999).
6. See S. D. Perlman, "Collateralized Mortgage Obligations: The Impact of Structure on Value," in Frank J. Fabozzi, ed., *Advances and Innovations in the Bond and Mortgage Markets* (Chicago: Probus, 1989), 417–436.
7. See, for example, J. Sterngold "Anatomy of Staggering Loss," *New York Times,* May 11, 1987; Lipin (1992).
8. Note that the yield on AA commercial paper is quoted on the bond equivalent basis while the Federal Funds rate is quoted at the bank discount basis.

CHAPTER 10

Options on Futures

Over-the-counter (OTC) options on currencies and interest rate products began trading among banks and other financial institutions in late 1970. The Chicago Mercantile Exchange (CME) introduced options in interest rates products in 1985. It was an extension of the currency options that began trading at the Philadelphia Exchange (PHLX) in 1982 in response to the needs of multinational corporations to hedge currency exposure and to the needs of arbitrageurs and speculators to garner speculative profits (losses).

This chapter provides an overview of options on interest rates, currencies, indices, and commodity futures products, such as options on spreads position on Eurodollar futures, Treasury futures, currency futures, and commodity futures. Various options positions for hedging and speculating are illustrated using real-world–type exposures. Options on futures are very similar to options on equities and are priced accordingly, using standard Black-Scholes options pricing formula.[1]

Options on futures are more attractive to institutional and individual investors, as they are far more liquid than options on underlying spot instruments. The transaction costs are also smaller on options on futures. Options on futures allow institutions to leverage desired positions without tying up significant capital.

Exhibit 10.1 shows the volume of options on Eurodollar futures, the most actively traded futures in the world on the CME.[2]

Treasury futures options prices are quoted to the 64th of 1 percent of the Treasury futures price of $100,000, as seen in Exhibit 10.2. For example, the price of 1–56 on a December call on Treasury notes futures at the strike price of 112 per $100 face value is $1+56/64$ percent of the $100,000 Treasury futures of $1,875 per one contract.

Eurodollar futures options, however, are quoted as basis points times 10. The Eurodollar futures December put option premium quoted by the *Wall Street Journal* at 2.62—that is, 26.2 basis points times 25—is equal to $655 for a strike price of 98.50, implying 1.5 percent interest rate futures. The buyer of the options on the Eurodollar futures expects interest rates to drop; as interest rates drop (increase), the Eurodollar futures price increases (decreases) and the call option holder exercises (lets the option expire) its option to buy the underlying futures at the strike price, where the current futures price is higher than the strike price.

EXHIBIT 10.1   Volume of Eurodollar Futures and Options (1990–2001)

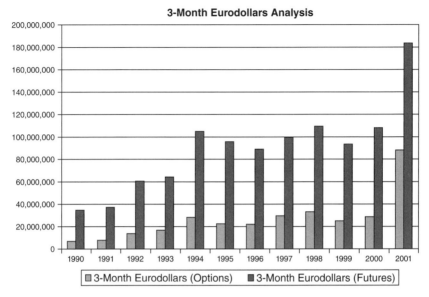

Source: Data from the Division of Economic Analysis of the Commodity Futures Trading Commission.

The seller of the call options on the Eurodollar futures has opposite expectations about interest rates than the buyer, as the seller expects rates to go up. The seller receives a premium of $655 up front and is obligated to sell the underlying futures if rates fall. However, if rates remain above 1.5 percent until expiration, the call buyer lets the call to expire worthless. The zero-sum payoffs of the options illustrate the dynamics, desire, and intensity of the bears (the buyer of the puts) and the bulls (the buyer of the calls) in performing a valuable function in the financial markets—that is, to discover the true price of the underlying assets.

Illustration 10.1

Assume that it is September 20 and the portfolio manager at GNC hedge fund who has $10 million 10-year 4.375 percent Treasury notes priced at 100–31+ to yield 4.25 percent is concerned about rising interest rates in the next three months. The fund manager wishes to hedge interest rate exposure with options on the Treasury notes futures. The put option on the Treasury notes futures for December contract at the strike price of 114 is quoted at 1–20, as shown in Exhibit 10.2. The premium per contract is 1 20/64 percent of the 100,000, that is, $1,312.50.

The fund manager buys 100 put options for December futures for a total premium of $131,250. Currently the yield on the bond is 4.2521 percent. The options on the futures contract are written on a 6 percent coupon, $100,000 par Treasury notes futures. The price of notes per $100 face value is 100−31+, which is equal to 100 63/64, or $100.983375. For hedging purposes, the notes in the portfolio have to be converted to their futures equivalent as if it pays 6 percent coupon interest. This is accomplished to identify which futures contracts have to be selected to hedge the underlying portfolio. The price of the underlying Treasury notes in the hedge fund portfolio, assuming they provide 6 percent coupon interest and all else remaining the same, is equal to $114 per $100 face value.

The fund manager wishes to protect the downside risk by buying put options at a strike price of 114 to protect the value of the portfolio if interest rates increase over the next three months.

The fund manager is not so keen to pay an up-front fee of $131,250 and contemplates financing the purchase of the 114 December puts by simultaneously selling December 115 calls for a premium of 1−31, as shown in Exhibit 10.2, or 1 31/64 percent of the $100,000, $1,484.375 per one contract. By selling 100 calls and receiving $148,437.5 premium, the fund manager more than compensates for the purchase of 100 puts for an up-front fee of $131,250. By being long in 114 December puts (114 refers to the strike price of the option) and short in 115 December calls, the collars created in this example eliminate the downside risk as well as the upside potentials, as selling calls obligates the fund manager to sell Treasury notes futures at the strike price of $115 if rates decrease.

The collars in this scenario produce net gains of $17,187.50 for the fund manager.

SPREADS

Spreads are created by combining long and short positions in one or two calls or puts in the underlying instruments such as stocks, bonds, commodities, indices, and interest rates. Spreads are intended to reduce risk and to limit the potential profit provided that the investor's expectations materialize. The following sections provide an example of various spreads using real market data on various derivative instruments traded in the organized exchanges in the United States and United Kingdom.

BULL SPREADS

Bull spreads are produced when an individual buys one call option at a given strike price while simultaneously selling another call at a strike price higher than the call purchased. For example, consider buying a Eurodollar futures option at the strike price of 98.25, implying a 1.75 percent interest rate on the Eurodollar December futures for 17.7 basis points, or paying $442.50 per contract as

EXHIBIT 10.2   Futures Options Prices

Metals

Copper (CMX)
25,000 lbs.; cents per lb.

Price	Oct	Nov	Dec	Oct	Nov	Dec
64	3.60	4.40	5.00	0.05	0.50	0.75
66	1.75	2.95	3.60	0.15	1.00	1.35
68	0.50	1.85	2.50	0.90	1.90	2.25
70	0.10	1.05	1.65	2.50	3.05	3.40
72	0.05	0.55	1.10	4.40	4.55	4.80
74	0.05	0.25	0.65	6.40	6.25	6.35

Est vol 125 Th 44 calls 12 puts
Op int Thur 3,607 calls 1,158 puts

Gold (CMX)
100 troy ounces; $ per troy ounce

Price	Nov	Dec	Feb	Nov	Dec	Feb
310	14.70	16.80	21.40	1.80	3.70	7.50
315	10.80	13.80	18.10	2.60	5.70	9.10
320	7.80	11.40	15.90	4.10	8.30	12.80
325	5.30	8.60	13.20	7.10	10.40	13.70
330	3.80	7.10	12.40	10.50	13.90	18.10
335	2.40	5.80	9.60	14.20	17.60	20.40

Est vol 5,000 Th 8,951 calls 2,991 puts
Op int Thur 115,881 calls 47,634 puts

Silver (CMX)
5,000 troy ounces; cts per troy ounce

Price	Nov	Dec	Mar	Nov	Dec	Mar
440	26.3	30.4	39.3	1.3	5.5	12.0
450	18.0	23.7	33.2	3.0	8.8	15.8
460	11.8	18.2	28.3	6.8	13.3	20.7
470	7.4	13.8	24.1	12.4	18.8	26.4
475	5.8	12.0	22.3	15.8	21.9	29.5
480	4.7	10.4	20.6	19.6	25.3	32.8

Est vol 700 Th 1,232 calls 699 puts
Op int Thur 52,979 calls 13,422 puts

Interest Rate

T-Bonds (CBT)
$100,000; points and 64ths of 100%

Price	Oct	Nov	Dec	Oct	Nov	Dec
111	2-04	3-01	3-37	0-01	0-61	1-34
112	1-04	2-24	2-62	0-01	1-08	1-58
113	0-07	1-53	2-28	0-03	1-49	2-23
114	0-01	1-24	1-62	0-60	2-20	2-58
115	0-01	1-01	1-37	--	2-60	--
116	0-01	0-47	1-15	--	3-43	4-10

Est vol 44,153;
Th vol 31,559 calls 62,630 puts
Op int Thur 382,668 calls 414,299 puts

T-Notes (CBT)
$100,000; points and 64ths of 100%

Price	Oct	Nov	Dec	Oct	Nov	Dec
113	1-44	2-18	2-40	0-01	0-38	0-60
114	0-44	1-39	2-00	0-01	0-59	1-09
115	0-01	1-05	1-31	0-20	1-25	1-51
116	0-01	0-44	1-04	--	2-00	--
117	0-01	0-27	0-47	--	--	--
118	0-01	0-16	0-32	--	--	3-52

Est vol 68,240 Th 47,329 calls 72,079 puts
Op int Thur 798,121 calls 725,270 puts

5 Yr Treas Notes (CBT)
$100,000; points and 64ths of 100%

Price	Oct	Nov	Dec	Oct	Nov	Dec
11200	1-10	1-40	1-56	0-01	0-30	0-46
11250	0-42	1-19	1-36	0-01	0-41	0-58
11300	0-13	1-00	1-17	0-01	0-54	1-07
11350	0-01	0-49	1-03	--	--	--
11400	0-01	0-37	0-53	--	--	--
11450	--	0-27	0-42	--	--	--

Est vol 25,515 Th 15,192 calls 30,682 puts
Op int Thur 140,415 calls 206,759 puts

Eurodollar (CME)
$ million; pts. of 100%

Price	Oct	Nov	Dec	Oct	Nov	Dec
9775	5.77	..	5.82	0.02	..	0.10
9800	3.30	..	3.55	0.05	0.15	0.30
9825	1.20	1.60	1.77	0.45	0.85	1.02
9850	0.35	0.65	0.87	2.10	2.40	2.62
9875	0.10	0.20	0.37	..	..	4.60
9900	0.05	0.07	0.20	..	..	..

Est vol 233,983;
Th vol 342,258 calls 98,502 puts
Op int Thur 4,803,733 calls 3,029,352 puts

1 Yr. Mid-Curve Eurodlr (CME)
$1,000,000 contract units; pts. of 100%

Price	Oct	Nov	Dec	Oct	Nov	Dec
9675	5.85	..	7.12	0.25	1.02	1.55
9700	3.72	4.80	5.40	0.62	1.70	2.30
9725	2.12	3.25	3.85	1.52	2.65	3.25
9750	1.05	2.05	2.62	2.95	..	4.52
9775	0.40	1.20	1.60	..	..	..
9800	0.17	0.70	1.00	..	..	..

Est vol 37,152 Th 45,130 calls 15,060 puts
Op int Thur 877,146 calls 465,065 puts

2 Yr. Mid-Curve Eurodlr (CME)
$1,000,000 contract units; pts. of 100%

Price	Dec	Mar	Jun	Dec	Mar	Jun
9575	7.07	7.22	7.12	1.25	2.85	4.20
9600	5.25	5.67	5.75	1.90	3.80	5.30
9625	3.75	4.35	..	2.90	..	..
9650	2.50	..	3.50	..	..	..
9675	1.55	..	2.65	..	..	..
9700	..	1.55	..	..	..	..

Est vol 4,720 Th 0 calls 0 puts
Op int Thur 62,791 calls 29,626 puts

Euribor (LIFFE)
Euro 1,000,000

Price	Oct	Nov	Dec	Oct	Nov	Dec
96500	0.42	0.42	0.43	..	0.00	0.01
96625	0.30	0.31	0.32	0.00	0.01	0.03
96750	0.18	0.21	0.23	0.01	0.04	0.06
96875	0.09	0.13	0.16	0.05	0.09	0.11
97000	0.04	0.08	0.11	0.12	0.16	0.19
97125	0.02	0.05	0.07	0.23	0.26	0.27

Vol Fr 115,104 calls 114,606 puts
Op int Thur 2,944,918 calls 1,158,210 puts

Euro-BUND (EUREX)
100,000;pts. in 100%

Price	Oct	Nov	Dec	Oct	Nov	Dec
11100	0.93	1.38	1.63	0.02	0.47	0.72
11150	0.49	1.07	1.34	0.08	0.66	0.93
11200	0.19	0.80	1.08	0.28	0.89	1.17
11250	0.05	0.59	0.87	0.64	1.18	1.46
11300	0.01	0.43	0.68	1.10	1.52	1.77
11350	0.01	0.30	0.52	1.59	1.89	2.11

Vol Fr 43,496 calls 62,567 puts
Op int Thur 461,817 calls 427,104 puts

Currency

Japanese Yen (CME)
$500,000 yen; cents per 100 yen

Price	Oct	Nov	Dec	Oct	Nov	Dec
8050	..	1.81	..	0.45	0.99	1.25
8100	0.96	1.52	1.79	0.64	1.20	1.47
8150	..	1.26	1.53	0.88	1.44	1.71
8200	0.51	1.05	1.31	1.19	1.73	1.99
8250	0.35	0.87	1.12	1.53	2.05	2.29
8300	0.24	0.72	0.96	1.92	2.39	2.63

Est vol 3,503 Th 1,207 calls 1,538 puts
Op int Thur 33,179 calls 47,603 puts

Canadian Dollar (CME)
100,000 Can$, cents per Can$

Price	Oct	Nov	Dec	Oct	Nov	Dec
6250	..	..	1.27	0.10	0.32	0.45
6300	0.54	..	0.95	0.22	0.49	0.63
6350	0.27	..	0.69	0.45	..	0.87
6400	0.12	0.36	0.50	0.80	..	1.18
6450	0.06	..	0.35	..	..	1.52
6500	0.03	0.14	0.25	..	..	1.92

Est vol 123 Th 61 calls 76 puts
Op int Thur 28,365 calls 6,753 puts

British Pound (CME)
62,500 pounds; cents per pound

Price	Oct	Nov	Dec	Oct	Nov	Dec
1530	2.08	2.84	..	0.46	1.22	..
1540	1.38	..	2.54	0.76	..	1.92
1550	0.88	1.68	2.02	..	..	..
1560	0.46	1.28	1.60	1.84	..	2.98
1570	0.30	0.98	1.32	2.68	..	3.70
1580	0.18	0.76	1.06	..	..	..

Est vol 341 Th 467 calls 116 puts
Op int Thur 4,868 calls 3,387 puts

Swiss Franc (CME)
125,000 francs; cents per franc

Price	Oct	Nov	Dec	Oct	Nov	Dec
6600	1.26	..	1.97	0.15	0.56	0.87
6650	0.90	..	..	0.29	..	..
6700	0.61	1.09	1.41	0.50	0.98	1.30
6750	0.38	0.86	..	0.77	..	..
6800	0.24	0.70	1.00	1.13	..	1.88
6850	0.15	..	1.54	..	..	..

Est vol 123 Th 185 calls 75 puts
Op int Thur 4,811 calls 418 puts

Euro Fx (CME)
125,000 euros; cents per euro

Price	Oct	Nov	Dec	Oct	Nov	Dec
9650	1.54	..	..	0.34	..	1.32
9700	1.21	1.83	2.23	0.51	1.13	1.53
9750	0.91	1.56	1.96	0.71	1.36	1.76
9800	0.66	1.31	1.72	0.96	1.61	2.02
9850	0.49	1.11	..	1.29	1.91	..
9900	0.35	0.94	1.33	1.65	2.23	2.62

Est vol 1,076 Th 2,602 calls 819 puts
Op int Thur 32,539 calls 22,836 puts

Index

DJ Industrial Avg (CBOT)
$100 times premium

Price	Sep	Oct	Nov	Sep	Oct	Nov
77	23.00	..	..	0.10	25.00	..
78	14.00	..	..	0.80	28.75	40.00
79	5.50	..	..	2.00	32.75	..
80	2.00	28.00	40.00	9.00	37.50	..
81	0.25	23.50	..	12.00	42.50	..
82	0.05	19.25	30.00	27.00	47.25	..

Est vol 2,262 Wd 348 calls 801 puts
Op int Wed 7,253 calls 12,480 puts

S&P 500 Stock Index (CME)
$250 times premium

Price	Sep	Oct	Nov	Sep	Oct	Nov
830	13.50	..	..	1.70	30.80	..
835	9.70	..	..	2.90	32.70	..
840	6.50	36.50	..	4.70	34.80	46.70
845	3.80	33.80	..	7.00	37.10	..
850	1.90	31.20	43.00	10.10	39.50	51.30
855	1.00	28.70	..	14.20	42.00	..

Est vol 24,045 Wd 8,787 calls 17,672 puts
Op int Wed 142,001 calls 213,008 puts

Other Options

Nasdaq 100 (CME)
$100 times NASDAQ 100 Index

Price	Oct	Nov	Dec	Oct	Nov	Dec
880	..	..	47.20	..	..	..

Est vol 668 Th 3 calls 71 puts
Op int Thur 3,915 calls 2,897 puts

NYSE Composite (NYFE)
$500 times premium

Price	Sep	Oct	Nov	Sep	Oct	Nov
460	0.00	15.85	20.65	0.68	18.35	23.15

Est vol 285 Th 101 calls 81 puts
Op int Thur 1,001 calls 1,822 puts

Source: Wall Street Journal, September 20, 2002.

shown in Exhibit 10.2, while simultaneously selling Eurodollar December futures at a strike price of 98.50 for 8.7 basis points, or receiving a $217.50 premium. Exhibit 10.3 present the behavior of these bull spreads.

The investor who purchased a Eurodollar futures call at a strike price of 98.25 and sold a Eurodollar futures call at a strike price of 98.50 is expected to have the following payoff, assuming interest rate changes +/− 75 basis points at the expiration of the contract (the Eurodollar futures index is at 99 or 97.50).

The profit in the long call as yield drops by 75 basis points is equal to 75 × $25, $1,875 less premium of $442.50 (remember, the change in the price of

EXHIBIT 10.3   Payoff of Bull Spreads Created by Call Options

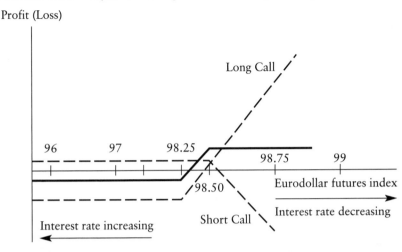

Eurodollar futures for 1 basis point change in the yield is +/− $25). The short call is obligated to sell the Eurodollar futures at the strike price of 98.50. The loss in the short call is equal to 41.3 basis points, or $1,032.50 (the yield dropped by 50 basis points minus 8.7 basis points the short call collected from the long call).

The investor's expectation about the direction of the interest rate has to be skewed toward a falling rate scenario as opposed to the rising rate case in this example.

Profit in the long call: $1,875 less premium of $442.50 = $1,432.50
Short call losses = $1,032.50
Total profit = $400

The maximum profit will be no more than $400 even interest rate drops to zero theoretically.

The payoff of these bull spreads, assuming the interest rate in the underlying Eurodollar futures increases by, say, 75 basis points in the next three months is:

The long call at strike price of 98.25 expires worthless: −$442.50
The short call at strike price of 98.50 expires: +$217.50
The profit of bull spreads: −$225

The maximum loss is equal to $225. The bull spread created with the call options provides protection for downside risk as well as limiting upside potentials.

BEAR SPREADS

Bear spreads are created when investors buy a put option at the higher strike price and simultaneously sell a put at a lower strike price. The upside potential is limited in this case and the downside risk is truncated at the strike price of the put option purchased. Consider a gold mining firm that is concerned about falling gold prices under $325/ounce in the next three months. It buys 325 December put futures at $10.40/ounce and finances the purchase of the puts by simultaneously selling 310 December put futures for $3.70/ounce, as listed in Exhibit 10.2. Exhibit 10.4 shows the behavior of the bear spreads.

Suppose the price of gold drops to $300/ounce by December. The long put provides protection, as the buyer sells the gold at the strike price of $325, for which a $10.40 premium has been paid. The profit is equal to $14.60/ounce of gold, or $1,460 per one contract; however, the upside potential is limited by selling the 310 (310 refers to the strike price) put, for which a premium of $3.70 has been collected. The seller is obligated to purchase the gold at $310/ounce for the short put, a loss of $6.30/ounce, or $630 per one contract. The net profit is $830 per contract.

However, if the price of gold futures is $340 by the expiration date of the contact, the puts are worthless and the loss stemming from the bear spreads is the differential in the premium paid and received. In this scenario, $10.40 is paid and $3.70 is received for a net loss of $6.70/ounce, or $670 per contract.

Investors taking such a position are actually bearish about the price of gold in the next three months, as demonstrated by their desire to purchase puts at a higher strike price while selling puts at a lower strike price.

BUTTERFLY SPREADS

A butterfly spread strategy involves buying a call at strike price of E_1, buying a second call at a higher strike price of E_3, while selling two calls short midpoint of E_1 and E_3 at E_2. For example, consider buying December 64 copper futures call at COMEX for 5 cents and December 72 at 1.10 cents (see Exhibit 10.2), while selling two December 68 calls short for 2.5 cents, as shown in Exhibit 10.5.

Strategy
Buy December 64 copper futures for 5 cents.
Buy December 72 copper futures for 1.10 cents.

EXHIBIT 10.4   Payoff of Bear Spreads Produced by Put Options

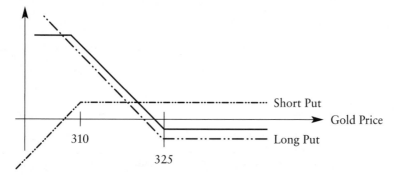

EXHIBIT 10.5   Butterfly Spreads on Copper Futures CMX
Produced by Call Options

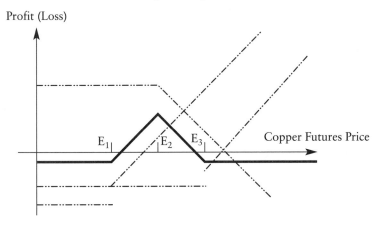

Sell two December 68 copper futures for 2.5 cents.

Net outflow is equal to 1.10 cents/pound.

The maximum loss is equal to 25,000 lbs.× \$.011/lb. = −\$275.

The loss of \$275 is realized if the copper price is below 64 or above 78 cents in this example. However, if the copper price remains in the range of 64 to 72 cents per pound, profit will be realized. For example, if the copper futures price is 68 at the expiration of the contract, maximum profit of 2.9 cents will be realized per pound of copper.

The maximum profit is equal to \$.029/lb.× 25,000 = \$725.

BOX SPREADS

The box spread strategy creates a synthetic long forward and a synthetic short forward by buying and selling options. For example, from the put/call parity, the relationship shown in Equation 10.1 exists.

$$\text{Long put} + \text{Spot price} = PV \text{ (Strike price)} + \text{Long call} \qquad (10.1)$$

The parity in the futures market for the options on interest rate futures, such as Eurodollar futures, needs to be restated as follows where PV is the present value:

$$\text{Long put} - \text{Long call} - PV \text{ (Strike price of futures)} = -\text{Futures price} \qquad (10.2)$$

In Equation 10.2, if the investor buys a put and simultaneously sells a call at the same strike price, the investor has synthetically shorted the futures. Similarly, by multiplying both sides of Equation 10.2 by a minus (−), the investor can synthetically produce long futures:

$$\text{Short put} + \text{Long call} + PV \text{ (Strike price of futures)} = + \text{Futures price} \qquad (10.3)$$

In Equation 10.3, the investor has effectively created long futures by buying a call and simultaneously selling a put at the same strike price.

Example: The treasurer of DuPont wishes to hedge the company's exposure to currency risk for deutsche mark (DM)250 million payables to BMW in one year. The spot rate and the one-year forward rate are DM3.2/$. The treasurer wishes to buy calls on U.S. dollars and simultaneously sell puts in U.S. dollars at the strike price of DM3.2/$. The strategy produces a synthetic long forward price of DM/$ assuming the premium of the call and put are equal to $.017/DM.[3]

Since the exchange rates of the spot and forward are the ratio of the two price indices, the call option in dollars is identical to the put option in foreign currency (e.g., deutsche marks, euros, etc.), and the put option in dollars is identical to the call options in foreign currency:

Call in $ = Put in DM

Put in $ = Call in DM

The treasurer can buy puts in deutsche marks by simultaneously selling calls in deutsche marks to synthetically create a short forward of DM/$ or a long forward of $/DM, as demonstrated in Exhibit 10.6.

The synthetic long (short) forward created by long put (short call) and short call (long put) produces a payoff identical to the payoff of the forward contract provided that the hedger used the futures contract to hedge the receivables (payables) denominated in the foreign currency. The payoff of the box spreads

EXHIBIT 10.6   Creating Synthetic Forward Using Box Spreads

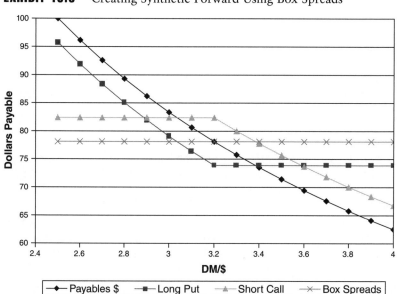

is equal to the payoff of the long (short) forward contract in the amount of DM250 million at the forward rate of DM3.2/$ or $78.125 million.

The buying of box spreads can be considered to be taking a long (lending) and short position (borrowing) at the same strike price and over the same time horizon with a payoff equal to that of a riskless asset. (This concept will be demonstrated shortly.) The question is, why bother to buy box spreads in the first place when one can invest in a risk-free asset? The answer may depend on the mispricing and the treatment of the payoff of the box spreads and the payoff of the risk-free asset as ordinary income or capital gains subject to different taxation.

Assuming interest parity holds and the risk-free interest rates in the United States and Germany are equal to 4.5 percent, DuPont can borrow dollars, use the proceeds to buy deutsche marks, and invest the deutsche marks for one year at 4.5 percent, using the payoff from the German bond to pay the DM250 million payable to BMW, as seen in Exhibit 10.7.

DuPont borrows the dollar equivalent of the present value of the DM250 million, that is [250 million/1.045]/DM3.2/$ equal to $74.7607 million to buy 239.234 million/deutsche marks at the spot rate of DM3.2/$. It invests this amount at 4.5 percent to yield DM250 million at maturity. The $74.7607 million borrowed at 4.5 percent to hedge the foreign exchange risk has the future value of $78.125 million. The ratio of the payables denominated in deutsche marks and dollars is [DM250 million]/[$78.125 million], equal to the implied one-year forward rate of DM3.2/$, that is, also equal to a one-year forward rate as corroborated by the box spreads in Exhibit 10.6. This is the money market hedge of payable, with the payoff identical to the forward contract, assuming interest parity is not violated.

As demonstrated in this example, it is possible to synthetically create a long or short position to replicate the payoff of financial assets such as stocks, bonds, commodities, currencies, futures, and so on. However, treating the resulting gains or losses as capital gains (capital losses) as opposed to ordinary income or loss for tax purposes will enable individuals to engage in the practice of tax arbitrage. Section 1258 of the U.S. tax code, enacted in 1993, explicitly states that income due to time value of money on bonds has to be treated as ordinary income. The gain or loss in an option is treated as capital gains or losses for tax purposes by the tax code.

The problem arises when investors use options to synthetically create a long or short position and treat the resulting gains or losses as capital gains or losses for tax purposes. Doing this makes it difficult for tax authorities to detect whether the gains (losses) are indeed ordinary or capital gains that are subject to asymmetric tax rate treatments.

EXHIBIT 10.7 Money Market Hedge

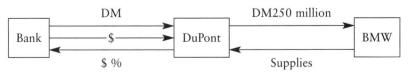

LONG STRADDLE

The long straddle involves buying a call and put simultaneously at the same strike price over the same delivery period. The payoff in this strategy depends on the volatility of the underlying assets. Profit will be realized if volatility is expected to increase for a variety of different reasons in the market. For example, consider the December 97.50 strike price in euro FX futures at CME. The speculator buys a December call at a strike price of 97.50 at CME for 1.96 cents and simultaneously buys a put with the same strike price for 1.76 cents (see Exhibit 10.2).

The speculator believes that the euro FX is expected to move one way or the other significantly against the dollar by the delivery date. Exhibit 10.8 presents the payoff of a long straddle.

As long as the euro deviates significantly from the strike price of 97.50 cents/€, the speculator will realize profit. For example, the speculator believes that the European central bank may not be able to maintain the current spot rate of $.9740/€, as this rate is making European goods and services unduly expensive, thereby intervention to support the currency is likely to fail. The exchange rate in this scenario is likely to fall, say, to $.80/€. However, the speculator is betting that the euro may revalue to $1.20/€ due to weak economic fundamentals in the United States as well as a bigger-than-expected deficit, which may be inflationary in nature.

Suppose the euro devalues to $.80/€ by December. The call expires worthless and the put is in-the-money and produces a net profit per unit of $.13766/€. The profit of the straddle is summarized in Illustration 10.2.

EXHIBIT 10.8   Payoff on Long Straddle

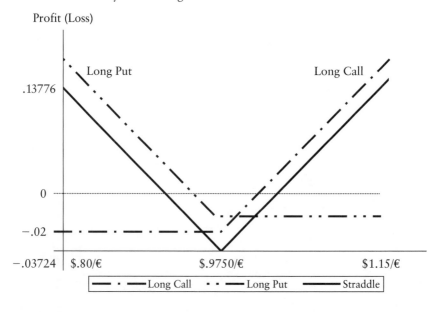

Illustration 10.2

It is September 20 and a FOREX speculator believes that the euro is expected to significantly move in one way or the other against the dollar by December. Buy December call at strike price of 97.50 cents/€ at CME for 1.96 cents/€ and simultaneously buy puts with the same strike price for 1.76 cents/€ (see Exhibit 10.2).

One contract for euro FX futures is for delivery of 125,000 units.

Long call premium paid: $.0196/€ × 125,000 = $2,450

Long put premium paid: $.0176/€ × 125,000 = $2,200

Results

Scenario I: December 21: Euro devalues to $.80/€ at the expiration.

Long Straddle: [.9750 − .0176 − .0196 − .80] × 125,000 = $17,225

Scenario II: Euro FX revalues to $1.15/€ by delivery date.

The profit of the straddle is as follows:

Long Straddle: [1.15 − .9750 − .0176 − .0196] × 125,000 = $17,225

The maximum loss on the long straddle is equal to $4,650; the premium for the call and put paid assuming the euro is $.9750/€ at expiration, the loss will be smaller than $4,650 in the range of $.9574/€ to $.9846/€.

The long straddle is effective as long as the underlying instrument is expected to move in one or the other directions due to a pending merger and acquisition, a spin-off and the likelihood of its collapse due to a regulatory block, the outcome of an election as to whether the winner will push spending toward defense or a social agenda, and its impact on the segment of the economy directly affected by such events, positively or otherwise. The central bank purchase or sale of its own foreign currency for stabilization purposes and the eventual collapse of such policy and any other events that trigger a massive purchase or sale of the underlying currency (assets) are expected to produce profit for speculators and arbitrageurs.

SHORT STRADDLE

The short straddle strategy involves selling a call and put simultaneously at the same strike price, where the investor believes that there will not be any major movement of the underlying instrument in one direction or the other. Provided that the underlying instrument price remains in the neighborhood of the strike price, the short straddle is expected to produce a profit of no more than the premium received by selling the call and put. For example, consider a March 2003 call and put on silver futures at a strike price of 470 cents that is quoted at the CMX for 24.1 and 26.4 cents, respectively, per troy ounce of silver in Exhibit 10.2. The option to buy or sell a call or put on silver futures at CMX is for delivery of 5,000 ounces.

Assuming the price of silver futures remains inside of the $4.22 to $5.23 range, the speculator will realize a profit. For example, if the price of silver futures is $5/ounce, the put expires worthless as the put seller keeps the premium of $1,320 per contract (.264 × 5,000). The call, however, is activated as the buyer forces the seller to sell at $4.70. The call seller realizes a loss of $.06/ounce or $300 per contract, as the sums of the strike price of $4.70 and the premium .241 received falls short of the current price of $5/ounce. The short straddle in Exhibit 10.9 will make a profit of $1,020, equal to gains in the put sold less the call sold ($1,320 − 300). If the price of silver futures is equal to $4.22 or $5.23, the short straddle profit is nearly equal to zero. At the $4.22/ounce, the call is out-of-the-money and call seller keeps the premium of $.241/ounce; however, the short straddle is obligated to purchase the silver futures at the strike price of $4.70 from the put buyer where the current price is $4.22/ounce. The loss on the short put is equal to −$.216/ounce as sums of $4.22 plus the premium of $.264/ounce received less the strike price of $4.70.

Outside of the $4.22 to $5.23 range, the short straddle is expected to realize a loss, as can be verified in Exhibit 10.9.

Illustration 10.3 summarizes the payoff of short straddle.

Illustration 10.3

It is September 20, and a speculator believes that the price of silver futures is expected to remain in the narrow range of $4.45 to $5/ounce in the next six months.

Sell March 2003 call and put on silver futures at strike price of $4.70 for a premium of $.241 and $.264 at COMEX.

Short call: Premium received $.241 × 50,000 = $1,205 per contract
Short put: Premium received $.261 × 5,000 = $1,320

Results

March 20: the silver futures price is $5 at the expiration and speculator closes out its position.

The put sold expires and the speculator keeps $1,320 premium, while the call is exercised and the short straddle is obligated to sell at strike price of $4.70 plus the premium of $.241 for loss of nearly $300 or ($.06/ounce) × 5,000.

Total profit: $1,320 − 300 = $1,020

CALENDAR SPREAD

The calendar spread strategy involves selling a call or put for a given expiration date and simultaneously buying a call and put for the same strike price with longer time to expiration. The trader is essentially betting that the volatility of the underlying option will remain fairly constant. For example, consider the options on gold futures at a strike price of $320. The trader sells a 320 November gold

EXHIBIT 10.9 Payoff on Short Straddle

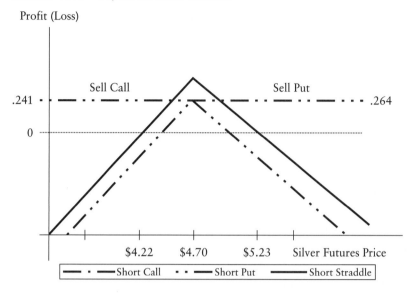

futures call for $7.80 and simultaneously buys a call at the same strike price for February 2003 at $15.90, as shown in Exhibit 10.2. The rate of time deterioration for the November short call is greater than the time decay for the February long call purchased.

Assuming the price of the gold futures remains in the neighborhood of the strike price by the expiration of the call sold and long call purchased is liquidated at the expiration of the short call the trader realizes a maximum profit. However, if the price at the expiration of the short call is significantly higher or lower than the strike price, the trader is expected to realize loss. Exhibit 10.10 illustrates the payoff of the calendar spread for the gold futures in this example.

Illustration 10.4 summarizes the profit (loss) for the calendar spread.

EXHIBIT 10.10 Calendar Spread

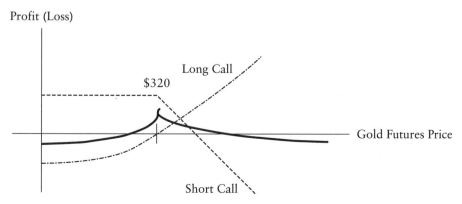

Illustration 10.4

A gold trader is expecting the implied volatility to subside and gold prices to remain around $320 strike price in the next three months.

September 20
Sell November 320 call at $7.80/ounce.
Buy February 320 call at $15.90.

Results
Scenario I: November 18, 2002
Gold futures price is $318/ounce.
November call expires and the seller keeps the premium of $780.
Long call is liquidated at the price of 14.50/ounce for loss of $140.
Profit: $780 − $140 = $640

Scenario II: November 18, price of the gold futures drops to $310/ounce
November call expires and the seller keeps the premium of $780.
February call is liquidated at 4.50 for a loss of $1,140 per contract.
Profit (loss) for calendar spread: −$1,140 + $780 = −$360

Scenario III: November 18, price of gold futures rise to $327.80/ounce
November call sold produces zero gain as the seller is forced to sell at strike price of $320.
February call is liquidated at $14 for loss of $190.
Calendar spread profit (loss): −$190

STRIPS

Provided that a trader is more bearish about the underlying instrument than bullish about it, a trader can buy two puts for every one call purchased at the same strike price. For example, suppose a trader is expecting that the British pound is more likely to devalue against the dollar in the next three months. The speculator buys two 156 cent December puts for 2.98 cents and simultaneously buys one December call for 1.60 cents. Exhibit 10.11 shows the payoff this strip is expected to have.

Each contract on the option for the pound futures is for delivery of 62,500 units of the pound at the COMEX.

Premium paid: 62,500 (2 × .0298 + 1 × .0160) = $4,725

The trader pays $4,725 to buy two puts and one call at a strike price of $1.56/pound. This is the maximum loss in three months if the pound price is equal to the strike price of $1.56 at the expiration of a call and two puts. The strike price

EXHIBIT 10.11 Payoff in Stripes Position

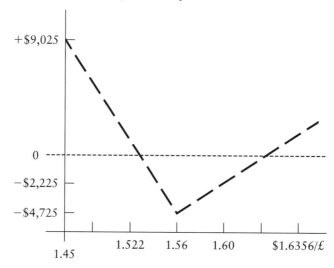

plus premium/minus 1/2 premium establishes the range of the exchange rates where the strips will be zero net present value; the payoff on the strips will be equal to zero. Let us assume the exchange rate is equal to a break-even price of $1.52220 or 1.6356/ pound[4]:

Strike price + .0756 = $1.6356, or Strike price $- \frac{1}{2}$ (.0756) = $1.5220/£

The two puts are activated as the buyer sells the pound for $1.56 when the price is equal to $1.5220. The profit of .0756 on the strips is exactly equal to the premium for two puts and one call.

  Suppose the spot price is equal to $1.6356 at the expiration. The put expires worthless, while the call is exercised for profit of .0756 that pays for the premium on the call and puts. However, assuming the exchange rate is outside of the range of 1.5220 and 1.6356, the stripes produce nonsymmetric profit tilted more on the bearish scenario than the bullish scenario. For example, if the exchange rate is equal to $1.45/pound, the profit of the stripes is equal to $9,025 for the stripes position. Illustration 10.5 examines this strategy.

Illustration 10.5

It is September 20 and a FOREX trader is more bearish than bullish about the British pound, as it expects the currency to devalue in the next three months rather than to revalue against the U.S. dollar, due to weak economic fundamentals and higher expected inflation. The trader buys two December puts and one call at a strike price of $1.56/pound.

September 20: Buy two December puts and one December call at strike price of $1.56.

(continues)

Illustration 10.5   *(Continued)*

Premium paid: 62,500 [2 × .0298 +1 × .0160] = $4,725

Scenario I: December 19
Spot price is $1.56.
Puts and call expire worthless for loss of $4,725.

Scenario II: December 19
Spot price is $1.45.
Two puts are in the money. The trader sells the pound at $1.56/£, for a profit of .11 per one put less premium.
Profit: [.11 × 2 × 62500] − $4,725 = $9,025

Scenario III: December 19
Spot price is $1.60.
Profit: [−2·× 0298 + .04 − .016] 62,500 = − $2,225

STRAPS

Straps involve buying two calls and one put at the same strike price, where a trader is more bullish than bearish about the underlying instrument for which the long positions are taken. Unlike a long straddle, where the trader believes large swings are imminent in one or the other direction on the underlying instrument by simply buying a call and a put at the same strike price, the straps trader is leaning more toward the bullish direction than a bearish outcome. Consider a FOREX trader who received a tip from the editor of foreign exchange magazine that the Swiss franc (SF) is more likely to appreciate against the dollar in the next three months than to depreciate. The trader buys two December calls and one December put at the strike price of 67 cents/Swiss franc. The premiums are quoted at 1.30 and 1.41 cent, respectively, for the put and call at COMEX in Exhibit 10.2.

Exhibit 10.12 shows the behavior of the straps. Illustration 10.6 presents the strategy.

Illustration 10.6

It is September 20 and a FOREX trader is more bullish than bearish about the Swiss franc, as it expects the currency to revalue in the next three months rather than to devalue against the U.S. dollar, due to stronger economic fundamentals in Switzerland and lower expected inflation. The trader buys two December calls and one put at a strike price of 67 cents/Swiss franc.

September 20: Buy two December calls and one December put at strike price of $.67/Swiss franc.
Premium paid: 125,000 [2 × .0141 + 1 × .0130] = $5,150

The break-even point is equal to the strike price plus half of the premiums for the calls and put when the underlying instrument price goes up: $.67 + \frac{1}{2}$ $(.04120) = \$.6906$/Swiss franc.

The break-even point is equal to a strike price minus premiums for the calls and put if the underlying instrument price goes down: $.67 - (.04120) =$ $\$.6288$/Swiss franc.

For example, if the exchange rate is at $\$.6906$/Swiss franc at expiration, the long calls produces profit of $5,150 that is offset by the premium of $5,150. However, if the exchange rate is $\$.6288$/Swiss franc at the expiration, the calls are out-of-the-money for a loss of $3,525 while the put is in-the-money for a profit of $3,525, for zero gain in the straps.

Scenario I: December 19

Spot price is $.68.

Put expires worthless for loss of $1,625. Two calls are exercised for loss of $1,025.

Profit (loss): $[-.013 - 2 \times .01411 + 2 \times .01] \; 125{,}000 = -\$2{,}650$

Scenario II: December 19

Spot price is $\$.6288$/Swiss franc.

Put is in-the-money for profit, and calls are out-of-the-money for loss.
$125{,}000[-2 \times .0141 - .0130 + .0412] = 0.0$

Scenario III: December 19

Spot price is $\$.72$/Swiss franc.

Put is out-of-the-money. Calls are in-the-money for profit on the straps.
Profit: $125{,}000[-2 \times .0141 - .0130 + 2 \times .05] = \$7{,}350$

EXHIBIT 10.12   Payoff in Straps Position

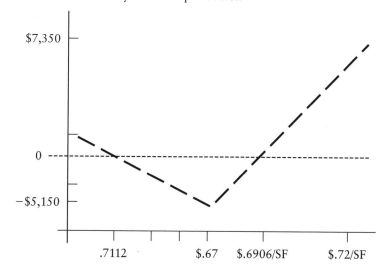

PRICE AND YIELD VOLATILITY

The price and yield volatility for the financial instruments traded in the market are related to one another assuming zero curvatures, as defined in Equation 6.6.

$$\Delta P = D \times P \times \Delta Y$$

where

D = duration of bond
P = price
Y = yield

Dividing both sides of this relationship by price and yield and rearranging, the following relationship emerges.

$$\Delta P/PY = D \times P \times \Delta Y/PY$$
$$\Delta P/P = D \times \Delta Y/Y \times Y \tag{10.4}$$

Price volatility ($\Delta P/P$) on the left-hand side of Equation 10.4 is equal to the duration of the bond at a given yield times the yield volatility ($\Delta Y/Y$), implied or historical, times the level of the yield (Y). The volatility tends to be highest as the option on the underlying instruments approaches the maturity. Options market makers tend to buy options when the volatility is low; otherwise they sell short. Exhibit 10.13 estimates the price volatility for a 6 percent coupon bond priced to yield 3 to 10 percent, assuming yield volatility of 5, 10, 15, 20, 40, and 60 percent.

The price volatility is nearly half of the yield volatility at the higher interest rates; however, it is only a fraction of the yield volatility at the lower rates. For example, the price volatility is 2.2 percent at an 8 percent interest rate when the yield volatility is 5 percent. As the yield volatility double, the price volatility

EXHIBIT 10.13 Estimates of the Price Volatilities for Various Yield Volatilities for 10-Year Swaps Futures

Interest Rate %	Duration	Yield Volatility					
		5	10	15	20	40	60
		Price Volatility					
3%	6.11	0.009	0.018	0.027	0.037	0.073	0.110
4%	5.99	0.012	0.024	0.036	0.048	0.096	0.144
5%	5.88	0.015	0.029	0.044	0.059	0.118	0.176
6%	5.76	0.017	0.035	0.052	0.069	0.138	0.207
7%	5.64	0.020	0.039	0.059	0.079	0.158	0.237
8%	5.52	0.022	0.044	0.066	0.088	0.177	0.265
9%	5.39	0.024	0.049	0.073	0.097	0.194	0.291
10%	5.27	0.026	0.053	0.079	0.105	0.211	0.316

doubles at the low rates; however, the price volatility tends to be slightly more than double at higher interest rates, as can be verified from the estimates in Exhibit 10.13.

The duration of the 10-year swaps futures is also estimated at the various yields, assuming the underlying instrument pays 6 percent coupon semiannually. As expected, there is an inverse relationship between the yield and duration; as yield increases, the duration of the bond decreases.[5]

Options traders on LIBOR-based instruments, such as options on Eurodollar futures, options on Euribor (options on euro-euro traded at LIFFE), and options on swaps futures consider the yield volatility, while options traders on the Treasury debt instruments and OTC options on the mortgaged-backed securities look at the price volatility. Exhibits 10.14 and 10.15 show the behavior of yield and price volatility for options on 10-year swaps futures as estimated by the Chicago Board of Trade over the July 2000 to June 2002 period.

Price and yield volatility tends to diverge significantly from the median of 7.5 and 16.8 percent, respectively, as the maturity of the option approaches its expiration. For example, the yield volatility for the option on the 10-year swaps futures is as high as nearly 40 percent and as low as under 5 percent, 21 days before the expiration date. The same is true for the price volatility; it goes up as high as 16 percent or as low as 4 percent, 21 days before the expiration date.

SPREAD TRADES ON TREASURY CURVES

Suppose a portfolio manager has a strong expectation that the spread on the Treasury notes in the portfolio and AA corporate is going to widen in the next

EXHIBIT 10.14   Price Volatility

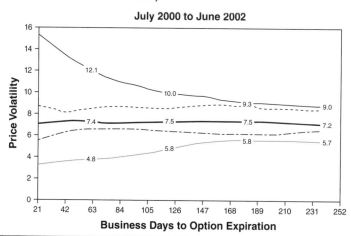

Source: CBOT estimates.

EXHIBIT 10.15   Yield Volatility

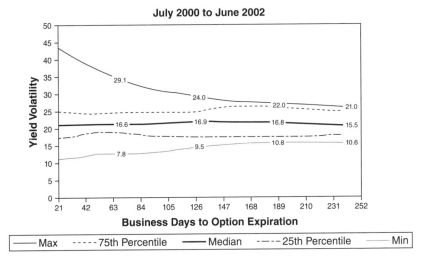

Source: CBOT estimates.

three months. The portfolio manager can buy the spreads, which requires going long in 10-year Treasury notes futures and short 10-year swaps futures, as shown in Exhibit 10.16. The underlying contract in 10-year swaps futures is a $100,000 par bond with 6 percent fixed coupon interest cash settled at the floating rate benchmark 10-year swaps rate quoted by the International Swaps and Derivative Association (ISDA).[6] However, the portfolio manager who expects a tightening of the spread may sell Treasury notes futures and buy 10-year swaps futures.

The price of 10-year Treasury notes futures is at 113–15, or 113.468, to yield 4.3266 percent. The price of 10-year swaps futures is at 109–31, or 109.968, to yield 4.73 percent as of October 29, 2002. The spread of 41 basis points reflects the credit risk of the 10-year swaps futures rate approximating the yield in AA bonds. The portfolio manager is expecting the spread to widen and wants to buy the spread. The spread has to be structured so that the price sensitivity of the long and the short position is identical. This is accomplished by estimating the hedge ratio for the spread. The hedge ratio is estimated using actual changes in the price of the Treasury notes futures and 10-year swaps futures for ±1 basis point change in the yield. For small changes in the yield, the actual yield and forecast yield based on duration is identical, as demonstrated earlier in Equation 6.6.

$$\Delta P = -D \times P \times (\Delta Y)$$

P = \$113,699.61	Yield = 4.30
P = \$113,525.46	Yield = 4.32%
ΔP = \$174.15	DVO1: \$174.15/2 = \$87.07/.8813 = \$98.79

EXHIBIT 10.16 Spread: Long Treasury Notes and Short 10-year Swaps Futures

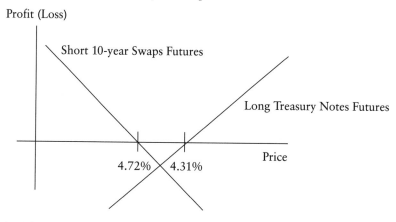

Initial Spread = −41 bps

Dividing 174.15 by 2, we arrive at the dollar value of 1 basis point DVO1 for Treasury notes spot price. The DVO1 for Treasury notes futures can be estimated by dividing DVO1 by the cheapest to deliver (CTD) conversion factor for a 6 percent coupon bond. The conversion factor for the CDT 10-year Treasury notes with 4.375 percent coupon is .8813 as of October 29, 2002. Therefore, the DVO1 for Treasury notes futures is equal to $98.79. The DVO1 for the 10-year swaps futures can be estimated as:

P	= $110,278.02	Yield = 4.70	
P	= $110,110.28	Yield = 4.72%	
ΔP	= $167.74	DVO1: $167.74/2 = $83.87	

The spread ratio or the hedge ratio (h) is estimated as the ratio of the two DVO1s, as defined in Equation 10.5.[7]

h = DVO1 (Treasury notes futures)/DVO1 (swaps futures)

  = $98.79/$83.87 (10.5)

  = 1.18

This ratio implies that the portfolio manager needs to short 118 swaps futures for 100 long positions in Treasury note futures to remain neutral to the direction of the change in interest rates (not so neutral, as is demonstrated later). In other words, the dollar change in the price of 118 swaps futures is identical to the dollar change in the price of 100 Treasury notes futures. As long as the spread widens, the portfolio manager is expected to profit regardless of the direction of the change in the yield (beware); if the spread narrows, the portfolio manager will lose. Consider the following four interest rate scenarios.

Scenario 1: Parallel Shift in the Yield; Spread Remains the Same

	Number of Contracts	Change in Yield	DVO1	Gains (Losses)
Treasury notes futures	100	+20	$98.79	−$197,580
10-year swaps futures	−118	+20	$83.87	+$197,933.20
Spread profit (loss)				+$353.20

The yield in both futures contracts increased by 20 basis points, the 100 long positions in the Treasury notes futures produced a loss of $197,580 as the product of the number of contracts times change in yield times (DVO1). However, the 118 short positions in the 10-year swaps futures produces profit of $197,933.20. The spread appears to be neutral as the loss of $353.20 is due to rounding error.

Scenario 2: Nonparallel Shift in the Yield; Spread Widens

	Number of Contracts	Change in Yield	DVO1	Gains (Losses)
Treasury notes futures	100	+10	$98.79	−$98,790
10-year swaps futures	−118	+30	$83.87	+$296,899.80
Spread profit (loss)				+$198,109.80

When the spread widens, as shown in this scenario, the yields are increasing for the underlying futures in Treasury notes as well as the swaps futures; however, the shift in the yield is nonparallel, as the yield in the swaps futures increases by 30 basis points for only a 10-basis-point increase in the Treasury notes futures. The spread in this scenario produces the largest profit. A word of caution: If the spread narrows and the Treasury notes increase, say, by 20 basis points while the yield in the swaps futures increases by 10 basis points, then the spread produces a loss, as the underlying long position in the Treasury notes futures suffers more losses than the profit of the short position to cover that loss, as shown in Scenario 3.

Scenario 3: Nonparallel Shift in the Yield; Spread Narrows

	Number of Contracts	Change in Yield	DVO1	Gains (Losses)
Treasury notes futures	100	+20	$98.79	−$197,580
10-year swaps futures	−118	+10	$83.87	+$98,966.60
Spread profit (loss)				−$98,613.40

Assuming the yield spread widens as in Scenario 4, the spread produces a profit as expected. For example, suppose the yield in Treasury notes futures decreases by 10 basis points while the yield in the swaps futures decreases by 5 basis points; the spread widens, resulting in a profit of $148,273.30. These scenarios are provided to demonstrate how the likely results shape the profit (loss) potentials for spread transactions and the actual outcome entirely depends on the behavior and evolution of the particular long or short futures.

Scenario 4: Nonparallel Shift in the Yield; Spread Widens

	Number of Contracts	Change in Yield	DVO1	Gains (Losses)
Treasury notes futures	100	−10	$98.79	+$ 98,790
10-year swaps futures	−118	−5	$83.87	+$ 49,483.30
Spread profit (loss)				+$148,273.30

EXOTIC OPTIONS

Exotic options are variants of ordinary options where the spot price, strike price, and maturity are embedded with options.[8] An example would be allowing the spot price to be determined over the option period (path dependent) as average spot as opposed to one price at the expiration or exercise date.

Asian Options

Asian options are traded over the counter on foreign currencies and other instruments, as the strike price is the simple arithmetic or geometric average of the price of the underlying instrument over the life of the option or the exercise date. The underlying volatility of the average price is always smaller than the volatility of the spot price. Therefore, premiums for Asian options are smaller than premiums for otherwise ordinary options.

Asian options as hedging instruments provide the end user the opportunity to manage risk at lower cost and at average as opposed to spot price, where most of the transactions in the international trade are settled. For example, most of the intercompany transactions in the OTC markets are settled at the average exchange rate as opposed to an exchange rate prevailing at the settlement date. The greater the sampling frequency, the smaller the dispersion of the outcome below the average, thus producing a smaller price for the option. Call (C) and put (P) for the Asian options at strike price (E) are defined as:

$$C = \text{Max}\ (A_s - E, 0)$$
$$P = \text{Max}\ (E - A_s, 0)$$

where

A_s = geometric average of the spot price, which is always smaller than its arithmetic counterpart

The estimates of the annual volatility based on monthly, weekly, and daily prices translating into 12, 30, and 252 observations produce the smallest standard deviations with the largest sampling frequency.[9] In other words, the average price per 12, 30, or 252 observations is expected to have the smallest standard deviations for the daily data. The call options written with an average price based on 252 observations is expected to have the smallest standard deviation and the smallest call premium, whereas the put option is expected to have the largest premium.

Rainbow Option

The rainbow option pays the maximum of the base interest rate or the return from the portfolio of two risky assets denominated in dollars and foreign currency. Consider a three-month option that pays a maximum of 90-day LIBOR, the returns on the S&P 500 index, or the return for the U.K. equities on the Financial Times Stock Exchange (FTSE):

$$C = Max \ (LIBOR, \ S\&P \ 500, \ FTSE)$$

Suppose an investor buys a call option whose payoff is the greater of the three-month LIBOR, the return on S&P 500 index, or the return on the FSTE. Assuming the return is equal to 7.5, 11.25, and 10 percent for the respective indices, the investor receives 11.25 percent on this rainbow option. The investor pays the lower of the three indices if all three declined from the time the option is acquired to the time the option expires. The rainbow option can be considered as a swap with cap/floors imposed on the payoff where a mutual fund pays the higher of the returns to a hedge fund for an up-front fee, while receiving the lower of the returns on the underlying instrument from the hedge fund. This synthetic securitization of risk is achieved as a mutual fund transfers its risk on the underlying assets without selling the securities in the portfolio similar to a total return swap.

The rainbow option allows investors to bet on the better or worse of the underlying assets, such as stocks, bonds, or commodities. An option to earn better of two classes of assets, such as stocks and bonds, allows investors to garner the higher return if one of the underlying instruments outperformed the other. For example, if the returns on the stocks as proxy by the return on the S&P 500 and return on the bonds is based on the Lehman Brothers Index are respectively equal to 5.5 and 8 percent over the option period, the investor realizes the higher return of 8 percent on the bonds. This type of option was popular in 1990, as investors were unsure of the direction of the markets for stocks and bonds.

The large mutual funds presumably are the writers of this type of option, with long positions in stocks and bonds. They sell call options for a premium to augment portfolio returns.

Quantos

The payoff in foreign-denominated assets exposes the investor to foreign exchange risk as well as market risk. To mitigate market risk, the investor can hedge the underlying instrument by taking an offsetting position in the forward, futures, or options market. However, the foreign exchange rate risk still remains, causing unexpected gains (losses) that may offset the gains (losses) in the underlying instrument as defined in Equation 2.1.

Quanto is an equity-linked forward or futures contract where the payoff depends on the value of an index denominated in a foreign currency and marked to market on a daily basis.

The Nikkei 225 futures traded in the CME is an example of a quanto, where the foreign exchange rate risk is mitigated. The minimum tick is priced at $5, and the futures position in the Nikkei 225 futures is marked to market on a daily basis, rendering foreign exchange risk irrelevant from the perspective of the U.S. investor speculating about the direction of the Nikkei 225.

For example, an investor in the United States who is bearish about Japanese stocks in the next three months can sell Nikkei 225 futures or buy put options in Nikkei futures without regard to exchange rate risk. The speculator's position is marked to market on a daily basis similar to any other futures contract. Assume the Nikkei 225 futures shorted at 11,000 and by the expiration the Nikkei has fallen to 10,275. The speculator's profit is equal to 725 times $5, or $3,625, on one contract. This profit (loss) is realized without regard to the yen/$ exchange rate when the position was taken and closed out on or before the expiration date of the contract without reference to the exchange rates at the inception and the closing date. The options on the Japanese index of 225 blue-chip stocks for speculative purposes is marketed as put warrants by Goldman Sachs in 1989.

Nikkei Put Warrants

To mitigate foreign exchange rate risk and to provide an opportunity for U.S. and Canadian investors to bet on the prospect of falling Japanese stock prices, Goldman Sachs launched Nikkei Put Warrants (NPW) on February 17, 1989, on the Toronto Stock Exchange. The NPW priced at Canadian (C)$3.55 allowed investors to cash in at the settlement value if the Nikkei dropped at least 500 points or more:

$$\text{Cash settlement value in C\$} = 100 \text{ NPW} = 11.68 \times \frac{[(32,174 - \text{Nikkei at exercise})]}{\text{¥/C\$ at exercise}}$$

For example, if the Nikkei dropped to 25,000 and the exchange rate at exercise was equal to 84 ¥/C$, then the investor will receive C$997.52 for 1 NPW. Taking into account the investor initial premium of C$355, the investors realized a profit of C$642.52.

Barrier Options

Barrier options depend on the underlying instrument value to reach a certain level or barrier to be activated or to expire when the price reaches a certain threshold level. The knockout option expires when the underlying instrument price crosses the prespecified barrier. The knock-in option is activated when the barrier is crossed.

Consider a few versions of synthetic barrier options as sums of the up-and-out (UAO) and up-and-in (UAI) put options that are equal to the ordinary put (P_0) and the sums of down-and-out (DAO) and down-and-in (DAI) call options equal to the ordinary call (C_0). The premium of the any barrier option, therefore, is smaller than its conventional counterpart.

$$P_0 = \text{UAO} + \text{UAI}$$
$$C_0 = \text{DAO} + \text{DAI}$$

Example: It is September 20 and a steel mill in Birmingham has SF12 million receivable in 75 days. Its treasurer is concerned about a devaluation of the Swiss franc. To manage its exposure to downside risk, the firm can buy ordinary put options on Swiss franc December futures at exercise price of 68 for 1.88 cents, as shown in Exhibit 10.2. However, buying up-and-out puts at the strike price of 68 and barrier at 70, will provide downside protection that the treasurer is seeking. Once the Swiss franc appreciates and crosses 70, the option expires. The premiums for the up-and-out put and down-and-in and down-and-out calls are always likely to be less than the premiums for the ordinary put and call options.

Example: It is January 14 and Enterprise USA has 35 million payables in Norwegian kron in 96 days. The treasurer is concerned about appreciation of the kron. Buying an ordinary call can mitigate the firm's exposure to foreign exchange risk. However, buying down-and-out call options will be less expensive, as the maturity of the DAO is less than the maturity of the ordinary call option. For example, the corporate treasurer for Enterprise may buy this option at a strike price of $.14/kron and the lower barrier of $.11/kron. Once the lower barrier is reached the option expires, leaving the treasurer exposed in the event the kron appreciates over the strike price of $.14/kron at the maturity of the payables.

NOTES

1. Options on futures are priced using F. Black, "The Pricing of Commodity Contracts," *Journal of Financial Economics* (1976): 167–179.
2. All futures and options contracts traded in the various U.S. futures exchanges aggregated across contracts over time.
3. The premium for the call and put is estimated by assuming 4.5 percent domestic and foreign interest rate predicated on the assumption that interest parity holds, the volatility is 14 percent, and the option has one year to expiration.
4. The stripes are nonsymmetric position tilted toward bearish sentiment. The break-even points for the stripes when the underlying instrument price falls as trader expects has to be weighted by strike price minus 1/2 of the premium for the stripes. In the example, the break-even point is equal to a strike price $-1/2$ (.0756) = $1.5220.

5. Duration is estimated assuming the bond pays semiannual coupon interest.

6. The price of the 10-year swaps futures is similar to the price of the Treasury futures, as the underlying contract is for delivery of $100,000 par bonds priced at the coupon of 6 percent to yield the 10-year swaps rate quoted by ISDA. The price of the 10-year swaps futures is determined in this way:

$$\$100,000 \times [6/r + (1 - 6/r) \times (1 + 0.01 \times r/2)^{-20}]$$

where

r = rate quoted by ISDA as the benchmark for a 10-year interest swaps expressed in percent terms

The ISDA benchmark for par swap rates is the weighted average collected by Reuters and Garban Intercapital and published on Reuters page ISDAFIX1.

7. Using the actual change in price as the proxy for the forecasted change in price, the duration of the Treasury notes futures (D_f) can be approximated after adjusting the futures price with 6 percent conversion factor of the cheapest to deliver for 10-year bond of .8813:

$$174.15 = -D \, (\$113,468 \times .8813) \, (+/-.0002)$$
$$D_f = 8.70$$

Duration of the swaps futures D_{sf} is estimated as:

$$166.52 = -D_{sf} (\$109,968) \, (+/-.0002)$$
$$D_{sf} = 7.57$$

8. See Rubinstein and Reiner (1991) for detail analysis of various exotic options.

9. There are approximately 252 trading days per year.

CHAPTER 11

Credit Derivatives:
Pricing and Applications

The last 20 years have witnessed phenomenal growth and expansion of off–balance sheet instruments such as swaps, options, forwards, and futures in the portfolios of financial institutions. Credit derivatives and default insurance are the new breed of on– and off–balance sheet financial instruments of the last five years, allowing banks and other financial and nonfinancial corporations to transfer or assume credit risk on the specific "reference" asset or portfolio of assets. The increased application of the derivatives has raised concerns about the default risk properties of these instruments. These concerns have been mitigated by the Bank for International Settlements (BIS), as it imposed a risk-based capital ratio in 1992, requiring banks to hold capital reserves to cover unexpected losses on the current and future replacement cost of these instruments in the event of default.

Credit derivatives such as credit default swaps (CDSs), synthetic collateralized loan obligations (CLOs), asset swaps, total return swaps, credit-linked notes (CLNs), credit spread options, and credit spread forward contracts allow an efficient allocation of economic capital, resulting in diversification of risk and improved shareholder returns.

The credit market provides essential information to various constituents in the form of the spread of default-free bonds with that of the defaultable debt instruments. The spread provides valuable information in the following ways:

- It conveys probability of default.
- It is a leading economic indicator.
- It is an efficient allocater.

The credit spread indicates the market-required risk premium on the risky debt as compared to the risk-free instrument, all else remaining the same. The higher the risk, the greater is the spread between the default-free bond and its defaultable counterpart. Central bankers around the world closely analyze the credit spread in order to set an effective monetary policy to strengthen financial stability and to manage assets. Using the spread, central banks analyze the interdependence among Treasury bonds, corporate bonds, and money market debt instruments to gain insight into what effect monetary policy changes of "easing" or "tightening" will have on real economic activities. For example, the widening spread on the bonds of two issuers both rated equally by rating agencies is the credit market response to ration credits to the less creditworthy issuer with financial problems. It will be difficult for that issuer to acquire capital in the market without providing higher rates. Central banks uses information embedded in the yield spread to make monetary policy recommendations for achieving financial stability in the credit markets.

The spread between the yield on corporate bonds and Treasuries tends to widen in periods during which economic downturn is expected and to tighten when economic boom times are expected; thus the yield spread on the corporate sector serves as a leading economic indicator.[1] The spread is likely to change between seemingly similar issues as the unique factor(s) peculiar to a particular issuer changes. For example, buyers of the CDS for an issuer are likely to pay a higher spread if the market is anticipating a downgrade in the reference entity's debt.

J.P. Morgan Chase, a firm rated AAA and the largest syndicated loan underwriter in the world, has seen its CDS spread rise after the collapse of Enron and default by Argentina, where the firm had substantial exposure. The cost of buying protection for J.P. Morgan Chase creditors increased as defaults by corporations and sovereign nations have landed the underwriter giant involved in most of the bankruptcy cases in the world.[2] Since December 2001, the CDS of the banking giant has increased from 30/37 to 80/90 at bid-offer. Lehman Brothers, rated AA, has its CDS trading at 65/75.

The CDS prices are quoted as basis points spread (bps) over LIBOR. For example, the bid-offer spread for the XYZ corporation debt may be quoted at 60/70 bps per $1 million at risk. Party A, the buyer of the protection, pays 70 bps to the seller in order to buy the CDS. Had party A elected to sell protection on XYZ debt, it would have received the bid rate of 60 bps.

The spread between the default-free and risky debt instruments can be used to estimate default probabilities in a one-period bond. The extension to multi-periods and embedded options on the risky debt instrument makes estimation of the default probabilities extremely sensitive to the underlying assumptions.

The credit market has grown phenomenally in the last five years. Various instruments will be discussed here briefly. The British Bankers Association (BBA) survey of global credit derivatives market in Exhibit 11.1 reveals some interesting statistics.

The survey reveals that credit derivatives are expected to reach over $1.95 trillion by the end of 2002 and are expected to more than double by 2004. The share of the London market is expected to be about 51 percent well over New York and Asia combined by 2004 in the amount of $2.45 trillion.[3]

CREDIT DERIVATIVES PRODUCTS

The number of credit derivatives is growing as new instruments are created by financial engineers in response to changes in regulatory climate, taxes, increased

EXHIBIT 11.1   Global Credit Derivatives Market Excluding Asset Swap

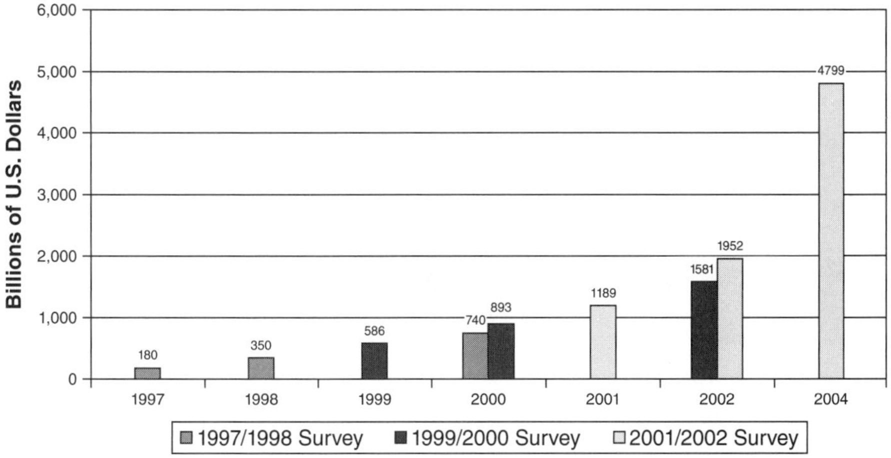

Source: British Bankers Association.

volatility, and changes in supply and demand conditions. Credit derivatives enable the parties to reduce credit exposure without physically removing assets from the balance sheet. For example, loan sales, unwinding or assignment of credits, require consent and notification of the counterparty. However, transactions on credit derivatives are confidential and do not require notification of the customer, thereby separating the fiduciary relationship from the risk management decisions.

Tax and accounting considerations may create disincentives for the sale of an asset in the firm's portfolio, such as long-term bonds. However, hedging a portfolio of bonds through buying credit default swaps not only protects the underlying bonds from default, but also provides disincentives for the outright sale of an asset for tax or accounting purposes. Credit default swaps provide hedging for the exposed credit instruments that would not be achieved through the sale or short selling of the underlying instrument.

The introduction and pace of new products has increased since 1998 as various currency crises and increased sovereign risk have shaken the stability of the financial markets. The following section describes the credit derivative products and their function in the global credit markets. Exhibit 11.2 shows the distribution of credit derivatives as a percentage of the global market share.

CREDIT EVENT/DEFAULT SWAP

This is an over-the-counter (OTC) contract between two parties, where *party A,* the buyer of the protection, pays an annuity (insurance premium) over the life of the contract or the occurrence of the "events," whichever comes first, to *party B,* the seller of the protection on the risky debt instrument "reference asset or assets" issued by *party C,* obligating party B to pay the face value of

EXHIBIT 11.2 Distribution of the Credit Derivatives as a Percentage of Global Market Share

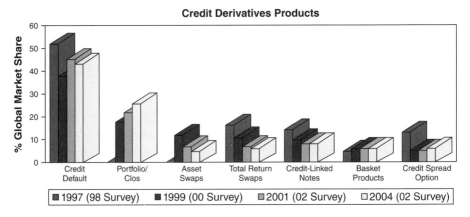

Credit Derivatives Products

Source: British Bankers Association.

the reference asset(s) triggered by the default or any other change in the credit quality of the issuer, as outlined in the contract. The CDS is therefore similar to an insurance policy where the buyer of the protection pays an annuity of, say, 80 basis points on a five-year debt issued by party C with the notional principal of $10 million over the period of the five-year or the occurrence of significant "events," whichever comes first, and is expected to receive the par value of the bond less the *recovery value* of defaulted reference asset, as shown in Exhibit 11.3.

Party A, for example, makes quarterly payments of $20,000 for five years to party B, the seller of the protection. In the event there is no default by the issuer of the reference asset, party C, the protection seller (the insurer), keeps the entire premium. The protection buyer buys the protection (buy insurance) and is *short* the credit exposure of the reference asset. The protection seller, however, sells the protection (sell insurance) and therefore is techniquely *long* the credit exposure, as shown in Exhibit 11.4.

The CDS convention for settlement is in cash or physical delivery of the "referenced" asset in the event of default. Physical delivery requires the delivery of defaulted debt to the protection seller, obligating the seller to pay the par

EXHIBIT 11.3 Cash Flow of Five-Year Credit Default Swap

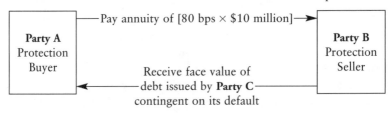

EXHIBIT 11.4   Credit Default Swaps Cash Flows

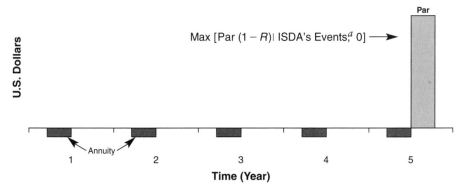

a The protection seller payout par times one minus recovery rate of R that is contingent on the
material trigger events as defined by the International Swaps and Derivative Association (ISDA)
Master Agreement.

value of the debt to the buyer of the protection. Cash settlement, however,
requires that the buyer's agent poll a minimum of three to five dealers to determine the fair value of the "reference" asset to set of the amount of compensation (par minus the fair value of the defaulted bond) the protection seller must
pay the protection buyer. Cash settlement is usually more costly to the protection seller, as the price of the defaulted bond falls well below the true intrinsic
value following the credit event.

The contingent credit event(s) that obligates the seller of the CDS to pay the
buyer may include some or all of these events[4]:

- Bankruptcy
- Counterparty failure to pay
- Material restructuring of the reference party's debt
- Capital control/moratorium involving sovereign reference entity
- Obligation acceleration or default
- Downgrade
- Receivership

The International Swaps and Derivatives Association (ISDA) has produced a
standardized letter of confirmation master agreements for executing credit
default swap transactions. The standardized master agreement confirmation
allows the parties to define precisely the underlying instrument and the types
of events that would trigger payments to the protection buyer. Exhibit 11.5 presents the over-the-counter (OTC) indicative term sheet for credit default swaps.

The actual ISDA confirmation document may be 40 or more pages long as
it details all the events that trigger payout by the protection seller. The protection buyer pays $93,750 every six months up until the occurrence of defined

EXHIBIT 11.5   Indicative Term Sheet for the Credit Default Swap

---

Protection Buyer: Investor

Protection Seller: J.P. Morgan

Notional Principal: $25 million

Transaction Type: Credit default swap

Protection Premium: 75 basis points, payable semiannually in advance of the period on actual/360-day basis. The protection buyer pays $93,750 to the protection seller until the maturity or trigger material event date, whichever comes first.

Transaction Date: To be determined by both buyer and seller.

Effective Date: Five business days from transaction date.

Termination Date: Three years from the effective date or the occurrence of material defined event in the ISDA Master Agreement.

Assignability or Unwinding: As defined in the ISDA Master Agreement.

Reference Obligation: $675 million issue of NBNI 7 1/4 bonds maturing 2007 rated Bbb by Standard & Poor's.

Materiality: The price of referenced credit falling below 90 percent of initial price as determined in good faith by the calculation agent.

Termination Payment by Seller: Contingent on the occurrences of material defined events as outlined in the ISDA Master Agreement. The amount is equal to notional principal times (1-recovery rate) plus accrued interest. The recovery rate is determined in the market by allowing a grace period of three months or longer as agreed from the event date by pooling major dealers on a weekly basis to allow the price of defaulted debt to settle to its true intrinsic value post event.

Settlement: Cash or physical delivery of defaulted debt for payment of the par after the trigger event.

Credit Events: Bankruptcy of referenced credit, restructuring, moratorium, acceleration, repudiation, and any other event as defined in the ISDA Master Agreement for default swap.

Calculation Agent: Protection seller.

---

material event or the maturity of the swap, whichever comes first. Assuming a 50 percent recovery rate on a defaulted reference credit, the protection seller is expected to pay out $12.5 million to the protection buyer.

PRICING CREDIT DEFAULT SWAP

Consider Transamerica, an AA-rated firm whose five-year interest rate swap rate is quoted at LIBOR plus 150 bps. The floating risk-free rate is quoted at London Interbank Bid Rate (LIBID) minus 12.5 bps, with a margin of 12.5 bps. The credit risk of Transamerica over the default-free floating rate note of LIBID minus 25 bps translates into a credit spread of 175 bps for the company's default swap in the credit market, as demonstrated elsewhere.[5]

To price the credit default swap, the credit spread in the bonds of the reference entity is usually adjusted up or down, depending on the expected financing rate of the counterparties in the repurchase agreement repo market. The implied repo rate is derived from the asset swap spread minus the credit default swap spread at the bid for the protection seller. Unlike the asset swap spread, the default swap spread is likely to embody the probability of default, the recovery rate of risky bonds, the funding cost of the protection seller, and the cost of capital of the protection buyer, and is likely to be higher than the asset swap spread. Exhibit 11.6 provides some interesting observations about the behavior of the default swap for selected credits.

The default swap spread is greater than the spread of the asset swap for every debt with the exception of the Republic of Korea's Ba2 credit, where the asset swap is at LIBOR plus 878 basis points and the default swap for the protection seller is 800 basis points. Furthermore, the default swap widened from July 8 to August 31 for all credits; however, some credit widened more than others, despite having virtually the same rating. For example, News Corp, Telecomm, and Time Warner's default swap, respectively, widened by 30, 25, and 30 basis points over the three-week period that coincided with the increased volatility and duress in the credit markets attributed to the events in Southeast Asia, Latin America, and Russia. The widening credit spread is due, among other things, to rising repo rates in the spot and the forward markets (implied repo). The last two columns of Exhibit 11.6 should be examined closely, as they relate to the implied repo rates for two dates, July 8 and August 31. Asset swap rates

EXHIBIT 11.6 Credit Default Swap Premium for Selected Bonds

	Implied Repo Premiums for Writing Default Protection for Five Years						
Credit	Rating	Spread	Asset Swap	Prot (bid) 31-Aug	8-Jul	Implied 31-Aug	Repo 8-Jul
Ford	A1/A	T + 96	L + 18	27	22	9	6
GMAC	A3/A	T + 98	L + 21	26	22	5	7
Philip Morris	A2/A	T + 115	L + 38	51	50	13	8
News Corp	Baa3/BBB−	T + 145	L + 68	80	50	12	12
Telecomm	Baa3/BBB−	T + 96	L + 19	55	30	36	10
Time Warner	Baa3/BBB−	T + 115	L + 36	70	40	32	10
RJR Nabisco	Baa3/BBB−	T + 300	L + 223	275	n.a.	52	n.a.
Republic of China	A3/BBB+	T + 365	L + 288	420	n.a.	55	n.a.
Republic of Korea	Ba2/BB+	T + 955	L + 878	800	n.a.	78	n.a.

Source: Andrew Kasapi, *Mastering Credit Derivatives* (Englewood Cliffs, NJ: Prentice-Hall, 1999) p. 155.

as quoted in the OTC market are not static and continue to change as the underlying floating interest rates change. Therefore, one has to be cautious in relating a default swap spread today to the asset swap spread yesterday, as the last two columns of Exhibit 11.6 incorrectly point out.

Example: Suppose a three-year default-free note pays LIBOR minus 12 basis points, and the three-year defaultable instrument pays LIBOR plus 120 basis points. If the financing rate for this bond in the repo market is equal to LIBOR, then the premium for the three-year default swap has to be equal to 132 basis points per year. Assuming the default swap is greater than 132 basis points, a swap dealer can short the reference bond and sell default swap protection, and will receive the difference between the higher swap rate and 132 basis points as a riskless arbitrage profit. However, if the default swap is less than 132 basis points, the swap dealer can buy the bond and buy default swap protection, producing a synthetic default-free instrument with a payoff greater than the payoff of the default-free debt as a riskless arbitrage profit.

The credit spread is the market-required premium over the default-free instrument in order to induce investors to hold the debt issued by the referenced entity. The price of the credit default swap for Transamerica turns out to be the present value of the spread of 175 basis points over the five-year period discounted at the five-year interest rate swap rate of 5.75 percent:

$$175 \times [(1 + .0575)^5 - 1] / [(1 + .0575)^5 \times .0575] = 7.422\%$$

The default swap price of 7.422 percent is likened to the price of floors (the put option) the investor has purchased, which insulates the buyer of the protection in the event the reference entity defaults. Default would trigger payment of the par less recovery value of the debt to the protection buyer. Unlike the premium for the floors that is paid up front, the buyer of the CDS pays effectively the amortized premium over the life of the underlying instrument, provided no material event occurs. To estimate the annual or semiannual spread, the price of the default swap as a put option can be amortized over the life of the option, similar to amortization of caps and floors premiums.

Alternatively, the price of CDS can be estimated as the portfolio of long position at the floating rate note (FRN) at LIBOR plus q basis points plus long on the default swap written on the same bond at the cost of z basis points to produce synthetic default-free FRN:

$$\text{Long FRN} + \text{long default swap} = \text{risk-free synthetic FRN} \quad (11.1)$$

Suppose the bid-offer spread is 1/8 on the LIBID/LIBOR, and Treasury over eurodollar (TED)[6] is 12.5 basis points, resulting at default swap spread of z:

$$\text{LIBOR} + q - z = \text{LIBID} - \text{TED}$$
$$\text{LIBOR} - \text{LIBID} = z - q - \text{TED}$$
$$z = q + 25 \text{ bps, assuming } q = 150 \text{ bps}$$
$$z = 175 \text{ bps}$$

In the absence of imperfection in the market, the credit spread of risky FRN has to be equal to the default swap premium written on the same issue by the seller of the protection to ensure a zero arbitrage condition. This condition establishes that the default risk of the cash bondholder is equal to that of the protection seller. Given the condition in Equation 11.1, the value of the credit default swap at origination is zero net present value. The value is likely to change over time due to macroeconomic changes as well as to factors unique to the issuing referenced asset entity.

The default swap price may differ from the cash market price of the FRN bond for a number of reasons:

- Liquidity
- Counterparty risk
- Delivery option
- Funding cost of the counterparties
- Other special features embedded on the cash bond
- Correlation between the protection seller and the reference asset

Credit default swap is usually more liquid than the underlying reference asset; therefore, the seller of the protection requires a lower premium. Many corporate and emerging market sovereign bonds do not trade actively in the secondary market, making their bid-offer spread quite large. The spread is therefore a compensation for default and for the absence of future liquidity. If a credit spread contains significant liquidity premium, the default swap premium should be significantly less than the credit spread. It is difficult and expensive to short corporate and emerging markets' sovereign bonds in the market. Buying credit default swaps is a convenient way of shorting the bonds. This fact may explain why buyers of protection are willing to pay more than the credit spread in the OTC market.

The buyer of CDS is exposed to counterparty risk; the seller may be unable to fulfill its financial obligations, unlike the cash bondholder. The delivery option affords the buyer of the protection to deliver any deliverable instrument that is the same seniority as the underlying instrument the protection is written. The party with the short position on the credit (the protection buyer) is likely to deliver the cheapest-to-deliver bond of equal seniority to the protection seller in the event of default. Bonds issued by U.S. agencies may trade below the LIBOR rate, requiring the seller to add a positive spread for writing protection on these issues.

UNWINDING AND ASSIGNABILITY OF CREDIT DEFAULT SWAPS

The parties to the credit default swap, like the parties to any other swap, may agree to terminate or assign it to another party. However, unlike interest rates or currency swaps, where one party makes a net payment to another party as the net present value of the cash flow (paid and received) over the remaining life of the swap at the termination date discounted at the fixed rate prevailing at the termination. The default swap can be unwound as the protection seller/buyer takes an offsetting position through buying/selling default swaps over the remaining life of the swap in fulfilling its obligation. In this process, the seller may unwind its position for a profit/loss if the underlying referenced credit tightens/widens. The next example illustrates this point.

Example: The protection seller on the XYZ default swap that is quoted at 55/65 basis points as of October 8, 1999, in Exhibit 11.7 at the bid-offer on the notional principal of, say, $25 million will receive $137,500 assuming annual reset.

$$.0055 \times \$25,000,000 = \$137,500$$

The underlying debt is XYZ's 10-year 7.125 percent note due 2010. The tenor of the swap is only five years. The protection seller assumes the credit risk of the referenced asset over five years for an annuity of $137,500 per year, is obligated to pay the par value of the bond upon material credit event, and receives the defaulted bond whose recovery value will be determined after a period of no more than three months by the pooling agent. Now consider these two scenarios, provided that the protection seller wishes to unwind its position after, say, two years through early termination or an assignment clause embedded in the swap.

Scenario I: The default swap for the referenced credit with three years to expiration has tightened to 30/40. The protection seller can buy a three-year protection for the referenced credit and pays 40 basis points per annum. The seller effectively locks at the riskless arbitrage profit of 15 basis points over the remaining life of the swap, or $37,500 per year.

Scenario II: The default swap for the referenced credit with three years to expiration has widened to 65/75. The protection seller can buy protection by paying 75 basis points to offload the credit risk to another party, losing net 20 basis points, or $50,000, over the next three years. The OTC bid-offer spread in Exhibit 11.7 reflects only the particular dealer's quote, which may be rated

EXHIBIT 11.7 Credit Default Swap Quotation: XYZ Company (A1/A)

Term	Bid	Offer	Reference Obligation
5 years	55	65	XYZ 7.125% 1/31/ 10
Payout/Settlement			
Physical, Par Versus			
Delivery, January 31, 2001			

A1/A. The same credit may be quoted at a higher or lower spread, depending on whether the market maker is a higher- or lower-rated bank or an insurance company. For example, a Aaa-rated market maker may quote the same instrument in Exhibit 11.7 at 70/80, while a Bbb-rated bank may quote it at 35/45. There is no arbitrage opportunity as the "buyer beware" of the quality of the counterparty.

The richness/cheapness of the spread is determined by the quality of the market maker that is the counterparty to the swap, by supply and demand conditions, by the relative value of the protection for the default swap, and by the liquidity of the hedging instrument. There is no point in buying protection where the counterparty may be unable to meet its financial obligations in the event of default. The party that is exposed to credit risk in a particular entity with relatively high concentration risk may pay higher spread at the offer to mitigate its exposure. However, a party with relatively little or no exposure—for example, an Australian firm—may accept a smaller spread at the bid or less for taking credit risk.

Illustration 11.1

An offshore entity set up by New York–based J.P. Morgan Chase purchased a series of forward gas trades in a five- to seven-year contract from Enron and advanced some payments to the now-defunct firm in 2000. J.P Morgan immediately purchased a surety bond with par value in excess of $1 billion from 11 underwriters for laying off its exposure to the Enron deal. The cost of buying protection with a surety bond was nearly 10 percent of the cost of buying a default swap in the OTC market. After the collapse of Enron in 2001, J.P. Morgan delivered the bond for payment of the par; the insurer denied payment and argued that the forward purchase from Enron was effectively a loan in disguise and the surety bond was not a loan guarantee. Litigation of the case took more than a year, and the lawsuit was settled when the presiding judge ruled that J.P. Morgan should receive 60 percent of the value of the surety bond.

> After suffering an Enron-related hangover throughout 2002, J.P. Morgan is ready to move on. Morgan's insurers have agreed to cover 60 percent of the losses associated with ill-fated Enron trading contracts. The bank can now look forward to a more prosperous 2003, when profits are expected to rise back up above $2 a share.

The settlement with 11 insurers will cover about 60 percent of the $1 billion the bank lost from complex financing deals arranged with bankrupt energy trader Enron. At issue in the Enron matter was whether 11 insurers had to pay out on surety bonds issued by insurers for a fee to guarantee a series of forward gas trades between Enron and offshore entities set up by New York–based J.P. Morgan.[7]

DEFAULT PROBABILITY

Buying protection against the default, creditors of risky debt effectively buy put options on the underlying bonds that transform the portfolio of long risky position and long put into riskless debt as defined in Equation 11.2.[8]

$$P_{df} = P_d + \text{long put} \tag{11.2}$$

where

P_{df} = default-free debt
P_d = risky defaultable debt

Buying risky bonds and buying protection (short the bond) produces synthetic long risk-free instruments, as expressed in Equation 11.2. However, selling the risky bond and selling protection (long the bond) produces a synthetic short position in a risk-free instrument, as can be verified in Equation 11.3.

$$-P_{df} = -P_d - \text{long put} \tag{11.3}$$

The negative sign indicates shorting the underlying instrument.

Assuming risk-free zero coupon bonds are priced to yield at 5 percent, while risky defaultable zero coupon debt is rated to yield a +5.90 percent with maturity of five years, the price of P_d and P_{df} are respectively equal to $75.08 and $78.35 per $100 par. The investor has essentially purchased a put option for $3.27 at a strike price equal to the price of a default-free bond that effectively insulates it from the default of a risky bond. The put option premium also can be interpreted as the default risk premium. The probability of default (PD) can be approximated assuming a zero recovery rate (R) in Equation 11.4.

$$PD = [1 - (P_d/P_{df})] \, (1 - R)$$
$$PD = [1 - (75.08/78.35)] \, (1 - R) \tag{11.4}$$
$$= .041$$

The actual probability of the default may be smaller than 4.01 percent in the example, provided that the recovery rate (R) (the rate that creditors recoup as the percentage of the par) in the event of the default is nonzero, as is evidenced from actual defaults by U.S. corporations as provided by Moody's.[9] At the limit when the recovery rate (R) approaches 100 percent, the PD approaches zero, as can be verified from Equation 11.4. Furthermore, the spread between the default-free and defaultable bond reflects not only the default risk but also the liquidity premium embedded in the risk-free bond. Exhibit 11.8 provides the average recovery rates for various classes of bonds.

The recovery rates are as high as 52 percent for the senior secured debts to as low as nearly 20 percent for the junior subordinated debts. The actual recovery rate for a particular issue could be as high as 77.46 to as low as 27.16 percent with a probability of 68 percent.

Altman has estimated the probability of default and mortality rates and losses for bonds using data from the 1971 to 1994 period.[10] The expected return (ER)

EXHIBIT 11.8 Average Recovery Rates on
U.S. Corporate Bonds

Class	Mean (%)	Standard Deviation (%)
Senior Secured	52.31	25.15
Senior Unsecured	48.84	25.01
Senior Subordinated	39.46	24.59
Subordinated	33.17	20.78
Junior Subordinated	19.69	13.85

Source: Moody's Investors Services, 2000.

on the fixed income portfolio is estimated as yield to maturity (*YTM*) (promised yield or yield to worst) minus the expected annual loss (*EL*)[11]:

$$ER = YTM - EL$$

Exhibit 11.9 summarizes the annualized mortality rates and losses. For example, the annualized cumulative mortality loss rate for a five-year BB-rated bond

EXHIBIT 11.9 Annualized Cumulative Default Rates and Annualized Cumulative Mortality Loss Rate (1971–1994)

Original Rate/Year	1 (%)	2 (%)	3 (%)	4 (%)	5 (%)	6 (%)	7 (%)	8 (%)	9 (%)	10 (%)
				Annualized Cumulative Default Rates						
AAA	0.00	0.00	0.00	0.00	0.01	0.01	0.01	0.01	0.01	0.01
AA	0.00	0.00	0.27	0.27	0.22	0.19	0.16	0.14	0.13	0.12
A	0.00	0.05	0.08	0.11	0.10	0.09	0.10	0.11	0.10	0.09
BBB	0.04	0.27	0.26	0.33	0.37	0.40	0.44	0.39	0.35	0.37
BB	0.00	0.35	1.26	1.44	2.10	1.91	2.02	1.81	1.68	1.59
B	0.99	2.14	4.61	5.01	5.14	4.71	4.58	4.25	3.97	4.09
CCC	2.24	8.35	11.75	10.50	9.87	9.78	8.82	8.07	7.21	8.35
				Annualized Cumulative Mortality Loss Rates						
AAA	0.00	0.00	0.00	0.00	0.00	0.00	0.00	0.00	0.00	0.00
AA	0.00	0.00	0.05	0.06	0.05	0.04	0.04	0.03	0.03	0.03
A	0.00	0.01	0.01	0.04	0.05	0.04	0.05	0.05	0.05	0.05
BBB	0.03	0.15	0.15	0.20	0.19	0.20	0.24	0.22	0.19	0.21
BB	0.00	0.20	0.86	1.01	1.22	1.11	1.09	0.98	0.94	0.91
B	0.42	1.23	3.29	3.64	3.81	3.46	3.36	3.12	2.91	2.89
CCC	1.51	7.19	9.79	8.69	7.82	7.57	6.87	6.13	7.06	7.25

Source: E. Altman, *Bankruptcy, Credit Risk, and High Yield Junk Bonds* (London: Blackwell, 2002), p. 199.

is 1.22 percent. Suppose the on-the-run issue of BB has a promised yield or *YTM* of 10 percent with a spread of 250 basis points over the five-year Treasury note. The expected return therefore is equal to 8.78 percent, or a risk premium of 128 basis points over the five-year T-note.

BREAK-EVEN HIGH-YIELD BONDS

The promised yield or the yield to maturity is expected to compensate investors for the expected and unexpected default, the timing of the default, and the recovery rate in the event of default that measures the severity of loss when the bond is sold at a distress price following the default or once the firm emerges from reorganization under Chapter 11. The promised yield to break even (R_b) with the yield equivalent to the same volatility (same duration and convexity) as the risk-free Treasury bonds yield (R_f), assuming expected default (D_f) and recovery rate (R), is demonstrated in Equation 11.5.[12]

$$R_b = [R_f + D_f(1 - R) + (D_f + C_a/2)]/1 - D_f \qquad (11.5)$$

where

C_a = average coupon rate on high-yield defaulted debts
(other variables are as defined)

The break-even promised yield (R_b) must compensate investors for the risk-free rate, lost interest in the event of default, and proportion of the performing bonds in the market at $(1 - D_f)$ rate. The break-even promised yield is estimated assuming the Treasury yield of 6 percent and the average coupon rate of 14 percent on duration-equivalent high-coupon bonds with various default rates ranging from 1 to 10 percent and recovery rates of 30 to 60 percent, as shown in Exhibit 11.10.

EXHIBIT 11.10   Break-Even Promised Yield versus U.S. Treasury Bonds

Default Rate	Break-even Promised Yield			
	Recovery Rates			
	0.3	0.4	0.5	0.6
0.01	0.068384	0.067374	0.065354	0.065354
0.02	0.076939	0.074898	0.072857	0.070816
0.03	0.08567	0.082577	0.079485	0.076392
0.04	0.094583	0.090417	0.08625	0.082083
0.05	0.103684	0.098421	0.093158	0.087895
0.06	0.112979	0.106596	0.100213	0.09383
0.08	0.132174	0.123478	0.114783	0.106087
0.1	0.152222	0.141111	0.13	0.118889

Assuming investors expect a recovery rate of 50 percent and a default rate of 5 percent on a high-yield bond, the break-even promised yield has to be equal to 9.31 percent. The yield realized over and above the break-even—the yield premium—is the compensation for the liquidity, unexpected loss, and flight to quality at a point in time. That is, assuming the promised yield of 14.56 percent for the high-yield bonds in 2000, the average yield premium (promised yield less break-even yield) can be estimated for various recovery and default rates. The yield premium for 2000 will be respectively equal to 7.73 and 8.03 percent, assuming recovery rates of 30 and 50 percent, with a default rate of 1 percent.

DEFAULT RISK/RETURN

The incidence of corporate downgrades in the 1970s and 1980s provides some interesting statistics about the rising probability of bankruptcy in the United States, particularly in the 1980s. For example, of new issues of AAA bonds in 1970, 8 percent were downgraded after three years and 20 percent after five years. Of the bonds issued in 1980, 33.1 percent were downgraded in the first three years and 50.7 percent after five years.[13] On the class of single-A-rated bonds in 1970, 7.9 percent of the bonds were downgraded after three years and 4.3 percent were upgraded; however, 21.4 percent of the bonds were downgraded and 10.7 percent upgraded in the 1980s.[14] The higher number of downgrades in the 1980s can be attributed to the wave of corporate restructuring and leveraged buyouts and to an overall increase in the leveraged capital structure and the rising share of junk bonds used in restructuring in the U.S. capital market.

CREATING SYNTHETIC ASSETS

Investors and portfolio manager can transform the relationship expressed in Equation 11.2 to create a synthetic risky asset as shown in Equation 11.6.

$$P_d = P_{df} - \text{long put}$$
$$- \text{long put} = \text{short put}$$

(11.6)

Investors can write a default swap (sell protection and receive premium) by posting required margins and simultaneously buying a risk-free instrument (P_{df}). The synthetic risky asset created usually has a higher yield than the yield on the cash market instrument, particularly when the implied repo rate in the default swap (the rate implied from the asset swap rate at a spread of LIBOR minus the CDS premium) is low. The counterparty risk is very negligible for the protection seller as the protection buyer is usually a highly rated entity. The maximum loss to the protection seller in the event of counterparty default is the loss of premium.

Example: Exhibit 11.11 shows the yield spread between various issues of Argentina bonds and their U.S. Treasury counterparts. The credit spread appears to be smaller than the credit default swap of the nearly same maturity. For example,

EXHIBIT 11.11   Argentina Bonds and Default Swaps

Fixed Rate Coupon (%)	Maturity	Time to Maturity (years)	Bid Price	Yield to Maturity (%)	U.S. Treasury Yield (%)	Spread
10.950	Nov. 99	1.03	94.50	16.99	4.03	12.96
9.250	Feb. 01	2.34	96.00	11.23	4.08	7.15
8.375	Dec. 03	5.16	93.00	10.14	4.21	5.16
11.000	Oct. 06	7.97	96.50	11.69	4.51	7.97

Time to Expiration (years)	Sell Default Protection(%)	Buy Default Protection(%)
3	9.00	10.00
5	8.00	9.00
10	7.50	8.00

Source: Morgan Stanley Dean Witter, Working Paper No. 7, A note on the pricing of default swap by Louis Scott.

the credit spread between two sovereign bonds on February 2001 with a maturity of 2.34 years is 7.15 percent, while the three-year default swap premium is 8 to 9 percent bid-offer. Likewise, the credit spread for the five-year issue is 5.16 percent, while the five-year default swap is quoted at 8 to 9 percent at the sell-buy rate. In this scenario it pays to sell Argentina's bond short and simultaneously sell default protection. However, obtaining the bonds for shorting is very difficult in most markets. Alternatively, the investor who wishes to be long in the Argentina bond synthetically can sell October 2006 at bid, use the proceeds to buy U.S. Treasury, and sell the default swap as expressed in Equation 11.3 for 7.50 percent, resulting in total yield of 12.01 percent versus the 11.69 percent yield with same credit risk.

The synthetic long Argentina bond created in this example produces 32 basis points more than the cash market: 12.01 minus 11.69 percent. Furthermore, it pays off to sell February 2001 and buy the U.S. Treasury yielding 4.08 percent and sell a three-year default swap for 9 percent. This scenario produces a total return from the synthetic long bond of 13.08 percent (4.08 percent plus 9 percent for selling CDS) as compared to the cash market yield of 11.23 percent picking up 185 basis points more in the synthetic transaction, as can be verified from Exhibit 11.11. In this example, if the bond does not default, the investor effectively realizes 13.08 percent. However, if the Argentine bond defaults, the investor can sell the U.S. Treasury to pay off the protection buyer and receives the recovery value of the defaulted bond and any accrued interest.

The CDS enables investors to expand the opportunity set by tapping into a larger market than the tradable debt securities. The CDS allows financial institutions to hedge their exposure without selling the assets in the market where the bid-offer spread for the exposure is relatively large due to the illiquidity of the issue in the cash market and runs the risk of damaging the banking relationship. Furthermore, the hedge is relatively inexpensive to establish and mitigates the tax consequences of selling. Like any other hedge, the CDS hedge involves basis risk that is relatively high for low-rated and distressed issues compared to investment-grade bonds. As a general rule, the hedge needs to be implemented when the market is not concerned about the risk.

The CDS also helps corporations to tap in to the far more accommodating commercial papers market without rationing capital, as the issuing firm can back the paper by buying protection for the entire issue. In essence, the issuer can synthetically raise its credit rating in the commercial paper market in securing short-term capital presumably not available without CDS backing.

SYNTHETIC CREDIT DEFAULT SWAPS

Rearranging Equation 11.6 produces synthetic long credit default swap as shown in Equation 11.7.

$$P_{df} - P_d = \text{long put (long CDS)} \qquad (11.7)$$

To hedge the swap written on a reference entity, the protection seller can short the reference asset $(-P_d)$ and use the proceeds to buy an equivalent default-free asset (P_{df}), thereby producing the payoff of a long put that is equal to the cost of long CDS, as demonstrated in the relationship expressed in Equation 11.7.

Consider the December 2003 bond in Exhibit 11.11. The theoretical CDS premium on this issue has to be 5.16 percent (from Equation 11.7); however, the quoted CDS for this issue is 9 percent for the protection buyer. Buying the December 2003 bond and buying protection produces a return of 10.14 minus 9 percent, or effectively 1.14 percent. This return is 3.07 percent less than the return in a default-free Treasury bond yielding 4.21 percent. The credit default swap appears to be overpriced; therefore, it pays to sell the default swap for Argentina for a premium of 8 percent and sell the Argentine bond and use the proceeds to buy the U.S. Treasury bond yielding 4.21 percent. The return on this portfolio is 12.21 percent versus a return of 10.14 percent on Argentine sovereign debt; 207 basis points are picked up. In the event the Argentine debt defaults, the protection seller can use the proceeds from the U.S. Treasury to pay to the protection buyer the par value of the Argentine sovereign bond less the recovery value of the defaulted debt.

CREDIT DEFAULT SWAP APPLICATIONS

Banks and other financial institutions with credit exposure to corporate or sovereign bonds can mitigate their risk through:

- Purchasing credit default protection
- Selling the loan in the secondary market or holding the loan in their portfolio

Banks that are willing to increase their exposure to a particular company in order to reduce their concentration risk[15] can

- Sell default protection
- Buy a bond issued by the obligor to which they wish to have exposure
- Lend money to an obligor to which they wish to have exposure
- Buy credit-linked notes

Buyers of the default protections are:

- Commercial banks
- Nonfinancial corporations
- Actively managed debt funds
- Hedge funds

Sellers of default protections are:

- Life insurance companies
- Reinsurance companies
- Major banks
- Collateralized debt obligations
- Commercial paper conduits

Banks and other financial institutions buy credit default protection and achieve efficiency without selling the loan by:

- Preserving the bank-clientele relationship in issues arising with the borrower
- Avoiding legal, regulatory, or tax issues related to the sale of the assets
- Avoiding the sell of an illiquid asset with a huge bid/ask spread

RESTRUCTURING

Corporate restructuring had become a serious source of contention when Conseco reached an agreement with 25 banks, led by the Bank of America and Chase Manhattan, to extend the maturities on its short-term debt of $2.8 billion on September 22, 2001. The market participants quickly interpreted this event as a loan restructuring for the Indianapolis-based life insurer. Under the terms of ISDA's 1999 Master Agreement on credit default swaps, restructuring is a credit event that triggers payment to the buyer of protection. Protection sellers that had written protection for counterparties exposed to Conseco were obliged to pay out.

The Conseco case highlighted one of the main problems that protection sellers have with restructuring as a trigger event—moral hazard. Some of the protection buyers of Conseco debts, such as Bank of America and Merrill Lynch, after extending the loan and collecting the underwriting fees, were quick to deliver in terms of maturity, coupon, and the like the cheapest deliverable instruments in return for the par value of the bond. The lenders effectively precipitated the restructuring of the debt when it paid for them to do so. Credit derivative dealers in New York, including the largest dealers J.P. Morgan, Deutsche Bank, Merrill Lynch, and Morgan Stanley, began quoting two-tier prices for credit default swaps—one without restructuring and one with restructuring, for 10 to 15 basis points more. When a firm defaults, the debt covenants outline the distribution of the assets based on seniority of the claims on the right-hand side of the balance sheet. The filing for bankruptcy protection reveals that Conseco listed $51.1 billion in debts and $52.3 billion in assets, which excluded its profitable insurance subsidiaries (see Exhibit 11.12).

The creditors will recover all or parts of their claims depending on the seniority of claims and representations in the creditors' committee in the bankruptcy proceedings. The recovery rate is the rate that creditors recoup as the percentage of the principal owed to them by the defunct firm and is likely to vary from one class of claimant to other. Bond ratings are assigned by rating agencies such as Standard & Poor's, Moody's, and Fitch in an attempt to assign probability of default to corporate agencies and sovereign debts. The frequency of the rating changes, also known as ratings transition, provides the market with the information that probability of default is increasing (downgrade) or decreasing (upgrade). Exhibit 11.13 presents Moody's average one-year credit ratings transition matrix over the 1920 to 1996 period.

The transition matrix in Exhibit 11.13 indicates that there is a probability of 6.15 percent for a change in rating (downgrade) from an Aaa-rated to an Aa-rated issue. The probability of the downgrade to single A from Aaa is nearly 1 percent and to Baa is .23 percent. Likewise the probability of the upgrade from Aa to Aaa is 1.21 percent. There are greater chances for downgrades than for upgrades for all issues rated Ba and above, implying nonsymmetric probabilities. However, the issues rated B buck the trend by having a 5.79 percent higher chance of an upgrade and 3.08 percent chance of a downgrade.

EXHIBIT 11.12   CONSECO's Balance Sheet on December 19, 2002, Bankruptcy Filing

Assets	Payables
	Policy liabilities
	Notes payables
	Senior debts
	Subordinated debts
	Other liabilities
Total Assets = $52.3 billion	Total Debts = $51.1 billion

EXHIBIT 11.13 Moody's Average One-Year Credit Ratings Transition Matrix (1920–1996)

Rating from:	Aaa (%)	Aa (%)	A (%)	Baa (%)	Ba (%)	B (%)	Caa–C (%)	Default (%)	WR (%)
Aaa	88.32	6.15	0.99	0.23	0.02	0.00	0.00	0.00	4.29
Aa	1.21	86.76	5.76	0.66	0.16	0.02	0.00	0.06	5.36
A	0.07	2.30	86.09	4.67	0.63	0.10	0.02	0.12	5.99
Baa	0.03	0.24	3.87	82.52	4.68	0.61	0.06	0.28	7.71
Ba	0.01	0.08	0.39	4.61	79.03	4.96	0.41	1.11	9.39
B	0.00	0.04	0.13	0.60	5.79	76.33	3.08	3.49	10.53
Caa–C	0.00	0.02	0.04	0.34	1.26	5.29	71.87	12.41	8.78

Source: Carty, "Moody's Rating Migration and Credit Quality Correlation," Technical Report, Moody's Investors Service, 1997.

CREDIT-LINKED NOTES

Credit-linked notes (CLNs) are created as hedging instruments for direct loans to corporations in which the lender (e.g., Citigroup) extends a five-year loan to a corporation (e.g., Enron) and simultaneously sets up a trust where the trust issues five-year notes linked to the default of the Enron bond to investors. The trust invests the proceeds of the loan in a bankruptcy-remote money market debt. In the event the borrower (Enron) defaults, investors receive the proceeds of the debt issued by the failed corporation; however, if Enron does not default, Citigroup is obligated to pay the principal and interest in notes issued by the trust.

The CLN notes enjoy high ratings because of the existence of the trust, as the note holders receive the principal and interest (P&I) in the event Citigroup defaults. The borrower's credit risk determines the interest rates on the CLNs despite the fact that they are essentially issued by the Citigroup trust. Exhibit 11.14 demonstrates the creation of CLNs.

After extending over $1 billion in loans to Enron in 2000 and 2001 and hedging its exposure to the Enron credit risk by issuing CLNs, Citigroup, through its trust, avoided large losses when Enron collapsed in late 2001, in the second largest bankruptcy filing in the United States.[16] The structure of the CLNs is similar to the catastrophe bond. The principal and coupon interest payment is linked to the occurrence and severity of the trigger event as the investors bear some of the losses in the form of forgiveness of the interest and some or all of the principal.[17]

In September 1996, J.P. Morgan issued $594 million CLNs through its trust tied to the spread of Wal-Mart, an Aa-rated firm, originally priced at 65 basis points over a 10-year Treasury note. Morgan embedded a materiality clause in the issuance of a note provided that the spread widens to 150 basis points over

EXHIBIT 11.14 Credit-Linked Notes

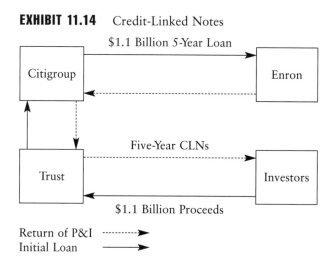

Return of P&I ┈┈┈┈┈▶
Initial Loan ━━━━▶

Treasury to trigger the default. In such an event investors will get the recovery value of the defaulted bond identified by pooling every two weeks five leading market makers over the period of three months. CLNs provide investors with relatively higher returns as well as higher risk as Wal-Mart comparable debts priced at a spread of 40 to 45 basis points over Treasuries.

SYNTHETIC COLLATERALIZED LOAN OBLIGATIONS

A collateralized loan obligation (CLO) is an asset-backed debt instrument that is supported by assets such as commercial or mortgage debts and revolving credit facilities and is usually backed by a variety of credit enhancement products, such as letters of credit, senior/subordinated structure, cash reserve funds, and excess servicing spread. Banks and other financial institutions use CLOs and their synthetic variants to manage and transfer credit risk to the capital markets. Banks transfer assets and loans to a special-purpose vehicle (SPV) trust, which in turn issues asset-backed securities consisting of classes of debts referred to as tranches and residual equity. The weighted average coupons of various tranches, including the so-called residual, support, or Z-bonds, will be less than the average coupon of the underlying loan by an amount equal to the service, administrative, and guarantee fees. The various tranches of debts with varying risk-return characteristics appeal to a broader range of investors in the market.

The CLO provides banks the opportunity to achieve, among other things:

- Reduced regulatory capital requirements
- Increased liquidity
- Access to efficient funding for lending

Assuming exposure to other issuers, banks reduce their concentration risk and off–balance sheet accounting treatment through CLOs.

The Basle committee on banking supervision (1988) set an 8 percent minimum capital requirement for the banks on their risk-based capital.[18] The 8 percent regulatory capital requirements are to be held against any risk-based asset classes, which includes all commercial loans, letters of credit, and unused revolving credit, reduce the relative attractiveness of these assets in a bank portfolio, given the small margins these loans offer in a highly competitive environment.[19] Therefore, through CLOs, banks are able to securitize (sell) some of their portfolio and free up significant amounts of capital for profitable redeployment in higher-yielding assets, diversification of overall risk, increased liquidity, and acquisition or origination of other loans resulting in origination fees.

In traditional CLO structures, assets are transferred into an SPV trust that fully funds the purchase of the assets through the issuance of securities (i.e., senior, subordinated, and unrated classes designed to enhance the rated notes, as shown in Exhibit 11.15). For example, a bank that wishes to securitize a $5 billion portfolio of its loans can free up $400 million (.08 times $5 billion) regulatory capital through a CLO transaction by selling the loans to SPV to support origination or purchase of $10 billion residential mortgage debts with 50 percent risk-weight (50 percent of 8 percent) or origination and the purchase of $25 billion, 20 percent risk-weight assets (20 percent of 8 percent or 1.6 percent) such as debts issued by the Federal National Mortgage Association (FNMA) or the Federal Home Loan Mortgage Corporation (FHLMC).

The risk-based regulatory capital benefits of the CLO hinges on the sponsoring bank taking no equity or subordinated interest in the debt issues of the SPV. Assuming the bank retains some subordinated issue on its book, the bank under the so-called low-level recourse rule must maintain capital on a dollar-for-dollar basis.[20] For example, if the bank in the earlier example holds $300 million of the subordinated or equity issue, it will be required to maintain a $300 million reserve capital and can free up only $100 million in the CLO transaction in order to support origination or purchase of $100/.08, $1.25 billion worth of securities risk-weighted 100 percent. Exhibit 11.15 shows the structure of the fully funded CLO.

EXHIBIT 11.15   Fully Funded Securitization

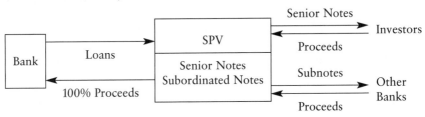

OBJECTIVES OF STRUCTURING COLLATERALIZED LOAN OBLIGATIONS

Once the loans are securitized through CLOs, the bank can use the proceeds to reinvest in other higher-yielding instruments and in diversifying its loan portfolio. CLOs enable an otherwise low-rated bank to restructure its loan portfolio by raising the ratings of its senior debt issues to be significant proportion of its loan portfolio balance. The structuring CLO provides other benefits:

- Through a CLO transaction, a bank can reduce its liabilities and improve on its higher-rated, lower-yielding assets, thereby increasing return on assets and return on equity.

- A CLO enables a bank to reduce concentration risk by transferring its credit exposure to a particular borrower and a particular industry to the capital market fairly efficiently. In the process of securitization, the bank assumes other credit risk to which it wishes to have greater exposure.

- Through its CLO transactions, a bank can manage its liquidity, credit spread, and concentration of assets tied to floating rate index, such as LIBOR, thereby improving asset/liability management.

- CLOs help preserve the bank-clientele relationship. The CLO enables the bank to sell its loan without damaging its relationship with its customer, since the sponsor and the portfolio manager of the SPV trust is the affiliate of the bank. There is no need to notify the client when selling or assigning the loans, as there is in the case of selling loans on a whole loan basis.

SYNTHETIC COLLATERALIZED LOAN OBLIGATIONS

Synthetic CLOs emulate cash CLOs by transferring credit risk of the reference assets to the capital market through credit derivatives such as total return swap, or credit default swap, or through issuing credit-linked notes without actually transferring the ownership of the assets to the bankruptcy-remote SPV trust. The banks therefore are able to preserve the bank-client relationship in issues arising from loan assignment, loan transfer, and client confidentiality. Synthetic securitization that transfers portfolio risk through credit default protection can be unfunded, partially funded, or fully funded. Exhibit 11.16 illustrates the synthetic partially funded CLO.

The first synthetic CLO was issued in 1997, where the trust created by the issuer of the CLO issued the same dollar amount of credit-linked notes to investors; and the trust invested the proceeds of the issue equal to the outstanding CLOs the issuer was hedging in its balance sheet in a bankruptcy-remote debt instrument. In a synthetic CLO, the sponsoring bank uses a credit default swap or credit-linked notes to transfer the exposure of its portfolio of loans to the

EXHIBIT 11.16   Synthetic Partially Funded CLO

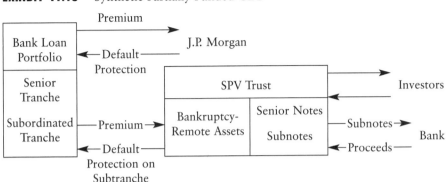

capital market, thereby allocating economic capital more efficiently by reducing regulatory capital requirements.

For example, Citigroup mitigated its exposure to its Enron loan through the issuance of CLNs that transferred the credit risk of its loan to Enron to the capital market. To the extent the Enron loan in the Citigroup book is fully collateralized by cash, to be assigned the zero risk weight category for regulatory capital requirements.

There are two types of synthetic CLO: *arbitrage* and *balance sheet.* Arbitrage CLOs are usually undertaken by insurance companies to exploit yield mismatch (spread) on the underlying pool of assets as well as the lower cost of servicing CLO liabilities.

Balance sheet CLOs are employed by banks to mitigate and manage regulatory and risk-based capital. Synthetic CLOs are more efficient in transferring risk and are less costly, since the amount of the issuance is usually small relative to the reference portfolio and less burdensome to administer as compared to cash CLOs in transferring partial claims on a particular credit. Synthetic CLOs allow banks to acquire exposure to a particular asset that may be difficult to acquire in the cash market through CDS. The bank that wishes to take credit exposure on a particular firm can sell protection on the reference asset of the entity. However, a bank can buy protection and therefore synthetically short the credit risk of the reference entity. Furthermore the synthetic structure allows the bank to transfer the balance sheet risk subject to a given threshold, over a given interval.[21]

The cash CLO on corporate exposure is 100 percent risk-weighted. The risk-weighting is much less, for synthetic CLOs, reflecting the funded portion of the structure that is backed by government securities that is zero risk-weighted. This phenomena has prompted European banks to issue synthetic CLOs by taking advantage of the fact that capital adequacy requirements (8 percent minimum capital on corporate exposure) do not differentiate among various levels of operating, market, and credit risks.

SYNTHETIC ARBITRAGE COLLATERALIZED LOAN OBLIGATIONS

This structure replicates a highly leveraged exposure to a portfolio of syndicated loans and bonds. An SPV trust in a typical structure enters into total return swap (TRS) on the portfolio of credits that is ramped up at the origination, where it pays to the sponsoring bank LIBOR plus a spread normally equivalent to the bank's funding/administrative costs and receives total returns from the referenced portfolio. The trust issues a series of debts with senior/subordinated structure and uses the proceeds to invest in a high-quality/liquid instrument that earns a return approximating LIBOR, which defrays the coupon on the referenced notes and funds the first loss exposure to the referenced portfolio. As with any swap, the TRS is marked to market periodically and may be subject to market value triggers (as outlined in the confirmation master agreement of the swap). Examples of these synthetic transactions where the risk of the referenced portfolio is transferred to the capital market via credit default swap, total return swap, and credit-linked notes are J.P. Morgan BISTRO, Citibank ECLIPSE, Bank of America SERVES, Chase's CSLT, and J.P. Morgan SEQUILS/MINCS.

J.P. Morgan BISTRO is the synthetic securitization of risk achieved through a credit default swap, where an originating bank buys credit protection on a portfolio of exposed credit from J.P. Morgan via a portfolio of credit default swaps and J.P Morgan simultaneously buys credit protection from BISTRO SPV Trust. The originating bank usually takes a 5 percent first loss that is equivalent of taking 20×1 leverage position in the referenced portfolio in aligning its interest with that of the note holders. This leverage position has the potential to increase and/or decrease the return on regulatory capital, not economic capital, by a leverage factor of 20, as a single default on the referenced portfolio increases the severity of loss by leverage factor of 20.

The SPV issues tranches of notes—that is, credit-linked notes at spread over LIBOR—where the return/risk to the note holders is augmented by the premium of the CDS as well as the losses arising from actual default and recovery value of debts according to the priority of their debt. The proceeds of the notes are invested in highly liquid government debt instruments in collateralizing notes and are pledged first to the sponsoring bank to satisfy default in the CDS transaction on the first loss and second to the repayment of principal to the note holders.

Large banks usually buy whole loans from smaller banks and repackage and securitize them, thereby earning an arbitrage profit in the process. Motivations for structuring a synthetic CLO/CBO could be:

- Regulatory capital relief
- Risk transfer
- Arbitrage profit
- Restructuring balance sheet

The synthetic arbitrage CLO is created, where the SPV enters into total return swaps with the sponsoring bank on the referenced portfolio of loans paying LIBOR plus spread and receiving total returns from the referenced portfolio. The SPV invests the collateral loans in bankruptcy-remote debt instruments and issues layers of securities to investors, as shown in Exhibit 11.17.

In a synthetic CLO, the bank or its affiliate keeps the assets on its books, while securitizing the risk by transferring it to SPV. Ultimately the SPV transfers the credit risk to investors in the capital market through credit-linked notes, credit default swaps, or total return swaps, thereby realizing regulatory capital relief. The synthetic CLO does not provide any benefit to the sponsoring bank for the purpose of calculating its Tier 1 capital, because the reference assets remain on the bank's book. In cash CLOs, the loans/bonds are physically removed from the bank's balance sheet, allowing the bank to reduce its risk-based capital and giving it the ability to originate and purchase other loans, producing origination fees for the sponsoring bank.

SYNTHETIC BALANCE SHEET COLLATERALIZED LOAN OBLIGATIONS

Banks use synthetic balance sheets CLOs to transfer the credit risk to the capital market and to improve the risk/return profile on their portfolios of regulatory capital. Synthetic CLOs can be structured by issuing credit-linked notes through the sponsoring bank or its affiliate SPV or by writing a credit default swap by the bank or the SPV affiliate for a premium, thereby providing the sponsor the opportunity to achieve regulatory capital relief at lower all-in cost funding than cash CLOs (see Exhibit 11.18).

The sponsoring bank usually takes the first loss on the underlying reference obligors; this is intended for credit enhancement of the remaining issues in the synthetic CLO structure.

EXHIBIT 11.17   Synthetic Arbitrage CLO: Total Return Swaps

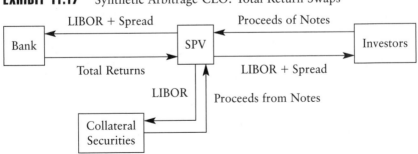

EXHIBIT 11.18   Synthetic Balance Sheet CLO

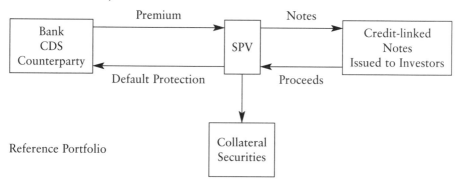

CDS: credit default swap
SPV: special-purpose vehicle

CAPITAL ADEQUACY REQUIREMENTS

The BIS capital adequacy requirements allow banks to estimate the minimum capital for off–balance sheet derivative transactions using two methods: (1) the original exposure method and (2) the current exposure method. Exhibit 11.19 presents the original exposure method.

As shown in the exhibit, BIS requirements for risk-based off–balance sheet swaps assign a risk-weight of 0, 20, and 50 percent, depending on the relative riskiness of the counterparty to the swap transaction. The BIS capital requirements for various classes of debts for on–balance sheet requirements are:

- The sovereign government debt of the member of Organization of Economic Cooperation and Development (OECD) is assigned zero BIS risk-weight. These debts are treated as risk free, and banks are not required to hold any reserve capital against them.

- The senior debts of the banks from OECD are assigned 20 percent BIS risk-weight. The banks are required to hold 1.6 percent (.20 × .08) of reserve capital for these types of debts. For example, a bank has to hold $320,000 in reserve capital (.20 × .08 × $200,000,000) for $200 million investment in a Mexican bank note.

- Unfunded corporate revolving credits are assigned a 50 percent risk-weight. The banks are required to hold 4 percent (.50 × .08) of reserve capital.

- For all others, including corporate debts, funded revolving credit, non-OECD sovereign debts, 100 percent BIS risk-weight is assigned. Financial institutions must hold 8 percent reserve capital against the risk-based assets.

EXHIBIT 11.19   BIS Capital Adequacy Requirement
Original Exposure Method

	Conversion Factor	
Maturity	Interest Rate Swaps (%)	Foreign Exchange Swaps (%)
Less than 1 year	.5	2.0
One year and less than two years	1	5
For each additional year	1	3

Capital requirements = Notional value of swap × conversion factor × risk weight

Examples of capital requirements:

   A. Five-year interest rate swaps, $200 million notional principal, counterparty OECD bank.

     $200,000,000 \times .05 \times .20 = \$2,000,000$

   B. Three-year interest rate swaps; $20 million notional principal, counterparty AAA-rated manufacturing firm.

     $20,000,000 \times .03 \times .50 = \$300,000$

   C. Three-year currency swap, $100 million notional principal, counterparty GM.

     $100,000,000 \times .08 \times .50 = \$5,000,000$

Source: Basle Committee on Bank Supervision, *Treatment of Potential Exposure for Off–Balance Sheet Items* (Basle, Switzerland: BIS, April 1995).

The capital adequacy requirement distinguishes credit derivatives from other derivatives and whether the derivative transaction is booked in the bank's trading desk or in the bank's balance sheet. In 1997 the Federal Reserve Bank and the Bank of England allowed banks to book credit default swaps and options like total return swaps in the bank trading desk. Thus banks had a smaller risk-weight than the 8 percent required capital had banks booked the swaps and options in their balance sheets.

When there is a basis risk as most hedges do have basis risk; the hedge is not perfect in mitigating the exposure of the underlying instrument with credit derivative, the bank may be charged capital not only for the counterparty risk, but also for the reference asset being hedged thereby increasing capital requirements that can reduce the relative attractiveness of the deal.

CREDIT EXPOSURE METHOD

This method is estimated by marking to market the value of the swap, plus potential exposure as determined by an add-on factor for swaps with positive, negative, or zero mark-to-market value are provided in Exhibit 11.20. The

EXHIBIT 11.20   BIS Capital Adequacy Requirement Current Exposure Method

	Add-on Factor for	
Maturity	Interest Rate Swaps (%)	Foreign Exchange Rate Swaps (%)
Less than one year	0	1
One to five years	.5	5
Five years or more	1.5	7.5

Capital requirement = Credit Exposure × Risk-weight

Example
1. Three-year, $25 million interest rate swap, counterparty is Microsoft, assuming swap is in the money by $360,000.00

   Current exposure = Max (360,000) = $360,000
   Potential exposure = $25,000,000 × .005 = $125,000
   Capital requirement = (360,000 + 125,000) × .50 = $242,500

2. Five-year currency swaps $/euro $20 million notional principal, assume swap is out of money by −300,000

   Current exposure = Max (−300,000) = 0
   Potential exposure = 20,000,000 × .075 = $1,500,000
   Capital requirement = (1,500,000 + 0) × .50 = $750,000

Source: Basle Committee on Bank Supervision, *Treatment of Potential Exposure for Off–Balance Sheet Items* (Basle, Switzerland: BIS, April 1995).

capital requirement under this method is estimated as the product of the credit exposure and risk-weight applicable to the counterparty.

The BIS capital adequacy requirements continue to evolve as new instruments and associated risks emerge in the capital market. The regulatory agency on bank supervision has mandated the minimum capital for banks on their derivative transactions to be three times the 10-day value at risk (VAR) with 99 percent confidence interval, as discussed in Chapter 8. The BIS capital requirements do not distinguish between two-currency swaps denominated in two currencies with significantly different amounts of volatility. The BIS capital adequacy requirements fail to take into account the volatility of interest and exchange rates, which need to be addressed in the near future.

TOTAL RETURN SWAPS

Total return swaps (TRS) are an on-off–balance sheet transaction for the party that pays total returns composed of capital gains or losses plus the ordinary coupon or dividend and receives LIBOR plus spread related to the counterparty's credit riskiness on a given notional principal. The bank paying total returns is effectively warehousing, renting out its balance sheet, while transferring economic value and risk to a preferably uncorrelated counterparty to the referenced assets. For example, it makes little sense for a bank to lay off its exposure to a portfolio of credits in a Singapore bank rated Baa with a counterparty bank in Singapore rated A.

There is a strong correlation between the referenced debt and the counterparty; the fortunes of both are directly related to that of the Singapore economy. The counterparty in another part of the world—say, in New Zealand —whose performance is unaffected by the banking crisis in Singapore is said to be an uncorrelated counterparty.[22] The bank pays all the cash flows from the loans—coupons, commitment fees, and perhaps some of the origination fee— as well as any positive increase in the value of the underlying debt to the counterparty, while receiving floating rate LIBOR plus spread, which defrays its funding cost. The bank receives any decrease in the value of the referenced assets from the counterparty.

Total return swaps are highly leveraged transactions (HLTs) that motivate the receiver to take on the credit risk of referenced assets it does not own. The bank that is trying to reduce its concentration risk to a particular entity and free up regulatory capital may enter into a TRS with a hedge fund that is willing to post 5, 10, or 20 percent collateral and/or mark to market the position frequently for mitigating counterparty risk to the bank on the notional principal of, say, $50 million. The bank can free up $3.2 million of risk capital as the risk weight is reduced from 100 percent to 20 percent (.08 capital requirement × 100 percent risk weight for risky debt × $50 million) by transferring the total returns (coupon plus 300 basis points) as well as gains or losses due to risk of default of the referenced bond to the hedge fund in return for LIBOR plus 75 basis points (see Exhibit 11.21).

The bank's motivations are different from those of the hedge fund and may include:

- Reducing its exposure without selling the reference asset
- Preserving the banking relationship with the client whose debt is being securitized by bank
- Providing the regulatory capital relief to free up capital
- Managing balance sheets to originate other loans and earn origination fees

EXHIBIT 11.21   Total Return Swap

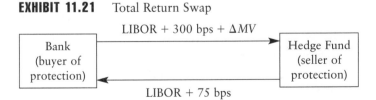

- Deferring unrecognized gains/losses on the referenced assets by paying total returns and receiving floating rate
- Diversifying risk

The debt underlying the reference asset is a par bond rated BBB with coupon equal to LIBOR plus 300 basis points. The hedge fund funding cost is assumed to be at the spread of 100 basis points over LIBOR. Suppose LIBOR is equal to 5 percent. The return received by the hedge fund is predicated on the amount of the change in the market value (*MV*) of the asset net of coupon (dividend) levered by the amount of collateral posted by the hedge fund. The leverage cuts both ways; assuming underlying debt price appreciates, then the return will be magnified by the leverage factor. However, assuming the debt price falls due to rising interest rates or a downgrade of the issuer, the leverage factor will have a devastating negative impact on the return realized by hedge fund.

The amount of the collateral posted depends on the extent of the bank's desire to securitize the credit risk of the referenced asset. A bank may enter into a TRS with a hedge fund that posts 5 or 10 percent collateral for mitigating the counterparty risk; a conservative bank may require larger collateral: 10, 15, or 20 percent. Where the counterparty is highly rated entity, there will be no requirement for posting collateral. For example, assume that CREF is the counterparty to the above swap as the receiver of the TRS. As an AAA-rated pension fund, CREF will be expected to post no collateral, thereby realizing the benefits/woes of the highly leveraged transaction in the TRS. The bottom line is that the swap allows economic use of capital without tying up 100 percent in a transaction. Exhibit 11.22 illustrates the impact of leverage on the TRS realized return for the hedge fund as a receiver and the bank as a payer, assuming the hedge fund will post 5 or 10 percent collateral.

EXHIBIT 11.22 Total Return Swap Payoff to Receiver Assuming 5 to 10 Percent Collateral Posted by Hedge Fund on Notional Principal of $50 Million

Bond Price in 1 Year	Capital Gain Loss	Coupon Net +225 Basis Points	Interest on 5% Collateral[a]	Interest on 10% Collateral[a]	Return Realized on 5% Collateral (%)	Return Realized on 10% Collateral (%)
103	1,500,000	1,125,000	125,000	250,000	110	60
100	0	1,125,000	125,000	250,000	50	27.50
97	−1,500,000	1,125,000	125,000	250,000	−10	−2.5
95	−2,500,000	1,125,000	125,000	250,000	−50	−22.50
92	−4,000,000	1,125,000	125,000	250,000	−110	−52.50

[a]Assuming 5 percent interest is earned.

As expected, the return realized by the receiver that is taking on the credit risk (risk of default), the market risk (interest rate risk due to rising interest rate), and the unique risk (possible downgrade of the debt issue) of the underlying debt instrument as a bank lays off all the risks to the receiver by paying total return while receiving LIBOR plus spread is extremely sensitive to the amount of collateral posted. For example, the receiver—the hedge fund—will realize return of 60 to 110 percent, assuming the amount of collateral posted is respectively 10 and 5 percent of the notional principal of $50 million and the underlying debt instrument appreciates only by 3 percent over the one-year period. However, assuming the underlying debt owned by the bank drops to 92, the hedge fund respectively will realize returns of −52.50 to −110 percent, where the leverage factor is 10 and 20 to 1.

By paying total returns, the bank in this example is essentially buying protection to lay off risk and realizes regulatory relief of risky capital as it no longer needs to hold the required reserve for the risk-based capital. The receiver of the total returns is selling protection for the reference assets it does not own, but that is financed by the bank for the receiver that posts some agreed amount of collateral.

NOTES

1. See Gertler and Lown (2000) for evidence that the yield spread is a leading economic indicator of the U.S. business cycle.
2. See February 18, 2002.
3. See BBA Credit Derivative Report 2000/2001.
4. See Ian Marsh, "What Central Banks Can Learn about Default Risk from Credit Market," *BIS Paper No. 12* (2001).
5. See Moorad Choudry, "Issues in Asset Swap Pricing of Credit Default Swaps," *Derivatives Week,* December 3, 2001.
6. TED refers to the spread of U.S. Treasury price over Eurodollar.
7. See *Multex Investors,* January 3, 2003.
8. This formulation is in the spirit of Merton (1974).
9. See Moody's Investor's Service, "Recovery Rates on Corporate Bonds," 2000.
10. See Altman (2000).
11. See E. Altman, *Bankruptcy, Credit Risk, and High Yield Junk Bonds* (London: Blackwell, 2002).
12. See J. Bencivenga, "A high-yield premium model for the high–yield debt market," p. 315, at Altman, *Bankruptcy, Credit Risk, and High Yield Junk Bonds* (London: Blackwell, 2002).
13. See Altman and Kao, "Corporate Bond Rating Drift: An Examination of Rating Agency Credit Quality Changes Over Time; and Lucas and Lonski, *Journal of Fixed Income* (March 1992).
14. See Altman and Kao, "The Implication of Corporate Bond Rating Drift," *Financial Analyst Journal* (May-June 1992): 64–75.

15. This is the risk of having disproportionately higher exposure to a particular party or parties in a given geographic location.

16. See Daniel Altman, "How Citigroup Hedged Bets on Enron," *New York Times,* February 8, 2002.

17. An example of this type of issue is the Tokyo Disneyland bond issued by Oriental Land, the operator of the theme parks in Japan, to raise $100 million at LIBOR plus 310 bps in May 1999 to manage earthquake exposure.

18. The Basle Committee on Banking Supervision consists of senior members of the G-10 central bankers that includes Belgium, France, Canada, Germany, Italy, Luxembourg, Netherlands, Japan, the United Kingdom, and the United States.

19. Based on the Basle Accord, the banks and their holding companies are required to maintain 8 percent capital against their risk-weighted assets. For example, some less risky assets, such as government and government agency–sponsored issues are risk-weighted by 50, 20, 10, or 0 percent of their face amount. Commercial loans are risk-weighted by 100 percent and therefore require an 8 percent capital. Mortgage debts are 50 percent risk-weighted, and assets issued by the government agencies Federal National Mortgage Association and Federal Home Loan Mortgage Corporation are assigned 20 percent risk-weight. Cash and near cash such as Treasury bills are assigned 0 percent risk.

20. Under the "low-level recourse rule" pursuant to 12 U.S.C. § 4808, the capital requirement for recourse cannot exceed the amount banks contractually obligated to fund.

21. See for details Kenneth Kohler and Mayer Brown, "Collateralized Loan Obligations: A Powerful New Portfolio Management Toll for Banks," Rowe & Maw, 1998, *Fitch Structured Finance* (February, 6, 2001).

22. To remedy the problem of finding an uncorrelated counterparty, the market has innovated the credit-linked note, where the seller of the risk has no exposure to the investors that assume the risk.

CHAPTER 12

Credit and Other Exotic Derivatives

Risk management continues to evolve as new financial service products are developed to mitigate risk in the 21st century. The biggest risk for an individual in the information economy is individual retirement equity exposure to market risk in its compensation tied to the stock price of its employer. A new breed of marketable, liquid, and highly specialized credit default swaps that enable individual employees to transfer the credit risk of their employer to the capital market can be an important risk management product. However, Robert Schiller makes the following arguments:

> For most individuals, the biggest risks are not euro-dollar exchange rate or oil prices. Instead, they are their pay packets or price of their home. It is reasonable to support that in coming years, our personal financial services software, with the assistance of professional organizations or trade union and pension funds will allow people to make essential contracts to reduce income risk. Individuals may be able to create financial swaps of average income in their region (as measured by a regional income index), thereby reducing risk.[1]

This chapter reviews some of the recent exotic innovations with credit and weather derivatives.[2] The regulatory changes in treatment of derivative transactions, whether booked in the bank balance sheet or the bank trading desk, continue to have a significant impact on the return on capital as the Bank for International Settlements (BIS) searches for an optimum capital reserve requirement that protects the integrity of the banking system and provides sufficient regulatory capital relief. The chapter starts with a discussion of highly leveraged transactions, such as credit spread forwards, credit spread options, options on credit exposure, asset swap switches, and callable step-ups.[3] These derivative products are designed to synthetically transfer risks in the capital markets.

Pricing and application of transfer and convertibility protection are illustrated with numerous examples followed by a discussion of emerging market bonds and stripped Brady bonds. Pricing and application of weather derivatives are presented at the end of this chapter.

CREDIT SPREAD FORWARD

A credit spread forward (CSF) is a contract where two parties agree to pay or receive a future spread that depends on the difference between the yield on two indices at the origination and that prevails at the settlement of the contract. In early 1992, Goldman Sachs, in a highly leveraged swap on principal of $5 million, designed this type of spread. Investors paid LIBOR to receive the total return based on the change in the value of the Goldman Sachs Commodity Index (GSCI) futures minus 150 basis points at the beginning and the settlement of the contract.[4]

Suppose an investor entered into a CSF transaction in three months over a period of 182 days with Goldman Sachs on notional principal of $5 million. Assume that in three months the LIBOR is at 3.75 percent and the GSCI is at 2,530. The GSCI is equal to 2,565 at the end of the contract. At the settlement of the contract, the investor pays $93,750 and receives $31,669.96 for a net payment of –$62,080.04:

$$\text{Pay: } (.0375) \times \tfrac{1}{2} (5,000,000) = \$93,750$$
$$\text{Receive: } \{[2565/2530 - 1] - \tfrac{1}{2}(.0150)\}(5,000,000) = \$31,669.96$$
$$\text{Net: } -\$62,080.04$$

CREDIT SPREAD OPTION

This over-the-counter (OTC) option contract allows two parties to enter into a contract where the buyer/writer pays/receives an up-front fee for contingent cash flow in the future if the spread (i.e., the difference between the yield on two financial instruments) widens/tightens above the strike price agreed at the origination and the settlement period. Credit spread options are like any other instrument for which there is an active exchange traded or the OTC call and put options such as options on foreign currency, commodity, and indices. The call/put options allow buyers that are expecting tightening/widening the yield spread between an AA corporate and identical maturity Treasury over the next six months, with limited exposure to risk. Consider the example of a European call and put credit spread between a bank as a writer and investor as a buyer shown in Exhibit 12.1.

For example, if the spread tightens to 200 basis points (XYZ credit improves) in the example in the next six months, the call is in-the-money and the call option buyer receives $468,750 equal to the duration multiplied by the notional principal multiplied by 15 basis points. The buyer of the call has paid an up-front fee of $137,500 (.0055 × $25 million) for this option. This is an off–balance sheet transaction that is highly leveraged, with a small probability of an enormous upside potential and downside risk limited to the amount of premium paid up front. Exhibit 12.2 presents the behavior of call and put on the spread option.

However, if the spread widens to 240 basis points (XYZ's credit deteriorates) as a result of worse-than-expected growth for the economy and likely

EXHIBIT 12.1   Call/Put Credit Spread on XYZ Bonds Due July 10, 2022, as of February 14, 2002

Spread/call put buyer: Investor

Spread/call put writer: Bank

Notional principal (NP): $25 million

Current spread: 2.25%

Strike (exercise) spread call/put: 2.15% (out-of-the-money forward call, in-the-money forward put)

Duration (DUR): 12.5 years

Exercise date: 6 months from today

Call option premium: 55 basis points of the notional principal payable by investor to the bank

Put option premium: 105 basis points of the notional principal payable by investor to the bank

Settlement date: Today, February 14, 2002

Underlying index: XYZ bonds due July 10, 2022

Reference benchmark index: 5.785% U.S. Treasury bond offer yield due September 2022

Index credit spread: Yield to maturity of the underlying index 6.25% coupon is estimated as (bid price net of any accrued interest) bid yield less the offer yield of the U.S. Treasury bonds at 12.00 P.M. New York EST time two days prior to exercise date.

Call option payment: NP × DUR × Max (2.15% − index spread, 0)

Put option payment: NP × DUR × Max (Index credit spread − 2.15%, 0)

---

downgrade of the issuer of the referenced debts, the put will produce profit. In this scenario, the buyer of the spread put enjoys a profit of $781,250 less the premium of $262,500. The change in the price of the referenced index reflects the duration and the convexity of the underlying bonds, particularly when the referenced index is a long-term debt. As discussed in Chapter 10, the price of

EXHIBIT 12.2   Payoff of Spread Call and Put

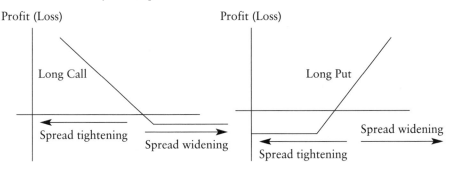

the options also reflects the volatility of the price of the underlying debt or the yield volatility.

Investors can use spread transactions in a number of ways to create a synthetic structure rather than dealing in the cash market. For example, buying calls and simultaneously selling puts will allow investors to lock in the current spread to buy the underlying instrument synthetically using the power of the leverage in the option market with limited capital. Likewise, selling the bonds in the portfolio and selling puts on the same bonds for a fee enables investors to buy back the same portfolio when buyers exercise their option. Active managers of bonds/stocks portfolios use this strategy to buy bonds/stocks by selling the put at a desirable strike price.

ASSET SWAP SWITCH

One potential source of profit in the cash or derivatives market is the identification of mispricing of the underlying cash or derivative instruments. The other source of profit is the ability to forecast the future direction of interest rates and use the duration-based approach in rebalancing the portfolio. There is no convincing evidence to support forecasters' notoriously poor track record in their endeavors. According to Homer and Liebowitz, one of five types of asset swaps can be used to rebalance a portfolio.[5]

1. *Substitution swap.* Consider two bonds, A and B, identical in every respect. Both are Aa-rated utilities; however, bond A's yield is 7.25 percent and bond B has a yield to maturity of 7 percent. The portfolio manager is expecting the mispricing to be corrected in the next three to six months. The yield spread is expected to tighten. The portfolio manager swaps the expensive bond (bond B is in the portfolio) for bond A (the cheap bond is not in the portfolio). This swap is the sale of bond B to purchase bond A. As long as the investor's expectation materializes, bond A is expected to outperform bond B in rising, falling, and stable interest rate scenarios.

2. *Intermarket swap.* Consider two bonds identical in every respect except bond A is an 18.5 year 6 1/4 corporate with a yield of 8.25 percent and bond B is an off-the-run issue 18.5 year 6 1/4 government bond with a yield of 7 percent. The yield differential is expected to tighten in the next three to six months. The portfolio manager swaps government bonds in the portfolio for the corporate bonds. This strategy pays off provided the yield spread tightens, as the corporate bond will outperform the Treasury under the assumed scenario.

3. *Pure yield pickup swap.* The investor swaps short-term bonds for long-term bonds in an upward-sloping yield environment. As long as there is no upward shift in the yield curve, this strategy pays off. However, the upward shift in the yield curve exposes the long-term bonds to higher interest rate

risk, as high-duration bonds suffer significant losses as rates increase. Savings and loans followed this strategy, borrowing short term and lending long term, for years until their demise in the 1980s.

4. ***Rate anticipation swap.*** The investor has an expectation concerning the direction of interest rates in this swap. Assuming the investor believes that the bottom has been reached in the bond market and a rally is expected in the next few months, it might swap short and intermediate bonds for long bonds of higher duration and vice versa.

5. ***Tax swap.*** A tax swap is the selling of bonds with capital losses to offset realized capital gains and the simultaneous buying of other bonds where recognition of losses is advantageous for tax purposes.

There are other types of swaps when the swap is triggered contingent on the changes in market conditions (i.e., rates increase or decrease, below- or above-average temperature, events like more rainfall or drought, and any other conceivable phenomena that may or may not happen, producing an exchange of one asset or its payoff with another asset). In years to come, undoubtedly we will see other as-yet unknown swaps.

Selling/buying an asset contingent on its widening/tightening its spread against, say, LIBOR with an agreement to buy/sell another asset is an option to enter into an asset swap (also known as asset swap switch).

Example: Consider a bank that is long on an Argentine bond at a spread of LIBOR plus 450 basis points. It wishes to offload this bond and acquire an alternative New Zealand sovereign bond currently trading at a spread of LIBOR plus 120 basis points if the Argentine spread widens to LIBOR plus 500 basis points without widening in the New Zealand spread in the next six months. The spread of the two issues against LIBOR is not correlated in this scenario.[6] The bank offers its counterparty 30 basis points for the right, but not an obligation, to exchange the Argentine bond for the New Zealand sovereign if and only if the Argentine spread widens to 500 basis points. The bank in this scenario has a long put in Argentine sovereign debts or a protective put (the bank owns the underlying debt) coupled with the obligation to purchase (short put, although it gets not a direct premium but an indirect premium that is embedded in the acquisition of another asset) the New Zealand sovereign debts triggered by the widening of the Argentine spread. Counterparties with different expectations about the term structure of interest rates for two sovereign debts are motivated to make this type of swap.

The investor (swap counterparty) may believe that the Argentine debt at a spread of 500 basis points over LIBOR can be an attractive deal to acquire (Argentine bonds are cheap at a spread of 500 basis points) without being overly concerned about the widening spread; that is, the widening spread may be due to alignment of the spread with that of the underlying economic fundamentals as opposed to an increased likelihood of default. The bank, however, may consider the widening of the Argentine spread a serious risk; therefore, it is willing to lay off the risk by paying 30 basis points to the counterparty in exchange for assuming the New Zealand exposure (see Exhibit 12.3).

The reverse transaction in Exhibit 12.3 is between two parties on two uncorrelated assets where the exchange of the assets takes place if and when the spread tightens, producing a nonsymmetric payoff. For example, consider an investor that owns a New Zealand bond and a bank that is long on Argentine credit. The investor is willing to pay some premium to the bank to have the right, but not an obligation, to purchase Argentine credit (buy call on Argentine credit), provided that the Argentine spread tightens, and simultaneously to sell call on New Zealand credit (the investor owns the bond) that obligates the investor to exchange New Zealand credit for Argentine credit. A long call in one asset plus a short call in another asset conditional on tightening of the spread produces an asset swap switch.

The derivatives market is obsessed with fancy and confusing nicknames for financial products. As the previous example reveals, the transactions are purely based on one's view of the interest rate spread in one asset vis-à-vis another asset conditional on tightening or widening spread.

Options on Credit Exposure

This over-the-counter option allows one party to lay off risk or to assume exposure for a short period of time by buying or selling protection. A bank can buy credit exposure options on its swap line linked to a particular counterparty without selling or assigning the swap and severing its relationship with a client. In this scenario, the bank buying the option on the particular exposure pays an upfront fee to reduce the concentration of its exposure (to free up swap line) to a particular country, region, or counterparty. The cost of this type of insurance depends on the supply and demand for this type of protection and is determined through negotiations. The bank, having freed up and reduced its concentration risk, can assume exposure in a more lucrative transaction with the same

EXHIBIT 12.3   Asset Swap Switch

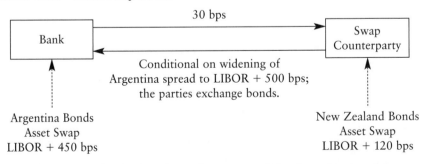

Long put in one asset plus short put in another asset conditional on widening of the spread produces asset swap switch.

counterparty to which it had no credit line. The bottom line is the amount of business the bank expects to get with a particular client over time, which depends on the variety of factors.

As long as the bank can lay off some risk over the next, say, nine months by buying protection, buying default swaps, or paying total returns in the TRS at the cost of 50 basis points to an uncorrelated counterparty and assuming the same amount of exposure for 75 basis points to a different party to which it had no credit line, the bank is effectively earning net 25 basis points and maintains a good bank-clientele relationship.

After the Latin American loan defaults in 1989, international banks have become far more innovative in mitigating concentration of credit risk in their portfolios. In simple plain-vanilla swaps, banks swap credit risk by exchanging the payoff of credit risk to obligors in manufacturing, retail, food, and high tech in certain geographical regions with credit risk to preferably uncorrelated obligors in other segments of the economy.

The swap could be contingent on a particular parameter or events that trigger the exchange of one credit risk for another as well as to attach an option to engage or terminate the swap (swaption) for a fee. Callable step-ups are callable swaps (swaptions) with embedded options to terminate the swaps after a given period by forcing termination through significant increase (step-ups) in the premium.

CALLABLE STEP-UPS

This OTC option was developed in the late 1990s by large banks for window dressing the balance sheet for a short period. It realized benefits of regulatory capital relief on the portfolio of credit risks denominated in dollars or foreign currency on transactions of $1 billion to $3 billion. Banks having exposure to investment-grade credits or unfunded commitments can reduce the risk-based capital by buying an option or default protection that may reduce the risk-weight from 100 percent of the 8 percent required reserve capital to 20 percent of the 8 percent for a short period of time. The reduced risk-based capital reserve through purchase of protection increases the return on regulatory capital five-fold, as the return is a levered complement of BIS requirements. Banks would normally have purchased a credit default swap or engaged in TRS by paying total return to achieve regulatory capital relief provided that protection is acquired over the life of the underlying referenced credit, which may have been 5 to 10 years. However, the option allows the bank to lay off risk (sell its risk to someone else who is willing to assume it for a fee) for a short period for reporting purposes to the Federal Reserve Board on the Fed call reports by the end of the quarterly reporting and call back the credit risk when the option expires forced through a significant increase (step-ups) in the premium.

The sell (securitize credit exposure) and buy-back (take credit risk) feature of the step-ups option forces the protection buyer to call back the exposure, as remaining hedged on the underlying referenced credits does not pay off when the premium increases by 100 basis points or more. The protection seller is paid an up-front fee and does not face any counterparty risk in this transaction that banks usually book in their trading book where the regulatory capital charges are smaller as opposed to bank book. The premium on this option that synthetically transforms the referenced credit-risky obligors into risk-free instruments is normally greater than the spread of these issues over LIBOR and the U.S. Treasury securities.

Example: Consider a German bank with a portfolio of credit risks is rated Baa2/Bbb with the weighted average coupon (WAC) of LIBOR plus 40 basis points, weighted average maturity (WAM) of 7.2 years, and duration of 5.3 years. This portfolio of credits is neutral its benchmark, the Lehman Brothers government/ credit index. The market value of the portfolio is $2.5 billion. The bank contemplates laying off the credit risk of the portfolio over the next reporting period to Bundesbank by purchasing an OTC option for 60 days. The annualized premium is 60 basis points. The bank pays an up-front premium of 10 basis points to the protection seller for assuming the credit risk. The protection seller realizes a $2.5 million premium for taking the credit risk of the portfolio of 200 obligors in this highly leveraged transaction that is booked in the bank's trading desk. The protection seller assumes the risk of default in any one of the referenced credits, however small in probability of default but substantial in severity of loss.

The protection buyer reduced the risk-based capital reserve from 100 percent of the 8 percent to 20 percent of the 8 percent; therefore, the return on capital increases by five times as the levered returns improve owing to regulatory capital relief complement of the BIS. At the expiration of the option, the protection buyer calls back the portfolio as the cost of buying protection step-ups to 180 basis points as the incentive to terminate the option substantially increases.

The risk shifting and retaking risk in the step-ups option scenario can be replicated in the organized exchange. The bank can buy put options on the Lehman Brothers index that provide protection for $2.5 billion worth of credit portfolios. In the event of default, the bank puts the defaulted bond(s) back to the put writer (the insurer) for the face value of the debt(s). By assuming the credit risk of the portfolio, the protection seller is required to hold reserve capital equal to 4 percent of the notional principal, provided that the transaction is booked in the trading desk and the exposure is footnoted without balance sheet impact. The BIS might change the rule in the future, mandating protection sellers to hold 8 percent capital for these transactions. This change will reduce the relative attractiveness of these transactions and the availability of protection.

TRANSFER AND CONVERTIBILITY PROTECTION

A new breed of the OTC product emerged in 1999 in a negotiated capital market. It mitigated the exposure to foreign currency–denominated deposits held by major international banks and facilitated debt issues in emerging market economies by attaching transfer and convertibility (T&C) protection to enhance the credit quality of the issue. In the past, the absence of convertibility of the foreign currency to hard currency was a major stumbling block for international trade, particularly to foreign direct investment. Major banks and insurance companies finally provided the T&C protection as a natural extension of their other products.

The convertibility of foreign-denominated debt to hard currency can be hampered by a number of factors, such as imposition of exchange rate control on the size and the price at which the foreign currency can be converted to hard currency, moratorium, runs in the banking system, war and civil unrest, expropriation, revolutions that defy the law of land and disrupt currency flows, and other events as defined by the protection seller in the confirmation agreement. The T&C protection (insurance) is not a guarantee of the payment; it is a guarantee to convert local currency to hard currency, provided that the issuer has sufficient local currency and is in compliance with the terms of the T&C protection. The T&C protection seller effectively insures the buyer of the protection for an up-front fee on the given notional principal and over the life of the protection.

When banks in an emerging market economy are unable to convert the usually soft local currency to hard currency due to political upheaval and official imposition of the exchange control, a dual exchange rate emerges, as we have witnessed postrevolution in Iran and other countries. Dual exchange rates refer to two distinctly different exchange rates on the same currency, an official government rate and the black market rate, where the latter is the market-equilibrating rate to satisfy the demands of the individual and businesses in the economy. The official exchange rate is the only way individuals can get a limited amount of hard currency for overseas travel. It also is available to certain exporters/importers for procuring essential goods and services. The official exchange rate offers great potential for abuse.

T&C protection originated through the World Bank—specifically the International Development Association and the Multilateral Investment Guarantee Agency (MIGA)—to encourage investment and finance trade in the world's poorest countries. The MIGA guarantee mitigates providers of capital against risks such as transfer restriction, imposition of capital control, war, political upheaval, and expropriation. To align the interest of investors with the underlying project guarantor against T&C restrictions, investors are expected to remain at risk for up to 10 percent of the equity investment and 5 percent of the loan. MIGA receives an annual premium for providing protection with the term extending 15 to 20 years for eligible member projects that is expected to expand, modernize, and structure the financing of the existing projects. Eligible projects are expected to enhance a country's overall growth, adhere to MIGA guidelines, and be financially viable.

Example: Light Service de Electricidade Brazil recently secured a $23 million loan from foreign investors to upgrade electricity services to Rio de Janeiro and the surrounding low-income areas. The loan was guaranteed against T&C restrictions and expropriation (see Exhibit 12.4).

EXHIBIT 12.4   Structure of Transfer and Convertibility Insurance

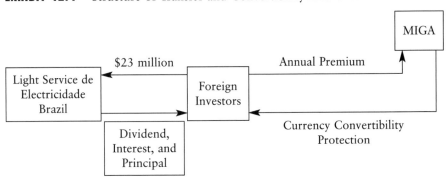

Without the T&C protection, investors either would not have provided the capital for the project or would have required a hefty risk premium that would have made the project economically unfeasible. The premium for the insurance varies from project to project and is negotiated between the buyer and seller. It depends on, among other things, the volatility of the local exchange rate, interest rate, the size of the protection, the length of the coverage, political risk, and other factors as related to the soundness of the project. MIGA's provision of convertibility protection has been in response to private investor demands for risk mitigation services. Private providers of T&C protection are major banks and insurance companies. Exhibit 12.5 presents a typical OTC indicative term sheet for the Brazilian real T&C risk.

Every six months the protection buyer pays in advance an annuity of $218,750 for the convertibility insurance over the life of the protection. According to the document shown in Exhibit 12.5, the protection buyer is required to pay in two business days the Brazilian real-dollar equivalent of the notional principal at the exchange rate at the time of convertibility. The protection seller in turn will deliver to a designated bank in London or New York $25 million to satisfy its obligation.

The T&C protection policy offered by the Overseas Private Investment Corporation (OPIC) to cash-strapped Asian and Latin American debt issuers allows the issuer to mitigate sovereign foreign currency risks (transfer and convertibility, expropriation, and social unrest) and access to international capital markets at a lower cost of funds. Rating agencies have always capped the ratings of individual companies domiciled overseas at or below the sovereign rating. For example, the rating of sovereign Argentina has hampered the ability of a private creditworthy Argentine oil company to raise foreign capital. Two sovereign risks cap the foreign currency rating of a company:

1. Transfer risk, where a sovereign decree prohibits the transfer of hard currency out of a country
2. Convertibility risk, where a sovereign decree imposes restrictions on the ability of a company to convert local currency into hard currency

EXHIBIT 12.5 Brazilian Real Transfer and Convertibility Protection Risk Indictive Term Sheet

Protection Buyer: Light Service de Electricidade Brazil

Protection Seller: Commercial bank, AAA rated

Notional Principal: $25 million

Protection Coverage: Transfer and convertibility

Protection Premium: 175 basis points, payable semiannually in advance of the period on actual/360-day basis. Protection buyer pays the convertibility amount to protection seller, and protection seller pays $25 million by wire transfer of funds available in two business days at the settlement date in London or New York City following the events that trigger payment.

Transaction Date: To be determined by both buyer and seller.

Effective Date: Five business days from transaction date.

Termination Date: Five years from the effective date.

Payment Terms: Contingent on occurrences of defined convertibility events.

Convertibility Amount: Equal to notional dollar amount times the Brazilian real per dollar exchange rate by wire transfer to a designated bank by protection seller two business days at the settlement date as triggered by defined events.

Brazilian Real Exchange Rate: The rate, determined by the calculation agent, to be equal to Brazilian real spot exchange rate per dollar two business days prior to settlement as published by the central bank of Brazil. If the rate is unavailable or unpublished, the calculation agent uses the Brazilian real exchange rate as quoted by major foreign exchange dealers in Brazil, London, or New York on financial or commercial transactions for buying Brazilian real for U.S. dollars.

Convertibility Events: Outlined in the International Swaps and Derivatives Association (ISDA) Master Agreement as any defined event that affects the exchange of the real for the dollar. These events include:

- Failure of the Brazil central bank to exchange real at spot for dollars
- War and civil unrest in which Brazil is a party
- Expropriation and confiscation or nationalization of foreign-owned assets in Brazil
- Imposition of material exchange control that limits the ability of the protection buyer to transfer and convert the Brazilian real at spot exchange rate to the U.S. dollar
- Run in the Brazilian banking system

Calculation Agent: Protection seller

Creditworthy companies in emerging market economies usually have an investment-grade rating in a local currency while having a below-investment-grade rating in foreign currency due to sovereign risks. Debt issuers ratings of the emerging markets economies in acquiring foreign capital have been enhanced through the use of T&C insurance by rating agencies such as Standard & Poor's (S&P), Duff & Phelps, and others. Therefore, T&C insurance adds value to the sovereign nation and to a company that issues foreign currency–denominated debts and acquires protection to mitigate sovereign risks. When evaluating the use of T&C insurance, S&P does not take into account the expected loss and recovery value of an investment, only the timely payment of interest and principal. Exhibit 12.6 presents the effect of the use of T&C protection on the rating of a company.

T&C insurance is expected to add value to the Asian economies listed in Exhibit 12.7 by raising the countries' foreign currency ratings.

The application of T&C protection is driven largely by the potential for rating elevation that it provides in the capital market. Under S&P's rating criteria, the use of appropriately designed T&C protection policy may increase the rating of a bond issuer up to the level of its local currency rating, as shown in

EXHIBIT 12.6   Rating Enhancement of T&C Insurance

Uninsured Rating			Insured Rating
LC Rating of Issuer	**Sovereign FC Rating**	**FC Rating of Issuer**	**Structured Issue FC Rating**
BBB	BB+	BB+	BBB

LC: Local currency

FC: Foreign currency

Source: Standard and Poor's, "New Rating Approach Gives Private Sector Issuers for Partial Coverage of Transfer and Convertibility Risk," October 19, 2000.

EXHIBIT 12.7   Local and Foreign Currency Rating

Country	FC Rating	LC Rating
India	BB+	BBB
Malaysia	BBB−	BBB+
Philippines	BB+	BBB
South Korea	BBB	A−
Thailand	BB+	BBB

Source: Duff & Phelps Credit Rating Co., "Political Risk Insurance for Asian Issuers to Breach Sovereign Ceilings," August 24, 1999, at *www.dcrco.com*.

Exhibit 12.7. The rating elevation provides some relief in terms of access to capital markets to secure debt or equity and a reduced cost of capital, which creates value for the issuing entity.

PRICING TRANSFER AND CONVERTIBILITY PROTECTION

The market for T&C insurance is in the early stages of the development and discovery period as participants in the market look at the treatment of T&C insurance payoffs to the buyer of the protection in Argentina that has been triggered due to the imposition of exchange control since December 2001. The value of the T&C protection depends not only on the speed at which claims are processed but also on the overall process of evaluating claims by the insurers. The types of risks for which insurance is acquired are hard to quantify in the OTC market, thereby making it fairly difficult to price this insurance. Historical reliable data, particularly on the markets for the emerging economies, are rare and at best cannot be trusted. There are only a few players in the T&C market. In addition, the lack of transparency plaguing the derivative markets in emerging economies renders publicly available information worthless. Buyers and sellers negotiate the price and the terms of T&C protection policies, depending on the supply and demand for the insurance. There are more buyers than sellers.

While current quotes provided by a few dealers are rare and more or less guesstimates, the relative riskiness of this insurance vis-à-vis other insurance can provide reasonable assurance to the buyer that the price is not entirely out of line with underlying factors that determine the premium for an insurance. Insurers must look at a few fundamental factors when pricing T&C protection, besides factors unique to the protection buyer. These factors are related to the current account as a percentage of gross domestic product; usually a negative 4 percent or more ratio signals a great deal of stress on the underlying currency, and the currency is likely to severely devalue. When debt service of the sovereign as a percentage of the sovereign annual budget is in excess of 3 percent, the sovereign's difficulty in servicing its outstanding debt obligation is implied.

On the surface, the risks are relatively higher for T&C protection than in credit default swaps, requiring higher premiums for the former insurance than for the latter. The OTC market prices of convertibility protection and default swaps quoted for Brazil, Argentina, Mexico, and Russia, as of July 14, 1997, in Exhibit 12.8 bears out this claim. However, when the market for this product matures, the premium for T&C insurance is expected to fall below that of the credit default swap. The actual loss to the insurer is expected to be lower than that of the default insurance, since the seller of the protection pays only after having received the convertibility amount from the protection buyer at the exchange rate prevailing on the date of the trigger event.

For Brazil, a six-month default swap for the buyer of the protection is 80 basis points while a six-month convertibility protection is 110 basis points at the bid (to sell protection) and not available at the offer rate. Convertibility insurance appears almost twice as expensive as default insurance for buying or

EXHIBIT 12.8   Sovereign Credit Default Protection versus Convertibility
Protection Prices, Bid-Ask Broker Indications (Basis Points
per Annum)

	6-month Default	6-month Convertibility	1-year Default	1-year Convertibility
Argentina			70/NA	NA/140
Brazil	60/80	110/NA	70/95	120/170
Mexico			65/75	NA/110
Russia	NA/195	150/185		

Source: Prebon Yanmane, Tullett Capital Markets, July 14, 1997.

selling a one-year protection on Brazil. As a general rule, buying protection from
an uncorrelated counterparty with a high rating may be the best way to mitigate counterparty risk.

SPECULATIVE CAPITAL

Large banks, hedge funds, and actively managed stock and bond funds fueled
the growth of the emerging market economies in the 1980s, particularly in
Asia for supplying unregulated capital to these markets in pursuit of a higher
yield; in the 1990s, they found the convertibility a major risk. The "hot capital" moved in and out of the emerging market economies, causing significant pain
for providers and end users. These movements are cited as the main reason for
the collapse of the currency, financial crisis, and bank run in Mexico in 1994,
for the Southeast Asian crisis of 1997, and for the Russian ruble devaluation of
1998–1999. When flight of capital starts in a country or a region, for whatever
reason, debt and equity investments denominated in the soft currency have to
be converted back into hard currency, which puts undue pressure on the local
banking system to honor those obligations. The end result is severe devaluation,
imposition of exchange control, and a contagion effect to other economies as a
spillover threatens the soundness of the banking system.

EMERGING MARKET DEBTS AND BRADY BONDS

The financial markets in Eastern Europe, Latin America, and Asia (not including Japan) make up what are known as the emerging markets. Sovereign nations
and firms in these economies issue mostly dollar-denominated and some euro-
denominated debts to undertake various projects. Like other bonds issued in the
major industrial countries, these bonds are rated by rating agencies. Due to higher
credit risk and sovereign risk, the yield is at significant spread over U.S. Treasuries. Sovereign local currency–denominated debt enjoys better ratings than
sovereign foreign currency–denominated debt because the sovereign has the

ability to raise taxes to fulfill its domestic obligations. However, the sovereign's ability to service its foreign currency–denominated debts is constrained by the amount and availability of hard currency, which is not under its control. Therefore, other things remaining the same, rating agencies assign lower ratings to foreign currency–denominated debts.

Financial markets in emerging economies are plagued by a lack of an orderly secondary market, transparency, higher price volatility, wider bid-ask spread, and the absence of reliable price quotes, among other things. The development of an orderly financial market hinges on the ability of banks, financial institutions, and finance and insurance companies to securitize their financial assets effectively.

In the early 1980s, major U.S. banks extended nearly $200 billion in credit for business and development programs to mostly Mexico and other Latin American economies. By the end of the decade, the emerging market economies found themselves hit by a double whammy: falling commodity prices and rising interest rates. The end result was a default on more than $200 billion denominated nonmarketable bank loans that threatened the soundness and the integrity of the U.S. banking system. Restructuring had to be worked out to allow the defaulted economies access to the international capital market to revive the troubled economies' debt.

Debtor banks created an organization called the Paris club. The development bank acquired the troubled nonperforming loans at almost 50 cents on the dollar and enhanced their credit so that the new restructured debts could be traded in the secondary market. The secondary market allowed the debtor banks to recoup some of their lost capital and provided a way for the emerging markets to access the capital market.

Some of the secondary market trading of emerging economy debts is in repackaged sovereign debts whose principal and some interest is backed by long-term Treasury zero coupon bonds known as Brady bonds. Brady bonds represent the repackaging and restructuring of nonperforming bank loans into marketable securities collateralized by long-dated zeros. They are named after former Treasury Secretary Nicholas Brady, who worked out a plan in 1989 with Mexico to mitigate a huge concentration of risk facing U.S. financial institutions. According to the plan, the U.S. government and lending institutions agreed to provide some relief in the form of forgiving some of the principal and interest provided that Mexico implemented certain structural reforms. The U.S. financial institutions, having written off some of the nonperforming loans, reduced their concentration risk and cleaned up their balance sheets. The Brady plan did not pay off the defaulted bank loans; however, it provided a plan where these loans could be paid off in the distant future. This program extended to debts of other emerging countries, which came to be known as Brady countries.

As of August 1996, 13 countries issued Brady bonds: Argentina, Brazil, Costa Rica, the Dominican Republic, Ecuador, Mexico, Uruguay, and Venezuela in Latin America, and 5 other countries: Bulgaria, Jordan, Nigeria, the Philippines, and Poland. More than 75 percent of the Brady bonds are issued by Argentina, Brazil, Mexico, and Venezuela.

Past-due interest bonds cover interest due on restructured loans and do not have collateral, except in the case of Costa Rica. Front-loaded interest reduction bonds (FLIRBs) have a rolling interest guarantee (RIG) that covers 12 months of interest over the first five-year period. However, FLIRBs have no guarantee of principal. Principal bonds cover the principal owed on the bank loans; there are two types of par or discount bonds. Principal par bonds are long-dated instruments with a 25- to 30-year maturity with a fixed rate coupon. The long-dated discount bonds with floating rate coupons have a principal partially collateralized by U.S. Treasury zero coupon bonds. The discount and principal bonds have 12 to 18 months of RIG in the event of default. The partial backing of the principal and interest by long-dated U.S. Treasury zeros has increased the relative attractiveness and liquidity of these issues and allows investors to invest in the emerging market and profit from the improvement of the sovereign credit.

Brady bonds are quoted at the spread over the stripped Treasury zeros, where the sovereign spread is quoted after accounting for the U.S. Treasury collateral. Investors investing in emerging market bonds have double exposure: to sovereign risk and to the U.S. interest rate risk. For example, tightening a sovereign spread as a result of improvement in the sovereign rating increases the value of the Brady bonds; however, rising U.S. interest rates are likely to adversely affect the value of the these bonds, other things remaining the same.

Tightening or widening credit spreads of Brady bonds over U.S. Treasuries provides opportunities for arbitrage profit. For example, the credit spread option can exploit the tightening (improving spread) or widening (deteriorating spread) scenarios that investors foresee over time. Say investors foresee a tightening of the spread of Brady bonds over the U.S. Treasuries in the next six months. Currently the Argentine spread is 230 basis points, and the investor believes that the spread is likely to tighten to 160 basis points (the price of Brady will go up) in the next six months. The investor can buy at-the-money call options at the strike price of 230 for 50 basis points. Assuming Brady tightens to 165 basis points, the call buyer will make a profit of 15 basis points or dollar profit of ($DUR \times .0015 \times NP$) where DUR and NP are respectively duration and notional principal of the bond.

Alternatively, buying the put option produces a profit if the credit spread widens. In this scenario the buyer, expecting deterioration of the Argentine spread over Treasuries due to weaker economic fundamentals and the likelihood of downgrade, has the option of putting the bond to the writer at strike price for a profit.

INTERNATIONAL SWAPS AND DERIVATIVES ASSOCIATION MASTER AGREEMENT

The ISDA Master Agreement is the bedrock of more than 90 percent of global derivatives transactions. A wide array of transactions on many different underlying products, such as equity, commodity, energy, currency, interest rate, and credit, are documented using the ISDA Master Agreement.

Close-out netting—"the right under the ISDA Master Agreement to treat the obligations under many different transactions as one amount owing between the parties upon termination of the Master Agreement, is a critical risk reduction tool"—is estimated to reduce the exposure to credit risk between counterparties by as much as 70 percent."[7] Netting is recognized for regulatory capital relief, providing an economic benefit for counterparties that use the ISDA Master Agreement to document transactions. Enforceability of the ISDA Master Agreement netting provisions has been confirmed in nearly 40 jurisdictions around the world." Exhibit 12.9 presents some of the key changes in the ISDA Master Agreement.

WEATHER DERIVATIVES

Weather affects the bottom line of businesses every year. Potential swings in earnings can be substantial due to weather-related phenomena, such as rainfall, drought, hurricane, and unusually cold or hot temperatures. Power producers—oil, natural gas, and electric utilities—are prone to reduced demand due to higher-than-average temperatures in the winter, where the demand for their product falls well below company expectations, or lower-than-average temperatures in summer, reducing the demand for an electric utility. Such situations expose producers to *volumetric risk*—the risk of falling revenue due to unfavorable weather conditions in winter and summer as demand for the products is adversely affected. Other businesses, such as hospitality, airlines, agricultural producers, and producers of consumer products, also are exposed to volumetric risk that needs to be mitigated.

In 1997 utility companies in the United States, whose revenues are highly correlated with weather, began to buy protection using derivative contracts to manage swings in profits from the effects of warmer-than-normal winters. The change in the regulatory climate that forced the industry to focus on profits and shareholder value more than ever was instigated by deregulation of the utility industry. For example, gas distributors in the United States reported nearly a 15 percent drop in first-quarter earnings when winter temperatures were milder than normal. According to a Major World Crop Areas and Climate Profiles report from 2001, "Climate and weather are significant factors affecting agriculture production around the world. Both seasonal and regional variability in weather directly influence crop yield potential."[8]

The overall growth in securitization of weather risk can be attributed to the El Niño winter of 1997–1998, when an unusually mild winter forced energy companies to hedge their exposure to weather risk. The agricultural, energy, and utility industries have used OTC products to manage their exposure to weather-related risk. The organized market for weather derivatives for mitigating weather-related risks started with the introduction of the first exchange-traded futures at the Chicago Mercantile Exchange in 1999 for 10 major cities in the United States.[9]

EHXIBIT 12.9 Key Changes in ISDA Master Agreement

New measure of damages provision: Close-out Amount.
Market Quotation and Loss, the standards in the 1992 ISDA Master Agreement, have been replaced by a single standard, Close-out Amount. The new approach to closing-out transactions is based on a standard of commercial reasonableness and describes the type of information that can be used in valuing terminated transactions and sets forth the procedures that can be followed in valuing those terminated transactions.

Introduction of Force Majeure Termination Event.
Force Majeure Termination Event was added as a new Termination Event in the 2002 ISDA Master Agreement. A force majeure provision was not included in the 1992 ISDA Master Agreement, as there was not member consensus on the need for such a provision at that time. The new provision is intended to ensure that force majeure events such as natural or man-made disasters, labor riots, acts of terrorism and other unanticipated events that prevent the performance of a party's obligations under the contract are considered. Once such an event occurs, a party is obligated to show that the event is beyond its control and that it could not overcome the event by using all reasonable efforts and that a waiting period of eight Local Business Days has expired. At that point, a party may move to terminate the transactions affected by the event.

Reduction of Grace Periods
Grace periods in Bankruptcy and Default Under Specified Transaction and Bankruptcy were reduced. For example, if a party failed to make a payment under the 1992 ISDA Master Agreement, notice of such failure was provided and the party was given a grace period of three Local Business Days to remedy its failure. Under the 2002 ISDA Master Agreement, the three Local Business Day grace period has been reduced to one Local Business Day. A similar change was made for the grace period in Default Under Specified Transaction. The Bankruptcy Event of Default in the 1992 ISDA Master Agreement provided for a 30 calendar day period during which the bankruptcy party could attempt to have the bankruptcy petition dimissed or stayed before an Event of Default was triggered. The new provision distinguishes between proceedings started by a party or its principal regulator, which become an Event of Default immediately, and proceedings started by third parties, which become an Event of Default after 15 calendar days.

Inclusion of Set-off Provision
The 1992 ISDA Master Agreement did not include a set-off provision. Set-off provisions are important in default situations because they allow the non-defaulting party to attempt to garner assets of the defaulting party other than the amounts it is owed. Thus, with a set-off provision, the non-defaulting party can explore whether there are other assets such as a deposit account that can be attached and then set-off against the amount the defaulting party owes the non-defaulting party.

Source: International Swaps and Derivatives Association, press release, January 8, 2003.

WEATHER DERIVATIVES MARKET

The value of the outstanding notional amount of weather derivatives since the first weather derivative transaction in late 1997 was $7.5 billion worth of deals as of June 2001, according to a survey conducted by the Weather Risk Management

Exchange-traded Weather Derivatives **359**

Association (WRMA) in conjunction with PricewaterhouseCoopers (PwC).[10] See Exhibit 12.10.

According to WRMA, nearly 70 percent of businesses in the United States are exposed to some type of weather-related financial risk.[11] The U.S. Department of Commerce estimated the corporate weather exposure at nearly $1 trillion, or one-eighth of gross domestic product.[12] Mitigating weather-related risk is expected to reduce the volatility of earnings and enhance value for shareholders as well as improve the credit ratings of the firms.

The deregulation of the utility industry has produced opportunities and challenges to the industry for hedging volumetric risk induced by changing temperatures. However, OTC products to deal with other weather-related phenomena, such as precipitation, rainfall, snowfall, and other extreme conditions to which firms in certain industries have been exposed and wish to acquire protection, are written by reinsurance and other risk arbitrageurs, such as large energy companies, energy merchants, and major commercial banks.

EXCHANGE-TRADED WEATHER DERIVATIVES

The Heating-Degree Day (HDD) and Cooling-Degree Day (CDD) indices were developed at the Chicago Mercantile Exchange (CME) as a measure of how much a day's average temperature deviates from 65° Fahrenheit.[13] While the problem of dealing with weather-related phenomena is an old and historic one, the

EXHIBIT 12.10 Survey Results of Notional Value of Weather Derivatives by Region (1998–2001)

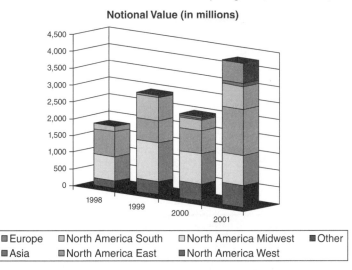

Source: WRMA/PwC Survey, April 2001–March 2002.

solution has been similar to managing other risks—foreign exchange, interest rate, and commodity price risk. The market has responded by introducing the risk management products such as:

- Futures
- Floors—put option
- Caps—call option
- Collars—combination of call and put
- Swaps

The HDD is a measure of the coldness of the one day's temperature deviation from 65° Fahrenheit or 18° Celsius as defined by the CME standard contract, as seen in Equation 12.1.

Daily HDD = Max (0, 65° Fahrenheit − daily average temperature)   (12.1)

A degree day defines a measure of how much a given day temperature deviates from 65° Fahrenheit. For example, if the average temperature is 50° Fahrenheit, then daily HDD will be 15° F colder than the standard 65° Fahrenheit; therefore, 15 HDD will be reported for the day. The CDD also measures the warmth of the daily temperature's deviation from the 65° Fahrenheit as shown in Equation 12.2.

Daily CDD = Max (0, average daily temperature − 65° Fahrenheit)   (12.2)

Assuming an average daily temperature is 70° Fahrenheit, then five cooling degree days will be reported for that day. However, if the average temperature is 48°, zero cooling degree days will result. Daily HDD and CDD as defined in CME contracts are respectively the put and call options at the strike price of 65° Fahrenheit and are priced using a standard option pricing formula, assuming the cumulative degree-day distribution is normal.[14] Furthermore, the option pricing in Equations 12.1 and 12.2 are Asian-type options, where the cumulative average prices are used as opposed to single prices at the unwinding or expiry of the option and therefore have smaller premiums attached, other things remaining the same.

Equations 12.1 and 12.2 are put and call options, respectively. However, an HDD call or CDD put is respectively equivalent to CDD call and HDD put:

HDD Call = CDD Call
CDD Put = HDD Put

CME FUTURES

The CME CDD and HDD indexes are the accumulation of the daily CDD and HDD over the calendar month. For example, if the average daily HDD in Atlanta for the month of February was 12 (65° Fahrenheit−53° Fahrenheit), then the

HDD index would be 336 (28 × 12), as there are 28 days in February. The value of the index would be equal to 33,600 (336 × $100). Likewise, if the daily average CDD for the city of Tucson in the month of January was 14° F (79° F − 65° F), then CDD index would be 434 as there are 31 days in January. The minimum tick for the CME weather futures is 1 HDD/CDD, or $100. Exhibit 12.11 presents the CME HDD futures quote on various delivery dates for Atlanta.

In Exhibit 12.11, the HDD index for February 2003 is valued at 49,800 (498 × $100). Suppose ice cream chain Baskin-Robbins is concerned about falling revenue due to a forecast of 10° F, which is a colder than average temperature in February. The chain is likely to hedge this risk by selling February 2003 CDD futures at CME or buying put options. Alternatively the chain can buy February 2003 HDD futures or buy call options to mitigate the risk of below-average temperatures that hurt the bottom line that could be offset with the futures or options hedge. However, had the hedger been proven wrong and the average temperature exceeds the forecast, the hedger enjoys an increase in profits. In such a case the hedge proves to be a minor nuisance with a cost that will be written off against the gains. The number of contracts to sell/buy depends on the amount of decrease in sales revenue the chain faces in the month of February for every one point drop in temperature.

Historical past observations on sales revenue and temperature have revealed that the correlation is nearly −90 percent between the two parameters during the cold season. One HDD point drop in temperature translates into nearly $5,000 loss in revenue.[15] Suppose the chain expects the revenue to fall by $500,000 due to cold-weather forecast as demand for ice cream is reduced. The chain is likely to buy 50 HDD February 2003 futures contracts to hedge against the risk of a 100 degree-day drop in temperature. The hedge is zero net present value at the

EXHIBIT 12.11 Atlanta HDD Futures

globex® quotes as of 01/21/03 10:12 A.M. (CST)

MTH/	SESSION					PT	EST	PRIOR DAY		
STRIKE	OPEN	HIGH	LOW	LAST	SETT	CHGE	VOL	SETT	VOL	INT
JAN03	----	----	----	----	----	UNCH	765.0	20		
FEB03	----	----	----	----	----	UNCH	498.0	10		
MAR03	----	----	----	----	----	UNCH	360.0	10		
APR03	----	----	----	----	----	UNCH	140.0			
OCT03	----	----	----	----	----	UNCH	118.0			
NOV03	----	----	----	----	----	UNCH	355.0			
DEC03	----	----	----	----	----	UNCH	595.0			
TOTAL						40 EST. VOL				

Source: www.CME.com.

origination and is likely to change as the temperature and its volatility changes over time, producing positive or negative cash flow for the hedger at the time the hedge is unwound or at the expiration of the contract.

In this example, suppose the HDD index for February 2003 closes at 585, as the hedger expected a colder-than-average month. Each future contract will produce profit of $8,700 (87 × $100), or $435,000, which offsets the lost revenue due to the colder-than-average temperature.

CME OPTIONS

A Florida citrus grower wishes to buy protection for the highly damaging frost during March-April through the purchase of Critical Temperature Day (CTD) below a certain strike price. This is a put option for an up-front premium, where the buyer transfers the risk of the temperature falling below critical freeze point, say, of 32° Fahrenheit, while the option provides the buyer the opportunity to remain unhedged if the temperature does not drop below the critical point and expires worthless, as defined in Equation 12.3.

$$\text{Daily CTD} = \text{Max} (0, 32° \text{ Fahrenheit} - \text{average daily temperature}) \qquad (12.3)$$

Assuming that the CTD index in Equation 12.3 is the daily accumulation of CTD over the option period of, say, three months multiplied by $100. Suppose the average daily temperature is 17° Fahrenheit during the option calendar period; the put option is in-the-money and produces 15 times $100, or $1,500 payoff. Had the average daily temperature been 40°, the option expires worthless.

Ski resorts and theme parks may use weather derivatives to offset the effects of a mild winter or rainy season. For example, a ski resort may use a weather derivative such as swap to cover the cost of offering rebates on lift tickets if weekly snowfall is less than expected. However, theme parks may use an option for protection against successive rainy days or extreme temperatures.

Exhibit 12.12 provides the HDD call and put options at strike price of 1240 for Des Moines for a January 2003 delivery month. According to the put-call parity:

$$\text{Put} + \text{average spot} = \text{call} + \text{strike price}$$

reveals that the call is priced at 101, it is at-the-money, and the premium is $10,100, while the out-of-the-money HDD put is priced at 16, or $1,600 per contract. For example, with the average HDD index at 1325 over the last two months, a ski slope operator in Des Moines is concerned about rising temperature in January and falling revenue as snow precipitation drops. The slope operator can hedge its exposure to milder-than-average temperatures by selling HDD futures or buying HDD put options at a strike price of 1240 for $1,600 per contract. The ski slope operator will be protected in the event the HDD falls below the 1240 strike price as a result of rising average temperatures. The operator will enjoy better business if proven wrong (average temperature drops, raising HDD and presumably more snow) and the option expires worthless.

EXHIBIT 12.12   Des Moines HDD Options

globex® quotes as of 01/21/03 03:21 P.M. (CST)

MTH/	SESSION					PT	EST	PRIOR DAY		
STRIKE	OPEN	HIGH	LOW	LAST	SETT	CHGE	VOL	SETT	VOL	INT
19 JAN03 DES MOINES HDD **OPTIONS CALL**										
1240	----	----	----	----	----	UNCH	**101.0**			
TOTAL						EST. VOL	VOL OPEN INT			
19 JAN03 DES MOINES HDD **OPTIONS PUT**										
1240	----	----	----	----	----	UNCH	**16.0**	30		
						EST. VOL	VOL OPEN INT			
TOTAL								30		

Source: www.CME.com.

SWAPS

A swap is an OTC contract where the two parties agree to exchange a series of cash flows in the future based on a given notional principal. For example, a utility company in Dallas could arrange an OTC swap where it receives "fixed normal" degree day and pays floating degree day to the swap counterparty. Suppose the "fixed normal" HDD for the month of January is 525° in Dallas. A utility company can enter into swap where it receives "fixed normal" HDD and pays floating HDD based on notional principal of $10 million, as shown in Exhibit 12.13.

The utility company enjoys higher (lower) demand for its product in January if the month turned out to be cooler (warmer) than forecast where it pays more (less) than receives in its swap transaction. For example, if the floating HDD drops to 385°, indicative of warmer temperatures than forecast, the utility company's cash flow is adversely affected by volumetric risk that is partly compensated by positive net cash flow of $1.4 million from the swap transaction. To mitigate exposure to abnormal temperatures, the parties may impose floors/caps on the floating degree-day HDD/CDD. However, if January turned out to be cooler than forecast, the floating HDD rises to 610°, and the demand for gas and electricity outweighs by far the negative cash flows associated with the swap, as the utility is expected to pay $.85 million more than it receives in its swap transaction.

EXHIBIT 12.13   Structure of Fixed for
Floating Swap

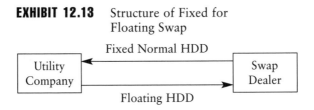

NOTES

1. Robert Schiller, *The Economist*, March 22, 2003.
2. See, for example Hull (2002) and McDonald (2003).
3. For theoretical derivations, see Jarrow and Turnbull (1996).
4. See Mason et al. (1995), p. 723.
5. Homer and Liebowitz (1971).
6. The uncorrelated counterparty provides diversification benefit as overall risk is reduced.
7. See ISDA Press Release, January 8, 2003.
8. See Weather Risk Management Association, 2001, report.
9. These cities are Atlanta, Chicago, Cincinnati, Dallas, Des Moines, Las Vegas, New York, Philadelphia, Portland, and Tucson.
10. See Weather Risk Management Association report at *www.wrma.org.*
11. The Weather Risk Management Association, formed in 1999, is a trade association dedicated to serving and promoting this industry. Membership is comprised of over 70 member companies, many of whom are the leading market makers and producers, in Europe, North America, and Asia.
12. See the report by Valerie Cooper, executive director for WRMA, 2001.
13. The average temperature is defined as the midpoint of the maximum and minimum temperature on a 24-hour period.
14. See Ross McIntyre at *weather derivatives.com*, who finds that the cumulative degree-day for London Heathrow Airport as reported by the U.K. Meteorological office has near-normal distribution.
15. The correlation weighted by the standard deviation of the sales and standard deviation of the HDD index is the hedge ratio as defined in Chapter 4.

references

Allayannis, G., and J. Weston. "The Use of Foreign Currency Derivatives and Firm Market Value." *Review of Financial Studies,* 14, no. 1 (2001): 243–276.

Allen, L., and C. Pantzalis. "Valuation of Operating Flexibility of Multinational Corporations." *Journal of International Business Studies,* 27, no. 4, (1998): 633–653.

Altman, E. *Bankruptcy, Credit Risk, and High-Yield Junk Bonds.* London: Blackwell, 2002.

Bansal, Vipul K.; James L. Bicksler; Andrew H. Chen; and John F. Marshall. "Gains from Synthetic Financings with Interest Rate Swaps: Fact or Fantasy?" *Journal of Applied Corporate Finance* 6, no. 3 (Fall 1993): 91–94.

Barro, R. J. *Black Monday and the Future of the Financial Markets.* E. T. Kamphius, ed. (McGraw-Hill/Irwin, 1989).

Bilson, J. "The Choice of an Invoice Currency in International Transactions." In *Economic Interdependence and Flexible-Exchange Rates,* J. Bhandari and B. Putnam, eds. (Massachusetts Institute of Technology Press, 1983), pp. 384–401.

Bishop, Matthew. "A Survey of Corporate Risk Management." *The Economist* (February 10, 1996).

Bodnar, G. M., G. S. Hayt, and R. C. Marston. "1998 Wharton Survey of Financial Risk Management by U.S. Non-Financial Firms." *Financial Management,* 27, no. 4 (1998): 70–91.

Brown, Gregory W. "Managing Foreign Exchange Risk with Derivatives." *Journal of Financial Economics,* 60 (2001): 401–448.

Buckley, P., and M. C. Casson. "Models of International Enterprise." *Journal of International Business Studies,* 29, no. 1 (1998): 21–44.

Burghardt et al. *Eurodollar Futures and Options* (Chicago: Probus Publishing Company, 1991).

Carow, Kenneth A., Gayle R. Erwin, and John J. McConnell. "A Survey of US Corporate Financing Innovation: 1970–1997." *Journal of Applied Corporate Finance,* 12, no. 1 (Spring 1999): 55–69.

Cassel, Gustav. "Abnormal Deviators in International Exchange." *Economic Journal* (December 1918): 413–415.

Chance, Don. M. *A Introduction to Options and Futures* (Dryden Press, 2000).

Chang, C., and J. Chang. "Forward and Futures Prices: Evidence from Foreign Exchange Markets." *Journal of Finance* 45 (1990).

Chang, E. C. "Returns to Speculators and the Theory of Normal Backwardation." *Journal of Finance* 40 (March 1985): 193–208.

Chang, Roberto, and Andrews Velasco. "Financial Fragility and the Exchange Rate Regime." National Bureau of Economic Research Working Paper 6469, March 1998.

Chen, Andrew H., and John W. Kensinger. "Puttable Stock: A New Innovation in Equity Financing." *Financial Management*, 17, no. 1 (Spring 1988): 27–37.

Chicago Board of Trade. *The Delivery Process in Brief for Treasury Board and Treasury Note Futures.*

———. *Understanding Duration and Convexity* (Chicago: Chicago Board of Trade, 1989).

Chowdhry, B. "Corporate Hedging of Exchange Rate Risk When Foreign Currency Cash Flow Is Uncertain." *Management Science*, 41 (1995): 1083–1090.

Chowdhry, B., and J. Howe. "Corporate Risk Management for Multinational Corporations: Financial and Operational Hedging Policies." *European Financial Review*, 2 (1999): 229–246.

Cornell, B., and M. Reinganum. "Forward and Futures Prices: Evidence from Futures Markets." *Journal of Finance*, 36 (December 1981): 1035–1045.

Cornell, B., and Alan C. Shapiro. "Managing Foreign Exchange Risks." *Midland Corporate Finance Journal* (Fall 1983): 16–31.

Corsetti, Giancarlo, Paolo Pesenti, and Nouriel Roubini. "What Caused the Asian Currency and Financial Crisis?" *Japan and the World Economy* (October 1999): 305–733.

Cox, J. C., J. E. Ingersoll, and S. A. Ross. "A Reexamination of Traditional Hypotheses about the Term Structure of Interest Rates." *Journal of Finance* (September 1981): 769–799.

———. "The Relation between Forward Prices and Future Prices." *Journal of Financial Economics*, 9 (December 1981): 321–346.

Culbertson, J. M. "The Term Structure of Interest Rates." *Quarterly Journal of Economics* (November 1957): 489–504.

Culp, C. L., and M. H. Miller. "Metallgesellschaft and the Economics of Synthetic Storage." *Journal of Applied Corporate Finance*, 7, no. 4 (1995): 62–76.

Cumby, R., and M. Obstfield. "A Note on Exchange Rate Expectations and Nominal Interest Differentials, A Test of Fisher Hypothesis." *Journal of Finance* (June 1981): 697–703.

De Giorgio, E. M. "Ashanti—The Full Story." *African Business*, 249 (December 1999): 34–36.

Diamond, Douglas W., and Philip H. Dybvig. "Bank Runs, Deposit Insurance, and Liquidity." *Journal of Political Economy*, 91 (1983): 401–419.

Dufey, Gunter, and Sam L. Srinivasulu. "The Case for Corporate Management of Foreign Exchange Risk." *Financial Management* (Summer 1984): 54–62.

Duffie, D. "Credit Swap Valuation." *Financial Analyst Journal* (1999): 73–87.

Eaker, et al. *International Corporate Finance* (The Dryden Press, 1996).

ECB. "The Information Content of Interest Rates and Their Derivatives for Monetary Policy." *ECB Monthly Bulletin* (May 2000): 37–46.

Edwards, F. R., and M.S. Canter. "The Collapse of Metallgesellschaft: Unhedgeable Risks, Poor Hedging Strategy, or Just Bad Luck?" *Journal of Applied Corporate Finance,* 8, no. 1 (1995): 86–105.

Edwards, Franklin, "Hedge Funds and Collapse of Long Term Capital Management." *Journal of Economic Perspectives,* 13, no. 12 (1999): 189– 210.

Eiteman, D., A. Stonehill, and M. Moffett. *Multinational Business Finance.* 9th ed. (Wellesley, MA: Addison Wesley Longman, 2001).

Evans, Thomas G., and William R. Folks Jr. "Defining Objectives for Exposure Management." *Business International Money Report* (February 2, 1979): 37–39.

Fabozzi, F. J. *Fixed Income Mathematics: Analytical and Statistical Techniques* (Chicago: Probus, 1993).

———. *Valuation of Fixed Income Securities and Derivatives.* 3d ed. (New Hope, PA: Frank J. Fabozzi Associates, 1998), p. 53.

Falloon, W. "MG's Trial by Essay." *Risk,* 10 (October 1994): 228–234.

Fama, Eugene F. "Forward Rates as Predictors of Future Spot Rates." *Journal of Financial Economics,* 3, no. 4 (1976): 361–377.

Figlewski, S. *Hedging with Financial Futures for Institutional Investors* (Cambridge, MA: Ballinger, 1986).

Finnerty, John D. "An Overview of Corporate Finance: An Overview of Corporate Securities Innovation." *Journal of Applied Corporate Finance,* 4, no. 4 (Winter 1992): 23–39.

———. "Premium Debt Swaps, Tax-Timing Arbitrage, and Debt Service Parity." *Journal of Applied Finance,* 11, no. 1 (2001): 17–22.

Finnerty, John D., and Douglass Emery. "Corporate Securities Innovations: An Update." *Journal of Applied Finance* (Spring/Summer 2002): 21–47.

Flesaker, B. "Arbitrage Free Pricing of Interest Rate Futures and Forward Contracts." *Journal of Futures Markets,* 13 (1993): 77–91.

Folks Jr., William R. "Decision Analysis for Exchange Risk Management." *Financial Management* (Winter 1972): 101–112.

Francis, J. C., and R. Ibbostson. *Investment* (Upper Saddle River, NJ: Prentice Hall, 2002).

Francis, Jack C., and Rakesh Bali. "Innovation in Partitioning a Share of Stock." *Journal of Applied Corporate Finance,* 13 no. 1 (Spring 2000): 128–136.

Frankel, J. "In Search of the Exchange Risk Premium a Six Currency Test Assuming Mean-Variance Optimization." *Journal of International Money and Finance* (December 1982): 255–274.

French, K. "A Comparison of Futures and Forward Prices." *Journal of Finance* (November 1983): 311–342.

Froot, et al. "A Framework for Risk Management." *Journal of Applied Corporate Finance,* 7, no. 3 (1994): 22–32.

Furman, Jason, and Joseph E. Stiglitz. "Economic Crises: Evidence and Insights from East Asia." *Brookings Papers on Economic Activity*, 2 (1998): 1–135.

Gaillot, H. "Purchasing Power Parity as an Explanation of Long-term Changes in Exchange Rates." *Journal of Money, Credit and Banking* (August 1971): 348–357.

Gastineau, G., D. Smith, and R. Todd. *Risk Management, Derivatives, and Financial Analysis under FASB No. 133*. The Research Foundation of AIMR and Blackwell Series in Finance, 2001.

Geczy, C., B. Milton, and C. Schrand. "Why Firms Use Currency Derivatives." *Journal of Finance*, 52 (1997): 1323–1354.

Gertler, M., and C. S. Lown. "The Information in the High-Yield Bond Spread for the Business Cycle: Evidence and Some Implications," NBER Paper no. 7549, 2000.

Gesky, R. "On the Valuation of Compound Options." *Journal of Financial Economics*, 7 (1979): 63–81.

Giddy, Ian H. "The Foreign Exchange Option as a Hedging Tool." *Midland Corporate Finance Journal* (Fall 1983): 32–42.

Goeltz, Richard K. *Managing Liquid Funds on an International Scope* (New York: Joseph E. Seagram and Sons, 1999), p. 171.

Graham, J., and C. Smith. "Tax Incentives to Hedge." *Journal of Finance*, 54 (1999): 2241–2222.

Graham, J. R., and D. A. Rogers. "Do Firms Hedge in Response to Tax Incentives?" Duke University Working Paper, 2000.

Graham, J. R., and C. W. Smith Jr. "Tax Incentives to Hedge." *Journal of Finance*, 54, no. 6 (1999): 2241–2262.

Gupta, A., and M. G. Subrahmanyam. "An Empirical Examination of the Convexity Bias in the Pricing of Interest Rate Swaps." *Journal of Financial Economics*, 55, no. 2 (2000): 239–279.

Haushalter, G. "Financing Policy, Basic Risk, and Corporate Hedging: Evidence from Oil and Gas Producers. *Journal of Finance*, 53 (2000): 979–1013.

Hendricks, Darryll. "Netting Agreements and the Credit Exposures of OTC Derivative Portfolios." *Quarterly Review*, Federal Reserve Bank of New York (Spring 1994): 7–18.

Hicks, John R. *Value and Capital*. 2d ed. (London: Oxford University Press, 1946), p. 141.

Homaifar, G., and B. P. Helms. "Distribution of Prices for Commodity Futures." *Advances in Futures and Options Research*, 4 (1990): 253–264.

Homaifar, G., and Joachim Zietz. "Official Intervention in the Foreign Exchange Market and the Random Walk Behavior of Exchange Rates." *Economia Internationale*, 48, no. 3 (August 1995): 359–373.

Homaifar, G., J. Zietz, and O. Benkato. "Determinants of Capital Structure for Multinational and Domestic Corporations." *International Economics*, 51, no. 2 (1998): 189–210.

Homer, Sydney, and Martin L. Leibowitz Jr. *Inside the Yield Book* (New York: Prentice-Hall and the New York Institute of Finance, 1971), Chapters 1–5, 8–13.

Horwitz, D. L. "*P&G v. Banker's Trust:* What's All the Fuss?" *Derivates Quarterly,* 3, no. 2 (1996): 18–23.

Houthhakker, H. S. "Can Speculators Forecast Prices?" *Review of Economics and Statistics* (1957): 143–51.

Hull, J. C. *Fundamentals of Futures and Options Markets.* 4th ed. (Upper Saddle River, NJ: Prentice Hall, 2002).

———. *Options, Futures, and Other Derivatives.* 4th ed. (Upper Saddle River, NJ: Prentice-Hall, 2000).

Hull, J., and A. White. "Valuing Credit Default Swaps I: No Counterparty Default Risk." *Mimeo.* University of Toronto, 2002.

Jackson, P., D. J. Maude, and W. Perraudin. "Bank Capital and Value at Risk." *Journal of Derivatives,* 4, no. 3 (Spring 1997): 73–90.

Jarrow, R. A. and F. Yu. "Counterparty Risk and Pricing of Defaultable Securities." *Journal of Finance* (2001).

Jarrow, R., and S. Turnbull. *Derivative Securities* (Cincinnati, OH: South-Western College Publishing, 1996).

Jensen, M., and W. Meckling. "Theory of the Firm: Managerial Behavior, Agency Costs, and Ownership Structure." *Journal of Financial Economics,* no. 3 (1976): 305–360.

Jorion, P. *Value at Risk: The New Benchmark for Controlling Market Risk* (Burr Ridge, IL: Irwin, 1997).

Kaminsky, Graciela, and Carmen M. Reinhart. "The Twin Crises: The Causes of Banking and Balance-of-Payments Problems." *American Economic Review,* 89 (1999): 473–500.

Kasapi, A. *Mastering Credit Derivatives* (Upper Saddle River, NJ: Prentice Hall, 1999).

Kowai, Masahiro. "The East Asian Currency Crises: Causes and Lessons." *Contemporary Economic Policy,* 14 (1998):157–172.

Kowai, M., et al. "Crisis and Contagion in East Asia: Nine Lessons." *World Bank 2001* (Washington, D.C.: World Bank, 2001).

Krugman, Paul. "A Model of Balance-of-Payments Crises." *Journal of Money, Credit, and Banking,* 11 (1979): 311–325.

———. "Pricing to Market When the Exchange Rate Changes." National Bureau of Economic Research Working Paper no. 1926, May 1986.

———. "What Happened to Asia?" Massachusetts Institute of Technology, Cambridge, MA (1998).

Laux, Paul A., Christos Pantzalis, and Betty J. Simpkins. "Operational Hedges and the Foreign Exchange Exposure of U.S. Multinational Corporations." *Journal of International Business Studies,* 32, no. 4 (2001): 793.

Lee, K. C., and C. Y. Kwok. "Multinational Corporations vs. Domestic Corporations: International Environmental Factors and Determinants of Capital Structure." *Journal of International Business Studies* (Summer 1988): 195–217.

Levitch, R. M. *International Financial Markets: Prices and Policies* (Irwin McGraw-Hill, 1998).

Lipin, Steven. "J.P. Morgan Had $50 Million in Losses in Trading Mortgage-Back Securities." *Wall Street Journal* (March 10, 1992): A4.

Litzenberger, R. H. "Swaps: Plain and Fanciful." *Journal of Finance,* 47, no. 3 (1992): 831–850.

Lothiar, J., and M. Taylor. "Real Exchange Rule Behavior: The Recent Float from the Perceptive of the Past Two Centuries." *Journal of Political Economy* (June 1996).

Lutz, F. "The Structure of Interest Rates." *Quarterly Journal of Economics* (1940–41): 36–63.

Mann, Catherine. "Prices, Profit Margins and Exchange Rates." *Federal Reserves Bulletin* 72 (June 1986): 336–379.

Marshall, J. F., and K. R. Kapner. *The Swap Market.* 2d ed. (Miami, FL: Kolb,1993).

Marston, Richard C. "Tests of Three Parity Conditions: Distinguishing Risk Premia and Systematic Forecast Errors." *Journal of International Money and Finance* (1997): 1345–1357.

Masiela, M., S. M. Turnbull, and L. M. Wakeman. "Interest Rate Risk Management." *Review of Futures Markets,* 12, no. 1 (1993): 221–261.

Mason et al. *Cases in Financial Engineering* (Upper Saddle River, NJ: Prentice Hall, 1995).

McDonald, R. L. *Derivatives Markets* (Addison-Wesley, 2003).

McKinnon, Ronald I., and Huw Pill. "Credible Liberalizations and International Capital Flows: The 'Overborrowing Syndrome.'" In Takatoshi Ito and Anne O. Krueger, eds., *Financial Deregulation and Integration in East Asia* (Chicago: University of Chicago Press, 1996).

Mello, A. S., and J. E. Parsons. "Maturity Structure of a Hedge Matters: Lessons from the Metallgesellschaft Debacle." *Journal of Applied Corporate Finance,* 8 no. 1 (1995): 106–120.

Merton, R. C. "Influence of Mathematical Models in Finance on Practice: Past, Present and Future." *Philosophical Transactions of the Royal Society of London,* series A, 347 (June 1974): 451–463.

Merton, Robert C. "Financial Innovation and Economic Performance." *Journal of Applied Corporate Finance,* 4, no. 4 (Winter 1992): 12–22.

Miller, M., and V. Culp. "Risk Management Lessons from Metallgesellschaft." *Journal of Applied Corporate Finance Journal,* 7, no. 4 (Winter 1995): 62–76.

Mishkin, F. "Are Real Interest Rates Equal Across Countries? An International Investigation of Parity Conditions." *Journal of Finance* (1984): 1345–1357.

Modigliani, Franco, and Richard Sutch. "Innovations in Interest Rate Policy." *American Economic Review* (May 1966): 178–197.

Myers, S. C. "Determinants of Corporate Borrowing." *Journal of Financial Economics,* 5 (November 1977): 147–175.

Obstfeld, Maurice. "Rational and Self-Fulfilling Balance of Payments Crises." *American Economic Review,* 76 (1986): 72–81.

Ogden, Joseph P. "An Analysis of Yield Curve Notes." *Journal of Finance,* 42, no. 1 (March 1987): 99–110.

Park, H. Y., and Chen. A. H. "Differences between Forward and Futures Prices: A Further Investigation of Marking to Market Effects." *Journal of Futures Markets,* 5 (February 1985): 77–88.

Petersen, M. A., and S. R. Thiagarajan. "Risk Measurement and Hedging: With and Without Derivatives." *Financial Management,* 29, no. 4 (Winter 2000): 5–29.

Pratt, Tom. "Salomon Unveils New Hybrid with PERCS like Features." *Investment Dealers' Digest,* 59, no. 26, June 28, 1993, p. 12.

Radelet, Steven, and Jeffrey D. Sachs. "The East Asian Financial Crisis: Diagnosis, Remedies, Prospects." *Brookings Papers on Economic Activity,* 1 (1998): 1–90.

———. "The Onset of the East Asian Financial Crises." NBER Working Paper 6680, 1998.

Rendleman, R., and C. Carabini. "The Efficiency of the Treasury Bill Futures Market." *Journal of Finance* 34 (September 1979): 895–914.

Rendleman Jr., R. J. *Applied Derivatives: Options, Futures, and Swaps* (Malden, MA: Blackwell, 2002).

Rosenweig, J., and P. Koch. "The U.S. Dollar and the Delayed J-curve." *Economic Review,* Federal Reserve Bank of Atlanta (July/August 1988): 2–16.

Rubinstein, M. "Double Trouble." *Risk,* 5, no. 1 (1991/92): 73.

———. "Option for the Undecided." *Risk,* 4, no. 4, 43.

———. "Somewhere Over the Rainbow." *Risk,* 4 no. 10, 63–66.

Rubinstein, M., and E. Reiner. "Breaking Down the Barriers." *Risk* (September 1991).

Schrand, C., and H. Unal. "Hedging and Coordinated Risk Management: Evidence from Thrift Conversions." *Journal of Finance,* 53 (1998): 979–1013.

Schwebach, R. and T. Zorn. "A Simple Derivation of the Fisher Equation Under Uncertainty." *Journal of Financial Education,* 23 (Fall 1997): 84–87.

Scott, L. "A Note on the Pricing of Default Swaps." Morgan Stanley Dean Witter Working Paper no. 7, 1998.

Shapiro, Alan C., and David P. Rutenberg. "Managing Exchange Risks in a Floating World." *Financial Management* (Summer 1976): 48–58.

Shepherd, B. "The Art of Hedging Gold." *Global Finance,* 13, no. 3 (March 1999): 6–9.

Simons, Katerina. "Measuring Credit Risk in Interest Rate Swaps." *New England Economics Review* (November/December 1989): 29–38.

Smith, C. W., C. Smithson, and L. Wakeman. "The Evolving Market for the Swap." *Midland Corporate Finance Journal* (Winter 1986): 20–32.

Smith, D. J. "Aggressive Corporate Finance: A Close Look at the Procter & Gamble-Bankers Trust Leveraged Swap." *Journal of Derivatives,* 5, no. 4 (1997): 67–79.

3/M. "The Arithmetic of Financial Engineering." *Journal of Applied Corporate Finance,* 1, no. 4 (Winter 1989): 49–58.

Solnik, Bruno. "Swap Pricing and Default Risk: A Note." *Journal of International Financial Management and Accounting,* 2, no. 1 (Spring 1990): 79–91.

Srinivasulu, Sam, and Edward Massura. "Sharing Currency Risks in Long-Term Contracts." *Business International Money Reports* (February 23, 1987): 57–59.

Statement of Financial Accounting Standards No. 52 (Stamford, CT: Financial Accounting Standards Board, December 1981).

Stutltz, R. M. "Option on the Maximum and Minimum." *Journal of Financial Economics*, 10, no. 2 (1982): 161–186.

Summers, Lawrence H. "Roots of the Asian Crises and the Road to a Stronger Global Financial System." Remarks made at the Institute of International Finance, 1999.

Tavakoli, J. M. *Credit Derivatives: A Guide to Instruments and Applications* (New York: John Wiley & Sons, Inc., 1998).

———. *Credit Derivatives and Synthetic Structures.* 2d ed. (Hoboken, NJ: John Wiley & Sons, Inc., 2001).

Telser, L. G. "Futures Trading and the Storage of Cotton and Wheat." *Journal of Political Econom,* 66 (June 1958): 233–251.

Torbenson, Eric. "Hedging Fuel Costs Can Pay Off the Airlines." *Tribune Business News* (July 19, 2001).

Tufano, P. "Agency Costs of Corporate Risk Management." *Financial Management,* 27 (1998): 67–77.

———. "Who Manages Risk? An Empirical Examination of Risk Management Practices in the Gold Mining Industry." *Journal of Finance,* 51 (1996): 1097–1137.

———. "Securities Innovation: A Historical and Functional Perspective." *Journal of Applied Corporate Finance,* 7, no. 4 (Winter 1995): 90–103.

Turnbull, S. M. "Swaps: Zero Sum Game?" *Financial Management,* 16, no. 1 (1987): 15–21.

Whitt, J. "The U.S. Current Account Deficit: Is There Trouble Ahead?" *Economics Update,* 11, no. 3 (July–September 1998).

Zenoff, David B. "Applying Management Principles to Foreign Exchange Exposure." *Euromoney* (September 1978): 123–130.

Zietz, Joachim, and Ghassem Homaifar. "Exchange Rate Uncertainty and the Efficiency of the Forward Market for Foreign Exchange." *Weltwirtsschaftliches Archive,* 130, no. 3 (1994): 461–475.

———. "Exchange Rate Uncertainty and the Efficiency of the Forward Market for Foreign Exchange: A Reply." *Weltwirtschaftliches Archive,* 131, no. 4 (1995): 789–791.

index